ANNUAL EDITIONS

Human Sexuality

05/06

A·N·N·U·A·L E·D·I·T·I·O·N·S

Human Sexuality 05/06

Twenty-Nineth Edition

EDITOR

Susan J. Bunting

Lincoln College

Susan Bunting is a child, adolescent, and family counselor at Chestnut Health Systems, a consultant for Employment Development Associates, and an instructor in sociology and psychology at Lincoln College in Illinois. Dr. Bunting received her B.S. and M.S. in sociology and her Ed.D. in curriculum and instruction from Illinois State University. She has taught, counseled, trained, and developed curriculum in human sexuality, sexual abuse, substance abuse, domestic violence, self-esteem, child and human development, learning disabilities, behavior change, family, and intimate relationships. Dr. Bunting publishes pamphlets, instructional materials, articles, and books in these areas.

McGraw-Hill/Dushkin

2460 Kerper Blvd., Dubuque, IA 52001

Visit us on the Internet
http://www.dushkin.com

Credits

1. **Sexuality and Society**
   Unit photo—© Getty Images/Ryan McVay
2. **Sexual Biology, Behavior, and Orientation**
   Unit photo—© Getty Images/PhotoLink/Jack Star
3. **Interpersonal Relationships**
   Unit photo—© Getty Images/Jonnie Miles
4. **Reproduction**
   Unit photo—© Getty Images/Geoff Manasse
5. **Sexuality Through the Lifecycle**
   Unit photo—© Getty Images/Bronwyn Kidd
6. **Old/New Sexual Concerns**
   Unit photo—© Getty Images/PhotoLink/Kent Knudson

Copyright

Cataloging in Publication Data
Main entry under title: Annual Editions: Human Sexuality. 2005/2006.
1. Sexual Behavior—Periodicals. 2. Sexual hygiene—Periodicals. 3. Sex education—Periodicals.
4. Human relations—Periodicals. I. Bunting, Susan J. *comp. II*. Title: Human Sexuality.
ISBN 0–07–291733–4   658'.05   ISSN 1091–9961

Twenty-Nineth Edition

Cover image © Photos.com
Printed in the United States of America   1234567890QPDQPD987654   Printed on Recycled Paper

Editors/Advisory Board

Members of the Advisory Board are instrumental in the final selection of articles for each edition of ANNUAL EDITIONS. Their review of articles for content, level, currentness, and appropriateness provides critical direction to the editor and staff. We think that you will find their careful consideration well reflected in this volume.

EDITOR

Susan J. Bunting
Lincoln College

ADVISORY BOARD

John D. Baldwin
University of California - Santa Barbara

Janice I. Baldwin
University of California - Santa Barbara

Kelli McCormack Brown
University of South Florida

Teresa Jean Byrne
Kent State University

Jeffrey K. Clark
Ball State University

Maureen A. Clinton
Suffolk Community College

Linda J. Coleman
Salem State College

Donald R. Devers
Northern Virginia Community College

Harry F. Felton
Pennsylvania State University - Worthington

Dan Goldman
Rancho Santiago College

Marylou Hacker
Modesto Junior College

Kathleen Kaiser
California State University, Chico

Gary F. Kelly
Clarkson University

John T. Lambert
Mohawk College - Fennell

Bruce D. LeBlanc
Black Hawk College

Theodore J. Maroun
McGill University

Fred L. Peterson
University of Texas, Austin

Dale Rajacich
University of Windsor

Mina Robbins
California State University - Sacramento

Martin S. Turnauer
Radford University

Deitra Wengert
Towson University

Staff

Preface

In publishing ANNUAL EDITIONS we recognize the enormous role played by the magazines, newspapers, and journals of the public press in providing current, first-rate educational information in a broad spectrum of interest areas. Many of these articles are appropriate for students, researchers, and professionals seeking accurate, current material to help bridge the gap between principles and theories and the real world. These articles, however, become more useful for study when those of lasting value are carefully collected, organized, and reproduced in a low-cost format, which provides easy and permanent access when the material is needed. That is the role played by ANNUAL EDITIONS.

Sex lies at the root of life and we can never learn to reverence life until we know how to understand sex.

The above quote represents a core belief of Havelock Ellis, a late nineteenth century sexologist, as well as the editor and publisher of this current anthology on human sexuality more than a century later. Some things haven't changed, but some things clearly have. In the 15 years that I have been involved with compiling the *Annual Editions: Human Sexuality,* one of the most remarkable changes has been in the amount and breadth of coverage sexuality-related topics and issues have received in media of all kinds. It is therefore, likely that you, as students reading this 05/06 edition, have already been exposed to far more discussion and information about sexuality than students of previous decades.

Despite this greater inclusion of sex and sexuality in the media and in social life, in general it is clear to experts in the fields of human sexuality and human relationships that the goal of most collegiate courses in human sexuality has not yet been accomplished. So readers, as you begin your planful examination of—or Ellis's goal above—human sexuality in the first decade of the twenty-first century, try to remember that some things have changed, some things will change, and many things are likely to stay much the same. Maybe that's why it's important to emphasize the "human" in human sexuality.

Annual Editions: Human Sexuality 05/06 is organized into six sections. *Sexuality and Society* notes historical and cross-cultural views and analyzes our constantly changing society and sexuality. *Sexual Biology, Behavior, and Orientation* explains the functioning and responses of the human body and contains expanded sections on sexual hygiene, diseases, and conditions affecting sexuality and functioning, and guides to preventive and ongoing sexual health care. *Interpersonal Relationships* provides suggestions for establishing and maintaining intimate, responsible, quality relationships. *Reproduction* discusses some recent trends related to pregnancy and childbearing and deals with reproductive topics, including conception, infertility, contraception, and abortion. *Sexuality Through the Life Cycle* looks at what happens sexually throughout one's lifetime—from childhood to the later years. Finally, *Old/New Sexual Concerns* deals with such topics as sexual abuse, rape, sexual harassment, and legal and ethical issues regarding sexual behavior and closes with this edition's focus section: Integrating the Erotic and the Spiritual.

Also, in this edition of *Annual Editions: Human Sexuality 05/06* are selected *World Wide Web* sites that can be used to further explore the topics. These sites will be cross-referenced by number in the *topic guide.*

The articles have been carefully reviewed and selected for their quality, readability, currency, and interest. They present a variety of viewpoints. Some you will agree with, some you will not, but we hope you will learn from all of them.

Appreciation and thanks go to Loree Adams for her suggestions and expertise; to Michael Fatten, Joe Strano, Al Sodetz, Sue LeSeure, and Marian Micke for their willingness to act as two-way sounding boards; to Mary Roy for her organization and assistance, to Ollie Pocs for inspiration, and to those who have submitted articles for this anthology or reviewed articles for previous editions. We feel that *Annual Editions: Human Sexuality 05/06* is one of the most useful and up-to-date books available. Please return the postage-paid article rating form on the last page of this book with your suggestions and comments. Any book can be improved. This one will continue to be—annually.

Susan J. Bunting
Editor

Contents

UNIT 1
Sexuality and Society

Unit Overview   xviii

Part A.   Historical and Cross-Cultural Perspectives

The concepts in bold italics are developed in the article. For further expansion, please refer to the Topic Guide.

UNIT 2
Sexual Biology, Behavior, and Orientation

The concepts in bold italics are developed in the article. For further expansion, please refer to the Topic Guide.

UNIT 3
Interpersonal Relationships

Unit Overview　　　　　　　　　　　　　　　　　　　　　　**82**

The concepts in bold italics are developed in the article. For further expansion, please refer to the Topic Guide.

The concepts in bold italics are developed in the article. For further expansion, please refer to the Topic Guide.

UNIT 4
Reproduction

The concepts in bold italics are developed in the article. For further expansion, please refer to the Topic Guide.

UNIT 5
Sexuality Through the Lifecycle

UNIT 6
Old/New Sexual Concerns

The concepts in bold italics are developed in the article. For further expansion, please refer to the Topic Guide.

The concepts in bold italics are developed in the article. For further expansion, please refer to the Topic Guide.

The concepts in bold italics are developed in the article. For further expansion, please refer to the Topic Guide.

Topic Guide

This topic guide suggests how the selections in this book relate to the subjects covered in your course. You may want to use the topics listed on these pages to search the Web more easily.

On the following pages a number of Web sites have been gathered specifically for this book. They are arranged to reflect the units of this *Annual Edition.* You can link to these sites by going to the DUSHKIN ONLINE support site at *http://www.dushkin.com/online/.*

ALL THE ARTICLES THAT RELATE TO EACH TOPIC ARE LISTED BELOW THE BOLD-FACED TERM.

Abortion
34. Under the Radar
35. Which Babies? Dilemmas of Genetic Testing

Abuse
4. A Deadly Passage to India
7. Slaves of the Brothel
13. Hear Sensuality, Think Sex?
44. Crimes Against Nature
45. New Hope for Sex Offender Treatment
46. A Cruel Edge
49. Breaking the Silence
50. The Mystery of Misogyny

Adulthood, young
9. The Princess Paradox
39. Choosing Virginity
44. Crimes Against Nature

Aging
2. Sex Around the World
10. The Manliness of Men
14. The New Sex Scorecard
15. The Hormone Conundrum
16. Sex, Drugs & Rock 'n' Roll
29. The Viagra Dialogues
30. The Secret Lives of Wives
41. Sex in the '90s

Bisexuality
3. The Beauty Pageant Prevails
20. Why Are We Gay?
41. Sex in the '90s
51. In Search of Erotic Intelligence

Contraception
31. Access Denied
32. What's New in Contraception? Understanding the Options

Counseling
4. A Deadly Passage to India
7. Slaves of the Brothel
17. What Problem?
18. When Sex Hurts
20. Why Are We Gay?
22. Great Expectations
24. How to Tell Your Potential Love About Your Chronic STD
27. Save Your Relationship
28. How to Rediscover Desire
29. The Viagra Dialogues
44. Crimes Against Nature
45. New Hope for Sex Offender Treatment
49. Breaking the Silence
51. In Search of Erotic Intelligence
52. The Merry-Go-Round of Desire

Ethical issues
4. A Deadly Passage to India
7. Slaves of the Brothel
8. Rock the Casbah
19. The Rise of the Gay Family
21. Dr. Sex
24. How to Tell Your Potential Love About Your Chronic STD
29. The Viagra Dialogues
30. The Secret Lives of Wives
31. Access Denied
34. Under the Radar
35. Which Babies? Dilemmas of Genetic Testing
37. A Tale of Two Mothers
39. Choosing Virginity
41. Sex in the '90s
44. Crimes Against Nature
45. New Hope for Sex Offender Treatment
46. A Cruel Edge
48. The Bible's Lost Stories
49. Breaking the Silence
51. In Search of Erotic Intelligence
52. The Merry-Go-Round of Desire

Female sexuality
1. Women's Ideal Bodies Then and Now
2. Sex Around the World
3. The Beauty Pageant Prevails
4. A Deadly Passage to India
7. Slaves of the Brothel
9. The Princess Paradox
14. The New Sex Scorecard
15. The Hormone Conundrum
20. Why Are We Gay?
27. Save Your Relationship
29. The Viagra Dialogues
30. The Secret Lives of Wives
36. Sex Without Sex? Keeping Passion Alive
38. The Sexual Revolution Hits Junior High
41. Sex in the '90s
42. What Turns You On? (Hint: It's Not Work!)
48. The Bible's Lost Stories
51. In Search of Erotic Intelligence
52. The Merry-Go-Round of Desire

Gender
1. Women's Ideal Bodies Then and Now
2. Sex Around the World
3. The Beauty Pageant Prevails
10. The Manliness of Men
14. The New Sex Scorecard
21. Dr. Sex
48. The Bible's Lost Stories
51. In Search of Erotic Intelligence
52. The Merry-Go-Round of Desire

Homosexuality
3. The Beauty Pageant Prevails
19. The Rise of the Gay Family
20. Why Are We Gay?

Sexually Transmitted Diseases (STDs)

World Wide Web Sites

The following World Wide Web sites have been carefully researched and selected to support the articles found in this reader. The easiest way to access these selected sites is to go to our DUSHKIN ONLINE support site at *http://www.dushkin.com/online/*.

AE: Human Sexuality 05/06

The following sites were available at the time of publication. Visit our Web site—we update DUSHKIN ONLINE regularly to reflect any changes.

General Sources

National Institutes of Health (NIH)
http://www.nih.gov

Consult this site for links to extensive health information and scientific resources. The NIH is one of eight health agencies of the Public Health Service, which in turn, is part of the U.S. Department of Health and Human Services.

SIECUS
http://www.siecus.org

Visit the Sexuality Information and Education Council of the United States (SIECUS) home page to learn about the organization, to find news of its educational programs and activities, and to access links to resources in sexuality education.

UNIT 1: Sexuality and Society

Department of State: Human Rights
http://www.state.gov/g/drl/hr/

The U.S. State Department's Web page for human rights includes country reports, fact sheets, reports on discrimination and violations of human rights, plus the latest news covering human rights issues from around the world.

SocioSite: Feminism and Women's Issues
http://www.pscw.uva.nl/sociosite/TOPICS/Women.html

Open this University of Amsterdam Sociology Department's site to gain insights into a number of issues that affect both men and women. It provides biographies of women in history, an international network for women in the workplace, and links to family and children's issues, and more.

Woman in Islam: Sex and Society
http://www.jamaat.org/islam/WomanSociety.html

This Web site is sponsored by the secretary general of Pakistan offering objective analysis and explanations regarding a woman's role in Islamic society. Topics include marriage, family matters, and sex within Islamic society.

Women's Human Rights Resources
http://www.law-lib.utoronto.ca/Diana/

This list of international women's human rights Web sites provides interesting resources on marriage and the family; rights of girls; sexual orientation; slavery, trafficking, and prostitution; and violence against women.

UNIT 2: Sexual Biology, Behavior, and Orientation

The Body: A Multimedia AIDS/HIV Information Resource
http://www.thebody.com/cgi-bin/body.cgi

On this site you can find the basics about AIDS/HIV, learn about treatments, exchange information in forums, and gain insight from experts.

Healthy Way
http://www.ab.sympatico.ca/Contents/health/

This Canadian site, which is directed toward consumers, will lead you to many links related to sexual orientation. It also addresses aspects of human sexuality over the life span, general health, and reproductive health.

Hispanic Sexual Behavior and Gender Roles
http://www.caps.ucsf.edu/hispnews.html

This research report from the University of California at San Francisco Center for AIDS Prevention Studies describes and analyzes Hispanic sexual behavior and gender roles, particularly as regards prevention of STDs and HIV/AIDS.

James Kohl
http://www.pheromones.com

Keeping in mind that this is a commercial site with the goal of selling a book, look here to find topics of interest to nonscientists about pheromones. Links to related material of a more academic nature are included. Check out the diagram of "Mammalian Olfactory-Genetic-Neuronal-Hormonal-Behavioral Reciprocity and Human Sexuality" for a sense of the myriad biological influences that play a part in sexual behavior.

Johan's Guide to Aphrodisiacs
http://www.santesson.com/aphrodis/aphrhome.htm

"The Aphrodisiac Home Page" provides links to information about a multitude of substances that some believe arouse or increase sexual response or cause or increase sexual desire. Skepticism about aphrodisiacs is also discussed.

UNIT 3: Interpersonal Relationships

American Psychological Association
http://www.apa.org/topics/homepage.html

By exploring the APA's "PsychNET," you will be able to find links to an abundance of articles and other resources related to interpersonal relationships throughout the life span.

Bonobos Sex and Society
http://songweaver.com/info/bonobos.html

This site, accessed through Carnegie Mellon University, includes an article explaining how a primate's behavior challenges traditional assumptions about male supremacy in human evolution.

The Celibate FAQ
http://www.glandscape.com/celibate.html

Martin Poulter's definitions, thoughts, and suggested resources on celibacy were created, he says, "in response to the lack of celibate stuff (outside of religious contexts) on the Internet," and his perception of the Net's bias against celibacy can be found on this site.

Go Ask Alice
http://www.goaskalice.columbia.edu

This interactive site provided by Healthwise, a division of Columbia University Health Services, includes discussion and insight into a number of personal issues of interest to college-age people—and those younger and older. Many questions about physical and emotional health and well-being in the modern world are answered.

UNIT 4: Reproduction

Ask NOAH About Pregnancy: Fertility & Infertility
http://www.noah-health.org/english/pregnancy/fertility.html

New York Online Access to Health (NOAH) seeks to provide relevant, timely, and unbiased health information for consumers. At this site, the organization presents extensive links to a variety of resources about infertility treatments and issues.

Childbirth.Org
http://www.childbirth.org

This interactive site about childbirth options is from an organization that aims to educate consumers to know their options and provide themselves with the best possible care to ensure healthy pregnancies and deliveries. The site and its links address a myriad of topics, from episiotomy to water birth.

Planned Parenthood
http://www.plannedparenthood.org

Visit this well-known organization's home page for links to information on the various kinds of contraceptives (including outercourse and abstinence) and to discussions of other topics related to sexual and reproductive health.

UNIT 5: Sexuality Through the Lifecycle

American Association of Retired Persons (AARP)
http://www.aarp.org

The AARP, a major advocacy group for older people, includes among its many resources suggested readings and Internet links to organizations that deal with the health and social issues that may affect one's sexuality as one ages.

National Institute on Aging (NIA)
http://www.nih.gov/nia/

The NIA, one of the institutes of the National Institutes of Health, presents this home page to lead you to a variety of resources on health and lifestyle issues that are of interest to people as they grow older.

Teacher Talk
http://education.indiana.edu/cas/tt/tthmpg.html

This home page of the publication *Teacher Talk* from the Indiana University School of Education Center for Adolescent Studies will lead you to many interesting teacher comments, suggestions, and ideas regarding sexuality education and how to deal with sex issues in the classroom.

World Association for Sexology
http://www.tc.umn.edu/nlhome/m201/colem001/was/wasindex.htm

The World Association for Sexology works to further the understanding and development of sexology throughout the world. Access this site to explore a number of issues and links related to sexuality throughout life.

UNIT 6: Old/New Sexual Concerns

The Child Rights Information Network (CRIN)
http://www.crin.org

The Child Rights Information Network (CRIN) is a global network that disseminates information about the Convention on the Rights of the Child and child rights among nongovernmental organizations (NGOs), United Nations agencies, intergovernmental organizations (IGOs), educational institutions, and other child rights experts.

Infertility Resources
http://www.ihr.com/infertility/index.html

This site includes links to the Oregon Health Sciences University Fertility Program and the Center for Reproductive Growth in Nashville, Tennessee. Ethical, legal, financial, psychological, and social issues are discussed.

Men's Health Resource Guide
http://www.menshealth.com/new/guide/index.html

This resource guide from *Men's Health* presents many links to topics in men's health, from AIDS/STDs, to back pain, to impotence and infertility, to vasectomy. It also includes discussions of relationship and family issues.

Third Age: Love and Sex
http://www.thirdage.com/romance/

This interactive site explores a current topic: relationships forged on the Internet. Browse here to hear various viewpoints on the issue. Advice columnists and psychologists add their perspectives.

Women's Studies Resources
http://www.inform.umd.edu/EdRes/Topic/WomensStudies/

This site from the University of Maryland provides a wealth of resources related to women's studies. You can find links to such topics as body image, comfort (or discomfort) with sexuality, personal relationships, pornography, and more.

We highly recommend that you review our Web site for expanded information and our other product lines. We are continually updating and adding links to our Web site in order to offer you the most usable and useful information that will support and expand the value of your Annual Editions. You can reach us at: *http://www.dushkin.com/annualeditions/*.

UNIT 1

Sexuality and Society

Unit Selections

Key Points to Consider

- Have you ever spoken to a young person from another culture/country about sexuality-related ideas, norms, education, or behavior? If so, what surprised you? What did you think about their perspective or ways?

- Do you feel the American culture is too permissive or too rigid with respect to sexual norms, expectations, and laws? Why? What changes would you recommend?

- What do you think can and should be done about HIV/AIDS, child sexual abuse, and prostitution in developing countries?

- In what ways does it matter whether the source of gender differences is biological or cultural? Do you feel that either gender has a "better" sex role or a wider range of acceptable behaviors? If so, which?

 **Links: www.dushkin.com/online/**
These sites are annotated in the World Wide Web pages.

Department of State: Human Rights
http://www.state.gov/g/drl/hr/

SocioSite: Feminism and Women's Issues
http://www.pscw.uva.nl/sociosite/TOPICS/Women.html

Woman in Islam: Sex and Society
http://www.jamaat.org/islam/WomanSociety.html

Women's Human Rights Resources
http://www.law-lib.utoronto.ca/Diana/

People of different civilizations in different historical periods have engaged in a variety of modes of sexual expression and behavior. Despite this cultural and historical diversity, it is clear that human sexuality is a dynamic and complex force that involves psychological and sociocultural, as well as, physiological facets. Our sexuality includes our whole body and personality while we learn what it means to be sexual and to behave sexually within the structure and parameters of our era through our family, social group, and society. By studying varying cultures and eras we see more clearly the interplay between the biological, psychological, and sociocultural, as well as between the person, generation, and society.

For several centuries, Western civilization, especially Western European and, in turn, American cultures, have been characterized by an "anti-sex ethic." This belief system includes a variety of negative views and norms about sex and sexuality, including denial, fear, restriction, and the detachment of sexual feelings and behavior from the wholeness of personhood or humanity. Indeed, it has only been in the last 50 years that the anti-sex proscriptions against knowing or learning about sex have lost their stranglehold so that people can find accurate information about their sexual health, sexual functioning, and birth control without fear of stigma or even incarceration. In fact, many Americans and others have become increasingly concerned in recent years about the ways in which sex and sexual topics have been talked and written about in various media formats. On the surface it might seem that the "anti-sex ethic" no longer reigns. However, it is still active, but now co-exists with an in-your-face, commercialized, and negative view of sex.

One generalization on which sociologists and others who study human behavior anywhere in the world can agree is that social change in beliefs, norms, or behavior—sexual or otherwise—is not easily accomplished. When it does occur, it is linked to significant changes in the social environment and usually happens as a result of interest groups that move society to confront and question existing beliefs, norms, and behavior. Changes in the social environment that have been most often linked to changes in sexuality and its expression include the invention of the car, the liberation of women from the kitchen, changes in the legality and availability of birth control, the reconsideration of democratic values of individual freedom and the pursuit of happiness, demographic shifts where particular (or different) age groups predominate, the growth of mass media, and the coming of the computer age and related technologies. The social groups that have been involved in the process of this sexual/social change have also been far-reaching. In the United States they include the earliest feminists, the suffragettes; Margaret Sanger, the mother of the birth control movement; mainstream religious groups that insist that "sexuality is a good gift from God"; publishers of sex education curricula for youth; pioneering researchers like Alfred Kinsey, Havelock Ellis, William Masters, Virginia Johnson, and others; and a panorama of interest groups who have advocated changes, demanded rights, or both.

Many events, people, and perspectives have played a role in sexuality beliefs and behaviors today. One of the most dramatic is from the "don't-talk-about-it" to an "everyone's-talking-about-it" communication norm. Current examples range from baby-boomer women about menopause and hormone replacement therapy, to prominent politicians, athletes, or entertainment celebrities about erectile dysfunction, sexually transmitted diseases or prostate cancer and public service and paid advertisements on television, radio, and the internet for contraceptives, erectile dysfunction medications, and sexual lubricants. However, it is also clear that some things have not changed as much as we might expect given the increased talk, information, and availability of birth control and other sexual health products and services. It is not characteristic for the majority of people of any age to feel comfortable with and communicate about sexual feelings, fears, needs, and desires. Negotiating, even understanding, consent and responsibility seems even harder today than when we were not talking. The incidence of unplanned, unwed, and teenage pregnancies, sexually transmitted diseases (some life-threatening), molestation, incest, rape, and sexual harassment continue to be troubling, especially because rates of these sexuality-related problems are not lowest in what we perceive as the "most developed" or enlightened country, the United States. At the same time, despite more knowledge than ever before and the efforts of many in the educational, medical, and political spheres, the dream of healthy, positive, and fulfilling sexuality still eludes individuals and society as a whole.

This unit overviews historical, cross-cultural, and current issues and trends in order to illustrate the connectedness of our values, practices, and experiences of sexuality. In so doing it is meant to challenge readers to adopt a very broad perspective through which their examination of today's sexuality, and their experience of it, can be more meaningful. Only in so doing can we hope to avoid a fear-based return to the "anti-sex ethic" of the past while striving to evaluate the impact and value of the social changes that have so profoundly affected sexuality at the dawn of the twenty-first century.

Women's ideal bodies
then & now

Just 100 years ago, the Chinese worshipped a woman's round belly as a symbol of fertility and sexual desire. Today, they strive for a flat, Westernized ideal. And in South Africa, women's once-revered big hips have given way to skin and bones. Every day, TV, the Internet, and the inevitable creep of modernization force women around the globe to abandon their unique body ideals. *Marie Claire* investigates the changing shape of women

By Julia Savacool

China

china 1900 slim body, soft belly

THEN For centuries in China, the most desirable women were slim by Western standards with "a modest touch of fullness" in their midsection (the Chinese actually had a term for it: *feng man*). This body ideal was related to traditional Chinese-medicine principles that said a woman's *qi*, or vital energy, has its central reservoir in the abdomen. "For the Chinese, a rounded belly translated into a woman of sexual desire, fertility, and strength," says anthropologist Susan Brownell, Ph.D., an expert on Chinese culture at the University of Missouri-St. Louis.

china 2004 thin body, flat belly

NOW The thin are getting thinner! According to a recent study, up to 70 percent of Chinese college women now think they're too fat, even though their weight is normal. And Dr. Sing Lee, director of the Hong Kong Eating Disorders Clinic, says he sees 25 to 50 times as many patients as he did 15 years ago. "Fatness is subjective in these women's minds," Dr. Lee explains. "In one study we

did, more than half the women were at normal or below-normal weight, but they were all trying to lose at least 10 pounds." The growing Chinese fixation on skinniness is apparent in the proliferating weight-loss ads in their women's magazines—as many as one in every two ads is for diet products, pills, or teas.

The decline of *feng man* can be traced directly to the 1966 Cultural Revolution and the influence of communism. "With the rise of communism, femininity and softness were discouraged," Dr. Brownell explains. "A masculine ideal was associated with revolutionary fervor and was emulated because it is also associated with hard work, a communist ideal." And China's strict one-child policy today means that women's bodies are less appreciated as fertility symbols. "In China, thinness and a flat belly are in," says Dr. Brownell.

Fiji

Then, fat

THEN When Harvard Medical School anthropologist/psychiatrist Anne Becker, M.D., Ph.D., was studying the women of Fiji in the 1980s, she found that two-thirds of the population were overweight or obese. Amazingly, almost one in five obese women surveyed said they wished to gain even more weight. "In Fiji, social position was partly determined by how well you were fed. At any meal, you were supposed to eat beyond the point of fullness." In particular, large calves were a mark of attractiveness. "Thick calves were equated with a woman's ability to do work—a valued attribute," explains Dr. Becker. "Calling someone 'skinny legs' was the ultimate insult."

Now, slim

NOW When Dr. Becker visited the villagers in 1988, eating disorders were unfamiliar, and women laughed at her description of the Western world's quest for thinness. But today, being thin is the goal of many young women on the island. "The change in women's thinking about their bodies has been remarkable," says Dr. Becker.

So what happened? In a word: television. In 1995, TV came to the rural island villages, and young women started spending hours watching soaps and sitcoms. The quality of life portrayed in these shows far surpassed the Fijians' own, says Dr. Becker, and native women equated those higher living standards with the willowy look of the Western actresses—an ideal they began to emulate. Thirty-eight months after TV's arrival, 15 percent of girls surveyed had vomited to control their weight. "Fijians are leaping from an isolated agricultural society into the information age," says Dr. Becker, "and the psychological impact has been immense."

Jamaica

Then, coca cola-bottle shape

THEN "In my mother's generation, proper proportion was king," says Gail Marcia Anderson, M.A., the Jamaican co-author of a new study in the *Journal of Cross-Cultural Psychology* that compares body-image attitudes of white American and black Jamaican youth. "It was believed that the bust should be moderate, the waist smaller, the hips larger—all in proportion, like an old-fashioned Coca-Cola bottle." Moreover, says Anderson, it has always been more attractive for a Jamaican woman to be 10 pounds overweight than 10 pounds underweight: "Jamaicans have traditionally valued the curvy, voluptuous figures of women."

Now, large butts

NOW Voluptuousness is still valued, but today, big butts are emphasized— and proper proportion is a thing of the past. In pursuit of a supersize rear, some women even risk their health by taking animal-hormone pills, used by

farmers to fatten chickens, in a misguided attempt to "grow" a larger butt. (There's no scientific evidence that it works.) "These pills are extremely dangerous," says Dr. Manuel Peña, representative of Jamaica's Pan American Health Organization. "They are not meant for humans. Taking them can have severe health implications, including high blood pressure and metabolic problems."

A driving factor behind Jamaica's big-bottom fascination comes from the rise in popularity of Jamaican "dancehall" music, which exploded with the current generation, says Anderson. "In dancehall, most dance moves center around the hips and buttocks."

"There's even a popular song that explicitly celebrates 'mampi-size' women—a colloquialism for the big-bodied female," adds Carolyn Cooper, Ph.D., a professor of literary and cultural studies at the University of the West Indies in Jamaica and author of *Sound Clash: Jamaican Dancehall Culture*. "Some foolhardy women are taking chicken pills in an attempt to give themselves the full figure celebrated in dancehall lyrics."

Reinforcing the image of voluptuous hips are the super-curvy "dancehall queens"—women who win the annual dance contests and wow the crowds with their overtly sexual gyrations. "These women sit at the pinnacle of what most young Jamaicans want their bodies to look like," says Anderson. "In previous generations, women covered up their bodies out of modesty; their figures were less on display. Today, dancehall queens are just about showing it all." She adds, "Women in Jamaica have always liked curves; it's just that the type of curve has changed."

Mongolia

Then, plump and short

THEN "Mongolians traditionally described the ideal woman as plump enough and short enough to 'fill your eyes' when you look at her," says Naidan Tsogzolmaa, a native Mongolian guide and program director for Nomadic Expeditions. This body ideal was suited to the harsh way of life of Mongolia's nomadic horseback riders—extra flesh is imperative for survival in a country where temperatures drop to negative-26 degrees Fahrenheit at night. "Skinny women will not survive the extreme Mongolian winters, and tall women will not fit on the native horses, which are quite small," says Tsogzolmaa. "And, because nomadic Mongolians are so isolated, husband and wife must depend on each other for keeping the family healthy and fed. A man would not want a wife who looks like she might not be strong enough to carry her share of the work." Moreover, high-fat horses' milk and cheese have long been dietary staples for nomadic Mongolians, encouraging their rounder physiques.

Now, thin and tall

NOW Among nomadic tribeswomen, plump and short is still considered ideal, but the nomadic population itself is in decline. More than 50 percent of Mongolians now live in urban centers (a 20-percent increase over the past two decades), where the physical ideal closely resembles that of Western culture. In Ulaanbaatar—Mongolia's capital city, where nearly one-third of the country's people live—tall and thin is in vogue.

The influence of Western culture can actually be traced back to the 1930s, when "young, affluent girls were sent to Russia and Germany to study," says Tsogzolmaa. "They brought back with them a certain notion of body shape, which has grown stronger over time. Now Ulaanbaatar women are striving to get that slim shape you see in the West."

Better infrastructure and jobs have also lured more Mongolians to urban centers. And modern amenities have negated nomadic concerns about surviving long, cold winters, while giving women instant access to global trends. "We have the same technology in our cities as every other city in the world," says Tsogzolmaa. "So Ulaanbaatar women see images of Western models in the media." Dieting is very popular, she notes, and fitness centers, which didn't even exist here 10 years ago, are now starting to take off.

South Africa

Then, big legs and hips

THEN For centuries, large lower bodies were the mark of sexiness for South Africa's indigenous women. In fact, women of the Ndebele—one of the largest native populations—wore large, beaded waist and leg hoops called golwani, stuffed with rubber to produce a larger-than-life bottom half. These padded costumes symbolized rolls of body fat, considered marks of beauty. The Zulu, another South African tribe, created rituals to highlight women's hips and legs. "Among black natives, large buttocks and thighs were considered signs of womanliness," says anthropologist Carolyn Martin Shaw, Ph.D., of the University of California Santa Cruz. "Large buttocks were the focal point of celebratory dances that required women to turn their backsides to the audience and show off fantastic muscle control by contracting their buttocks to the music."

Now, slim all over

NOW All-around thin is in. A new study reports that Zulu women have the fastest-growing rate of eating disorders of any group in the country. "In our study of black female university students in a rural area, 45 percent had some form of disordered eating," says researcher Julie Seed, senior lecturer in psychology at Northumbria University in the U.K. "Considering that bigness has traditionally been seen as a sign of wealth and beauty, this was a shock."

"Thin" has even become a political statement. "Prior to the end of apartheid in 1995, there were no documented cases of eating disorders among blacks in South Africa," says Seed. "But today, women in the black community equate 'thin' with being educated and having rights—in other words, being more like a white person. Younger black women don't want to look big, because big symbolizes their past, and their past has not been particularly rosy." Seed and her colleagues' study also reveals that some Zulu and Ndebele women feel being thin will improve their job prospects.

Kenya: the last holdout

Then and Now

The Maasai are one of the last global cultures to remain true to their natural look (long and lanky). Why are they holding on to their body ideal? For one, their shape is already similar to the Western ideal that other countries are importing. But lifestyle also plays an important role: The nomadic Maasai, who often walk dozens of miles a day, expend a tremendous amount of energy. Meanwhile, their food sources are poor: The traditional diet consists of milk, cow's blood, and meat on special occasions. And finally, the warrior Maasai (who also inhabit parts of Tanzania) have enormous pride in their culture. Their coming-of-age rituals strengthen the ties of women to their community, and language barriers limit their contact with outsiders.

Sex Around the World

more takes a revealing look at the intimate lives of women in seven countries. When we dispatched our foreign correspondents around the globe, even they didn't know if women in traditional societies would talk about sex and love. They did—in detail. Here are their true confessions

PRODUCED BY SHARLENE K. JOHNSON

ITALY
LOVE, ITALIAN STYLE

MARA MEMO, 53
A divorced professor of urban sociology at the University of Rome, she has two daughters, 23 and 12, by two different men. She has managed to carve out both a career and what she calls a "joyous existence."

BEAUTIFUL BEGINNING "I was almost eighteen, and he was my first great love. We were in an alpine field full of flowers, and we took off our clothes and made love on the grass—the first time for both of us. Afterward, I said, 'How marvelous!'"

TODAY "Sex is a wonder—the most joyous thing. If it's missing from my life, I feel sad, depressed, nervous, like a lion in a cage. It's not enough to have children or work. I want to be cuddled, embraced and caressed, and to reciprocate. I can make love two or three times a night, as many as five times a week, with my current partner."

IMPROVISING "I like variety: making love on the ground, on the table, wherever."

LOOKING GOOD "I'm proud of my legs. When I'm ninety, I'll still pinch men's bottoms and wear miniskirts."

YOUNGER LOVERS "I've often been with younger men—once a twenty-three-year-old when I was forty-four. They are more open to playing soccer or taking a walk at one in the morning."

THE MAIN ATTRACTION "He has to be a great lover. Attractiveness is second."

MOTHER KNEW BEST "When I lived with my first daughter's father without marrying him, my mother said, 'People will think you're a whore.' I told her that was silly; we're no longer in the nineteenth century. But she was right: People did think that, and I was really hurt."

SURVIVING HEARTACHE "When a great love ends, it's painful, but you pick yourself up and discover that you can be lighthearted once more. You can fall in love again and again."

—*Elisabetta Povoledo*

ITALY: "I'm Proud of my legs. When I'm ninety, I'll still pinch men's bottoms and wear miniskirts."

EGYPT: "I like being on top best. Here, women call the missionary position 'the roach,' because the woman is on the bottom with her legs and arms flailing."

EGYPT
FROM DESERT TO OASIS

HALA, 40-something
A career woman and veiled Muslim with two school-age children, she divorced her first husband a few months after their arranged marriage. Several years later, she married for love. She asked that

neither her full name nor her photo be published.

A BAD START "My first time was at the hotel after my first wedding. I was tense. I didn't know him well. I didn't love him. I thought afterward, 'Sex isn't romantic, it's animalistic.'"

THE BLOODY SHEET "His family wanted to be reassured about my virginity. My husband's sister asked him, 'Is everything okay? Is she good?' Sometimes the husband's female relatives want to see the "blood on the sheet."

NOT A VIRGIN "In the villages, if the girl is found not to be a virgin, I hear they may kill her—even nowadays."

NO FOREPLAY "My first husband would just come and then finish. After sex with him, I would go to the bathroom and cry. I heard from friends that they enjoyed sex, but I was in pain."

A SECOND CHANCE "It's about feelings, not just sex. My second husband wants me to enjoy intercourse as well. We try everything. He tells me, 'I've taught you fifty positions. During our lifetime, I'll teach you ninety-nine.' I like being on top best. Here, women call the missionary position 'the roach,' because the woman is on the bottom with her legs and arms flailing."

CHANGING TIMES "I never spoke to my mother about sex—not when I got my period, not on the day of my wedding, not to this day. Now, my daughter has sex education at school, and I talk to her, too. I tell her not to have intimate relations before marriage. When she is older, I will talk to her about sex itself and tell her not to be passive."

FEMALE CIRCUMCISION "I wasn't circumcised, but all my aunts were. It was common in the villages until recently; girls were thought to be excitable, so their clitorises were cut. It's not a religious idea. It's for

men's benefit. It's bad, because it makes a woman cold sexually."

RELIGION AND SEX "The Koran says that sex is important within marriage, because from it comes life."

—*Sarah Gauch*

MEXICO
SEX AS THE SPICE OF LIFE

ALEJANDRA ALLEN MAGANA, 41
Magana, an advertising sales executive, lost her virginity at 16 to a rapist and then had an unsatisfying marriage. The widowed mother of two teenage boys now still has an adventurous sexual relationship with her boyfriend.

FIRST THINGS FIRST "You can't have sex without love."

THE CALM AND THE STORM "I can guarantee you that my mother has never had an orgasm in her life. Furthermore, my father left my mother years ago, and she never had another relationship. She has passed the time so calmly. I would go crazy after one month. When I have sex, all my problems dissipate, and I feel so good."

TIMES HAVE CHANGED "I tell my two sons that sex is a very important and beautiful part of life, but that they need to be careful to avoid STDs."

FAVORITE POSITION "I could be making love in all sorts of positions with my partner, but if I don't have the last orgasm on top, I don't feel satisfied."

FAKING IT "When I was married, I followed the lead of Donna Summer—I copied her ahs, ohs and ooohs. But I didn't feel anything.

Now I scream, cry, kick, and it's all real."

CULTURAL NORMS "Most women are not open about sex; many don't have orgasms. I tell girlfriends how wonderful it feels, and they say, 'He lets me know when it's over.' That's not worth it."

SELF-GRATIFICATION "It's considered normal for men to masturbate, but not for women to do so."

RAPE "Rapes occur on the streets, but I think they also happen within the family. A single woman might invite a boyfriend to live with her, and he turns around and rapes her daughter."

SEXUAL GOAL "Sex is more important for me today than ever before. I want to reach menopause feeling that I have the same satisfying sex life that I do now."

—*Eliza Hughes*

SWEDEN
NORTHERN LIGHTS SHINE ON

GUN MARIANNE KRISTOFFERSSON, 57 Kristoffersson, a translator in Stockholm, has a "cozy relationship" with the man she has been dating for three years. Never married, she says she has had her most intense sexual experiences in the years since she turned 40.

HER FIRST TIME "Just before I turned twenty-two, I looked for a 'deflowerer.' I had never dated and thought my virginity was embarrassing. It was a blood-bath and didn't feel good in any way, but I was glad to have it over with."

SWEDEN: "I never longed for marriage and

children and had scores of lovers. I always do what I want and fulfill my dreams."

INDIA: "I had a very close friend with whom I talked about many things. We were closer than if we had had sex. He died and I've never found that tremendous bond again."

SINGLE BY CHOICE "I'm very unusual, almost unique, because I've never longed for marriage and children and had scores of lovers. I always do what I want and fulfill my dreams. I do love, but I also fear becoming dependent and vulnerable."

BEING THE OTHER WOMAN "I've often had relationships with married men, and was smitten with a few of them. I thought they suited my way of life—the silver lining without the everyday nagging."

IS LOVE NECESSARY? "No. I might be a virgin if that were the case."

PILLOW TALK "It turns me on to talk in bed about what you're going to do. But my current partner is a bit shy about this, and I have to accept it."

TABOO "Anal intercourse."

GENERATION GAP "Miles wide. My mother didn't know how her body worked. She thought she menstruated and ovulated at the same time. We never, ever talked about sex. My generation is the first to be able to make decisions about our bodies and our lives. Friends my age who have daughters are very open with them."

HOMOSEXUALITY "Sweden is pretty free of prejudice. Homosexuals

are allowed to marry, through so-called registered partnerships. I think that sexual preference is a private matter."

CHANGING PRIORITIES "Earlier in my life, I chose men for their physical attractiveness and was disappointed and hurt. Those men conquer woman after woman. Now, I'm mature enough to choose a warm and loving man whom I can trust."

—Anna Pandolfi

INDIA
LOVE LOST, TWICE OVER

RENU BHASIN, 55
Defying her parents and India's rigid social norms, Bhasin married for love 33 years ago. At first, she enjoyed an active sex life with her husband, a businessman in New Delhi. But as she became busy with their daughters, now 25 and 28, and he with his career, they grew apart. Five years ago, he took a mistress. Bhasin asked that her face not be shown.

WEDDING NIGHT "I was nervous. My first night was not as exciting as succeeding ones, because I got more and more comfortable."

MOTHER AND DAUGHTER "My mother never talked to me about sex. What little I knew was from discussions with friends. With my daughters, I let them know that they could say what they wanted to me about the subject. There is nothing wrong with sex."

THE OTHER WOMAN "I don't know what he sees in her, and I cannot see where I was lacking."

HIS PUNISHMENT "I say I'm tired, and I think he understands what I'm saying. This is the only way I can pay him back. Having a sexual relationship with him just doesn't

make me feel comfortable these days."

HER TEMPTATION "I had a very close friend, with whom I talked a lot. We were closer than if we had had sex. It was more satisfying, because sex is a one-time thing, and then it's finished. Our relationship was an ongoing process. He died, and I've never found that tremendous bond again."

WHY SHE STAYS "I'm over fifty. It's too late for me to start earning a living. And why should I? He married me, so he has to take care of me. It's my birthright. If he's been indiscreet, let him live with it."

BOTTOM LINE "Today, I find that I can dictate my own terms—even though there is something missing in my life. Still, I have no regrets."

—Martha Ann Overland

BARZIL
THE GIRL FROM SAN PAULO

CACILDA CAMARGO, 45
An accomplished ceramicist with her own studio, Camargo lives with her husband of 23 years, their 22-year-old daughter Gabriela and Gabriela's boyfriend. Deeply involved in spiritualism, Camargo spends hours on the Internet, meeting like-minded people.

FIRST AND FOREVER "The first person I had sex with was my husband, right after he asked me to marry him. I was nineteen. It was during Carnival, and we were at a farmhouse. Our friends threw us together in a room. I thought we were just going to sleep."

MOTEL SEX "When we were dating, we'd go to motels. We'd

schedule a wake-up call for about four o'clock, so we could get home before sunrise. My mother and my mother-in-law still think I was a virgin bride. After we got married, we kept going to motels for the big beds, hot tubs and mirrors."

THE MORE THINGS CHANGE "My daughter is embarrassed to talk about all the things that my mother couldn't tell me about. I don't know if my daughter has a good sex life, but I prefer that she have sex here in the house, rather than sneak around."

TOTAL TRUST "Sometimes I go out dancing with a group from my ceramics class. I'm not interested in having affairs, and my husband knows that. He trusts me. I know a lot of couples who could never have the open relationship that we have."

BRAZILIAN CULTURE "Until recently, women weren't thought of as having orgasms. That's changing now. Women talk about multiple orgasms. Men talk about impotence and sexual dysfunction. That was taboo for a long time."

DIFFERENCE OF OPINION

"Men here love the rear-entry position, and most women don't like it at all."

ADVANCED LESSONS "I've been reading a lot lately about techniques to strengthen the vaginal muscles. A woman who perfects that will keep her man forever."

ADULT TOYS "There is no reason why an old married couple can't have their toys. Why not improve your sexual performance?"

—Jennifer L. Rich

BRAZIL: "I've been reading a lot lately about techniques to strengthen the vaginal muscles. A woman who perfects that will keep her man forever."

JAPAN: "I envy the younger generations freedom. My daughter says she'll live with boyfriends before marrying. If I had wanted that, my mother would have disowned me."

JAPAN
LOOKING BACK, AND FORWARD

MIDORI SEKIYAMA, 49
With five kids between 7 and 21 and a busy architect husband, this Tokyo public-health worker says her sex life has deteriorated. She allots time weekly to go a movie or take a day trip—unusual for a married woman in Japan.

A GOOD START "To me, sex is spiritual and physical. That is why I had no sex with my boyfriends until,

at twenty-one, I met the man who would become my husband. After we got married, we enjoyed sex and experimented a lot—having intercourse anywhere and often."

BABY TALK "Things changed after I devoted my time to our first child and was usually tired. My husband woke up early for work, so we often slept in separate rooms. Sex became routine."

DIFFERENT PRIORITIES "I want to have a satisfying sex life that expresses my love for my husband. But he believes his work is most important. To him, I am just the children's mother; he does not expect me to be attractive. We have intercourse once or twice a month. I keep quiet and pretend to be a good wife."

AN AFFAIR TO REMEMBER

"I had a lover for about two years. It was so romantic. I was happy to be cared for by him. Then his wife found out, and our affair ended. I was heartbroken."

SILENCE "Affairs are not common among married women my age, so I would never talk to my friends about my lover."

HER LIFELINE "My children."

HER MOTHER'S WAY "My mother and I never discussed sex. I suspect her marriage was not entirely happy—which did not stop her from being a loyal wife and devoted mother."

NEW FREEDOMS "I envy the younger generation's freedom. My daughter says she'll live with boyfriends before marrying. If I had wanted that, my mother would have disowned me."

—Suvendrini Kakuchi

The Beauty Pageant Prevails

As snow flickers across the bleak, colorless Moscow sky, eight young women walk into a Soviet-era building that houses a cramped indoor firing range. They're all very dewy and innocent-looking, so the military-style fatigues they're wearing seem more like a fashion statement than a uniform. But the women are here today for a shooting contest that's part of the newest Russian beauty pageant; Miss Ugolovno-Ispol'nitel'naya Sistema or, literally translated, Miss Criminal Execution System.

Less literally, I suppose, you'd call it Miss Bureau of Prisons. Its youngest contestant, 17-year-old Katya Zagrebina, is studying to be a criminal lawyer at the Ministry of Justice's Pskov Law Institute. Katya has a gorgeous smile, and her sleek body ripples with muscles. When it's her turn, she slowly holds the gun out in her right hand, aims and makes me go deaf as the gunpowder spark flashes. No shaking, no hesitation. After her target is brought forward, we can see that all of her shots were accurate, with one dead-on in the bull's eye, giving her a top rating of five out of five points. She'll make a perfect employee one day.

Katya tells me she learned all about guns at the institute, "I like shooting," she says through a translator, smiling. "I especially love Kalashnikovs." When I ask why she would want to enter such a contest, she says that all 15 of the women (with 400 men) in her school were "strongly encouraged" to take part in the two earlier regional contests. Still, Katya says she hopes to become the first Miss Bureau of Prisons (M-BOP? Ha). Yesterday there was a short swimming competition, and today they get to show off their abilities to accurately shoot a target and run 1,000 meters before indulging in the standard beauty-pageant fare: talent show, etiquette, diplomacy and evening gowns. The winner gets a crown with precious stones and may get to travel to Western Europe with the Minister of Justice.

Half of the women display various hues of red dye in their dark hair, ranging from fire-engine to maroon, but despite that, they're all very attractive. I'm slightly disappointed that none of the contestants is six feet tall, 250 pounds or wearing head-to-toe gray, because that's what I picture when I think of Russian women working in prisons (a random stereotype I've never really pondered before this instant). Russia has the second-highest incarceration rate in the world, behind the U.S.—partially because of the high amount of crime after the country

switched over to capitalism, partially from civil unrest and partially because the government will still lock you up at the drop of a hat. Actually, I guess I'm not the only one who thinks badly of prison employees. That's sort of why they decided to have this pageant in the first place.

"We are reforming the bureau of prisons. We are trying to be more humanitarian, more liberal," says Alexander Juravski, the Ministry of Justice Cultural Center employee who masterminded this event. "Many people have the opinion that those who work in the corrections facilities break rules, that they're rude, vulgar, impolite and mean. But it's not really like that. There are around 400,000 workers, about one-third women, in the Russian corrections system. A great majority of them are educated, cultured, goodwilled, well-meaning, good workers." And they look hot in ball gowns.

We all squish into the tiny firing range for the contest. One of the coordinators asks the women if they've shot guns before, and they laugh and say, "Yes, of course." None of them has had to shoot her gun on the job, they tell me later, but most are required to practice at least once a month.

The women, who represent different regions of the country, look delicate and sweet even as they raise their guns. But each of their targets has at least one puncture wound in the bull's-eye or in the first ring. Don't mess with these chicks.

In the U.S., we're used to hearing about tiny pageants at every county fair and shopping mall across the nation—Ms. Wheelchair, Most Glamorous Grandmother, Miss Hell Hole Swamp. But apparently, Colombia, known as the "country of queens," is giving us a run for our money. Colombia has hundreds of pageants year-round crowning queens of everything from cattle to coal. And each November, various surgically enhanced women from every region compete in a 17-day extravaganza called the National Beauty Contest to try to become Miss Colombia, who goes on to compete in the Miss Universe pageant. Last year, one of the judges was a plastic surgeon. In this country, where the daily headlines are filled with stories about drug deals, murders, massacres and brutal kidnappings, the citizens seem to look to the beauty queens for inspiration and hope for a better future. The contestants are considered heroes, ideal citizens who are not only beautiful and elegant but who also do good deeds—last year, the queens released endangered turtles into the ocean and visited developmentally disabled children during the pageant. Celebrities, entrepreneurs and politicians show up at the daily festivities, which are broadcast throughout the country via every type of media outlet. This is by far the biggest event of the year for Colombians.

Now we're inside an impressive track-and-field facility in northeastern Moscow. About 25 young, fine-looking, non-smiling male and female athletes-apparently Olympic hopefuls—are pole-vaulting, jumping hurdles, lifting weights and sprinting. They seem annoyed that they have to put their sports on hold for five minutes while the M-BOP ladies run 1,000 meters. One sprinter nearly knocks me down when we all step onto the track. To lend importance to our little event, the organizers have invited four old guys clad in dozens of shiny medals to be guests of honor: legendary Soviet-era Olympic athletes. "I've run 6,900 miles in my lifetime!" one boasts to me, awards clanging.

As the girls change into their Nike and Adidas gear, I speak with Marina Kibenko, a stylish blond instructor from the law institute who is here to support Katya. Her answers sound like propaganda: "This contest is good for the girls because this will help them succeed! This will increase the prestige of the employees of the penal system!"

The announcer interrupts. "We welcome you to participate in a fair and uncompromised race," he says. The athletes totally ignore us. "Please cheer on these beauties!"

The eight girls begin running, and Katya takes the lead. The rest don't look so happy. The announcer yells, "You're doing well, you only have three laps to go—no big deal!" A few minutes later Katya wins, and a purplish-haired woman named Irina Kolchina, 30, sputters over the finish line last.

I turn back to Marina and ask if she enjoys working for the prison system. "I have a very specific job," she says carefully. "You have to get used to it, and you have to love it."

"So do you love it?" I ask. She squirms.

"I'm trying to avoid the question," she says, smiling and looking away. "I've spent my life teaching. I'm doing what I love. It's difficult to work here. You have to be a very strong woman. A weak woman wouldn't survive in this system."

During Colombia's National Beauty Contest, a much smaller local one also takes place. It's called the Popular Beauty Contest, and it's where the less affluent, mainly black contestants go from the local barrios to be crowned the Popular Queen. And even though it would make sense that the winner would automatically go on to compete in the national pageant, this traditionally has not been the case. Instead, Cartagena's official contestant has historically been chosen by a special committee, which generally picks someone who is much whiter and wealthier and willing to have plastic surgery if deemed necessary. But this past year, the mayor of Cartagena stepped in and appointed the winner of the Popular Beauty Con-

test, who was black and from a humble background, to be the local rep. Jeymmy Paola Vargas Gomez went on to place second in the big pageant, a prestigious position known as Vice Queen, and Cartagena's masses went crazy for her, like she was royalty they could relate to. Like she could take away some of their problems for a while.

An instrumental version of "Nights in White Satin" is playing over the PA system in the theater at the Ministry of Justice building on the morning after the running event. Onstage, some very girly young men are escorting the contestants in a dress rehearsal. One of the guys keeps leaping spontaneously, while a big screen above him displays dreary aerial shots of the contestants' hometowns and on-the-job photos involving rifles, barbed wire and modest smiles.

I ask Alexander why he decided to include ballroom dancing and an etiquette contest in the grand finale, which will be the next day. "My belief is that there is a movement in music, movies and the press which idealizes crime and rape, sex, blood, murder. And we are trying to go against that," he answers. "The challenge at the top is to develop a high-quality culture among the workers and to raise their moral system. We want to show our employees as role models, saying, 'There's another way of life, in which people love one another and have sincere friendships that say nice words to one another and smile and do good deeds.' And we are inviting everyone to this kind of lifeincluding you!" he says, motioning to me. I beam at him.

"THE MISS BUREAU OF PRISONS WINNER WILL INCREASE THE PRESTIGE OF THE PENAL SYSTEM!" SAYS MARINA, A GOVERNMENT EMPLOYEE.

Then I get it together. "But if the general public sees how beautiful the women are, do you think they'll commit more crimes just to be near them?" I ask.

He laughs. "I think there are more interesting ways to meet these girls. Legal ways without complications and headaches,"

In 2002, the first Miss Tibet pageant was supposed to "highlight the Tibetan identity," according to its organizers, and bring a little glitz to the lives of those who want more attention for their cause of independence from China. Thirty women registered for the pageant, which included a controversial swimsuit competition. But there was such an uproar in Dharamsala, the Indian city where the pageant was to be held, that only four women showed up. Many exiled Tibetan locals there, who favor long skirts and long-sleeved shirts to cover their bodies, said it trivialized their cause and was "un-Tibetan." Then last year, only one registered. The ceremony still took place, in a modified form: After they re-capped the accomplishments of the previous Miss Tibet, showcased a musical act and gave a speech about freedom, 20-year-old Tsering Kyi was crowned the new Miss Tibet and given a $2,000 scholarship. Shortly after she was crowned, she met Prince Charles. Which all makes me wonder what's more disturbing: when society dictates that females are most valued if they're wearing revealing clothes, or when women are ostracized if they actually choose to take part in a swimsuit competition.

Now I'm backstage, interviewing the women who have put on their evening gowns for the Miss Bureau of Prisons dress rehearsal. The Tom Jones song "Sex Bomb" is playing loudly and Alyona Kazlova, the pageant's artistic director, is telling the girls to really feel the music. They start to shake their hips more, and some flick their skirts and throw their hair around their shoulders. They're finally relaxing.

I corner Irina when she walks offstage. "This pageant shows that we're able to be different, strong, sexy and beautiful," she says enthusiastically. Irina is responsible for safety in one of the bureau of prison departments. Like the other women I interview, she seems to find no hypocrisy in this contest. Irina says she thoroughly enjoys her job and has never felt discriminated against. Quite the opposite. "I like working there because I'm the only woman in a group of men. The men in our system are very controlled, self-possessed and cultured," she says. "I like the discipline ... and I like the uniform."

Contestant Marina Kulkova, 21, also mentions the uniform as one of the perks of her job figuring out pensions for inmates. "With this pageant we will not only discover our hidden talents, but we will prove to others that the penal system has many pretty girls in it," she points out. "A girl with a gun is always scary. No one would expect anything good to come out of it. But we want to show that's not true."

Irina heads onstage to practice for the talent competition dressed in a bondage-like outfit-fake leather, gold belt and slimming stilettos. She sings a song interspersed with spoken-word bits extolling the virtues of Russia over an instrumental version of "Pretty Woman." After that, the professional dancers do a modern-ballet-type routine to a brass version of "Power of Love." By the end, it's late and the ladies are tired, so we say good night.

Why do American pageants seem so much cheesier and less meaningful, even when they're giving out pro-woman scholarships? Maybe it's because they appear to benefit only the beauty queen who wins and the advertisers who bought time slots during the event, instead of giving the nation any sort of hope. Still, I just wonder when all these countries will find more direct ways to affect society—say, if the Colombian government were to set aside some of the money it normally spends on the National Beauty Contest and put it toward microcredit loans for women. Because attempting to create social change via human Barbie dolls? That's not going to get anybody very far.

TO SHOW OFF THEIR TALENTS, A RUSSIAN CONTESTANT DID A GEISHA-STYLE DANCE, AND IN TIBET, A WOMAN SANG CELINE DION'S "MY HEART WILL GO ON."

Which brings us back to Moscow. I wake up on the last morning eager to watch the pageant's grand finale. Then I turn on the news and see pictures of bloody people being carried on stretchers out of a Moscow subway station. A terrorist—presumably a Chechen rebel—set off a bomb in one of the cars, and at least 39 people are dead, 130 wounded. The Chechens want to secede from Russia to have their own autonomous state and, with the presidential elections coming up, this was maybe a good time to get attention.

The locals I encounter don't seem afraid so much as resigned to the fact that nothing can really be done to stop such acts of violence. Suddenly, I get a phone call from one of the pageant's coordinators. "We're postponing the pageant and sending the girls home," she says. "It doesn't seem right to celebrate now."

A Deadly Passage to India

More than 20 million people could be infected with the AIDS virus by 2010. A journey to the heart of a suffering nation.

By Geoffrey Cowley

Wonder, degradation, hope—it's all on parade on a torrid summer night in Kolkata's Kalighat district. Pilgrims are swarming in the jasmine-scented mist outside the Dakshineswar Kali Temple. They've come from all over India to pay homage to Kali, the fearsome Hindu goddess who continually devours whatever life the earth generates. The lane leading up to the temple is a joyful riot of rickshaws, mopeds, stray goats and street vendors. Inside, the mood approaches ecstasy as worshipers burn incense and lay garlands and balloons at the feet of Kali's statue. But the scene grows darker, and death more mundane, as you wander the torch-lit lanes that extend behind the temple to the bank of the Hugli River. Pigs forage freely at the waterfront for garbage and funeral-pyre leftovers (open fires make imperfect incinerators). Men lounge on cots in front of small huts while, inside, their wives perform sex acts on strangers for a few rupees. Kids play on the pavement amid pimps and johns who hunger to put them to work. The AIDS virus thrives in places like Kalighat, and Asia has many of them. That's one reason the region is now in such peril.

As the vanguard of what the CIA has dubbed the "next wave" of the global AIDS crisis, India and China could have 40 million HIV-positive people by the end of this decade—the same number the entire world has today. The CIA predicts that India alone will have 20 million to 25 million infections, up from 4 million today, "even if the disease does not break out significantly into the mainstream population." That's not to say that disaster is inevitable. Despite its widespread poverty, India has a growing economy and the rudiments of a health-care system. It also enjoys substantial support from international donors such as USAID and the Bill and Melinda Gates Foundation, which last week announced a new $100 million India initiative. But it will take more than money to stop this juggernaut. The challenge, says Dr. Helene Gayle of the Gates Foundation, is to create a national network of AIDS prevention programs to reach all those in need. As anyone traversing this vast country soon learns, that is a tall order.

AIDS has varied faces in a country this vast, but those of the women stand out. As I discovered in the Tamil town of Namakkal, a monogamous woman can earn her in-laws' contempt by getting infected by her husband. With their bright saris, almond eyes and shiny black hair, Chitra, Selvi, Suganda, Selvamani and Vanilla look more like college girls than widows. When the girls were in their late teens or early 20s, all five married truckdrivers and, in keeping with tradition, stayed home to care for babies or in-laws while their husbands plied the highways. All five are now HIV-positive, and all but one have nursed their mates through their own illness and death. The women still wear their wedding necklaces, still care for their young children. Yet each is now reviled by her in-laws. "The family always blames the wife," Suganda explains matter-of-factly. "Very few husbands will admit their own responsibility."

It's easy to feel for Suganda, harder to sympathize with whatever truck-stop prostitute propelled the virus into her life. Then you meet her, or someone like her, and realize what a small role that choice has played in her life. Pattamal is one of 500 young women working the trucks that stop for gas or repairs on a 30-mile stretch of road outside Chennai. She is not a derelict, not a party girl; she's a mom. Seated on a stool in the roadside office of a service organization called Santoshi, she strokes the hair of her quiet 6-year-old daughter and explains her strategy for keeping the child fed. When a driver propositions her on the roadside, she secures a commitment of 100 rupees ($2), then gives him 10 minutes behind a bush or in the cab of his truck. If the driver pays up, she makes as much as she would from a day of scrubbing floors, and hardly has to leave her daughter's side.

How did India get into this mess? In many ways the country has been an AIDS disaster waiting to happen. Poverty and illiteracy are rife, and the commercial sex trade is huge. Women have little if any say in their sexual and reproductive lives. And a well-developed transportation system ensures that a sexually transmitted virus will spread widely once it arrives. When HIV arrived, in 1986, it had been battering other countries for five years, and its dynamics were well known. But instead of mobilizing to contain the virus, public officials blithely asserted that India's "moral character" and conservative sexual mores would keep it from spreading. The virus quickly defied that prediction, racing through red-light districts, infecting both sex workers and their clients. So the police started rounding up sex workers for mandatory blood tests, sometimes jailing the infected instead of promoting safer sex. Hospitals took a similar tack, using blood tests to expose and evict infected patients.

The political landscape is more hospitable today. The leaders of both major parties now acknowledge the urgency of the threat, and the country's AIDS-control agencies have won worldwide acclaim for their work with high-risk groups such as sex workers and street kids. Unfortunately, many average Indians are still living with more risk, and less protection, than they realize. Some 7 percent of the nation's adults harbor sexually transmitted infections—and nearly four men in 10 recall at least one homosexual encounter, according to surveys conducted by the Delhi-based Naz Foundation Trust. Sexuality was once—a major theme in the culture. Tamil Nadu's temple sculptures offer elaborate taxonomies of sensual pleasure, both for couples and for trios ("One lady, two gents," as my guide politely observes). But the Kama Sutra spirit is not much in evidence today. Sex is largely absent from the Bollywood cinema, the mass media and casual conversation. Schools offer little or no sex education. And homosexuality is not only a moral offense but a legal one under Section 377 of the Indian Penal Code. If sex has become a difficult topic for ordinary Indians, AIDS is often an impossible one. Groups providing care for patients or orphans risk eviction if their landlords or neighbors discover their true mission. In several recent instances, local cops have detained or harassed outreach workers for distributing the government's own safe-sex education materials.

Where, then, is the basis for hope? A mom with other options would not turn $2 tricks on a roadside. A wife with other options would think twice about waiting on her in-laws while sex workers waited on her spouse. And children with options would surely look beyond the alleys of Kalighat for their livelihoods. No one—not even Bill Gates—can create such choices by fiat. But at every level of Indian society, one sees hints that change is possible. Pattamal may live humbly, but she learned about HIV in time to avoid contracting it herself. She has used condoms consistently for the past five years. As an educator for Santoshi, she now distributes them to her clients and her peers. In a benevolent pyramid scheme, she then enlists them to do the same. Similar programs have sprouted in most of India's red-light districts in recent years, and some have shown dramatic results.

In Kolkata's Sonagachi district, a grassroots sex workers' collective called the Durbar Mahila Samanwaya Committee (DMSC) has held its 30,000 members' HIV rate below 10 percent for the past decade, even as the rates among other cities' sex workers has topped 50 percent. When members talk about the years before DMSC started in 1992, it's as though they're recalling bad dreams. Manju Biswas is typical. She was barely 13 when a neighbor in her village brought her to Kolkata on the pretext of finding her a job and sold her for $30 to a brothel keeper. Manju's father, a subsistence farmer, had died and her mother and brother were facing starvation. She was completely illiterate. "I was kept in a small, dark room locked for days by the madam," she told me. "Then one night I was forced to drink something that made me dizzy, and then this huge, drunken man was on top of me. I was screaming in pain but I fainted. When I woke up I was bleeding heavily. The madam told me I was now a fallen woman and should stop pestering her to let me go home. These men, 10 to 15 a day, would call on me. It was a horrible life."

Through simple coalition-building, the DMSC gradually transformed the surrounding district and became a legitimate power broker. "We have now branches in almost all the towns and cities in West Bengal," says Swapna Gayen, DMSC's president. "We now sit across from officials and discuss matters relating to our health and welfare." The group also runs a 24-hour AIDS hot line that offers free medical and legal guidance to anyone seeking help.

Whatever their circumstances, few sex workers would choose prostitution for their daughters. While standing up for their own rights, most also do whatever they can to see their own children liberated entirely from the trade. On that front, too, signs of progress are easy to find. On the edge of Mumbai's crumbling Kamathipura red-light district, a group called Apne Aap has created a safe place for school-age girls (they call themselves "Sparrows") to read, paint and socialize. Another group, Sanlaap, runs a similar operation in Kolkata's Kalighat. Because this district's prostitutes work in their huts, the kids are essentially homeless from dusk until midnight. But for the past few years they have spent their evenings in Sanlaap's two concrete shacks, getting the encouragement and electric lights a kid needs to become literate. As I sat down with a dozen of the teens who frequent the drop-in center, its impact was palpable. All but two are in school. Seven are planning for college. And any one of them, even the 10-year-olds, can tell you how to avoid contracting HIV. The Sanlaap kids have recently launched a campaign to raise AIDS awareness within the red-light district—and the older ones are now seeking a wider audience. "We want to be leaders," says Sushmita, a poised 18-year-old who has just completed her college-entrance exam. "We want to show people outside Kalighat that a youth group from this district can make a difference."

Small victories add up, but neither the Kalighat kids nor the Sonagachi sex workers will transform a nation of 28 states, 24 languages and a billion people. It's one thing to get a child through school, quite another to shatter a legacy of fear, ignorance and stigma. Fortunately, bigger players are now embracing that goal. The Gates Foundation has yet to work out the details of its new $100 million program, but its immediate goal is to target the country's huge mobile population—not only truckers but also soldiers, railway workers and oil workers. The foundation has the clout to foster alliances among employers in all those sectors, and the freedom to cross the public-private divide. One can only guess how all these efforts will play out. What's clear is that Asia's infant plague does not have to grow into a disaster.

Victims by Sex/Age Group	
Men	2.3 million
Women	1.5
Children	0.17

Sources: NACO, National Intelligence Council., UNAIDS; written by Josh Ulick.

Portrait of a Public-Health Crisis

A mobile population and a reluctance to acknowledge risky sexual behavior have hindered efforts to control AIDS in India. It could become the most HIV-afflicted country by 2010:

1. Mumbai: More than 50% of the city's thousands of sex workers are infected with HIV.
2. Tamil Nadu: Truckers patronizing prostitutes have helped spread HIV in southern states; 15% of drivers are infected.
3. Manipur: A conduit for Burmese heroin; 56% of the state's injecting drug users have contracted HIV.

AIDS: 20 years of terror

AIDS—Africa's looming disaster

Bernard Otabil

Another brave HIV/AIDS campaigner has finally succumbed to the disease. Nkosi Johnson, the brave 12-year-old South African died on June 1. Certainly, he is not the only person who died as a victim to the deadly disease on that day. What makes Nkosi Johnson's death so unique is his fight and bravery—that despite the despair and a shattered world that accompanies AIDS, he found the strength that made him one of the best campaigners on this deadly disease. Nkosi symbolised hope. Hope that the disease will certainly be overcome. He strove hard for the removal of stigma and discrimination that so many people suffer as a result of this disease. And at the 13th International AIDS Conference in Durban in July 2000, he called for HIV-positive people to be treated as equals. This, according to many commentators, was the turning point in the fight against AIDS on the continent.

The world has lost a true champion, a hero in the fight against AIDS. This is the human reality of the disease in the African continent. There are many like the late Nkosi who are willing to champion the cause of the fight against the deadly disease in the African continent. But who will listen to them? Gradually, deliberation on the epidemic has occupied the priority sessions at most international meetings of the powerful institutions of the world. Money—the lack of it and its mobilisation—has become the most actively discussed topic. According to some experts, international institutions and creditor organisations should tie debt relief and aid to some developing countries to an AIDS epidemic reduction strategy as in the case of the numerous poverty reduction and strat-

egy papers. But is this the real solution? Certainly, it could help. But those actually suffering from the disease know that it is not only the lack of funds which is the problem, but also the need to have a properly integrated community that treats HIV/AIDS patients as no different in society. Many are really suffering from emotional abuse. And African leaders have a great deal of work to do in addressing this issue.

In the campaign to win the masses at elections, many politicians go to great length to reach remote parts of their countries' extremely difficult to reach areas. But such political will is often absent in the fight against the spread of HIV/AIDS. The taxpayer's money should be used to cater for their own needs. The state of the health sector in most African countries is not supportive of programmes aimed at fighting the spread of the disease. In Ghana for instance, expectant mothers in the main maternity ward of the country's leading hospital, Korle Bu Teaching Hospital, sleep on the floor. So how will HIV/AIDS sufferers be treated? In some parts of Africa, the isolation of AIDS patients has led to early deaths of sufferers. Most patients have lost the will to fight on, preferring to die rather than go through the humiliation of being a sufferer. The consequence is now there for everybody to see. The disease is now alarming. Many sufferers prefer to keep the knowledge to themselves, infecting others instead.

As the impact of HIV/AIDS has placed increased strain on health institutions, HIV care will increasingly fall onto the homes as primary care givers, and onto the communities as support services. This is where the role of African governments is much more crucial. The important role of gov-

ernment in providing basic health care and support to people living with HIV/AIDS or to those affected by other disease could prove vital as an effective strategy for home care or community-based response. The talking must now be left with the bureaucrats and the academicians, now is the time to act.

President Obasanjo of Nigeria, as part of his numerous overtures, organized a seminar on the subject in Abuja in April this year. The attendance was good and the conference was termed a success. But will it help the sufferers—most of whom live in shantytowns and villages with very poor hygienic conditions? The very surroundings of most sufferers even increase the death rate. The sad reality is that the continent of Africa is on the way to extinction, if this issue is not properly addressed. Africans have a fighting instinct, and indeed, this is the only way that the continent can be protected.

President Festus Mogae of Botswana has sounded a battle cry. "We really are in a national crisis. We are threatened with extinction," he said. He is completely alarmed by the rate of infection in his country. Experts say about 36 per cent of the population is HIV-positive. And this figure is bound to double within the next 20 years if the spread is not checked. Botswana is not a poor country. The country has foreign reserves of over $6 billion and in the past 20 years, it is the only country that has been able to graduate from least-developed status. The diamonds industry is growing and Botswana's capital market is now one of the most cherished by foreign portfolio managers. So why is it that the scourge is eroding all the gains that it has made over the past years? Money certainly is not an issue. The disease, from the current trend in the African continent, could still be controlled by basic grassroot level initiatives. Volunteers could play a vital role in this regard and African governments should take the leading role. It is all too easy to blame cash-strapped economics in Africa as the driving force behind the spread. But the failure of most African governments to properly address the issue is as responsible a factor as the big pharmaceutical companies willing to put profits before human lives. The subject

in some parts of Africa is treated more like malaria. But AIDS is more deadly, crucial to the continent's growth and survival.

Sadly, even some scientists and respected learned people in the continent have gone to great length to prove that Africa's AIDS pandemic is not as it is told. Many of these so-called experts attribute the continent's death rate problems to tuberculosis but not HIV/AIDS. Sad indeed. The bare facts are that in many developing countries, people are suffering from the double burden of poverty combined with the explosion of communicable diseases,

which are responsible for around 60 per cent of all illnesses.

AIDS is now the number one killer—and that is official! The pandemic is now reducing life expectancy in some countries. Last year alone, it is estimated that HIV/AIDS was responsible for two million deaths in Africa, while more than one million lives were lost through malaria and tuberculosis. A country like Zambia is one that is at the brink of total disaster. The issue is now at such a critical stage that Africans are the best people to put an end to the pandemic.

AIDS: not all about money

Brigitte Syamalevwe has lived with HIV/AIDS for the past 10 years.
Here, she explains how Africans can help fight the disease without necessarily waiting
for more money, in this interview with Bernard Otabil

When the epidemic assumed such an alarming proportion on the African continent, the issue of money took centre stage. Yes, Africans are poor. So raising well over $5,000 a year for the cocktail of drugs needed to fight against the bout of infection that accompanies a suppressed immune system would surely be a problem for many Africans. But according to Brigitte Syamalevwe, it is not all about money.

Brigitte, an educationist and mother of 11 children, was diagnosed as being HIV-positive 10 years ago. She certainly knows what she is talking about. As a United Nations Volunteer, she is an international consultant and speaker on HIV/AIDS issues, particularly in her native country of Zambia. And though she struggles at times to complete her speech at conferences, she is never short of making her mark.

At a press conference in Brussels during the Third United Nations Conference on Least Developed Countries, the reality of the disease dawned on many. "My speech is not going to be one of the most fantastic ones that you have become used to all day," she said. "But rather, one that appeals to your conscience, and the fact that it takes you and me to properly address this issue of AIDS on the African continent," she continued. And she did indeed appeal to the conscience of the many gathered in the room.

As one of the privileged few to spend some time with her after her presentation, it was really a relaxing moment. Was she

really ill? Certainly, you couldn't tell without asking. She really looked younger than her age, bright and very apt. Her thoughts were very focused and very sharp. Brigitte emphasised repeatedly the fact that living with AIDS is not all about money, but rather the very little help that one can get in terms of education as to how one can take preventive measures. "The lack of HIV/AIDS education is rather going to kill and destroy Africans. At present, there is no cure for the disease and the infection rate is increasing by the day. Our behavior [with respect] to the disease is still very negative," she explained.

The illiteracy rate and the growing poverty problems on the continent are certainly aggravating the issue of AIDS in Africa. The issue is now multidimensional. It is now a development issue. When the South African President, Thabo Mbeki stressed the fact that HIV does not cause AIDS, his message was misinterpreted or rather he missed the point slightly. Perhaps, as he is not suffering from the disease, many did not see the logic in what he was trying to portray. Mbeki's stand, I suppose, was the belief that the continent of Africa has several depressing factors, all playing different parts in the spread of the disease. The ultimate immune deficiency syndrome and the resulting problems are only a manifestation of the many problems of malnutrition, hunger, starvation and the numerous diseases on the African continent.

Brigitte sees along the same lines. Africans, she says, do not treat the epidemic with the kind of attention needed to properly control the disease.

"In many parts of Africa, the political will that is needed to support the structures… and to ensure that it is directed to the communities where HIV/AIDS is much more rampant is not there," she stressed. She believes that most of the time, African governments and indeed some in the Western world have spent time on the bench, writing and campaigning, "but the sad reality is that the house is burning". African governments, she says, have spent most of the time talking about the disease without taking that needed decisive action that would ensure that people are properly made aware of the dangers of the epidemic. And although the Executive Director of UNAIDS, Peter Piot, may agree otherwise when he said at Abuja: "The political momentum is there, let nobody question the strong commitment of Africa's leadership to fight AIDS", he also stressed the need for commitment to be expanded at all levels in society, and turned into action and budgets.

In fact, up until as recently as the Abuja meeting in April, African governments had not made that much noise about the disease. Most of the campaign has been done by some nongovernmental and voluntary organisations. And Brigitte believes that the lack of involvement of African governments has only helped spread the disease.

Discrimination and the stigma associated with a declaration that one is infected with HIV/AIDS ensured that people stayed put and infected other people—causing the pandemic on the African scene. "The stigma associated with AIDS is the biggest worry… the government's support is very much needed," she said. Married to a pastor and health worker, Brigitte voluntarily decided to go for the AIDS test. Her reason? As a secondary school teacher of French, she was greatly alarmed by the rate at which some of her students were losing their parents and loved ones. It was therefore necessary, according to her, to take the test to ensure that she would not leave her children in sorrow one day. But though the results did not go the way she wanted, she never lost hope.

"We all have two instincts—an instinct to fight back and an instinct to flee," she said. And certainly, she had the courage to fight back and help others in her community. However, it wasn't all that rosy in the beginning. "The initial stages were tough. I did not have all the support I needed. Again, it is not all about money. The only support I had was sympathy. You know sympathy will only kill you. Sympathy… makes you addicted to only the good things that you would supposedly be missing," she said. "I had to be angry. An anger that stirred up my spirit in order to fight on all the way. That is why I have now channelled all my energies towards the creation of the necessary awareness that would help the future generation."

The AIDS epidemic rate of spread on the African continent is attracting more lip service than actual help from the international community. Quite often, the international agencies like the IMF have called for the reduction of the price of drugs, thereby making it affordable for the ordinary African. But the issue is far more than that. If the IMF and its sister organisation, the World Bank are so committed to the plight of Africans, then why can't they step in? This is not necessarily infringing on the rights of the pharmaceutical companies but rather buying the drugs at a specially agreed price and selling them cheaply to most African countries. Such a strategy does not sound as cosy as HIPC (the Heavily Indebted Poor Countries Initiative), so one does not expect much attention from the international institutions. And the way some Western pharmaceutical companies attempted a lawsuit to prevent the use of cheaper drugs in South Africa leaves much to be desired.

According to Brigitte, the international community is still largely unaware of the extent of the problem. "HIV/AIDS has diminished the gains that we (Zambia) managed in the late sixties and early seventies. To date, we are losing about three teachers a day in Zambia. And if you look at the fact that it takes 25 years to train and equip a teacher in Zambia, then we are effectively losing 75 years of trained skilled manpower," she stressed. It is really going to take much of a struggle to reverse this trend in Zambia. There is a crisis. The very fabric of society is now destroyed. The education system in most African countries is now getting worse and worse, with most social amenities like healthcare fully stretched. Some key sectors of some countries will collapse if these issues are not properly addressed. With a breakdown in the educational system, it is more likely that the rate of infection of children will increase.

The denial of the reality in most parts of Africa, according to Brigitte is a big threat to the control of the disease on the continent. "It saddens me that there is a total denial of the reality in most African countries. As a result, in most of these countries, people are not empowered enough to plan strategies and devise policies aimed at combating the issue," she stressed. "We declared last year the need for all African countries to declare HIV/AIDS as an emergency or a crisis situation that needed prompt action. But government commitment is not as it would have been thought. There is commitment at the community level as people living with AIDS and have seen the death of loved ones have tried to help each other. But the resources, mobilisation mechanisms, that would have ensured more volunteers and care workers needed to run these communities are not there," she explained.

The African culture, perhaps, needs some serious attention if the issue of AIDS is to be addressed in the manner befitting for all. In Zambia, the Copperbelt region is one of the areas with the highest infection. According to some commentators, the earthy behaviour of the mineworkers is what is driving the infection rate up. And according to Brigitte, it is all to do with poverty and education. Brigitte also believes that the length of denial in the country and the lack of political will of past presidents have all aggravated the problem. "The country has a history of inconsistency in its political life. Governments have not shown that boldness enough, and until the son of our president Kenneth Kaunda died of AIDS, not many people really had the knowledge about the disease," she stressed.

But that is not all. The very nature of the social organisation in most African countries, and for that matter the man-woman relationship, all have a negative impact on the disease. "In most African countries, women, for example, are not part of the decision making process at home. The men always dominate. And this in a way has transcended across all aspects of society so much so that even in the bedroom, the woman is even powerless to ask a man to put on a condom even to protect both parties," she said.

This cultural issue needs to be addressed if the AIDS pandemic is to be controlled. No matter the amount of money that is raised through funds and donations from the international community, the conduct of people in the continent in terms of sexual relationship can only cause the infection rate to increase. The new generation holds the key to addressing some of these cultural issues. The abject poverty on the continent is pushing more people onto the street, causing most of them to be vulnerable to the disease. The definition of masculinity in most African countries has much to be blamed for the spread of HIV/AIDS on the continent. The male African may sometimes use his position in such a way that puts all his family members at risk of infection.

It is all down to the policy makers. And Brigitte believes that if people with responsibilities in society tackle these issues critically, then we will have a different set of behaviour in the future. "The cultural issues are a problem. As a mother and an African, I see this as a severe pain on both our present society and the future children. We need a different approach and attitude towards this particular wrath. It is all about building the right relationships, attitudes and approach."

So wearing the hat of a United Nations Volunteer, Brigitte has been able to affect the community in which she lives. She runs an orphanage and has played leading roles in ensuring that people with HIV/AIDS play an active part in the community. Brigitte believes in the work of volunteers, believing that money is necessary, but not the only factor that can help address the issue on the African continent. The future, according to Brigitte is very bleak, unless African governments and indeed individuals put their act together to properly address this issue.

Africans are fighting back

Interview by B. A. Otabil with Sharon Capeling-Alakija, Executive Co-ordinator, United Nations Volunteers

WA: Looking at the emotional appeal made by most of the speakers at this session [of the Third United Nations Conference on LDCs], how certain are you that the international community will give the needed funds to fight the global AIDS epidemic?

SC-A: I truly wish I knew or had the answer to that. The answer I have to give you, truly, is that I'm not sure. Certainly, I feel that the knowledge of the cost of this pandemic on Africa is well understood. We cannot hide behind any ignorance any longer because I think that the problem has been articulated in eloquent and passionate terms. Certainly, here… the information is available. But whether or not this time, we are really going to be able to create the momentum that is necessary and sustain it, for me is still a question. I am cautiously optimistic, very cautious because, as the representative from the WHO said,… for this new funding to be positive and meaningful, more is needed. There are some criteria here. There is the need for this new money (funding) and it needs to be sustained over a long period of time. So that once we do build up the momentum of getting people aware and willing to come forward, the funds must be there to support the programmes. This is because part of it will be given to African people themselves. When the resources are not available for testing, for giving care, for education that is going to be necessary for the use of condoms; if the resources are not there once you build the momentum, you are really going to disappoint. So, it is a big question as to whether or not the donors are going to come forward. I certainly think that there are no excuses any longer.

WA: Looking at the rate of spread of AIDS and its impact on Africa, one can see that it needs more of a grass root approach. What is your organisation doing with regard to getting African governments to support your initiatives at this level?

SC-A: You know, you are absolutely right. These problems will be solved within countries themselves by mobilising the population to address the issue. However, as a part of international solidarity, we are all on one planet, there are responsibilities for the global community to support the efforts of countries in Africa and also to help countries in Africa build the capacity so that they can address the question themselves. As the UNV, we have a very excellent mechanism called national volunteers. We are mobilising people within countries in West Africa, sometimes to go to the countries on the continent and sometimes to stay and work in their own countries as national United Nations volunteers. Particularly people who are already HIV-positive and this set of people are part of our whole campaign of volunteers in Africa. This is to encourage people who are HIV-positive to speak out. What can be more compelling with respect to prevention is to listen to the words of someone who is HIV-positive, who may not see his or her own children grow. Those kind of issues are really compelling and these people who are not United Nations volunteers [are] doing this advocacy work or also engaged in counselling people and helping people who are HIV-positive to form community associations for the care of each other, also dealing with the whole phenomenon we now see in Africa. So I think that our UNV are able to support the mobilisation of people within countries themselves. The volunteers are often able to give some form of protection. As you know, people are often very afraid of people with AIDS. They tend to stigmatise, so any UNV helps people come out from this stigma to help fight against this pandemic. It also helps to give them some self-esteem because you often see them marginalised in the community in which they live. We are really helping Nigerians, Ghanaians, Sierra Leoneans and Malians to help themselves. You know, we all need solidarity, we all need friendship.

WA: Do you think African governments have been forthright in their fight against AIDS?

SC-A: I think what we have seen, for example in Abuja… where we had a summit of African leaders is that this issue was very much on the agenda. I think we have had a breakthrough now. I remember the tragedy when one of the first African leaders to come forward and really speak out on this was Kenneth Kaunda of Zambia. And of course what provoked it was actually the death of his own son. He began to realise that his countrymen and women were dying and it was his responsibility as the president to come out, but it takes tremendous amount of courage because it is the most intimate of subjects. The disease is transmitted through intimate sexual relations which people are not comfortable to talk publicly about and… people are afraid. There are all sorts of taboos and myths associated with the disease, how it is contracted and the contagious nature of it. It, therefore, takes tremendous amount of courage for people to come out and talk. I think we have seen African leaders beginning to give each other a little bit of courage to speak about the disease. Now, they are helping to mobilise the others. You need both a two-way means of communication from the top down and from the bottom up. You need people to be mobilised in the struggle, which will need the leadership that is creative enough to speak out candidly about the disease because it is still very sensitive.

WA: How would you say your partnership with UNCTAD and UNAIDS is helping to fight the disease globally?

SC-A: We have a very close working relationship with UNAIDS. In fact, they have been a major source of funding for us through this programme of getting greater involvement of people with AIDS. And in fact, with the current role of Ex-President Rawlings of Ghana, they have been very active in helping him with preparing briefings and preparing him for this new endeavor. We are working very close with them. I think the very major contribution of UNAIDS has been an advocacy and getting the issue on the agenda of governments and decision makers around the world. I think they have really done that. UNCTAD's contribution as the main secretariat running the LDCs, has been in term of development. This conference, for example, has not been only about trade issues, but rather… a conference about the whole myriad of changes that need to happen in order for the LDCs to enjoy the benefit that the rest of the world is beginning to experience from economic growth and globalisation.

WA: What do you think the future holds for the African continent?

SC-A: I have lived in Africa for 10 years myself, eight years in West Africa.

Besides, … I am married to a Nigerian and I have strong ties to West Africa to this day. One of the lasting things that I have seen all of these years since I left West Af-

rica is the resilience of the people. No matter what besets West Africa, somehow, people will fight back and I believe Africans will fight and find solutions. I am not

so optimistic about the world community, I am more optimistic about the resilience of African people. They deserve better.

---

20 years of HIV/AIDS

In June 1981, scientists in the United States reported the first clinical evidence of a disease that would become known as Acquired Immunodeficiency Syndrome or AIDS. Twenty years later, the AIDS epidemic has spread to every corner of the world. Almost 22 million people have lost their lives to the disease and over 36 million people are today living with HIV, the virus that causes AIDS. But two decades of struggle to control the epidemic have also yielded a growing arsenal of breakthroughs.

1981

The first cases of unusual immune system failures are identified among gay men in the USA.

1982

Acquired Immunodeficiency Syndrome (AIDS) is defined for the first time. In the course of the year, the three modes of transmission are identified; blood transfusion, mother-to-child, and sexual intercourse.

1983

The Human Immunodeficiency Virus (HIV) is identified as the cause of AIDS. In Africa, a heterosexual epidemic is revealed.

1985

The scope of the growing epidemic becomes manifest. By 1985, at least one case of HIV/AIDS has been reported in each region of the world. Film star Rock Hudson

becomes the first international icon to disclose he has AIDS. In the USA, the Food and Drug Administration (FDA) approves the first HIV antibody test. HIV screening of blood donations begins in the USA.

1987

Africa's first community-based response to AIDS (The AIDS Support Organisation or TASCO) is formed in Uganda. It becomes a role model for similar activities around the world. The International Council of AIDS Service Organisations (ICASO) and the Global Network of people living with HIV/AIDS are founded. In February, the World Health Organisation (WHO) establishes the Special Programme on AIDS, later to become the Global Progamme on AIDS. The first therapy for AIDS—azidothymidine (AZT)—is approved for use in the USA.

1988

In London, health ministers from around the world meet to discuss the HIV/AIDS epidemic for the first time.

1991–1993

In 1991–1993, HIV prevalence in young pregnant women in Uganda begins to decrease—the first significant downturn in a developing country. The success is attributed to countrywide mobilisation against the epidemic.

1994

Scientists develop the first treatment regimen to reduce mother-to-child transmission.

1995

An outbreak in Eastern Europe is detected among injecting drug users.

1996

The joint United Nations Programme on HIV/AIDS (UNAIDS) is created. Evidence of the efficacy of Highly Active Antiretroviral Therapy (HAART) is presented for the first time.

1998

Brazil becomes the first developing country to provide antiretroviral therapy through its public health systems. The first shortcourse regimen to prevent mother-to-child transmission is announced.

1999

The first efficacy trial of a potential HIV vaccine in a developing country starts in Thailand.

2000

The UN Security Council discusses HIV/AIDS for the first time.

2001

UN Secretary-General Kofi Annan launches his call to action, including the creation of a global fund on AIDS and health.

From *West Africa* (London), June 11-17, 2001, pp. 10-16. © 2001 by Afrimedia International Ltd. Reprinted by permission.

A MAN OF WORDS, A MAN OF ACTION

From Sixties Protester to AIDS Activist, DANNY GLOVER Shares with *A&U*'s Dann Dulin Why He Fights AIDS in Africa and at Home, and His Global Vision for a Sustainable World

Danny Glover. Danny Glover. Danny Glover. His name pops up repeatedly when you surf the Internet for HIV/AIDS-related Web sites. Whether he's lobbying South African President Thabo Mbeki to take bolder steps to battle Africa's AIDS pandemic, participating in the One Billion Against AIDS Benefit Concert in Johannesburg, or announcing the launch of the Black Media Task Force on AIDS to increase AIDS coverage—Glover is out there making a difference.

Since 1998, Glover has served as the first Goodwill Ambassador for the United Nations Development Program, traveling and speaking extensively throughout Africa; in 2000, Danny was the only Hollywood celebrity to attend the International AIDS Conference in Durban, South Africa; and, this past April, just days prior to our encounter, he attended the Day of Hope: Fight AIDS in Africa rally held on the West Capitol steps in Washington, D.C., to demand that Congress appropriate more money and provide necessary life-saving treatment for people with AIDS worldwide.

Glover seems to be in constant motion, even on the day of our interview. Having just arrived from Oakland, his flight delayed, our interview is bumped ahead one hour, and sandwiched between meetings with his agent, in whose conference room in Beverly Hills I await Glover's arrival. As life goes, when you wait for something, it never comes; the moment you leave, it shows up. Case in point: Glover arrived while I was in the loo. What timing. When I return to the conference room, Danny is standing by the spread of snacks and soda, munching on a pretzel. His large stature belies his gentle nature. He has a handsome, striking appearance. As I introduce myself, he apologizes for being late. I inquire about the Day of Hope. "It went well," he says, taking a sip from a bottle of Calistoga mineral water. "We had a variety of speakers, including rabbis, ministers, as well as a group of participants who are living with AIDS."

The photographer sets up and asks Glover to sit briefly by the window for the photo shoot. Glover seems surprised, almost agitated for an instant, that he may not be properly dressed for the photography. After momentarily considering it, he lets out a sigh of relief, "It's a good thing I have a dinner event this evening, otherwise I wouldn't have on a suit." After a few snaps, we convene at the conference table. Danny is a bit tired, yet focused and forthcoming.

"I first became aware of the devastation of AIDS when I lost a fellow actor to the disease back in 1985," Glover notes, sitting in an executive-style chair and radiating a business-like demeanor. "I remember while working on a film, I would take him food during the day. At the time, he was in denial. He never said he had AIDS, and he never indicated to me a lot about who he was in his life. I was there to provide comfort—to honor his privacy and to be his friend." In 1990, the circle grew smaller as Glover's brother, Rodney, was diagnosed with AIDS. "He is currently doing well, but for a period of time, his lifestyle did not embrace the fact that he was dealing with something very serious. He continued the lifestyle that had caused his infection because he had been incarcerated for a period of time. But recently he has changed his lifestyle for the sake of his two young children."

> **"I first became aware of the devastation of AIDS when I lost a fellow actor to the disease back in 1985."**

Besides Glover's brother, Danny's family includes his wife of twenty-five years, Asake Bomani, and their daughter, Mandisa. Raised in San Francisco, Glover lived in a public housing project until the age of ten. After graduating from San Francisco State College, he worked as a civil servant. At twenty-eight, he became interested in acting, and attended the Black Actors' Workshop at the American Conservatory Theatre. Glover weaved his way to Broadway, eventually starring in Athol Fugard's *Master Harold...and the Boys* and received wide critical acclaim. He made his film debut in a small role in the 1979 Clint Eastwood movie, *Escape From Alcatraz*. Subsequent films include: *Iceman, Places in the Heart, Witness, Silverado, The Color Purple, Grand Canyon, To Sleep With Anger, Antz, Lonesome Dove, Bopha!*, and *Beloved*. Glover's latest film, *The Royal Tenenbaums*, was recently in national release.

Though best known as Mel Gibson's lovable partner in the *Lethal Weapon* film series, of which there are now four, Danny portrayed Nelson Mandela in *Mandela*, a 1987 TV bio movie, and in 2000, he co-starred with Angela Bassett in *Boesman and Lena*, a film adapted from Athol Fugard's classic play. The love story takes place under apartheid in South Africa, and apartheid is an issue that is very deeply heartfelt to Glover, as is the current AIDS situation in Africa. Despite a busy acting career with over fifty movies to his credit and being a dedicated family man, Danny is active and committed to ending the AIDS crisis. What made his activism reach a global level? "To answer that question, you have to understand where I come from," Glover reflects. "I had been so close to the continent of Africa perhaps from the time I was about nineteen- or twenty-years-old. I had to define my life in such a way that I would spend time working in Africa in some capacity. I majored in economics at San Francisco State. I wanted to be a part of a larger community that encompassed Africa. When President Kennedy created the Peace Corps and VISTA as a way for America to become a more generous country, I wanted my level of generosity to be expressed on the continent of Africa. So I came out of that consciousness—that experience. I've never abandoned my relationship with the continent."

Since Glover's late arrival, our allotted time has been cut. Knowing this, Danny is very intent on unleashing what he thinks, and his excitement propels him to exude a passionate and continuous flow of thoughts.

"To answer your question, the decisive moment when my activism reached a global level was when I accepted the post of Goodwill Ambassa-

dor," he says. "In order to deal with the pandemic, I felt we had to deal with issues of infrastructure, poverty, and all those issues because—as we all know—AIDS is an opportunistic disease. Poverty, internal conflict, and an array of other problems are contributing factors to the strength of this pandemic. Healthwise, Africans are worse off now than they were thirty years ago. People are more vulnerable and, as a result, I've made it clear that in the fight against AIDS we have to link the issue of AIDS to all of these other issues."

"Today we have a youth culture that deals with a certain level of self-destruction."

With whole communities being wiped out in Central and sub-Saharan Africa, Glover encourages others to tighten the connection between the U.S. and Africa. "Right now there are a number of funding bills in Congress and, in addition, there are other things that are happening outside of Washington to strengthen this tie. Portland, Oregon [Glover's home] has a sister city in Africa which supports the fight against AIDS by heightening public awareness of the problem and by providing monetary support. Telluride, Colorado, has a similar relationship." Glover eases back in the chair for a moment, then suddenly sits erect. "America is one of the most stable, the most economically enhanced, and powerful countries in the world and we should certainly advocate for more resources in the fight. U.N. Secretary General Kofi Annan estimates that we need in excess of ten million," he clears his throat and arches his eyebrows, "excuse me, ten *billion* dollars a year for this fight. And we're not getting anywhere that amount."

Consequently, Glover is not very enthusiastic about the Bush administration, or its new director of the Office of National AIDS Policy, Scott Evertz. When I mention Evertz's name, Glover quizzically looks off in the distance, trying to recall who he is. "I don't hear a lot about Scott Evertz so that means he certainly is missing in action on the job," chuckles Danny, then adds, "but maybe

he's been drowned out by the other concerns of the nation and national policy." He thinks for a second. "But even when there's been an opportunity, I haven't heard his name mentioned as we talk about AIDS. This is not acceptable in a leadership role. I don't think the present administration and the leader of that administration have provided the leadership necessary in the fight against AIDS."

For the past few moments, Glover's assistant has been silently flagging him, warning that the meeting with his agent commences in a few minutes. He acknowledges, assures me that we will continue the interview afterward, and then proceeds back to where he was before the interruption.

"When do you see the U.S. administration on the forefront of AIDS?" Danny asks pointedly, sounding like Moze, the wise and insightful character that he portrayed in *Places in the Heart*. "Even when the primary AIDS population at one point in time happened to be homosexual, white males, even then you had a hard time getting the public officials to come out. And what's disappointing now is that we are *twenty years* down the road, and we haven't had a more forceful announcement from the administration about our willingness to fight the issues that surround AIDS." Glover pauses and looks out the huge window that frames a spectacular view of Century City. "We have lost friends, but the first prism through which we viewed AIDS was connected primarily to homosexual men. But now we see the demographics changing."

Indeed, according to the recent CDC stats, African-American women and men now have the highest rates of HIV infection. Although African-American males only make up thirteen percent of the nations population, it is estimated that they account for more than half of all new AIDS cases in the U.S. Furthermore, nearly half of all men newly infected with the virus are black, and sixty-four percent of all women with AIDS are black. According to a study by the Kaiser Family Foundation, African-Americans now consider AIDS as the number-one health problem facing the country and the world. What is Glover's take on this? "You need to make a distinction between the various segments of the African American community. If we look at certain age groups, HIV infection is more prevalent than in other age groups. Teens are being hit hardest and are the most vulnerable and also, in particular, African-American women."

With that, we stop and Glover departs for his meeting. Almost two hours later, true to his word, he returns—ready and revved. He picks up where he left off with AIDS in the African-American community. "Today we have a youth culture that deals with a certain level of self-destruction. Despair within certain segments of the community adds to this. I also believe there is a kind of macho arrogance that comes out of the repressive, marginalized existence that one has in which one's sexuality is expressed in very unhealthy ways. All this has an historical connection to it; media imagery connected to it that is often false, often conjured, and often misguided. To some degree, in all those dynamics, there is a certain level of urbanization—and what has happened with that urbanization?" Glover sternly questions. "So we take all those elements and throw those in some sort of caldron. It then explains some of the dynamics and some of the challenges, I believe, in creating a dialogue that addresses teens and speaks to them in a way that reflects the fateful kind of existence, or journey, they are on."

Glover's journey has brought him to a high profile advocacy position for human rights. In 1989, Danny and other artists founded Artists For A New South Africa (ANSA), an organization dedicated to furthering democracy and equality in South Africa, and confronting the AIDS disaster. Coincidentally, on the morning of our interview, a blurb appeared in the newspaper about Anglo American, a London-based mining conglomerate in South Africa that reversed its decision to cover the expense for AIDS drugs for its workers, twenty percent of whom are HIV-positive. When hearing this,

Danny tenses slightly. "It is unacceptable! Unacceptable!" he firmly repeats in his low and eloquent voice. "This is sending the wrong signal. You're sending a signal that you don't care. It's important that we call attention to this and organize to bring about a reversal."

This trademark of passionate activism also extends into other causes besides AIDS: from serving on the board of a math empowerment program, to being an advocate for literacy, to giving a million dollars to TransAfrica Forum, an African-American lobbying organization. What motivates this busy actor to be a civil rights crusader? "I'm fascinated with knowing more about people's stories. It comes from my grandparents, from my parents, in some sense, and from a degree of activism that was prevalent in my family life. It is part of the cultural memory that I have. I'm fueled by that," he says zealously. "As an actor, you are always trying to understand the human dynamic. Philosophically, as an artist, you always try to understand the context of that and your relationship to it. Even someone like myself, who has studied economics and political science and has listened to the voices of those all around the world, I always wanted to know what their connection was to me."

He continues: "I'm a product of speaking to the highest ideal of who we can be as human beings. That's what my activism comes out of. Whether it comes out of strong people like Martin Luther King or Malcolm X, or artists such as Ozzie Davis, Ruby Dee, Maya Angelou, Harry Belafonte, Paul Robeson, and I can go on and on and on—I am an extension of that. I try to understand what the possibilities are," insists Danny resting his hand on his jaw momentarily. "How do we build a sustainable world? That's one of the questions I ask myself each morning. And maybe you can say that I have the luxury to ask myself those questions because I've been relatively successful as an actor and it has provided me a degree of financial security. But, I used to work at San

Francisco's Office of Community Development in the poverty program. In the late sixties, I worked as a volunteer with groups that were supporting more democratization and participation in redevelopment programs in San Francisco. If you run into a person who says they remember me saying I wanted to be an actor in high school, then there is a little fallacy behind that," he says bemusedly, with a subtle nod.

Danny is scheduled to attend his dinner engagement shortly, and must depart. As our meeting ends, he sums up his thoughts: "AIDS is now on a whole other level. We have to deal with this fact, and that's the scary part. Containment was initially the easy part of the battle. We have to access how we can now elicit the support and the input of those who've already gone through the struggle, who have dealt with the struggle, and how can we import their understanding of the dynamics of it," he implores, referring to long-term HIV survivors." Glover continues: "Now, AIDS has really broken out of its cage. It's no longer simply a homosexual problem. Today, we're talking about South Africa; soon, we'll be talking about South Asia, and about South America. Where do you go then? I think we're all grappling. We have three weapons: education, treatment, and prevention. How far can we run with them and what impact can we have with them?" he asks. "That is another one of our challenges. We have to say, 'Let's do it now!' Let's put out all forces in all three of those areas. And since we know they involve a variety of other dynamics and concerns, we have to create a climate in which we can win."

Opinionated, articulate, and committed, Danny Glover serves as a fitting role model for the Hollywood community. Lending his notoriety, his charisma, and his strength to the AIDS war, he is an actor who enlightens—a star in every sense of the word who casts his light onto issues and causes that are now shaping our world, and will continue to impact our lives well into this new century.

SLAVES OF THE BROTHEL

**A virulent Mafia business is thriving in postwar Kosovo:
the $7 to $12 billion traffic in Eastern European women lured by promises of
work, then forced into prostitution. Despite international efforts, sex
slave traders have been nearly impossible to prosecute, thanks to corruption, local
laws, and the victims' fear of testifying. Tracing the path of one
young Moldovan woman, SEBASTIAN JUNGER conducts his own investigation
of a vicious cycle that traps as many as 200,000 women a year**

The plan called for a "soft entry," which meant that the police officers would ask to come in, rather than break down the door. It was 1:45 on the morning of July 6, 2001, and a convoy of white-painted U.N. police vehicles were gunning through Pristina's deserted streets on their way to raid the infamous Miami Beach Club. The convey passed a dead dog and a row of overflowing garbage bins and the destroyed post office and groups of tough-looking young men who turned to stare at the S.U.V.'s as they went by.

The owner of the Miami Beach, Milam Maraj, was suspected of trafficking in women and forcing them into prostitution. What to all outward appearances was a regular strip club was, in fact, a brothel, and the girls who worked there—teenagers from the former Soviet Union—were in all likelihood being held in conditions amounting to virtual slavery. Several months earlier, Maraj had been crippled by a bullet to the knee because he was willing to testify against a local strongman named Sabit Geci, who was also involved in trafficking and prostitution. Geci was sentenced to six years in prison—the first major victory against organized crime in Kosovo—but it cost Maraj his knee. Now he had to walk with crutches and carry a gun for protection and was suspected by the U.N. of engaging in the same kind of crimes that had put his arch-rival in jail.

The convoy of S.U.V.'s ground up the dark, pitted streets of Jablanica Hill and came to a stop a hundred yards from the bar. The raid went down fast. A team of heavily armed U.N. soldiers stood guard on the perimeter while half a dozen police officers rushed the front door and flattened the two bouncers up against the wall. From there they moved into the dimly lit bar and screamed for more light as they pushed the men to one side of the room and the women to the other. Maraj hobbled out on his crutches and played host with as charming a smile as he could muster. "Please, do your jobs," he invited, sweeping one hand toward the girls, who were already sitting at a table, waiting to be questioned by police. "There is no problem. You will see."

And in fact he was right. An hour later the police left, empty-handed. Of the dozen or so girls found at the club that night, not one had a forged visa, not one had entered the country illegally, not one admitted having been trafficked, beaten up, raped, or threatened. They just flirted with the police officers and then waved good-bye prettily when the officers trooped back out the door. The incident was all too typical of the failure to combat forced prostitution, which has spiraled out of control, becoming one of Europe's major problems.

Most of the prostitutes in Kosovo have been trafficked illegally from the poorest parts of the ruined Soviet state. They are lured by the promise of a good job, usually in Italy or Germany, their passports are confiscated, and they generally wind up sold to Albanian pimps, who force them to work in brothels to pay off their "debt," i.e., what it cost the pimp to buy them. Not surprisingly, the system is set up so that that is virtually impossible, and the women essentially become trapped in the dark, violent world of the Albanian Mafia. A moderately attractive young woman goes for around $1,000. Tall ones are worth more, and very beautiful ones are worth more. Moldovan women are preferred because they are particularly desperate—the living wage in their country is calculated at $100 a month, and the average income is a quarter of that—and they are remarkably beautiful. Moldova seems to have beautiful women the way Sierra Leone has diamonds—peculiar national treasures that haven't done either country much good.

The problem with investigating human trafficking in Europe is that the women themselves often deny needing help. They are too scared, manipulated, or desperate for money to dare admit anything to the police. The only way around the problem is undercover work, but the U.N. mandate in Kosovo until very recently did not include such intelligence gathering. Journalists, however, have never been bound by such rules. One weekday night in the pouring rain, photographer Teun Voeten and I drove out of Pristina toward the Macedonian border, where there are dozens of brothels tucked away in the smaller towns. We were with two Albanian translators, Erol and Valon, who spoke Serbian and whose appearance let them pass for anything—Serb or Albanian, Kosovar or

Macedonian. Our idea was to walk into a brothel, pretend to be American servicemen in Kosovo, and buy an hour or two with one of the women. In the privacy of a motel room, out of sight of the Albanian Mafia, which runs the brothels—in fact, some would say, runs the whole country—we could interview the woman with a tape recorder and get the real story of how she got there.

The highway was two narrow lanes of ruined pavement. Convoys of trucks blasted past us in the oncoming lane, and U.N. tanks and armored trucks slowed traffic heading south, toward Macedonia, to a crawl. Albanian rebels had seized a large part of the mountainous border between the two countries, and the U.N. peacekeepers were building up their presence in case they had to intervene on short notice. Off in the distance we could see the diffuse yellow glow of Camp Bondsteel reflecting off the cloud cover. Bondsteel is an enormous American base built close to a nasty little industrial town called Ferizaj. As a result, Ferizaj has an inordinate number of brothels, and at a gas station outside of town, with the rain drumming down and the trucks roaring past, the pump attendant advised us to check out one called the Apaci. It had the best girls in town, he said, so that was where all the American officers went. We thanked him and drove around the ghastly apartment blocks and ruined factories of Ferizaj until we found a low concrete building covered in camouflage netting. It had a photograph of an Apache attack helicopter on the door. We parked by some railroad tracks and walked in.

There are very good reasons why something amounting to slavery has been allowed to thrive in the middle of Europe. Not only is the Albanian Mafia notoriously violent—Kosovo has one of the highest murder rates in Europe—but it has attempted to infiltrate and buy off both the local police force and the government. "Those who have money here have power," as one United Nations police officer says. "And the Mafia has money." Undercover work in the brothels is dangerous, and attempting a police action that the Mafia doesn't get tipped off to is ex-

tremely difficult. Furthermore the Mafia is deeply intertwined with the Kosovo Liberation Army (K.L.A.), which fought the Serb Army and then started an insurrection in Macedonia, and it has access to plenty of weapons. Last year a German relief worker made the mistake of talking to some trafficked women about the possibility of escape, and that night someone attempted to throw a grenade into his hotel room. It was tossed into Room 69, which was empty; the relief worker was staying in Room 96.

No one paid us much attention when we walked in. There was a group of tough-looking Albanians in one corner, talking very seriously among themselves, and an American officer in uniform in another corner with his back to the wall. He was sitting with two Albanian translators and a blonde in a very short skirt who was feigning interest in whatever he was saying. Between her bad English and the music, she couldn't have understood much. We sat up front by the stage and made sure that the bartender couldn't get a clear view of Teun, who had a small, low-light camera in his pocket. He carefully took it out and put it under his hat.

There were 8 or 10 girls ranged at the table in front of us, drinking soda and smoking cigarettes and barely talking. Some had hair dyed jet black, and the rest had hair bleached so blond it almost looked blue. Occasionally I'd catch one of them looking at us, but then I'd realize she was looking through us and was too bored even to make eye contact. They sat with their legs crossed, waiting for their next shift on the stage, occasionally getting up without much enthusiasm to go talk to the table of Albanian men. They were pretty, but not extraordinarily so. A couple looked to be straight out of the Romanian peasantry—big, strong girls with rough faces and too much makeup—but one stood out from the rest. She was petite and had platinum-blond hair pulled back tight across her skull and dark glossy lipstick and one of those heartbreaking Slavic faces—high cheekbones, dark eyes, a slightly Asian cast—that you remember for years. She sat off by herself, oblivious to everyone around her, and when the D.J. put on an Algerian song called "Aicha," she stubbed out her cigarette and got up to dance.

There was something different about her—she was distant from the other girls, almost disdainful. I thought that maybe she would speak more openly than the others. "Her," I said to Erol before she'd even finished her dance. Erol waved the bartender over, a young guy with his hair bound improbably into a topknot, and negotiated the deal: we were to wait until closing time and then go out to our car and follow the security guys to a motel. The girls would already be there. Erol would go up alone at a cost of about $150. If he wanted to take her home with him he had to put down a deposit of her full price—$2,000—and if she escaped he would forfeit all of it.

After she finished her dance the bartender sent her over to our table. She was young—in her late teens, maybe—and unnervingly self-possessed. She sat there playing with her hair and smoking cigarettes and said that it was her first night at the Apaci and she was not happy to be there. She also said that her name was Niki and that she was from a small town in Moldova. (In order to protect her, I have changed her name.)

"Where did you work before here?" I asked.

"Banja Luka."

Banja Luka was the capital of Serb Bosnia, the site of some of the worst ethnic cleansing in the war.

"What did you think of Banja Luka?"

"If I could drop a bomb on Banja Luka," she said, "I would do it tomorrow."

It was around two in the morning when the lights went up. A hard, ugly rain was coming down outside, and the place had cleared out except for us and the thugs and the girls, who had been herded into the corner. The thugs who ran them were putting on their leather jackets. We were getting ready to go when a heavyset man—later thought by U.N. investigators to be Bashkim Beqiri—walked in the door. Beqiri was a local boxing champion who ran a strip bar called Europe 2000. One hand jammed in his pocket, he planted himself before an Apaci security guy and started yelling. The security guy didn't say much, and his buddies stood around, shifting from foot to foot while the girls looked away and Beqiri hollered. I asked Erol what was going on.

"That man wants his money," Erol whispered back. "He says he wants [$2,000] right now or he's going to kill the girl."

We couldn't tell which woman he was talking about. Beqiri turned and walked out the door, saying he would be back the next day. The security guys held a quick council and then herded the women outside into the pouring rain to a couple of late-model BMWs parked next to the railroad tracks. They looked dumb and well-muscled, and they squeezed themselves into a couple more cars and motioned for us to follow. We trailed them in our car through the dark streets of Ferizaj to a place called the Muhaxheri Motel, off a side street at the center of town.

The Muhaxheri was a slapdash five-story modern building with a cheap plastic sign outside and no one at the front desk. The thugs got out of their cars and looked around and then pulled the women out and shoved them toward the door. A police car drove by slowly but didn't stop. One of the men motioned to Erol, who got out of our car and nodded to us and disappeared into the motel. Another carload of men pulled up and went into the Muhaxheri and came out 10 minutes later and drove off. We waited an hour like that, the rain coming down, an occasional car pulling up and then driving away, and Erol never emerged from the motel.

War has been good for the Albanian Mafia. In February and March 1998, Serb military and paramilitary forces carried out a series of massacres in the Drenica region of central Kosovo that quickly grew into a massive campaign of ethnic cleansing. By the time NATO intervened a year later, as many as 10,000 ethnic Albanians had been killed and an estimated 800,000 driven across the country's borders. A massive NATO bombing campaign finally forced the Serbs to concede defeat, and they withdrew on June 10, 1999. Within hours, approximately 43,000 NATO troops poured into Kosovo to impose order, but it wasn't fast enough. Groups of young Albanian toughs were already patrolling the streets of Pristina and other large towns, establishing control in a society that had been completely sundered by the Serb occupation. Already in a position of power because they had helped fund and arm the K.L.A., the Mafia bought off local officials, infiltrated the police force, and killed anyone they couldn't intimidate.

Kosovo was, and still is, the perfect place to base a criminal network—chaotic, violent, and ringed by porous borders. Local and international authorities can't hope to control the trafficking routes. To the north are Serb gangsters who work closely with the Russian Mafia and are only too happy to overlook old ethnic hatreds in the interest of business. To the east are Bulgarian *moutri*—"thick-necks," mostly graduates of wrestling schools—who work for security firms that double as racketeering outfits. Criminal clans in Albania proper, given free rein by a corrupt, bankrupt, and utterly impotent government, have taken over the port town of Vlorë and use 500-horse-power inflatable rafts called *scafi* to run illegal immigrants and drugs across the Adriatic into Italy. An estimated 10 percent of the population of Vlorë are in business with the local Mafia, and two-thirds of the cars on the streets have been stolen from Western Europe.

Worldwide, the effect has been disastrous. The Balkan drug trade, which moves more than 70 percent of the heroin destined for Europe, is valued at an estimated $400 billion a year. By early 2001 the Albanian Mafia had muscled its competition out of the way and all but taken over London's crime-ridden red-light district, Soho. Albanian organized crime has established alliances with the Italian Mafia and with criminal gangs in Turkey. In February 2001 an Albanian insurrection started in Macedonia, and the Mafia quickly moved in to help arm and pay for the guerrilla movement that went from several hundred to several thousand men in a matter of months. In some cases, Mafia bosses simply became local rebel commanders and funded their military operations through criminal enterprises that could operate much more effectively under the cover of war.

The Organization for Security and Cooperation in Europe (O.S.C.E.)—part of the temporary governing body in Kosovo—estimates that around 200,000 women each year are trafficked from Eastern Europe and Central Asia, most of them as prostitutes. The value of their services has been estimated at between $7 and $12 billion. Even before the Kosovo war, human trafficking in Europe—much of it through the Balkans—was worth as much as $4 billion a year. Bulgaria alone loses 10,000 women a year to the traffickers. Moldova—a country so poor that a quarter of the population has emigrated in search of work—reportedly supplies two-thirds of the prostitutes working in Kosovo. Romania is a distant runner-up, followed by Ukraine, Bulgaria, Albania, and Russia.

Prostitution became a mainstay of the criminal economy within months of NATO intervention in Kosovo. With 43,000 men stationed on military bases, and spending by international reconstruction groups making up 5 to 10 percent of Kosovo's economy, the problem was bound to arise. There are now as many as 100 brothels in Kosovo, each employing up to 20 women. Thousands more women are trafficked through Kosovo and on into Western Europe. In southern Macedonia, the town of Velesta has dozens of brothels under the control of a strongman named Leku, who has reportedly paid off the local police and operates in the open with complete impunity. When national authorities tried to crack down on his empire, he threatened to take to the hills and start his own private war. The highway south of the Macedonian town of Tetovo—long a hotbed of Albanian nationalism and organized crime—is lined with brothels as well.

Unable to use local women easily—they aren't so poor, and their families would come looking for them—men such as Leku have turned to the hundreds of thousands of illegal migrants fleeing the former Soviet Union. Young women who have been promised innocent-sounding jobs in Western Europe, particularly Italy, are typically escorted by Serb or Bulgarian gangsters into Kosovo and Macedonia and then sold to Albanian pimps. By the time they realize what is going on, it is too late. Deprived of their passports, gang-raped, often forced to take drugs, and disoriented by lack of food and sleep, these women find themselves virtual prisoners of whatever brothel they wind up in.

"Once, Leku told a Bulgarian girl to take off her bra when she was dancing," a Moldovan woman I will call Elena told me. Elena had managed to escape the Macedonian Mafia after months of brutality and servitude. "She didn't want to, because she was ashamed, so Leku took a belt from the bartender and started beating her. Then he made her go onstage bruised and bleeding and crying." Another bar Elena worked at was owned by a man she knew as Ayed. "Ayed put three new girls in a car and made the rounds of his friends—they all took turns raping them. They made the girls do things they'd never done before because they were very young. We all lived in one room and slept on mattresses next to each other. There wasn't enough room, so we had to sleep on our sides. We only ate once a day, and we had to beg toothpaste and soap from our clients. Ayed had a huge ring on his hand, which was shaped like a lion's head. One day he started beating us one by one in the face." According to Elena, if they fell down he kicked them, if they cried he beat them, if they looked at him he beat them, if they didn't look at him he beat them.

"I learned about good and evil," she says. "I saw so many evil people."

After an hour and a half Erol still had not come out, so Valon decided to look for him. He walked into the hotel lobby and heard men talking in the hallway and was spotted by them as he slipped closer. They wanted to know who the hell his friends in the car were. "They're from the United States," Valon said. For some reason he added, "One of them is a basketball coach."

That seemed to satisfy the thugs, who kicked him out and said Erol would be out in a few minutes. Erol emerged 10 minutes later, smoking a cigarette and looking shaken. He got into the car and told Valon to get us out of there. "They found the tape recorder," he said. "They had a lot of questions." Valon pulled the car into the street, and we drove off through Ferizaj, keeping watch behind us to make sure no one was following. It

was three in the morning, and Ferizaj was completely deserted. Erol said they'd found the tape recorder when they patted him down outside Niki's room, and five or six of them had gathered around and started yelling, demanding explanations. Erol said that it was just his tape recorder and that he took it everywhere with him.

They confiscated it and then wrote down his name from his passport. They were very angry and kept telling him not to fuck with them. "Listen," one of the men had finally said, "Go in the room, finish your job for one hour, or you can go, right here and now."

Erol screwed up his nerve and went into the room. There was one bed and a window with a narrow balcony and a shower but no toilet. Niki was sitting on the bed, and she started to undress when he walked in. "You don't have to do that—I'm not here for that," he said. "I just want to talk to you."

She'd probably had stranger requests before—they all must have. He asked her where she was from and how she'd gotten here, and she became very serious and told her story. This is what Erol could remember of it on the drive back to Pristina:

Niki was from Moldova; her father was dead, and she had lived with her mother. She'd been promised a good job by a recruiter in Moldova who was actually in league with the Mafia, and she wound up trafficked to Banja Luka. Banja Luka was hell on earth, she said. Every customer was drunk and many were violent—one even grabbed her belly-button ring and ripped it right out. A month ago she had been trafficked in Ferizaj, where she wound up at Europe 2000. She escaped from there the day before and sought refuge in the Apaci. Tonight her previous "owner"—Beqiri— had come looking for her at the Apaci and said he was going to kill her if he didn't get back her purchase price. She didn't have the money, and neither did the owner of the Apaci. That was the argument we had witnessed. She was the girl they'd been arguing over.

"I like life very much. I'm too young to die," Niki had told Erol. "I'm just 18 years old."

Erol asked her if she was free to go home to Moldova if she wanted. She said that she was, but then admitted that she didn't actually have her passport. (In all likelihood, Beqiri did.) She wasn't even sure that any of the $150 Erol had paid for her would wind up in her pocket, so he gave her all the money he had on him, a 10 deutsche-mark note (about $5). On it he wrote, "For Niki, the most beautiful girl." She gave him a cigarette lighter in return. His last question was whether she ever had feelings for the guys she was with, or were they all the same?

"Of course sometimes I have feelings," she said. "I'm human."

Erol told her he was sorry and said goodbye and walked out of the room.

The next day we went to the police station in Gnjilane to report what we'd seen. Not only was there plenty of evidence of trafficking and prostitution in Niki's case, but there was reason to believe her life was in danger. The deputy police chief in Gnjilane was an American named Bill Greer, who quickly organized a group of Kosovar police to raid the Apaci. (U.N. police officers are training local Albanians—many of them taken from the ranks of the disarmed Kosovo Liberation Army—and Serbs in basic policy procedure.) The newly trained cops crowded into Greer's office and strapped on their guns and flak jackets while he explained through a translator: "We're going to get a young lady who's been threatened with being exterminated. She ran away from one pimp to the Apaci, and he came after her and demanded [$2,000] or she'd be killed."

The owner of the Apaci, Sevdush Veseli, was well known to the authorities. He'd already been detained for trafficking a young Romanian woman, but when it came time to make a statement to the judge, she was too frightened to repeat what she'd said earlier to the police, so they had to let him go. Veseli was a former member of the K.L.A. who wasn't known to be particularly violent, but Greer wasn't taking any chances. He sent half a dozen local police, backed up by a couple of U.N. officers, and they picked up reinforcements at the Ferizaj police station before bursting through the door at the Apaci. All they found was an old guy mopping the floor.

If Veseli hadn't been tipped off before, he certainly knew something was up now. Our little escapade the night before couldn't have escaped his notice, and he must have figured out that Niki had been the object of today's raid. Between the police and Beqiri, she was causing him more problems than she could possibly be worth. That meant that, one way or another, he would probably try to get her off his hands. That afternoon Ali Osman, Turkish police officer who headed the Trafficking and Prostitution Investigation Unit in Gnjilane, sent word to Veseli that he was to appear at the police station the following morning with all of his dancers.

Technically the Apaci was just a strip joint on the outskirts of Ferizaj. And technically the police could round up the employees anytime they wanted to check their visas and work papers. At nine the next morning, Teun and I showed up at the police station to watch the interrogation of a dozen or so women employed by Sevdush Veseli at the Apaci.

The women were seated in a small room, smoking and looking annoyed. Teun and I walked in, glanced around, and told Osman that Niki was not among them. That was no surprise. We went into Osman's office; the next step was to question the women individually, where we could speak freely without the other girls or their bosses listening in. Not only might they know what happened to Niki, but some of them might want out. Those were the ones who could provide testimony of trafficking and prostitution at the Apaci, which was what Osman needed to put Veseli behind bars.

Since undercover investigations were not allowed at this time under the U.N. mandate, convicting someone like Veseli usually depends on testimony from the prostitutes. It's a delicate game, though. First, there are plenty of prostitutes who—no matter how desperate their lives—have decided that anything is better than what they escaped from back home. Their pimp may be a violent alcoholic, but maybe their husband or father was, too, and at least here they have the

possibility of making a little money. "You're fighting against the most appalling economic condition," says Alison Jolly of the O.S.C.E. in Pristina. "And one of the worst myths is that these women want to become prostitutes. I mean in a sense, yes, but how much of a choice is it when the alternative is to stand in a breadline trying to feed your child? You're a paid slave, but you're still a slave. I personally consider it a very clever ruse by the pimps to pay the women something. This is a recent development. These guys are very smart, and a little intimidation goes a long way."

Even for the ones who are desperate to escape, though, making the leap into police custody is risky. To begin with, the pimps have convinced their prostitutes that the police will simply throw them in jail for prostitution or visa violations—which was true until U.N. regulations were recently established that overrode the Yugoslav Criminal Code. Furthermore, the women know that—since they were recruited back home—the Mafia network extends into the smallest villages of their home country. When a pimp promises to harm a prostitute or her family, it is not an idle threat.

The first woman they brought into Osman's office was a short, dark-haired Moldovan who pretended barely to understand Serbian. She said she had come by taxi through Romania into Serbia, then across the internal border into Kosovo. She claimed she was just a stripper, not a prostitute, and made about $50 a month at the Apaci. "Tell her we are here to help her," Osman said to the translator. "She has no problem with the police." She said nothing, so Osman sent her out.

The next woman was Romanian, dressed in tight black pants, a purple spandex halter, and the same high-heeled white sandals as the previous girl. When she also claimed to be just a dancer, Osman told her that her owner had sold his girls to customers, had threatened them, had beaten them. She feigned surprise and said that her owner was very nice. "One day everything will change, you will see," Osman told her. He was playing tough cop, but I could see concern softening his eyes. Maybe he had a teen-

age daughter back home. "And when it does, I may not be able to do anything."

Finally a tall blonde came in. I recognized her as the one who had sat with the American officer at the Apaci. She said that her name was Kristina and that she was from a small village in Moldova. She was wearing the same tight vinyl pants as the second woman but had different sandals and a lot less makeup. In the light of day she looked rougher, a more hardened version of her dancefloor self. I could see what she would look like as an old woman. She sat smirking with her legs spread and her feet cocked provocatively back on her high heels. She was smart and confident and said she spoke five languages well— all the countries she'd worked in. She said that she had come here by taxi from Moldova, and that her trip was paid for by a friend back home named Oleg. She had stayed in a house in Serbia for a while and then crossed the internal border into Kosovo two weeks ago.

"I heard about those houses with women waiting there," Osman said. "People come from Kosovo to pick you out." He pretended to be a buyer: "You, you, and you!"

"I don't know anything about it," Kristina said.

"I am sure you were trafficked. You were sold."

"No."

"Someone paid for you. Someone paid money for you."

"Nyet."

"Da."

"Nyet."

"Da. You have no trouble with the police. Our job is to arrest the pimps, not you."

"I am telling you the truth, sir."

Before he let her go, Osman allowed me to ask her some questions. I described Niki and asked if she knew her. Kristina furrowed her brow in a parody of concentration and finally shook her head.

"Do you remember sitting at a table with an American officer at the back of the room two nights ago?"

"Yes."

"Do you remember four men at a table sitting close to the stage?"

"No."

"One more question," I said. "Have you ever seen me before in your life?"

We'd spent an hour about three feet from her—at one point she'd even given us a smile. Now, she looked straight at me, touched one hand to her hair, and laughed.

"No," she said. "Never."

Some do escape. The International Organization for Migration (I.O.M.), which is charged with sheltering migrants and sending them back to their home countries, rescued more than 700 women from the Balkans and Italy during the year 2000. Elena, who was "owned" by Leku, escaped into police custody in a Macedonian town named Kumanovo, only to be sold by the police back to another bar owner. Through the help of a sympathetic client, she finally managed to make it to an I.O.M. office in Macedonia, where she was taken care of and eventually put on a plane for home. There she was installed in an I.O.M. safe house in Chisinau, the capital of Moldova, and given psychiatric counseling and job training.

Another Moldovan woman, whom I'll call Nina, left her husband to work in Italy as a waitress or cleaning lady because her son had a degenerative disease and she needed money to pay for his treatment. She wound up getting trafficked to Romania, where she was drugged and put on a train to Belgrade. Unable to buy her freedom, she wound up being sold again, this time to a brothel owner in the Bosnian town of Doboj, where she discovered that her husband had gotten her pregnant before she left. Her owner—unable to persuade her to have an abortion—took her to a corrupt doctor, who she suspects gave her an injection that induced miscarriage. A customer at the bar who found out what had happened slipped her the equivalent of $200 and offered his help. She eventually escaped to a local I.O.M. office and made it back to Chisinau, although she never told her husband the details of what had happened to her.

Inevitably, the women who are driven to escape are the ones who have suffered the most trauma and are most urgently in need of care. But they are also the ones who have the most damning evidence against the traffickers and, theoretically, the most reason to want to put them in jail. This is where the agendas of the I.O.M. and U.N. prosecutors diverge slightly. With no witness-protection program yet in place to shelter the women, the I.O.M. argues that their safety will be compromised if they are detained in Kosovo. Furthermore, there is insufficient funding to lodge them in safe houses for the duration of a criminal trial. For their part, U.N. prosecutors argue that in the long run the problem cannot be solved—in other words, the traffickers will never end up behind bars—if these women don't provide testimony.

The problem is made more complicated by the thicket of legal issues surrounding trafficking and prostitution. In the United States, gathering evidence of prostitution is fairly straightforward. Since it is nearly impossible to prove that a customer is not the prostitute's boyfriend, undercover cops pose as customers in order to prove prostitution charges. In Kosovo, however, the U.N. police force was until very recently prohibited from surreptitious intelligence gathering, and the Kosovo Police Service—the local police corps—has not yet been sufficiently trained in undercover work. (K.P.S. officers, who are paid only $230 a month, are also highly vulnerable to corruption, making security breaches almost unavoidable.) In addition, most of Europe has extremely rigorous standards for admitting into a trial evidence gained by an agent provocateur. A police action that in this country would be considered a standard "buy and bust" operation is more likely in Europe to be considered entrapment and therefore excluded as evidence.

As a result, the prostitutes themselves are needed to provide testimony against the pimps. Witness-protection concerns aside, this raises legal issues. A woman who accuses someone of being her pimp is implicitly admitting to prostitution, which is in itself punishable by jail. To get around this, Section 8 of United Nations Regulation 2001/4—which supersedes pre-existing local laws—declares that providing evidence of trafficking protects the woman against charges of prostitution. "Section 8 understands that in many cases, but not all, a foreign woman in Kosovo finds herself a stranger in a strange land," says Michael Hartmann, an international prosecutor for the U.N. in Kosovo, "and that she was basically not given a choice. Even though she became a prostitute voluntarily, one could assume that she is someone who would not ordinarily do that."

Because she is at risk, it is not in her best interest to remain in Kosovo long enough to provide testimony against her owner in a criminal trial. As a result, U.N. regulations allow for videotaped testimony to be admitted in court. This has its own shortcomings, however. A good defense attorney can argue that his inability to cross-examine his client's accuser weakens the value of the evidence, and—more insidiously—video testimony can even be viewed skeptically by a biased judge. Major criminal trials in Kosovo have two international judges sit on a panel with three local, or "lay," judges. This panel hears all evidence and then comes to a verdict. The lay judges, however, occasionally display the prejudices of the highly patriarchal Kosovar culture. They tend to blame the woman for her troubles, in other words. "The majority of rape cases are fabricated by the alleged victims, seeking revenge, or trying to pressure the defendant to force a marriage proposal," one judge, according to an O.S.C.E. report, declared before a rape trial.

Even a perfect system, however, would face daunting enforcement challenges. New U.N. regulations have made trafficking itself a crime, apart from the related issues of assault, rape, forced prostitution, etc. Trafficking is defined, in part, by the level of deception involved: if a trafficker tells a woman she is going to be a waitress and then transports her across a border to sell her into prostitution, he is guilty of trafficking whether she went voluntarily or not. As a result, traffickers have changed their strategy to get around this new, looser definition of the crime. Instead of slipping across borders at night, for example, they pay off border guards so that the women have legitimate visas in their passports. They coach the women in what to say if they are questioned by the police—some of whom are corrupt and have been bought off in the first place. They have placed informants throughout the local and U.N. administrations. And they have started offering the trafficked women just enough money to keep them in the game.

"Ultimately the problem is the economic conditions that make prostitution the only thing these women can do," says Alison Jolly. "Even when jobs come onstream, it's not going to be the women who get them. For some countries it will be decades before the economic situation is such that you don't need to take risks associated with trafficking. They think, Maybe, just maybe, I'll find something better out there."

In late March 2001, two women were arrested in Chisinau for selling illegal meat in plastic bags. Suspicious, the authorities tested it and confirmed their worst fears: the meat was human. The women said that they had gotten it at the state cancer clinic, and that they had been driven by poverty to sell it.

Only weeks earlier, the World Health Organization had warned that Moldova's economic collapse had created a thriving transplant market in human kidneys and other body parts. Some people were voluntarily selling their organs for cash, and others were being tricked into it in a ruse similar to the one used to lure women into prostitution. Moldova—pummeled by droughts, cold spells, and the 1998 Russian financial crisis—has become by far the poorest country in Europe. The average salary is $30 a month, unemployment is reportedly at 25 percent (though much higher in rural areas), and up to one million Moldovans—nearly a quarter of the country—have gone abroad to work. Some villages have lost half of their population, and virtually all their young people. Every year these migrants wire home an average of $120 million, which is equivalent to half the national budget. Two-thirds of the budget, however, is sent right back overseas to service the nation's foreign debt. With productivity only 40 percent of what it was under the Soviets, Moldova has voted back in a Communist government.

It is the only former Soviet republic to have returned so unabashedly to its past.

Teun and I have left Kosovo. It is now several months later, and we're driving through the emptied and sullen countryside of Moldova. We have come to see this place where, according to a significant proportion of the trafficked women, life is even worse than in the brothels of Kosovo. It's a low, dark day that will soon deteriorate into a pounding rainstorm that will fill up the rivers and wash out the roads and force the villagers to take off their shoes and carry them under their jackets. That's what you do when you own only one pair.

Village after village stands nearly empty, the brightly painted wooden gates of the houses hanging open and the weeds growing up around the palings. Cornstalks are piled against the fences to dry, and an occasional horse cart rattles by with an old man at the reins. Sodden hills checkered with woods roll southward to the town of Kagul and the Romanian border. There are no workers in the fields, no cars on the roads, no children in the houses. It is as if a great plague had swept through, leaving behind a landscape out of medieval Europe, out of *Grimm's Fairy Tales*. Kagul is the center of trafficking in southern Moldova, and we are with a woman I'll call Natalia, who was trafficked through Kagul and just made it home a few weeks ago. Natalia's story is so horrendous that I'm tempted to think she has embellished it, but at this point I've heard and read so many accounts of trafficked women, and the brutality is so consistent, that I've given up looking for some other explanation. These are troubled, traumatized women who may have distorted, misremembered, or even fabricated details of their experience, but their testimonies are unfortunately too similar to be doubted.

Natalia grew up in a desperately poor village named Haragij, where people survived on whatever they could grow, and children had to bring their own firewood to school in the winter. At age 16 she was married against her will to a violent alcoholic who wound up beating her so badly that he fractured her skull and almost killed her. She says the police

in her town were so corrupt that they had to be bribed in order to even consider arresting him, so she decided to leave and look for work in Chisinau instead. She had two young children, and she was determined to support them.

She wound up being trafficked twice. The first time she fell for the standard scam: a trafficker offered her a good job in Italy, but she was sold to a brothel in Macedonia. With the help of the I.O.M., she eventually escaped, but when she made it back to Moldova, she found out that her younger sister had been trafficked as well. Now knowing that world inside out, she decided to go back to Chisinau and get herself sold into prostitution one more time. It was the only way she could think of to get back to the Balkans and bring her sister home.

It didn't take long. Within a few days she met a woman who passed her the phone number of a man who supposedly could get her work in Italy. She met with him—a well-dressed and impressive businessman of 35 or so—and he offered to put her up in his apartment. She soon found herself with about 40 other women in an apartment somewhere in Chisinau. From this point on, her life would no longer be her own.

The women who didn't have passports were given fake ones and charged for them, which was the beginning of their debt. They were first taken by car to Constanta, Romania, and from there to the banks of the Danube, which they crossed at night by boat. Now they were in Serbia. There they were forced to walk across fields at night to a road, where they were picked up by a man named Milos, who she says took them to the White Star café-bar in the town of Kraljevo. There were dozens of women—Moldovans, Ukrainians, Romanians—being held in the basement of the bar, waiting to be bought by brokers for the Albanian Mafia.

Natalia spent several weeks there and was then moved across the lightly guarded internal border from Serbia into Kosovo. There she was sold to a place called #1, in the town of Mitrovica. The women at #1 were all on drugs—pot, morphine, pharmaceuticals, coke—and fell into two categories: slaves and girlfriends of the owner, a Serb Natalia referred to as Dajan. The girlfriends were the most beautiful ones and were given a certain degree of privilege in exchange for keeping order among the regular prostitutes, whom they held in contempt. One girlfriend tried to force a new Moldovan girl to have sex with her, and when Natalia stood up for the girl, she was beaten by the owner. In revenge, Natalia says, she found some rusty thumbtacks and put them on the woman's office chair, and when the woman sat on them she got an infection that sent her to the hospital. Natalia never saw her again.

The schedule was brutal. They had to strip-dance from eight P.M. until six A.M., taking time to go in back with clients if called upon, and they had to be up at eight A.M. in case there were clients during the day. She says the customers were a mix of local Serbs and United Nations personnel. The prostitutes made around $30 per client and $1 for each drink the client bought, which was all put toward their debt. Natalia owed $1,500, but the owner deducted for food, lodging, clothes, and, of course, drugs, particularly cocaine, which the girls freebased in back. The new girls lived at the bar, and the ones who had repaid more than half their debt lived in an apartment, because the owner didn't want the experienced ones warning the new ones about what was going to happen to them. If a particular girl got close to repaying her debt, the owner sold her off to someone else, and she had to start all over again.

One day, according to Natalia, Dajan's brother killed an Albanian man at the bar, and the police finally came and shut the place down. The girls were hidden from the police before the raid, and Natalia was sold off to another bar in Mitrovica, but there her luck changed. The toilet had a small window in it, and she managed to crawl out and escape. She walked all night and made it to Pristina, but instead of turning herself in to the I.O.M., she hitched a ride to Ferizaj. She had heard a rumor that her sister was in one of the Ferizaj bars, and she wanted to try to find her.

Natalia could not track down her sister, but at the Alo Bar she started talking to a beautiful and morose Moldovan woman named Niki. Niki was the girlfriend of the owner, an Albanian named Tus, and she said that she had been trafficked to Bosnia and then to the Apaci bar in Ferizaj, where she wound up in some kind of trouble.

"She told me that someone tried to help her and she thought that the owner noticed and so he sold her," Natalia says.

We are squeezed into the backseat of a Russian Lada on the way to Kagul. It has been raining hard all morning, and the creeks are up over the roads; the locals are using horses to drag cars through the washouts. "She told me there was something special on their faces," Natalia goes on. "She was afraid they were journalists and she didn't want to screw up her reputation back home. One of them questioned her, but he wasn't in love with her—she said he was either a journalist... or maybe the police."

Natalia spent hours talking to Niki, almost certainly the same woman we had tried to help. Either Natalia somehow heard about our experience and just repeated it to us, or the Kosovo underworld is so small and sordid—and the girls get shuffled around so much—that they just wind up meeting one another. Niki kept a diary, and during the time they were together she had let Natalia read it. I had told Niki my name when she came to our table, and in her journal she had referred to me as Sebastian Bach. She wrote that she must somehow have deserved the terrible things that happened to her, and so it didn't make sense that we were trying to help her. The owner had been tipped off that there was going to be a raid, and she had actually hidden herself when the police came looking for her after we left. She was scared of them because she knew that most of them were also customers at the bar. She knew that only the O.S.C.E. could help her, but she didn't want to escape before she had a little money to return home with. Also, she feared going to jail if she turned herself in to the police. In the meantime, she had taken some photos at the Alo Bar that she would try to send home to her mother. That way—however unrealistic the hope—her mother might be able to help her.

We arrive in Kagul in early afternoon, and Natalia takes us to the Flamingo Bar, which is near the bus station. It's a cheap-looking place with Formica tabletops and louver blinds on the windows. This is where the traffickers try to pick up girls who are waiting for buses to Chisinau or Bucharest. Well-dressed men come and go from the tables, and Natalia hides her face from them because she's afraid of being recognized. She got a crew cut a couple of weeks ago in an attempt to disguise herself, but she still lives in fear that they'll somehow find out she escaped. I ask her if she would testify against her traffickers if she had the chance.

"What would I do about my family?" she asks. "The police would lock up one guy, and there are 10 more.... We'd have to leave the country. It's better that I forget. I just pretend I don't see anything, and I go on with my life."

It was not until July 2001 that Moldova passed an anti-trafficking law. Recruiting for and organizing the trafficking of a human being abroad for the purpose of sexual exploitation, slavery, criminal or military activity, pornography, or "other loathsome purposes" is now punishable by up to 15 years in jail. Traffickers can get up to 25 years if their crimes involve minors, groups of people, the use of violence, or the taking of internal organs.

The Moldovan law is modeled after U.N. regulations, but enforcing it is even more daunting here than in Kosovo. In a country where doctors make around $30 a month, buying off the entire justice system—from the police right on up to the judges on the bench—presents no particular difficulty for the Moldovan Mafia. There are honest cops and judges, but they face a trafficking system that is so fluid and hard to pin down that it is almost impossible to crack. The process often starts with a completely legal classified ad in the newspaper: "Hiring girls without complexes for the work abroad" is a common one. The ad includes a phone number, and the initial contact is usually a woman, often one who was trafficked and has been blackmailed or otherwise coerced into doing the job. From there, the recruits are handed over to the traffickers themselves, whose job it is to get them across the border into Romania. In many ways that is the smallest obstacle in the entire process. Passports can be bought or forged for just a few hundred dollars, border guards can be bribed for even less, and the border itself is so porous that until recently the authorities didn't even bother to keep records of who went back and forth. (The Moldovan government is still hoping for an international loan that will allow it to buy a computer system to handle that task.) Once the girls are in Romania, they're almost always beyond help.

Vastly adding to the problem is the psychology of both the new recruits and the ones who have made it back. Not only are they poor, uneducated, and desperate, but they have grown up in a society that tolerates such astronomical levels of domestic violence that almost any kind of abuse could be considered normal, even deserved. "During the Soviet times there weren't as many social problems," says Lilia Gorceag, an American-trained psychologist who treats women at the I.O.M. safe house in Chisinau. "There was some kind of stability. Now that everything is gone, all our frustrations and fears have been converted to a fear about tomorrow, and it really increased the levels of violence."

According to Gorceag, one of the more common reactions to a violent childhood or marriage—not to mention a violent trafficking experience—is massive feelings of guilt. Niki's conviction that she somehow deserved her fate is a classic example of this sort of psychological defense. "Most trafficked women have very negative sexual experiences during childhood," says Gorceag. "Many were raped when they were young—I have many patients who had been raped by the age of 12, sometimes by their own father. They adopt a perspective that they have been created to satisfy someone else's sexual needs. They consider themselves depraved, unacceptable to family and friends. And very few men here

would tolerate it if they found out a woman had been trafficked. I know one 19-year-old woman who says her brother would kill her if he found out."

Such a woman is perfect prey for a trafficker, and a good candidate for relapsing into prostitution even if she makes it back to Moldova. Gorceag says that women who are trafficked to Turkey, Greece, and Italy generally survive their experiences psychologically intact, but the ones who wind up in the Balkans are utterly destroyed as people. They exhibit classic symptoms of severe post-traumatic stress disorder: they can't focus; they can't follow schedules; they're apathetic to the point of appearing somnambulistic; they fly into violent rages or plunge into hopeless depression; some even live in terror that someone will come and take them away. Their condition keeps them from functioning normally in a family or a job, and that puts them at even greater risk of being trafficked again.

"One of my patients ate napkins," says Gorceag. "When I took away the napkins, she started eating newspaper. She wasn't even aware of what she was doing. There is another patient who counts. She counts everything. When she can't find anything to count, she turns her sleeve and counts the stitching. These are people with completely destroyed psyches. It's a form of genocide. I know that's a very strong word, but I live with 22 of these women, and I see their suffering every day."

On our last day in Moldova, Teun and I meet Natalia to look at some photos she wants to show us. I have just received word from members of the U.N. anti-trafficking unit in Kosovo that they think they have found the bar where Niki is working, and they want me to fly back there to participate in a police raid. That way I can identify her so she can be sent home to Moldova, whether she wants to be or not. It's a beautiful fall day, and Natalia and Teun and I sit down at an outdoor café next to two puff-pastry

blondes who are wearing maybe an ounce of fabric between them. Natalia—tough, smart, and battered by her experience in Kosovo—tosses them a dismissive look.

"What do those women want?" I ask her. "What are they looking for?"

"Men with money," Natalia says. "Moldovan women have become very cold, very callous. They don't want to fall in love. They just want to meet a rich guy, and most of the guys with money are thugs. It's their mothers who push them into this—that's the worst part."

The photos Natalia shows us were taken at a bar when she was working as a prostitute. One was taken a few days after she arrived; she's very drunk and her eyes are red from crying. She has long, glamorous hair and very red lipstick and a forced smile that says more about her situation than any expression of hate or fear. There is none of the wry sarcasm in her eyes that I have become so fond of. I tell her that Niki has been located, and that if I go back to identify her she in all likelihood will be repatriated to Moldova.

"What should we do?" I ask. "Would we just be making things worse for her?"

"Yes, I think so," Natalia says without hesitation.

"So we shouldn't go to the police?"

Natalia takes a drag on the cigarette we gave her and crushes it in the ashtray. For her this is clearly not a question of principle; it's a question of guessing what Niki herself would want. If Niki were tied up in a basement getting raped, the answer would be easy: break down the door and save her. But she's not. She's imprisoned by a web of manipulation and poverty and threat and, much as I hate to admit it, personal choice. The answers aren't so obvious.

"She would just deny that she's a prostitute," says Natalia. "Look, there's nothing here for her. If you brought her home you'd have some sort of...." She casts around for the right words.

"Moral responsibility?"

"Yes," Natalia says, never taking her eyes off me. "Exactly."

From *Vanity Fair*, July 2002, pp. 112-117, 162-166. © 2002 by Sebastian Junger. Reprinted by permission of the Stuart Krichevsky Literary Agency, Inc.

ROCK THE CASBAH

IN IRAN, KIDS REALLY DO HAVE TO FIGHT FOR THE RIGHT TO PARTY. BUT NOW TWO-THIRDS OF THE COUNTRY IS UNDER 30. AND THAT COULD BE A REAL PROBLEM FOR THE MULLAHS.

BY T. Z. PARSA

THE HOTEL-ROOM MINIBAR STOCKS only Coca-Cola and water in this driest of dry towns. There's a prayer rug in the bedside drawer; a tin arrow on the wall points to Mecca. Flight time from New York is thirteen hours, and I already miss the crappy airline movies because television in Iran is three channels of media poverty. Some wet-eyed fellow gargling verses from the Koran; tulips swaying to a traditional Persian dirge; a low-budget soap opera with the hero in a white turban. It's in Farsi. Thankfully, there is also a complimentary English-language newspaper—the state-sponsored *Tehran Times,* whose lead headline might as well be the same every day: THOSE F*****G JEWS ARE AT IT AGAIN. As the sun sets into the smog (government subsidies and massive oil reserves keep gasoline at about 25 cents a gallon), I yearn for a bar—a lobby bar, a dive bar, a college bar, a gay bar, a strip bar, any kind of bar. No such luck in the Islamic Republic

of Iran. But then the phone rings and MC Kabob says the drugs are lined up, the girls are ready, and everything is good to go. Allah be praised—it's fiesta time in the Axis of Evil.

Undisclosed location: The police came down hard on Tehran's rave scene last year, so now the kids drive far outside the city. Secrecy is crucial: Invite only people you trust. Don't tell anyone until a few hours before. And make sure you're not followed.

"Hey, buddy—call me back from outside the hotel," Kabob whispers. "We're leaving in half an hour. Don't use the phone in the lobby. They're all tapped. And make sure you're not followed." Kabob is a twentysomething Iranian hedonist with a justified fear of flogging. He's lived

most of his life in the United States but returned to Tehran a few years ago; he's been reveling in the country's nascent party scene ever since.

The government runs the economy in Iran, so instead of a plug for Pepsi or Perrier, my phone card features two long-bearded martyrs. They're on display all over the place in Tehran—martyrs to the 1979 Shah-shafting revolution on bus stops, martyrs to the brutal eight-year war with Iraq on billboards. This religious propaganda bears a guilt-inspiring message directed at the nation's hordes of restless youth, including its million or so college students. Shame on you, it says. We died to protect the beautiful Islamic values of the revolution, and you ungrateful smurfs want to trade all that for a cold six-pack, a Moby CD, and a furtive pre-marital hummer.

In Iran, all the naughty fun Western sybarites take for granted—mood-enhancing drugs, strip poker, co-ed dancing—is illegal under

Sharia, the Islamic law derived primarily from the Koran as interpreted by religious scholars for whom Jessica Simpson is Satan's inflatable hump doll. Punishments range from bloody lashings to jail time in Tehran's notorious Evin prison, by all reports, a howling nightmare in the great *Midnight Express* tradition.

And so the kids here plan their parties in secret, like bank robbers or coup plotters. It's a spy game: Don't tell anyone until a few hours before. Keep it small—just people you can trust. Boys and girls in separate cars. Girls, keep your hair covered like a mullah's wife. (All women in Iran are required by law to wear the *hejab*—at a minimum, they must cover their hair with a head scarf and hide the curves of their body in a baggy trench coat.) You may be wearing a thong, tight jeans, no bra, and a tiny tee under your manteau, but to all appearances you are the reincarnation of Fatima. Don't bring alcohol—it is more difficult to stash than drugs. Keep the music low until you are outside the city. Watch out for police checkpoints.

"I cannot f*****g believe we're bringing you with us," MC Kabob shouts above the Snoop track that pounds from his tricked-out car stereo. "You are a total heatscore." We are climbing into the Alborz mountains at the head of a caravan of about four cars spaced a half-mile apart. The destination is Shemshak, a small ski resort an hour north of Tehran.

Turban renewal: The government worries a great deal about protecting Iranians from "corrupting influences." Although satellite dishes are banned, foreign television broadcasts are still pirated, and the Internet offers tantalizing glimpses of other outside temptations.

"Total heatscore," agrees Kabob's buddy G., who is riding shotgun. G.

recently returned from a university abroad to work in his family's import-export business. "It's worth it, though, if you write about these corrupt f*****s in the government."

"And the *basij*," Kabob adds.

The *basij* are volunteers in a quasi-official organization established after the revolution to do good works under the banner of Islam. Today, they are best known as religious enforcers who make it their business to raid parties, confiscate cars playing Western music, crack the heads of political protesters, and hassle girls about their *hejab*. As with many hard-line (read conservative, religious, anti-Western, anti-democratic) elements in the government, there is a murky quality to the *basij*. They are often armed, but unlike the police, they are not subject to formal review. As I was repeatedly told in ominous tones, no one counts their bullets.

An element of class conflict pervades attitudes about the *basij*. Most of them are from the old neighborhoods of southern Tehran, where crumbling buildings house large religious families, and filthy addicts skanked out on Afghan smack prowl the streets at night. The party people live in the northern part of the city, where ugly new luxury, apartment towers are planted among the old villas favored by wealthy clans during the Shah's regime.

"The *basij* are a bunch of jealous, uneducated thugs," Kabob says. "We have an expression in Iran—if you want a palace, build yourself a fortress. These thugs see you in a nice car with a pretty girl and it pisses them off. It is not about religion."

The party is in a ski lodge that belongs to one of Kabob's friends—a good-looking Persian hipster with a Clark Gable mustache and a gym rat's physique. "Last year, lot of parties in Tehran," he says, in pretty good English. "But the police start coming—breaking parties is the way they show power. And so we start coming to Shemshak more. But, is f*****g cold, man!"

MAGIC-CARPET RIDE

President Muhammad Khatami of Iran persuaded the United Nations to decree 2001 the "Year of Dialogue Between Civilizations." As a supporting gesture, his Tourism Ministry also declared it the "Year to Visit Iran." With 2002 shaping up to be the "Year of Civilizations Flipping Each Other the Bird," tourists can expect a less enthusiastic welcome.

You need a visa to enter Iran, and the process—all applications must be approved in Tehran—is reportedly slower than ever, especially for holders of American and British passports. (Travel agencies that offer tours of Iran claim they can facilitate the process.) There are no direct flights from the United States, but you can catch a connection from several European capitals. Bring cash if your credit cards are U.S.-issued, and try extremely hard not to lose your passport, because the U.S. has no embassy in Iran. Foreigners are subject to Islamic law: Women must wear head scarves; men must keep a respectful distance from women. Nevertheless, the average Iranian warmly welcomes foreigners—although at the moment it's probably best to leave your MY ARIEL SHARONA T-shirt at home.—*T.Z.P.*

Is it ever. But this is precisely why Shemshak has become the funky Medina for party pilgrims during the long winter months: The nearest police station is a twenty-minute drive along snow-packed roads.

Inside, bear heads hang on the walls, the gas heaters are set on high, and a fire crackles in the hearth. Its smoldering orange glow illuminates the faces of about fifteen people between the ages of 18 and 30, all stamping their feet against the cold and smiling sneaky smiles. The lights dim as three-foot-high speakers appear from behind a false wall and a chest-thumping beat fills the room. It's Fat Boy Slim shouting, *Right here, right now.*

YOUNG PEOPLE ARE THE MAJORITY IN Iran—A fact that often fails to come through in Western media coverage, which tends to focus on the grizzled mullahs who run the show. Of the 66 million people in the world's largest theocracy, more than 70 percent of them are under 30. The clerics are partly responsible for this baby boom, having exhorted women to populate Iran with new soldiers and martyrs during the eighties.

The hard-liners are coming to regret this policy, which created a restless generation of kids in their late teens and early twenties who have no memory of 1979. They don't identify the revolution with the ideals of democracy and nationalism that were its driving force, but with restrictive laws and a flailing economy. The no-sex, no-dancing, no-fun rules strike most of them as ridiculously archaic, especially given widespread access to satellite television and the Internet, where the giddy liberties of Western pop culture are in heavy rotation. But what really bothers young people is the sky-high unemployment (upwards of 20 percent) and devalued currency (you need a small satchel to carry a hundred bucks' worth of rials). Conservatives attempt to blame these ills on U.S.-imposed trade sanctions, but even the anti-American chest-beating set off by Bush's Axis of Evil speech has not kept Iranians from asking why a country this educated and oil-rich should be so poor.

"Every dollar you make in Iran, you have to drag and pull it because every f*****g dollar has several very heavy turbans standing on it." This is Tirdad, a 30-odd-year-old businessman describing the epidemic of corruption in the government. He speaks in a low voice after making me swear on my father's grave that I won't use his real name. (I gave the same promise to everyone in this article, and changed some other identifying facts as well.)

"They ask for bribes or a percentage of your business. Five years ago there was nothing you could do

about it—complain, and they asked for twice as much. Complain again, and they send you to jail where maybe you sort of decide to commit suicide one day after signing your business over to the son of some minister," Tirdad says. "Today, it's different. Now I tell them to send me an official letter asking me for the bribe. One local official actually did, and I took him to court and got him locked up, the stupid f**k."

Death to Smoochy: "Iran is paradise for foreign men," says a European journalist living in Tehran. "The women are uninhibited behind closed doors. But you must be careful. Many women look at you and see only one thing—a visa out of Iran." There are other, more serious risks: In 1988, a German businessman who went behind closed doors with an unmarried Iranian woman was sentenced to death.

Tirdad's got what the English call the wide-boy look—big expensive watch, tiny cell phone, camel-hair coat slung over the back of his chair. We're in the swankest restaurant in Tehran, a beautifully calm new joint called Monsoon—blond wood on the walls, pan-Asian fusion on the menu.

"*This* is the real change in Iran since Khatami was elected," Tirdad says, holding a spring roll with his chopsticks. Muhammad Khatami was elected president in 1997 on a platform of reform (more freedom of the press, closer ties to the West, greater foreign investment, less government in business).

"He legalized egg rolls?"

"No, you idiot. Monsoon brings a good idea from the West to Iran and these guys make a lot of money. People see that and they say, '*Me too*—I want to make money and bring good things to Iran.' When people understand that the conservatives are

blocking the road to prosperity, that's when they will push them out. It is young businessmen who will bring change to Iran."

Tirdad recently acquired another wife (Islam permits four), a cousin with a degree from an American college. She had been arrested, along with 300 others, in a raid of a party in Tehran. The prison's female doctor performed a virginity check and arrived at the unscientific conclusion that the absence of a hymen proved that the girl's honor had been sullied. They would not release her until she told them who did it. Tirdad accepted blame, and they were hitched the same day.

"It's like the f*****g Middle Ages!" Tirdad says. "Islam is a beautiful religion, and it is a deep part of Iranian culture, as deep as the Persian part. But Islam should be a personal practice, not public law. It is incredible how the government makes such a beautiful thing so ugly."

Tirdad experienced that ugliness firsthand last year when he was thrown in jail for two weeks after the police stumbled on a small party he was hosting. On his last day in prison, guards surprised him at the toilet and beat him senseless for the un-Islamic act of standing while pissing. Excretion and sex are hot topics in the Koran, as they are in the Old Testament. The difference is that in today's Iran, those seventh-century admonitions legally bind the destinies of 21st-century citizens, be they true believers, infidels, or (as is the case of most modern Iranians) something in between.

"It's going to be beautiful when things change and the economy is working," Tirdad says. "Seventy million people—what a market!"

He sips green tea and sucks on an imported cigarette, blowing smoke at the ceiling.

"Then I'll piss how I want and no one can say a word. I'll write the supreme leader's name in the snow!"

"I MOVED FROM L.A. TO LIVE HERE three years ago, and now I don't think I'd ever live anywhere else." This is from Ali, who is sitting in an apartment in northern Tehran with ten or so other young Iranians. Ali recently opened a gallery and "design workspace" in central Tehran; he is one of the many nouveau Sufis who have returned from abroad to embrace their Iranian heritage. "The *Sharia* is ridiculous, especially the way it treats women," he says. "But the rules of life in Manhattan or L.A. can be just as strict and absurd—it's the other extreme. After a few months in Iran, you see there is more to life than parties, money, fame, and media."

Mansour, a hipster in his early twenties, rolls his eyes from across the room and takes a big gulp from his tumbler of dog sweat—the literal translation of *aragh-é sag*, the vision-blurring moonshine that is delivered door-to-door by hustlers everyone calls the Armenians. "At least you could make the choice to stay or go," he says.

Iran has suffered a massive brain drain as its best students, academics, and professionals have fled to the United States and Europe, yet it remains very difficult for young Iranians to procure visas to leave the country. Last year, Mansour traveled from Iran to the Dominican Republic carrying $10,000 to pay the smugglers who were supposed to take him to Canada, where he has family. He was rerouted several times and spent a month in a Singapore jail before his father brought him back to Iran.

Zara, a 30-year-old woman who was raised and educated in the States but has come back to Iran, proposes a toast: "Here's to my Armenian—he's not too bad." A round of "How good's your Armenian?" ensues. Some bootleggers sell only dog sweat, but the better ones offer a wide selection of hard alcohol, as well as cans of Turkish beer and the occasional bottle of wine. There are also "film guys" who make the rounds with illegal videocassettes. Pot, opium, heroin, and cocaine are readily available in the streets of Te-

hran, but the trade in action movies and ale is highly clandestine.

"Five years ago, we would make our own wine," says a French journalist who has been stationed in Iran off and on for the past six years. "Big truck of grapes come to our house. Now I just order a bottle of Scotch from my Armenian. And so, *santé!* To progress in the Islamic Republic!"

"To progress!" shouts Zeba, a twentysomething woman with long, curly brown hair. "Five years after Khatami and now women don't have to wear socks in the summer. Wow! We can show our feet without being whipped! Here's to our country's amazing reform movement!"

Veiled allusions: Women in Iran are required to wear the *hejab*—to keep their heads covered and hide any alluring curves beneath folds of fabric. Young men who've spent time in the West hate these rules, and so do many women. But for one rebellious girl, the restrictions aren't so bad. "Sometimes I don't wear anything under my coat," she says. "Everything is more exciting when it is prohibited."

Zeba, Zara, and their friends represent a new female phenomenon. They're called *tokhs*, which literally means "stubborn" but is used to describe women who are unabashedly bohemian and defiant. They love Iran and manage to have lives that are fairly normal by Western standards, despite all the official religious restrictions.

"What's so bad about the *hejab*?" one of them asks. "Sometimes I don't wear anything under my coat. It's exciting—everything is more exciting when it is prohibited."

"*Hejab* is dignity!" shouts another girl, mocking the slogan of a religious propaganda billboard across the street from the apartment.

"Iran is paradise for foreign men," the French journalist confides. "The women are very, very uninhibited behind closed doors. But you must be careful. Many women look at you and see only one thing—a visa out of Iran." (That is not the only risk. In 1998 a German businessman was condemned to death for having sexual relations with an unmarried Iranian woman. He was later released, after pressure from the German government.)

"So you are basically a sex tourist in our country," Zeba snaps. The journalist's face drops. "Wouldn't Thailand be easier?" Then she cackles. "Who cares! Did it ever occur to you that some Iranian girls just want to have sex? That they want to stay in Iran? That you are a good-looking guy?" A spark jumps between the two.

Zeba voted for Khatami during his first election run (the voting age in Iran is 16) and says that she was very hopeful. In the last election she didn't even bother to vote, and she wasn't alone. Khatami was re-elected, but voter turnout dropped from 88 percent to 67 percent. Like many young Iranians, she became disillusioned as the conservative mullahs blocked most of Khatami's attempts at reform. (Public protest by young people has been limited—vandalism and dancing in the street following a World Cup qualifying match last October, students shouting support for their striking teachers in January.) The supreme leader, a severe and unpopular fellow by the name of Ayatollah Ali Khamenei, controls the judiciary, the police, the army, and the elite Revolutionary Guard, so he rarely feels obliged to concede any points to the popularly elected reformists.

Disillusioned or not, the *tokhs* and their friends were not sympathetic to the saber-rattling rhetoric in Bush's State of the Union address, which condemned Iran for its development of missile technology and its support of the armed Hezbollah group. Irascible ex-president Ali Akbar Hashemi Rafsanjani responded that Bush had "a sparrow's brain in a dinosaur's head," and it is likely that the majority of Iranians agree. They see missiles as necessary to their national defense and the Hezbollah boys as freedom fighters who forced Israel to abandon illegally occupied territory in Lebanon and who may succeed in kicking it out of Gaza and the West Bank as well.

"I suppose your president thinks that reformists in Iran will take his speech as a sign to rise up and overthrow the supreme leader," the lean, soft-spoken boyfriend of one of the *tokhs* says. "But no one wants sudden change like that. We had a sudden change in 1979, and look what it gave us!"

"I don't care about political freedom anymore, I just want to be able to do what I want," Zeba says. "I am sick of hearing about politics! Talk to me about love, art, history, culture—anything but politics!"

BACK AT THE SHEMSHAK SKI LODGE, our mini-rave is in full swing. "I'm the man you've got to talk to—I brought partying to Tehran!" MC Kabob says. "I started it all three years ago. And I will open the first nightclub here when things loosen up, which will be sooner than anyone thinks."

A balding fellow who has shucked down to a skin-tight black tank top passes around some home-grown hydroponic Tehran reefer. He recalls how he brought 50 MDMA tablets back from his last trip to Paris. "It's the easiest thing in the world," he says in French. "These officials wouldn't know an ecstasy pill if you stuck it up their ass; if you get caught you just tell them it's aspirin."

The kids roll their joints with tobacco here, but otherwise, familiar U.S. rave semiotics are in full effect. Pills are passed around and banged down as the music is pumped up. The girls' head scarves come off and, after about an hour, so do their overcoats. Everyone grips water bottles and wears sunglasses. Some of the girls even break out those idiotic little flashing-light gadgets. They wave them in the air and hoot like owls. It gets hot and sweaty and more clothes are shed until the girls are stripped down to baby T-shirts and tight pants, belly buttons winking.

"They've never been to a real rave, but they've heard about them from friends who live in the West," Kabob shouts, eyeing a lanky blonde girl who has tied a bandanna around her leg à la Hendrix and is whirling like a Sufi dervish. His pupils are obsidian dinner plates. "They see MTV on satellite television and they imitate."

Although satellite dishes are illegal, two of the three homes I visited in Tehran had them in order to pull in pirated television channels from the United States and Europe. One of these, L.A.-based National Iranian Television, broadcasts interviews with the Shah's oldest son (and heir to the Peacock Throne), making it the bane of the hard-liners and inciting another ineffectual roundup of the banned dishes. If the mullahs' hold on power depends on their ability to "protect Iran from corrupting influences," as they put it, then big changes are on the way.

The Persian Clark Gable is chanting something over and over as he hops around underneath a stuffed bear head.

"He's saying *Aaaaaa-Liyeh*," G. tells me. "It means 'sooooo perfect.' Can you feel it?" Sure can, but it's 6 A.M. and that post-peak torpor is starting to set in. Outside, dawn is breaking on the smooth white façades of the ski slopes.

"Don't look at your watch!" G. shouts in reprimand. "*Aaaaaa-Liyeh!* Don't look at a map. You're in Iran, my friend. How about that? *Aaaaaa-Liyeh!* Don't think about anything. Don't worry. This is only the beginning."

The Princess Paradox

Hollywood's newest Cinderella stories seek to inject some feminist messages into the age-old fantasy. But can you really wear your tiara while spurning it too?

By James Poniewozik

It's the recurring nightmare of high-minded modern parents of daughters. You ask your relatives to lay off the pink pinafores at the baby shower. You give your daughter Legos and soccer balls, not Barbies. You encourage her to play fire fighter and immerse her in *Dora the Explorer* videos. Then one Halloween rolls around, and your empowered, self-confident budding Marie Curie tells you that she wants to be... a princess.

Call it nature or nurture, harmless fantasy or insidious indoctrination, but Hollywood is discovering that it still pays not to fight the royal urge. Following 2001's $108 million-grossing *The Princess Diaries*, Hollywood has waved its wand and conjured a set of Cinderella stories for girls, including next month's *The Prince & Me* and *Ella Enchanted*, as well as *A Cinderella Story* in July and a *Princess Diaries* sequel in August. That's not to mention other fairy-tale projects (*Shrek 2*) and transformational stories like *13 Going On 30*, in which a gawky teen is magically morphed into a fashion-plate magazine editor played by the perpetually miniskirted Jennifer Garner.

We've come a long way, it seems, from the girls-kick-ass culture of just a few years ago (*Charlie's Angels, Crouching Tiger, Hidden Dragon*) in which a 360° flying-roundhouse kick was a girl's best friend. (On the proto girl-power cartoon, *Powerpuff Girls*, one of the heroines' worst enemies was a spoiled brat named Princess Morbucks.) But brush off the fairy dust, and you find a new kind of Cinderella, one who would rather save Prince Charming, thank you, and who has learned the lessons of feminism—or at least learned to pay lip service to them. You can have the girly dream of glass slippers and true love, these films say, as well as the womanly ideal of self-determination and independence—and any contradictions between them are no match for the movies' magic.

Ella Enchanted, for instance, is a spoof of *Cinderella* in which the title character (*Diaries'* Anne Hathaway, Hollywood's queen of princesses) spends her free time protesting the discriminatory anti-elf and -giant policies of the family of Prince Charmont (Hugh Dancy). What she wants at first is not love but to free herself of a fairy's curse that forces her to be obedient. In *The Prince & Me* (what, *The Prince & I* would have been too egghead-y?), Paige Morgan (Julia Stiles) is a workaholic soon-to-be medical student who rolls her eyes at friends rushing to get their M.R.S. degrees. When she falls for Eddie (Luke Mably), a rakish-but-sweet exchange student who turns out to be Danish Crown Prince Ed-

vard, the prospect of becoming queen upsets her dreams of working for Doctors Without Borders. (Stiles, who played Ophelia in the 2000 film *Hamlet*, should know that dating the prince of Denmark can be a pain.) "The Cinderella story has always frustrated me," Stiles says. "What I like about *The Prince & Me* is that my character is a lot more active and is ready to live a life by herself and be independent."

SPOILER ALERT: Skip this paragraph if you don't want to know how these movies end. O.K., here's the shocker—they end happily. What is surprising, however, is that, in the original ending of *The Prince & Me*, Paige broke up with Edvard to go to med school (in the final version, she gets to have both the guy and the career). And what's downright shocking is that Paramount approved the first, decidedly non-fairy-tale ending. "But when I saw it," says director Martha Coolidge, "I knew it was wrong. What was wrong about it was not what we thought—whether she got together with him or not. The real issue was about him making a compromise and the monarchy making a compromise."

Reinventing fairy tales has been a favorite project of feminist authors from Angela Carter (*The Bloody Chamber*) to Marlo Thomas (*Free to*

Be... You and Me), who understood that wish-fulfillment stories are about teaching people what they should wish for. Among an earlier generation of women, the wish was to be able to do everything men could. For the modern Cinderellas' audience, which takes that freedom as a given, the wish is to also be able—unashamedly—to fall in love and go to the ball. Indeed, in *Prince*, Paige realizes that she needs to be "rescued" from her disciplined but single-minded careerism as much as she needs to assert her independence. Girls asserting their right to choose the fairy-tale ending is not a bad thing, says Thomas, since now the movies are balanced by varied depictions of young women in films from *Whale Rider* to *Blue Crus*. "What women have tried to achieve for other women," she says, "is choice in every step of their lives."

But to succeed on both the feminist and the fantasy level, the new Cinderella has developed rules and conventions as strict as a Joseph Campbell template. She should be pretty, but in a class-president way, not a head-cheerleader way. She should be able to stand up for herself (recall the *Crouching Tiger* moves of *Shrek's* Princess Fiona). She must be socially conscious—a result, says Meg Cabot, author of the *Princess Diaries* books, of Princess Diana's charitable work. And she should above all not want to be a princess—at least until she changes her mind. In *Diaries*, *Prince* and *Ella*, it's not the girl who must prove herself worthy of princesshood; princesshood must prove itself worthy of the girl.

There's something a little have-your-tiara-and-disdain-it-too about making your protagonists ambivalent about the very fantasy that people paid $9 to see them live out. But that may make the fantasy more palatable to parents and filmmakers: men and, especially, women who are educated professionals. "I don't want to sound like an archfeminist," says Sherry Lansing, chairman of Paramount, which produced *Prince*, "but it really is important that it imparts contemporary values. It's a good love that allows both people to remain whole in it." Still, the fantasy couple that this earnestness yields in *Prince* is more yuppie than romantic: she, committing to years of med school; he, giving up his love of car racing to strap on a necktie and negotiate labor disputes. Goodbye, Chuck and Di; hello, Abbey and Jed Bartlet.

But it's easy for someone who has been through college to say a diploma and career are not cure-alls. The movies' audience of young girls makes the filmmakers much more message conscious—at least as far as the girls are concerned. The princes in these stories have fewer options than their Cinderellas. Edvard and Charmont are both reluctant to become king, but they learn, through the love of a good woman, to mature into the role and use it for good. The girls fight to control their destiny; the boys good-naturedly learn to accept theirs. Of course, they're not the target audience. "It's nice to have something that's not toxic or repellent to men," says Nina Jacobson, a top executive at Disney (*Diaries'* studio). "But we know we don't need guys to make a movie like that successful." You just need a feisty girl, a prophylactic dose of skepticism and a fabulous ball gown—about which no ambivalence is necessary.

The Manliness of Men

by Harvey Mansfield

Today the very word "manliness" seems obsolete.

There are other words, such as "courage," "frankness," or "confidence," that convey the good side of manliness without naming a sex. But to use them in place of "manliness" begs the question of whether moral or psychological qualities specific to each sex exist. Our society today denies that such differences are real, and seeks to abolish all signs of such qualities in our language. To the extent that feminism recognizes gender differences at all, it presents them as bad, and as the fault of men.

The women's revolution has succeeded to an amazing degree. Our society has adopted, quite without realizing the magnitude of the change, a practice of equality between the sexes never before known in human history. My intent is not to stand in the way of this change. Women are not going to be herded back into the kitchen by men. But we need to recognize that there have been both gains and losses in this revolution.

Manliness can be heroic. But it can also be vainly boastful, prone to meaningless scuffling, and unfriendly. It jeers at those who do not seem to measure up, and asks men to continually prove themselves. It defines turf and fights for it—sometimes to defend precious rights, sometimes for no good reason. Manliness has always been under a cloud of doubt—raised by men who may not have the time or taste for it.

But such doubts about manliness can hardly be found in today's feminism. Contemporary feminists, and the women they influence, have essentially a single problem with manliness: that it excludes women. Betty Friedan's feminist classic *The Feminine Mystique* is not an attack on manliness, but on femininity. It insists women should be strong and aggressive—like men.

Though the word is scarce in use, there is an abundance of manliness in action in America today. Young males still pick fights, often with deadly weapons. What we suffer from today, is a lack of intelligent *criticism* of manliness. Feminism has undermined, if not destroyed, the counterpart to manliness—femininity—and with it the basis on which half the population could be skeptical of the excesses of manliness.

Of course, women are still women. While they want men to be sensitive to women, they don't necessarily want them to be sensitive in general. That's why the traditional manly male—who is protective of women, but a sorry flop when it comes to sensitivity—is far from a disappearing species.

The manly male protects women, but is a sorry flop when it comes to sensitivity.

Manliness offers gallantry to women. But is gallantry fundamentally insincere because it always contains an element of disdain? The man who opens a door for a woman makes a show of being stronger than she, one could say. At the same time, the woman does go first. Manly men are romantic about women; unmanly men are sympathetic. Which is better for women?

The "sensitive male" who mimics many female emotions and interests, while discarding the small favors men have traditionally done for women, is mostly just a creation of contemporary feminists who are irritated with the ways of men, no longer tolerant of their foibles, and demanding new behavior that would pave the way for ambitious women. Feminists insist that men must work harder to appreciate women. Yet they never ask women to be more understanding of men.

Manliness is a quality that causes individuals to stand up for something. It is a quality that calls private persons into public life. In the past such people have been predominantly male, and it is no accident that those who possess this quality have often ended up as political rulers and leaders.

Manly men defend their turf, just as other male mammals do. The analogy to animals obviously suggests something animalistic about manliness. But manliness is specifically human as well. Manly men defend not just their turf but their country. Manliness is best shown in war, the defense of one's country at its most difficult and dangerous. In Greek, the word for manliness, *andreia*, is also the word for courage.

For good and for ill, males impelled by their manliness have dominated all politics of which we know. Is there something inevitable about this domination or are we free to depart from it? With more and more countries moving toward democracy and peace, perhaps manliness will become less necessary.

Yet there might also be a democratic manliness. In democracies, Tocqueville said, a manly frankness prevails—an open and fearless stance of "man to man" in which all are equal. Does democracy, then, tend to produce, and require, manliness?

Feminists find all sexual roles objectionable. They are insulted by the idea that nature has determined different social parts and purposes for the sexes. They have largely forced the abandonment of any idea of sexual nature in favor of the feminist notion of "choice." A woman today has the choice of every occupation that used to be reserved for men, *plus* traditional women's roles. Inevitably, "choice" for women opens up choices for men too. What happens when men are no longer pressed to face the duties that used to go with being a man? Traditionally, the performance of a man's duties has required him to protect and support his family. To be a man means to support dependents, not merely yourself.

But the modern woman above all does not want to be a dependent. She may not have thought about what her independence does to the manliness of men (it might make men more selfish). And she may not have considered carefully whether the protection she does without will be replaced by sensitivity, or by neglect. The statistics on male abandonment of their children in our day are not heart-warming.

According to feminists, any traditional notion that the different sexes complement each other serves merely to justify the inferiority of women. On its face, complementarity suggests real equality—each sex is superior in its place. But if you are sure that the best positions have been the men's, and that women have been the "second sex," then in order to achieve equality you must go for full interchangeability of the sexes. You must deny any natural preponderance of one quality or another in men and women.

Do men and women have different natures that justify different social roles? Or are these natures just "socially constructed"? If women can conclude that their roles have been designed artificially by society, then they are free to remake themselves without constraint. But the latest science suggests that being a man or a woman is much more than having certain bodily equipment. Perhaps men and women are characterized more by how they think than by their sexual organs.

While maleness is partly just a fact of biology, in humans it is linked to thinking and reason in ways that make manliness something much more than mere aggression. In humans, masculinity is more than just defense of one's own; it has been extended to require noble sacrifice for a cause beyond oneself.

Certainly, women reason and sacrifice too, and they are not devoid of aggressiveness. But their participation in these things is not "equal." As Aristotle said, men find it easier to be courageous—and women find it easier to be moderate. Of course, you cannot avoid Aristotle's qualifier, "for the most part."

For the most part, men will always have more manliness than women have, and it is up to both sexes to fashion this fact into something good.

Harvey Mansfield is professor of government at Harvard University.

THE NEW GENDER
WARS

EXPERTS AGREE THAT MEN AND WOMEN HAVE MORE THAN
JUST BIOLOGICAL DIFFERENCES. BUT WHAT DOES THAT MEAN
FOR SOCIETY? CULTURE? FAMILY? WORK? WITH PRIMARILY
WOMEN RESEARCHERS ON ONE SIDE AND MEN ON THE OTHER,
THE BATTLE OF THE SEXES RAGES ON.

BY SARAH BLUSTAIN

It's boys against girls yet again. Schoolyard taunting, but the stakes are higher. In place of spitballs, though, this time they're hurling serious research at one another.

The latest skirmish in the war between the sexes has flared up between psychologists studying the origins of gender differences. Research has shown that despite feminist advancements, gender differences persist. The question no longer is whether there are differences between the sexes but what to make of them.

> This gender split raises important questions about the current research. Each of these social scientists has looked at hundreds of studies to support his or her claims.

On one side are those who claim that it is evolution and biology that make us significantly different, and that no amount of feminist agitation will change that. Men will continue to be philandering, non-nurturing and sex-focused, and women will continue to be mothering keepers-of-the-hearth. On the other side are those who claim there's a lot more variation to our gender roles. Society, they say, and not our genes, determines how we react to our biological course. Change, this latter group says, is possible and evident.

So to what extent *does* biology, despite feminist objections, mean destiny? How willingly does our biology re-spond to our environment? And even if biology plays a role, how much of the male/female split is nonetheless reinforced by the culture we live in? During this era of great change in women's and men's roles—as we work out collectively who we will be in the coming generations—we need to know: Where do these differences come from and where might they go?

No little amount of rancor has been stirred up in the attempt to answer these questions, in no small measure because the psychologists themselves who are studying the origins of gender differences seem divided along gender lines. In undertones, some researchers suggest that all the evolutionary psychologists (EPs) are men, and those with theories about more varied etiology are women. Some accuse male EPs of seeing feminists as "the enemy," while others accuse female researchers of dismissing evolutionary theories which seem to reinforce male dominance out of hand. Each side tries to take the scientific high ground, pointing to the gender split with a cough or a sly look. They mean that, perhaps, these details are no accident: Maybe men, who still hold positions of relatively high status in American society, are promoting theories that maintain the patriarchal status quo; women, some of them self-described feminists, see a science that allows for more change.

This gender split raises important questions about the current research. Each of these social scientists has looked at hundreds of studies to support his or her claims.

There's relevant data from cultures on every continent, from cultures in every era dating back hundreds of thousands of years, and from every species from chimps to phalaropes (a small shorebird) to mice. Faced with thousands of studies, each theorist must look selectively at the data. And if theory drives research, we need to ask how much of the narratives of human development we read come from the way the personal narratives of the individual researchers color their world view.

The latest round of hostilities in this gendered war started in the mid-1990s, when a group of evolutionary psychologists began publishing research that looked at the origins of gender differences through Darwin's eyes. These EPs claimed (and continue to claim) that differences between the sexes do exist and that, try as we might, we can't change them. (That's the spark in the political tinder-box.) Whether in pre-modern Africa or current-day America, they say, gender-specific skills come from distinct psychological mechanisms that can be traced back directly and very nearly wholly to the Darwinian principle of sexual selection. In other words, it's in our genes.

The narrative of sexual selection goes something like this: In the mating and survival game, we all have a choice. One option, as David Geary, Ph.D., of the University of Missouri-Columbia puts it, "is to take all your energy and focus it on competing to get as many mates as you can. The other option is to have few mates and invest your reproductive energies on raising [offspring]." Men—who for biological reasons can have as many children as women they impregnate—follow the former path. Women, bound to their offspring by pregnancy and nursing, follow the latter.

True in many species, this drama is complicated among humans because many men parent their children, albeit not as much as women. Women, for their part, will compete for those men who invest in their children, thus raising their value. While the impact of these elements varies from one culture to the next, the pattern remains: Women invest in children more than men, and men, all other things being equal, prefer more sexual partners than do women.

Given these facts, the EPs suggest, men will naturally be inclined to pursue multiple partners. Their efforts, from an evolutionary point of view, will be put into finding a beautiful woman (genetically more appealing), finding as many partners as possible, and honing their physical skills in order to battle with other men for desirable women. Emotional skills that might lead to long-term relationships, in this view, have little role. Women, on the other hand, will pursue men who are more likely to stick around the morning after and help provide the food and protection mother and child will need to survive.

Sounds a lot like gender stereotypes today: a species of aggressive philandering men and nurturing, monogamous women. (Much cited research to bolster this view

by David Buss, Ph.D., a leader in this field at the University of Michigan, found that male college students who were offered the chance to sleep with a beautiful stranger that night, were more likely than their female counterparts to say yes.)

The situation may vary among cultures but, says Geary, culture will never change the fact that men can potentially reproduce more frequently than women. "It will always lead to some level of conflict of interest between men and women. Women want men to invest in their kids and them, and by doing so, men lose the opportunity to have multiple mates." And, he adds, there is no culture in which there is equality between men and women in childcare. "Women," he adds, "hate to hear that."

He's right. Women do hate to hear that. Not only women of the general public, but women researchers as well. Riled psychologists, many of them women, sat up in alarm when the evolutionary psychology theories started snowballing in academic journals and in the popular press as well. Articles appeared, television shows hosted EP spokespersons. Social conservatives started using the "biological" evidence of gender differences to claim validity for the women-as-natural-homemaker model of society.

Upsetting to critics of EP theories is the suggestion, popularized in the press, that what is biological is unchangeable. "One of my objections to evolutionary psychology," explains Mary Gergen, Ph.D., professor of psychology and women's studies at Pennsylvania State University-Delaware County and a hard-core believer that gender is primarily a social construct, "is that it tends to stabilize and justify existing patterns of social relationships. They say they are presenting 'just the facts ma'am,' but it justifies the status quo"

Certainly, the idea put forth by evolutionary psychologists about the origins of gender differences is a conservative take on the matter. Conservative in the old sense of the word: inclined to preserve existing conditions and to resist change. Conservative, too, in the political sense of the word, as these debates quickly descend from the ivory tower and onto the ground, where policy is determined and intimate relationships are worked out. It's a position that offers an in-your-face challenge to feminists and other women activists who have tried to move American society in the direction of the egalitarian ideal, bolstered by the philosophical perspective that human psychology is eminently mutable.

> Women harassing their men [over childcare] will lead to more investment in their children.

Researchers, a good number of them self-identified feminists, who had been happily testing sex differences, suddenly felt called to action not only to "put out fires," as one said, but to come up with alternative solutions to the question of origins.

"I started to address [the origins question] because it was being addressed very directly by evolutionary psychologists," explains Alice Eagly, Ph.D., a professor of psychology at Northwestern University who had been working on questions of sex differences for 20 years. To her, their explorations of evolution were becoming "imperial," suggesting that all sex differences had biological basis.

All of these researchers agree on some theoretical basics: the nature-versus-nurture debate is moot; the differences between men and women are the result of humanity moving through the environment. Even EPs, though they believe change is slow, agree that "evolution," as Geary explains, "does not lead to a fixed point. Women harassing their men [over childcare] will lead to more investment in their children. There's some kind of wiggle-room."

"This is more than wiggle room," Eagly insists, and it's there that the battles begin. "Yes, there is a lot of sexual selection for the biological side of things," agrees Janice Juraskca, Ph.D., professor of psychology at the University of Illinois, "but one of the things that got selected that these guys [EPs] often forget is a flexible human brain." It's the flexibility question that's key, and it's on that question—a question that has major political and personal implications—that all battle-lines between the girls and the guys are drawn.

Eagly and a former student, Wendy Wood, Ph.D., now a professor at the Texas A&M University, have been working together to offer an alternative, what they call their "bio-social" model. Their work spans the fields of psychology, investigating hormones, cultural bias and other cross-cultural and cross-species evidence to determine what they consider a more complex understanding of gender differences.

Like the EPs, Eagly and Wood reject social constructionist notions that all gender differences are created by culture. But to the question of where they come from, they answer differently: not our genes but our roles in society. This narrative focuses on how societies respond to the basic biological differences—men's strength and women's reproductive capabilities—and how they encourage men and women to follow certain patterns. If you're spending a lot of time nursing your kid, explains Wood, "then you don't have the opportunity to devote large amounts of time to developing specialized skills and engaging tasks outside of the home." And, adds Eagly, "if women are charged with caring for infants, what happens is that women are more nurturing. Societies have to make the adult system work [so] socialization of girls is arranged to give them experience in nurturing."

According to this interpretation, as the environment changes, so will the range and texture of gender differences. At a time in Western countries when female reproduction is extremely low, nursing is totally optional, childcare alternatives are many, and mechanization lessens the importance of male size and strength, women are no longer restricted as much by their smaller size and by child-bearing. That means, argue Eagly and Wood, that role structures for men and women will change and, not surprisingly, the way we socialize people in these new roles will change too. (Indeed, says Wood, "sex differences seem to be reduced in societies where men and women have similar status," she says. If you're looking to live in more gender-neutral environment, try Scandinavia.)

Certainly these are more optimistic theories for women who have themselves moved into the "male" world of work outside the home. "I think," continues Eagly, that "we would expect the shift only toward women taking on masculine qualities, because that's where the social change has been in terms of roles," she explains. "Women have moved into a lot of male-dominated [areas]. You don't see the reciprocal shifts psychologically—men becoming kinder and more nurturing," she says, because the social changes haven't produced more contact between men and babies. What's critical for more equality, she says—equality being one of her goals—is a "less sharp division of labor."

In a footnote in his book *Civilization and Its Discontents*, Sigmund Freud offers a bizarre account of the origin of differences between the sexes. When left alone with a campfire, he explains, primitive man could not help but urinate on it. It was in his nature, a working out of his homosexual struggle with a competitive penis-symbol, the flame. It was part of being anatomically able and competitively-prone. See a fire, piss it out. That's how women—clearly less able in this sport—become the tenders of the hearth.

Certainly no one would debate that—were we able to put Freud on his own couch—this theory would tell us more about its author than about the origins of gender differences. We might interpret the theories of some liberal psychologists in a similar vein. In the heady revolutionary 1960s and '70s, they believed you could banish gender differences with a little re-education. "We thought," explains Diane Halpern, Ph.D., a professor of psychology at California State-San Bernadino, who began her research in the late 1970s, "that there weren't going to be many [differences], that they weren't going to be significant, and those that there were could be attributed to bias." (She has since revised her thinking.)

In the development of current theories, there's a lot more research going on. Eagly and Wood are working on a series of papers to prove their "social roles" theory. In his recent book, *Male, Female* (APA, 1998), Geary used some 1,200 references. "I had to do overkill in order to prove the point," he reflects, "because there's so much resistance to the idea that there are real biological differences."

But even with all this research, dramatic differences in interpretation come into a relief, along with a clear gender divide over the question of whether men and women must—biologically—adhere to certain behaviors. That story of philandering fathers developed by the EPs, for instance, could be just a story.

Indeed, says Lynn Miller, Ph.D., professor of communication and psychology at the University of Southern California, it's possible to tell an entirely different evolutionary tale. Forget the abandoning fathers. To her, "we were adapted for the important role of fathers as well as mothers." Miller argues that because human birthing is so difficult—the newborn's head is larger than the birth canal—and because human infants are so fragile, humans depend on fathers' active involvement. "We probably are the descendants of men who gave that additional care," she says. And, she adds, "When you look across cultures, where fathers are more heavily involved with offspring, their children are more likely to delay sexual activity, less likely to be violent, and more likely to be in a monogamous and more enduring relationship."

Raises eyebrows, doesn't it? The guys are telling us that men will naturally wander, and the gals, whether they follow evolutionary, social-role or social-constructionist theory, are telling us that's not so. They've all got something to back up their narrative, but there's one thing to remember: Each of these narratives was born creatively, at least in part, from the head of the researcher who promotes it. So before we are drawn into their battle of the sexes, perhaps we should be putting today's gender explorers on the couch as well.

READ MORE ABOUT IT

Gender Differences At Work, C. Williams, Neil Smelser (Univ. California Press, 1991)

Sarah Blustain is associate editor of Lilith Magazine *and a freelance writer living in New York.*

"THE UNIFORM FOR TODAY IS BELLY BUTTONS"

The number of nudist women our age has doubled over the past six years. Gigi Guerra strips down to uncover the scoop.

I don't get excited about being naked in group situations. Sure, I've skinny-dipped, played strip poker, streaked, and gone on my fair share of gyno visits—but it's not as if these things helped define who I am as a person. I did what I had to do and then put my pants back on. Simply put, I love wearing clothes. I love buying clothes even more. Strip me of the joy of shopping and you've removed half the woman.

So now I hear that nudism is trendy. Not for old hippies, but for people our age. The American Association of Nude Recreation says the number of their 18- to 34-year-old members has increased by 50 percent since 1994. According to Nicky Hoffman, the administrative director of the Naturist Society (another organization for nudists), almost a third of their members are in their 20s and 30s. And though there are still more guys than girls, Nicky says she wouldn't be surprised if women soon start to outnumber men. To see what the big deal is, I flew to suburban Sacramento, Calif., site of Laguna del Sol, one of the biggest nudist resorts in the country. Needless to say, packing was a breeze.

"I never want to buy a swimsuit again."

"Most people come here for the first time out of curiosity," explains 36-year-old Patty Sailors, a perky, intelligent brunette who, along with her husband, manages Laguna. "The relaxing atmosphere keeps them here." I'm standing with her in the carpeted main office. We're both clothed, defying the hand-painted sign on the wall announcing: THE UNIFORM FOR TODAY IS BELLY BUTTONS. People around us are forking over four bucks a night for campsites, $12 for RV hookups and 90 bills for modern, air-conditioned rooms. Patty says she expects a crowd of at least 500 this weekend.

Tie-dye T-shirts hang on a rack in the back of the room. They're promoting Nudestock, a yearly Laguna blowout that brings hot dogs, a cover band, and vast expanses of uncovered genitals together under the sun. Nudists seem to like theme events. There's even a Truman Capote-esque Black-and-White Ball in April. I ask Patty how a nudist can properly "dress" for such an event. "Oh, people use lots of body paint," she laughs. "Some guys even draw their tuxes on." Is that with or without the cummerbund?

Patty gives me a tour of the grounds in a silver golf cart that looks like a mini Rolls-Royce. As we putt along, she explains that all guests are taken on tours like this—not just as a courtesy, but also to weed out freaks. "We make sure this is not a sexual environment," says Patty. Laguna bills itself as a family resort, and everything here whiffs of kids, couples and young singles keeping their hands to themselves. But about one in 70 people is turned away because they're married and try to come without their spouse. Occasionally, Patty says, others are denied entry because they gawk too much, make crude jokes, or give off weird vibes.

"Most have their first taste of nudism by getting N.I.F.C.," says Patty, as we cruise by a row of mobile homes. I see my first naked person and giggle to myself. "That means Nude In Front of the Computer," she continues, reining in my amusement. "Or, they'll walk around the house nude." We pass a volleyball game. One guy—clad only in a cropped T-shirt—jumps up to spike the ball. His penis follows. I'm simultaneously mesmerized and horrified. Does it hurt?

Patty's first taste of nudism came when she stopped wearing pj's in high school. "Then I started skinny-dipping," she explains. "The main reason I became a nudist is because I don't ever want to have to buy a swimsuit again." She's serious: Bathing attire is one of the biggest taboos in the world of nudism. Resort-wear designers, take note.

"Clothing hides who you are."

I stay in one of the motel-like rooms. It's spacious and clean, with a huge bed, generic art and a switch-on fireplace. There's even an indoor pool down the hall. It feels like I'm at the Marriott—except for the naked people who keep walking by my door. A water volleyball game is in full swing. (No, not that kind of swing. Get your mind out of the gutter.) I realize that this is the perfect time to get naked—I can run and hide in the pool; everyone will be too busy to notice.

I'm buck-naked in a room full of imperfection, and strangely, it feels comforting.

I strip, grab my towel and leave the room. Within seconds, I have a panic attack. I've never had issues with my body, but now I start to obsess: My butt feels too bony, and suddenly a Brazilian bikini wax doesn't seem like such a bad idea. I pray nobody looks at me.

But as soon as I enter the pool area, I'm relieved. Two women on lounge chairs have 10 times the pubic hair I do. A college-aged girl sitting by the hot tub has cellulite. Droopy breasts abound. The variety of penis sizes and shapes is astounding. I'm buck-naked in a room full of imperfections, and strangely, it feels sort of comforting.

Late Friday evening, a DJ kicks off a dance in the clubhouse. I'm perched by the bar, clad only in a gauzy cotton top (it's a little chilly). Though it's strange to socialize with my pubes showing, it's also refreshing to be around broads who aren't constantly in the rest room inspecting their asses in the mirror. Emily, a curly-haired accountant in her early 30s, couldn't care less about pathetic preening. She's been dancing all night with only a sky-blue butterfly clip in her hair, a big diamond ring on her finger and the determination to have a good time. She's here with her daughters, her brother and her fiancé, whom she met through a dating game on the radio. Emily tells me that one of her girls, who has a surgery scar on her chest, likes coming to Laguna because nobody is freaked out by her body. "I don't think [women] should be ashamed to be naked," she shouts over the pounding beat. "Here, it doesn't matter what your body looks like. Clothing is a way for people to hide who they really are."

Back in my room, I stare at my pajamas. I put them on and feel like I'm committing some kind of terrible crime.

"We're naked, not nuts."

It's Saturday. The temperature is supposed to top 100 degrees. Outside there's a sea of flesh that's 50 times more tan than mine. Thank God for SPF 45—I slather it on every square inch of my pasty white body. *Every* square inch.

On my way to Laguna's restaurant for breakfast, I feel beyond exposed. This is my first time fully naked in the light of day. Strangers wave and say hi, but nobody stares. By the time I arrive, I'm feeling unusually relaxed. I spread a towel down on a vinyl booth (nudist etiquette) and eat my melon, cottage cheese and muffin platter.

Post-dining, I walk to the main lawn. There's a volleyball match going on. The organizers are Neil, a tall, tanned engineer, and his 34-year-old wife, Gigi (hey, nice name!), a shy costume designer with long blond hair. Between games, Gigi tells me that nudism helped her become comfortable with her body. Back when she was 20, she and some friends came across a nude beach. Her friends joined in but Gigi thought she was "too fat" to participate. So she sat on a towel all day, sulking. "By the afternoon, I gave in and took all my clothes off," she explains.

Today, she and Neil participate in some form of nude recreation every summer weekend. Gigi has, at last count, windsurfed, square-danced, hiked, biked, and Jet Skied in the buff. Oh, and played volleyball. The couple has a Web site, *www.nakedvolleyball.com*, dedicated to the sport. "People e-mail us and say we need more pornography on the site," Gigi says, rolling her eyes. "They don't understand that nudism is not a sexual thing. We're naked, but not nuts."

Even though I suck at volleyball, I decide to give it a try. Gigi has inspired me. I forget that I'm naked as I jump around, run and punch. It's actually kind of liberating to feel the wind whistle through new places. Then I dive to catch a low ball. I end up sliding across the grass on my butt. A spiky burr wedges itself into one cheek. No more volleyball.

I head off court and run into Lisa. She's 23 years old and about to graduate from college with a degree in business management. She's stunning—sort of a Natalie Wood/Katie Holmes hybrid. But surprisingly, she hasn't been getting unwanted attention from any of the guys. Lisa says her real problem is dealing with the judgments of clothed people. For example, her roommate: "She saw my ass [one day]," says Lisa, "and asked me why I don't have any tan lines." Lisa doesn't think she'll tell her she's a nudist. "People can be really immature about it when they find out," she sighs.

Nudist myths: Guys walk around with erections. I did not see a single one. All nudists like volleyball. A survey of nudists found that they most favor swimming, walking and hiking. *Nudists are white trash.* Almost a quarter have a masters or Ph.D. and nearly half make upwards of $50K a year.

"This whole place is a dressing room!"

Late in the afternoon, I stop by the boutique, which is run by Lois, a spirited redhead. As I sift through racks of chiffon floral wraps and try on a Nipple Necklace—a tiny spray of colorful beads that dangles from your dockyard rivets—Lois makes small talk. "Some women ask where the dressing room is," she says, taking a sip of her Koozie-housed Diet Coke. "I tell them that this whole place is a dressing room!"

Next, I head to the river. The trail is gorgeous—fields of tall grass spread in one direction, willow trees dot the landscape in the other. In the distance I see a sign tacked to a fence. It's a warning: YOU ARE LEAVING LAGUNA DEL SOL. CLOTHING REQUIRED BEYOND THIS POINT. I later hear that farm workers on the other side of the fence snoop on the nudie people.

I jump into the cool water of the river. It feels great to swim naked. I climb up on some rocks, and think about how I'm actually starting to enjoy being nude. It now feels liberating. But then yelling interrupts my meditative moment. It's the photographer. I can't hear her over the rushing water. She points at my leg in desperation. I see a big bug crawling up my inner thigh, inches from my genitals. The insects here seem more sexed than the people do.

"I had a nude bridal shower."

"The good thing about being nude," says India, a bubbly 24-year-old with chunky highlighted hair, "is that when [my baby] spits up on me, I just hop in the shower." We're sitting outside the mobile home that she lives in year-round with her 30-year-old husband, Bobby, and their cute son. It's the end of the day and everything is moving slowly. Cows loll about in a nearby field. A big American flag flaps lazily from a pole in their immaculately groomed yard.

Bobby is Laguna's groundskeeper, and India works in town as a hairdresser. They met a few years ago when she gave him a cut. He soon brought her to Laguna for a weekend with his parents. "I grew up strictly religious," she says. "I wouldn't even wear a spaghetti-strap tank top in public." But she appreciated the nudists' nonjudgmental attitude. By Sunday, India was naked. "At first it was weird being naked around my boyfriend's parents, though," she notes.

Bobby proposed to India, nude, at Laguna. "I even had a nude bridal shower," she adds, smiling. India wants to stay here for a long time. She likes the "gated community" feel. "And each weekend, we meet a new young couple," she says excitedly. "I see more people our age here. It doesn't matter who you are or what you do."

Nudist truths: *Tampons are acceptable attire.* "But we advise women to tuck the cord," explains Patty. *Nudists are clean.* One woman told me that she showers up to five times a day. *Nudity is more accepted in Europe.* In France, there's a summer community of 40,000. Everything is done in the buff, from banking to grocery shopping.

"Attitudes are changing."

I think about what India says. I haven't heard one person start a conversation with: "Where do you work?" Instead, people chat about simple things like, "How are you today?" or "What SPF you got on?" It's nice to be at a place where your career (or lack thereof) doesn't dictate who you are—housewives and CEOs are on equal footing here. But perhaps the main reason why we women are drawn to nudism is because it makes us feel good about our bodies. Emily, Gigi, Lisa and India all told me as much. And pop culture might actually be helping the call.

"Attitudes are changing," says Nicky. "Larger-sized models and actresses are out there. Nudist organizations are popping up on campuses. At U Penn, there's a Naturalist Student Association. Wesleyan University has a clothing-optional dorm. I even saw an ad for salad dressing that showed a young naked couple on the beach. What does nudity have to do with salad dressing? I have no idea, but it sends a message that naked bodies are okay."

By late Sunday, I've forgotten that I'm naked. At first, I thought nudism was freaky. Now I realize that it's just a way for people to get comfy with themselves. And if you ask me, that's a way better way to go about it than dieting or getting plastic surgery.

Nudists also seem to have found a safe way to escape the pressures of daily life. For me, that's an appealing concept. I'm simultaneously trying to make it on my own, establish my career, pay off debt, and figure out what the hell it is I'm headed for—just like anyone my age. It's weird, but when you take away your clothes, it's like you take a vacation from a lot of your worries. Too bad I'm still addicted to shopping.

From *Jane*, August 2000, pp. 144–147. © 2000 by Jane Magazine/Fairchild Publications. Reprinted by permission.

Hear *Sensuality,* Think *Sex?*

Why we're so leery of our sensuous selves

By Jon Spayde

It's a shame what's happened to some good old words. *Tragic* used to point to a noble struggle between human beings and the forces of fate; today it means "really, really sad." *Irony* stood for the recognition that human knowledge of the universe is profoundly limited—before it morphed into that smirky feeling of superiority we get when we watch *The Brady Bunch.*

And *sensuousness*—a warm receptiveness to the gifts that our eyes, ears, noses, mouths, and skin can bestow upon us— well, baby, we've turned that over to Barry White. It's a 12-letter word for SEX. Our senses—which, if they were nourished as they should be, would triple the joy and juiciness of everything we do, from napping to mailing a letter to mountain climbing—are allowed free rein only in the boudoirs of our imagination.

Sex has been a pretty weird custodian of sensuousness in America. Which of our leading symbols of sexuality have actually affirmed the languorous joys of the receptive body? Hugh Hefner's airbrushed, jiggly girls next door? The massively endowed powerpumps of gay male erotica? The labia-pierced insurrectional sexuality of the riot grrrl underground? No, these manufactured turn-ons are little more than fantasies that mask deeper fears that sex is just one more arena in which we must perform with unerring precision. The eternal, slow, simple, complex pleasures of the wide-awake body opening itself to sweet sensation get lost in the shuffle of silk sheets.

So how do sensuous-seeking Americans do outside of the bedroom? At vacation time we line up to visit places of certified relaxation: the beach, the trout stream, the mountaintop. We're there to *unwind, recharge,* or *play.* The prospects for surrendering to our senses couldn't be better: The warmth of the sun. The shoosh of the surf. The tang of a hot pepper. And then something—one of any number of big things or noodgy little things—insinuates itself into the space between our senses and

their naked, happy communion with the world. Oh yeah, a voice in our head reminds us, we're at a cabin in the woods to catch up on our reading; we're hiking in the desert to conquer that steep peak; we're on a Caribbean island to get drunk, play beach volleyball, and score.

I don't mean to imply that our sexual encounters and precious days off are failures because they include a little anxiety or goal-setting or windsurfing. I just want to suggest how sneaky our resistance can be to real sensuality. Sensuality is a form of giving up: of our goals, hopes, agendas for the next five years or five minutes. A surrender of our purposeful, planned, caretaking, self-improving personas to the sheer presence of the world. Being sensuous means being endowed with senses, and that taking voluptuous pleasure in them is enough. Enough, at least, for this moment, which ought to feel like forever.

America's Puritan heritage and our long-running business culture both abhor idleness, the only true prerequisite for sensuousness.

There is, of course, a great deal in our American heritage that makes us run away, screaming, from this proposition. Puritan holiness and our long-running business culture both abhor idleness, the only true prerequisite for sensuousness. Idleness can seem at the same time too aristocratic and too plebeian for our relentlessly middle-class outlook: Only the most effete exquisites, says the anxious striver residing inside most of us, have the money and the time to savor the difference between five different kinds of green tea. Only the hopeless ne'er-do-well, with nothing left to lose, can afford to spend an afternoon on the public beach, happy for the lukewarm water between his toes and the sun on his back. Drunks, junkies, and those who can't handle life as we know it are the ones who surrender to their senses.

And it's not just mainstream Anglo culture that frowns at sensual indulgence. Recent immigrants, wherever they may hail from, are strivers. And they see folks who take too many sensuous breaks from the demand for bustle and uplift as letting down the team.

The biggest block to sensuous enjoyment may simply be the strange painfulness that many of us feel when our minds are not occupied. This is more than a socio-historically induced sense of guilt. It's visceral: our intolerable inner voices, a restlessness we can't explain, an emptiness we think we need to quickly fill. And even deeper inside, there's what Buddhists call *the monkey mind*, the endless, buzzing productivity of the psyche: memories, dreams, reflections, fantasies; all manner of mental flotsam, churning endlessly upward from some inexhaustible source. We swerve, almost by reflex, away from this experience of chaotic psychic activity. We may fear, too, that we will be overwhelmed by feelings—that will swarm over us like an army of ants if we try to open up to the sensuous by simply sitting back, exhaling, and being here now in blessed idleness.

But here's some good news: Sensuousness does not have to mean a still, empty, meditative state. Sensuousness, after all, is really a profound turning outward of our bodies, not a turning inward of our minds. It doesn't thrive on overstimulation, but it welcomes everything that's swirling around us: the color of the rose on the desk, the play of the breeze across our skin, the sound of a faraway train, the whiff of a lover's shampoo coming from the bathroom.

You don't have to work diligently to achieve sensuousness. It is a benefit our bodies receive from wandering onward and outward into the world: now hearing, now seeing, now feeling, now smelling, now tasting. Yes, it is lazy, gloriously so. Also aristocratic: Thanks to it, we inherit, immediately and at no cost whatsoever, the immense riches of the great world that surrounds us.

Jon Spayde is a contributing editor of Utne Reader.

From *Utne Reader*, November/December 2001, pp. 57-58. © 2001 by Jon Spayde. Reprinted by permission of the author.

UNIT 2

Sexual Biology, Behavior, and Orientation

Unit Selections

14. **The New Sex Scorecard**, Hara Estroff Marano
15. **The Hormone Conundrum**, Amanda Spake
16. **Sex, Drugs & Rock 'n' Roll**, Sue Woodman
17. **What Problem?**, Gerald Weeks and Jeffrey Winters
18. **When Sex Hurts**, Lisa Collier Cool
19. **The Rise of the Gay Family**, Dan Gilgoff
20. **Why Are We Gay?**, Mubarak Dahir
21. **Dr. Sex**, Robin Wilson

Key Points to Consider

- How have (or would) you react if a friend confided in you that he or she was having sexual functioning problems, for example, erections or painful intercourse problems? What if the person confiding in you was a co-worker? A stranger? Your mother or your grandfather? Who would you talk to if it were you with the problem and what response would you want from the other person?

- Let's assume you were shown research that predicted that behaviors you currently engage in could cause you to have serious health problems in the future. What likelihood of future problems and what nature of problems would make you change the behaviors in question?

- It is rare for people to wonder why someone is heterosexual in the same ways as we wonder why someone is homosexual or bisexual. What do you think contributes to a person's sexual orientation? Do you think it is possible for people not to feel threatened by sexual orientations different from their own? Why or why not?

 **Links: www.dushkin.com/online/**
These sites are annotated in the World Wide Web pages.

The Body: A Multimedia AIDS/HIV Information Resource
http://www.thebody.com/cgi-bin/body.cgi

Healthy Way
http://www.ab.sympatico.ca/Contents/health/

Hispanic Sexual Behavior and Gender Roles
http://www.caps.ucsf.edu/hispnews.html

James Kohl
http://www.pheromones.com

Johan's Guide to Aphrodisiacs
http://www.santesson.com/aphrodis/aphrhome.htm

Human bodies are miraculous things. Most of us, however, have less than a complete understanding of how they work. This is especially true of our bodily responses and functioning during sexual activity. Efforts to develop a healthy sexual awareness are severely hindered by misconceptions and lack of quality information about physiology. The first portion of this unit directs attention to the development of a clearer understanding and appreciation of the workings of the human body.

Over the past decade and a half, the general public's awareness of, and interest and involvement in, their own health care has dramatically increased. We want to stay healthy and live longer, and we know that to do so, we must know more about our bodies, including how to prevent problems, recognize danger signs, and find the most effective treatments. By the same token, if we want to stay sexually fit—from robust youth through a healthy, happy, sexy old age—we must be knowledgeable about sexual health care.

As you read through the articles in this section, you will be able to see more clearly that matters of sexual biology and behavior are not merely physiological in origin. The articles included clearly demonstrate the psychological, social, and cultural origins of sexual behavior as well.

Why we humans feel, react, respond, and behave sexually can be quite complex. This is especially true regarding the issue of sexual orientation. Perhaps no other area of sexual behavior is as misunderstood as this one. Although experts do not agree about what causes our sexual orientation—homosexual, heterosexual, bisexual, or ambisexual—growing evidence suggests a complex interaction of biological or genetic determination, environmental or sociocultural influence, and free choice. In the early 1900s sexologist Alfred Kinsey introduced his seven-point continuum of sexual orientation. It placed exclusive heterosexual orientation at one end, exclusive homosexual orientation at the other, and identified the middle range as where most people would fall if society and culture were unprejudiced. Since Kinsey, many others have added their research findings and theories to what is known about sexual orientation including some apparent differences in relative contribution of biological, psychological, environmental, and cultural factors for males versus females and sexual orientation. In addition, further elaboration of the "middle" on the Kinsey scale has included some distinction between bisexuality—the attraction to males and females—and ambisexuality—representing individuals for whom gender is no more relevant than any other personal characteristic—height,

hair color, right or left-handedness—with respect to sexual attraction and/or orientation. A final addition to our understanding of sexuality and sexual orientation comes from Anne Fausto-Sterling, a professor of biology and women's studies at Brown University, who has become the leading advocate for intersexuals, people who are not clearly male or female by anatomy or behavior. As a result of these and other findings about sexual orientation, leaders in the field now recommend that we pluralize our terms in this area: human sexualities and orientations.

The fact that the previous paragraph may have been upsetting, even distasteful, to some readers emphasizes the connectedness of psychological, social, and cultural issues with those of sexuality. Human sexuality is biology, behavior, and much, much more. Our sexual beliefs, behaviors, choices, even feelings and comfort levels are profoundly affected by what our culture prescribes and proscribes, which has been transmitted to us by the full range of social institutions and processes. This section begins our attempt to address these interrelationships and their impact on human sexuality.

The subsection, *The Body and Its Responses,* contains informative and thought-provoking articles that illuminate the interplay of biological, psychological, cultural, and interpersonal factors that affect sexual functioning. The articles explore differences and similarities in the functioning of male and female bodies.

The subsection, *Hygiene and Sexual Health Care,* deals with articles that address common sexual functioning problems. Each contains clear information and explanations of symptoms, available treatments, and resources.

The *Human Sexualities and Orientations* subsection contains articles that explore the full breadth of what has historically been reviewed as "alternate" sexuality. However, as more gay, lesbian, bisexual, and transgendered people have publicly acknowledged their orientation, and have become more visible in the public eye via popular magazine stories, television, and movies, they are asserting their desires to be understood and accepted simply as people who are human, and therefore, sexual. In this subsection readers will meet some of these people, as well as some of their families, supporters, and critics. At the end, readers can make their own predictions about whether the first decade of the new century will bring a greater understanding and acceptance of the wide range of human sexualities, further entrenchment of homophobia, or an increased polarization of both.

The New Sex Scorecard

TALKING OPENLY ABOUT SEX DIFFERENCES IS NO LONGER AN EXERCISE IN POLITICAL INCORRECTNESS; IT IS A NECESSITY IN FIGHTING DISEASE AND FORGING SUCCESSFUL RELATIONSHIPS. AT 109 AND COUNTING, *PT* EXAMINES THE TALLY.

By Hara Estroff Marano

Get out the spittoon. Men produce twice as much saliva as women. Women, for their part, learn to speak earlier, know more words, recall them better, pause less and glide through tongue twisters.

Put aside Simone de Beauvoir's famous dictum, "One is not born a woman but rather becomes one." Science suggests otherwise, and it's driving a whole new view of who and what we are. Males and females, it turns out, are different from the moment of conception, and the difference shows itself in every system of body and brain.

It's safe to talk about sex differences again. Of course, it's the oldest story in the world. And the newest. But for a while it was also the most treacherous. Now it may be the most urgent. The next stage of progress against disorders as disabling as depression and heart disease rests on cracking the binary code of biology. Most common conditions are marked by pronounced gender differences in incidence or appearance.

Although sex differences in brain and body take their inspiration from the central agenda of reproduction, they don't end there. "We've practiced medicine as though only a woman's breasts, uterus and ovaries made her unique—and as though her heart, brain and every other part of her body were identical to those of a man," says Marianne J. Legato, M.D., a cardiologist at Columbia University who spearheads the new push on gender differences. Legato notes that women live longer but break down more.

Do we need to explain that difference doesn't imply superiority or inferiority? Although sex differences may provide ammunition for David Letterman or the Simpsons, they unfold in the most private recesses of our lives, surreptitiously molding our responses to everything from stress to space to speech. Yet there are some ways the sexes are becoming more alike—they are now both engaging in the same kind of infidelity, one that is equally threatening to their marriages.

Everyone gains from the new imperative to explore sex differences. When we know why depression favors women two to one, or why the symptoms of heart disease literally hit women in the gut, it will change our understanding of how our bodies and our minds work.

The Gene Scene

Whatever sets men and women apart, it all starts with a single chromosome: the male-making Y, a puny thread bearing a paltry 25 genes, compared with the lavish female X, studded with 1,000 to 1,500 genes. But the Y guy trumps. He has a gene dubbed Sry, which, if all goes well, instigates an Olympic relay of development. It commands primitive fetal tissue to become testes, and they then spread word of masculinity out to the provinces via their chief product, testosterone. The circulating hormone not only masculinizes the body but affects the developing brain, influencing the size of specific structures and the wiring of nerve cells.

25%
of females experience daytime sleepiness, versus 18% of males

But sex genes themselves don't cede everything to hormones. Over the past few years, scientists have come to believe that they too play ongoing roles in gender-flavoring the brain and behavior.

Females, it turns out, appear to have backup genes that protect their brains from big trouble. To level the genetic playing field between men and women, nature normally shuts off one of the two X chromosomes in every cell in females. But about 19 percent of genes escape inactivation; cells get a double dose of some X genes. Having fall-back genes may explain why females are far less subject than males to mental disorders from autism to schizophrenia.

What's more, which X gene of a pair is inactivated makes a difference in the way female and male brains respond to things, says neurophysiologist Arthur P. Arnold, Ph.D., of the University of California at Los Angeles. In some cases, the X gene donated by Dad is nullified; in other cases it's the X from Mom. The parent from whom a woman gets her working genes determines how robust her genes are. Paternal genes ramp up the genetic volume, maternal genes tune it down. This is known as genomic imprinting of the chromosome.

For many functions, it doesn't matter which sex genes you have or from whom you get them. But the Y chromosome itself spurs the brain to grow extra dopamine neurons, Arnold says. These nerve cells are involved in reward and motivation, and dopamine release underlies the pleasure of addiction and novelty seeking. Dopamine neurons also affect motor skills and go awry in Parkinson's disease, a disorder that afflicts twice as many males as females.

XY makeup also boosts the density of vasopressin fibers in the brain. Vasopressin is a hormone that both abets and minimizes sex differences; in some circuits it fosters parental behavior in males; in others it may spur aggression.

Sex on the Brain

Ruben Gur, Ph.D., always wanted to do the kind of psychological research that when he found something new, no one could say his grandmother already knew it. Well, "My grandmother couldn't tell you that women have a higher percentage of gray matter in their brains," he says. Nor could she explain how that discovery resolves a long-standing puzzle.

99%
of girls play with dolls at age 6, versus 17% of boys

Gur's discovery that females have about 15 to 20 percent more gray matter than males suddenly made sense of another major sex difference: Men, overall, have larger brains than women (their heads and bodies are larger), but the sexes score equally well on tests of intelligence.

Gray matter, made up of the bodies of nerve cells and their connecting dendrites, is where the brain's heavy lifting is done. The female brain is more densely packed with neurons and dendrites, providing concentrated processing power—and more thought-linking capability.

The larger male cranium is filled with more white matter and cerebrospinal fluid. "That fluid is probably helpful," says Gur, director of the Brain Behavior Laboratory at the University of Pennsylvania. "It cushions the brain, and men are more likely to get their heads banged about."

White matter, made of the long arms of neurons encased in a protective film of fat, helps distribute processing throughout the brain. It gives males superiority at spatial reasoning. White matter also carries fibers that inhibit "information spread" in the cortex. That allows a single-mindedness that spatial problems require, especially difficult ones. The harder a spatial task, Gur finds, the more circumscribed the right-sided brain activation in males, but not in females. The white matter advantage of males, he believes, suppresses activation of areas that could interfere with work.

The white matter in women's brains is concentrated in the corpus callosum, which links the brain's hemispheres, and enables the right side of the brain to pitch in on language tasks. The more difficult the verbal task, the more global the neural participation required—a response that's stronger in females.

Women have another heady advantage—faster blood flow to the brain, which offsets the cognitive effects of aging. Men lose more brain tissue with age, especially in the left frontal cortex, the part of the brain that thinks about consequences and provides self-control.

"You can see the tissue loss by age 45, and that may explain why midlife crisis is harder on men," says Gur. "Men have the same impulses but they lose the ability to consider long-term consequences." Now, there's a fact someone's grandmother may have figured out already.

Minds of Their Own

The difference between the sexes may boil down to this: dividing the tasks of processing experience. Male and female minds are innately drawn to different aspects of the world around them. And there's new evidence that testosterone may be calling some surprising shots.

Women's perceptual skills are oriented to quick—call it intuitive—people reading. Females are gifted at detecting the feelings and thoughts of others, inferring intentions, absorbing contextual clues and responding in emotionally appropriate ways. They empathize. Tuned to others, they more readily see alternate sides of an argument. Such empathy fosters communication and primes females for attachment.

Women, in other words, seem to be hard-wired for a top-down, big-picture take. Men might be programmed to look at things from the bottom up (no surprise there).

Men focus first on minute detail, and operate most easily with a certain detachment. They construct rules-based analyses of the natural world, inanimate objects and events. In the coinage of Cambridge University psychologist Simon Baron-Cohen, Ph.D., they systemize.

The superiority of males at spatial cognition and females' talent for language probably subserve the more basic difference of systemizing versus empathizing. The two mental styles manifest in the toys kids prefer (humanlike dolls versus mechanical trucks); verbal impatience in males (ordering rather than negotiating); and navigation (women personalize space by finding landmarks; men see a geometric system, taking directional cues in the layout of routes).

26%
of males say they have extramarital sex without being emotionally involved, versus 3% of females

Almost everyone has some mix of both types of skills, although males and females differ in the degree to which one set predominates, contends Baron-Cohen. In his work as director of Cambridge's Autism Research Centre, he finds that children and adults with autism, and its less severe variant Asperger syndrome, are unusual in both dimensions of perception. Its victims are "mindblind," unable to recognize people's feelings. They also have a peculiar talent for systemizing, obsessively focusing on, say, light switches or sink faucets.

Autism overwhelmingly strikes males; the ratio is ten to one for Asperger. In his new book, *The Essential Difference: The Truth About the Male and Female Brain*, Baron-Cohen argues that autism is a magnifying mirror of maleness.

The brain basis of empathizing and systemizing is not well understood, although there seems to be a "social brain," nerve circuitry dedicated to person perception. Its key components lie on the left side of the brain, along with language centers generally more developed in females.

Baron-Cohen's work supports a view that neuroscientists have flirted with for years: Early in development, the male hormone testosterone slows the growth of the brain's left hemisphere and accelerates growth of the right.

Testosterone may even have a profound influence on eye contact. Baron-Cohen's team filmed year-old children at play and measured the amount of eye contact they made with their mothers, all of whom had undergone amniocentesis during pregnancy. The researchers looked at various social factors— birth order, parental education, among others—as well as the level of testosterone the child had been exposed to in fetal life.

Baron-Cohen was "bowled over" by the results. The more testosterone the children had been exposed to in the womb, the less able they were to make eye contact at 1 year of age. "Who would have thought that a behavior like eye contact, which is so intrinsically social, could be in part shaped by a biological factor?" he asks. What's more, the testosterone level during fetal life also influenced language skills. The higher the prenatal testosterone level, the smaller a child's vocabulary at 18 months and again at 24 months.

Lack of eye contact and poor language aptitude are early hallmarks of autism. "Being strongly attracted to systems, together with a lack of empathy, may be the core characteristics of individuals on the autistic spectrum," says Baron-Cohen. "Maybe testosterone does more than affect spatial ability and language. Maybe it also affects social ability." And perhaps autism represents an "extreme form" of the male brain.

Depression: Pink—and Blue, Blue, Blue

This year, 19 million Americans will suffer a serious depression. Two out of three will be female. Over the course of their lives, 21.3 percent of women and 12.7 percent of men experience at least one bout of major depression.

The female preponderance in depression is virtually universal. And it's specific to unipolar depression. Males and females suffer equally from bipolar, or manic, depression. However, once depression occurs, the clinical course is identical in men and women.

The gender difference in susceptibility to depression emerges at 13. Before that age, boys, if anything, are a bit more likely than girls to be depressed. The gender difference seems to wind down four decades later, making depression mostly a disorder of women in the child-bearing years.

As director of the Virginia Institute for Psychiatric and Behavioral Genetics at Virginia Commonwealth University, Kenneth S. Kendler, M.D., presides over "the best natural experiment that God has given us to study gender differences"— thousands of pairs of opposite-sex twins. He finds a significant difference between men and women in their response to low levels of adversity. He says, "Women have the capacity to be precipitated into depressive episodes at lower levels of stress."

Adding injury to insult, women's bodies respond to stress differently than do men's. They pour out higher levels of stress hormones and fail to shut off production readily. The female sex hormone progesterone blocks the normal ability of the stress hormone system to turn itself off. Sustained exposure to stress hormones kills brain cells, especially in the hippocampus, which is crucial to memory.

It's bad enough that females are set up biologically to internally amplify their negative life experiences. They are prone to it psychologically as well, finds University of Michigan psychologist Susan Nolen-Hoeksema, Ph.D.

Women ruminate over upsetting situations, going over and over negative thoughts and feelings, especially if they have to do with relationships. Too often they get caught in downward spirals of hopelessness and despair.

It's entirely possible that women are biologically primed to be highly sensitive to relationships. Eons ago it might have helped alert them to the possibility of abandonment while they were busy raising the children. Today, however, there's a clear downside. Ruminators are unpleasant to be around, with their oversize need for reassurance. Of course, men have their own ways of inadvertently fending off people. As pronounced as the female tilt to depression is the male excess of alcoholism, drug abuse and antisocial behaviors.

The Incredible Shrinking Double Standard

Nothing unites men and women better than sex. Yet nothing divides us more either. Males and females differ most in mating psychology because our minds are shaped by and for our reproductive mandates. That sets up men for sex on the side and a more casual attitude toward it.

Twenty-five percent of wives and 44 percent of husbands have had extramarital intercourse, reports Baltimore psychologist Shirley Glass, Ph.D. Traditionally for men, love is one thing and sex is . . . well, sex.

90%
of males and females agree
that infidelity is always wrong,
20–25% of all marital fights
are about jealousy

In what may be a shift of epic proportions, sexual infidelity is mutating before our very eyes. Increasingly, men as well as women are forming deep emotional attachments before they even slip into an extramarital bed together. It often happens as they work long hours together in the office.

"The sex differences in infidelity are disappearing," says Glass, the doyenne of infidelity research. "In my original 1980 study, there was a high proportion of men who had intercourse with almost no emotional involvement at all—nonrelational sex. Today, more men are getting emotionally involved."

One consequence of the growing parity in affairs is greater devastation of the betrayed spouse. The old-style strictly sexual affair never impacted men's marital satisfaction. "You could be in a good marriage and still cheat," reports Glass.

Liaisons born of the new infidelity are much more disruptive—much more likely to end in divorce. "You can move away from just a sexual relationship but it's very difficult to break an attachment," says Rutgers University anthropologist Helen Fisher, Ph.D. "The betrayed partner can probably provide more exciting sex but not a different kind of friendship."

It's not that today's adulterers start out unhappy or looking for love. Says Glass: "The work relationship becomes so rich and the stuff at home is pressurized and child-centered. People get involved insidiously without planning to betray."

Any way it happens, the combined sexual-emotional affair delivers a fatal blow not just to marriages but to the traditional male code. "The double standard for adultery is disappearing," Fisher emphasizes. "It's been around for 5,000 years and it's changing in our lifetime. It's quite striking. Men used to feel that they had the right. They don't feel that anymore."

LEARN MORE ABOUT IT:

Eve's Rib: The New Science of Gender-Specific Medicine and How It Can Save Your Life. Marianne J. Legato, M.D. (*Harmony Books, 2002*).

Not "Just Friends": Protect Your Relationship from Infidelity and Heal the Trauma of Betrayal. Shirley P. Glass, Ph.D. (*The Free Press, 2003*).

Male, Female: The Evolution of Human Sex Differences. David C. Geary, Ph.D. (*American Psychological Association, 1998*).

The Hormone Conundrum

An abrupt end to a major menopause study leaves women as confused as ever

By Amanda Spake

Seven years ago, Mary Lazarus read an ad in her local paper asking for volunteers for a clinical trial of hormone replacement therapy. It was part of the federally funded Women's Health Initiative, and the scientists were looking for postmenopausal women at least 50 years old. "I wanted to do it," says Lazarus, of Millbrae, Calif. "There was so little information on women's health." So she signed up.

Lazarus was just 50 at that time, but she had been taking estrogen since her hysterectomy at age 46. Her gynecologist prescribed the pills to relieve her severe hot flashes and night sweats. To be included in the landmark, 161,000-woman WHI study, she had to go cold turkey for several months to wash her body clean of estrogen. "I got all my symptoms back," she says, but it was a price she was willing to pay for potential payoff ahead.

Those hopes all but came to an end last week when Lazarus opened a letter from officials at the National Institutes of Health. The letter said they were prematurely stopping the estrogen study, which had enrolled 11,000 women. "We have stopped the study in the interest of safety of the study participants," said Barbara Alving, director of the WHI, at a briefing last week. The NIH believes that, based on the data so far, estrogen does not provide the reduction in heart disease that was anticipated and hoped for. Indeed, estrogen therapy is apparently increasing some health risks, especially the risk for stroke. The study did not increase the chance of heart disease or breast cancer, though a separate study revealed a trend toward increased risk of cognitive impairment and dementia. The actual data will be released in April.

This was the second bombshell from the WHI in its long-awaited review of hormone therapy, once believed to be a cure-all for aging women. The first exploded in July 2002, when the NIH stopped the combined estrogen plus progestin trial—the treatment most commonly used by menopausal women who have not had a hysterectomy. The end came after a mountain of data revealed that women on HRT had more invasive breast cancers, heart disease, strokes, and blood clots. That study's positive findings—a reduction in hip fractures and colorectal cancer—did not outweigh the added harm. A *New England Journal of Medicine* report last week contained a mixed message about HRT and colorectal cancer risk, while another report—showing twice the risk of dementia in the HRT group—cast an even darker shadow over the whole idea of hormone therapy for women. Before the WHI, observational studies of women choosing to take estrogen (usually alone, later combined with progestin) appeared to show that hormones were a fountain of youth. Indeed, hormone pills were credited with reducing heart disease, bone fractures, atherosclerosis, and overall mortality, including deaths from seemingly unrelated causes like accidents and homicide. Hormones were also said to improve mood, skin, hair, sex drive, concentration, and memory. These studies often conflicted on the possibility that estrogen increased the risk of cancer and stroke.

Not surprisingly, estrogen use skyrocketed through the 1970s, until researchers documented that women taking estrogen had four or more times the risk of developing endometrial cancer compared with those who did not use the drug. Estrogen use plummeted until doctors began prescribing another hormone, progestin, to be taken in combination with estrogen. The idea was to mimic women's natural hormonal cycles and eliminate the endometrial cancer risk. By 1999, an estimated 15 million women had prescriptions for hormones.

The WHI study changed all that. Today, according to Wyeth, the company that makes the two bestselling hormone pills, about 8.5 million women use some type of hormone therapy. The vast majority take estrogen, not estrogen plus progestin, and nearly half use Wyeth's Premarin. Clearly, the results of the estrogen-only trial are exceedingly relevant.

The problem is that nobody knows what the results are yet. So stopping the estrogen study is causing a firestorm among researchers. The WHI's Data Safety and Monitoring Board, a group of outside experts in the safety of clinical trials, advised stopping the earlier trial because the data clearly showed the drugs were causing more harm than benefit to women. The safety "boundary" was crossed when a steep increase in invasive breast cancers became evident within five years. "For the estrogen and progestin trial, we basically laid out everything for the world," says Marcia Stefanick, professor of medicine at Stanford University, a lead WHI investigator. But she questions whether the same consensus existed for stopping the estrogen study last week.

The findings translate to about 6,800 excess strokes per year among postmenopausal women.

The WHI's Alving concedes it did not. No safety boundary was crossed, she says, and indeed the board was divided over stopping the trial. Some members favored sending a letter to the participants describing the stroke risk and allowing the women to decide for themselves whether to continue. That's the route Sharon Lubbers, 60, of Portland, Ore., would have preferred: "Here you are, participating with a long-term commitment. You've invested seven years. I think it would have been better if we had been notified of the results and given the option to continue." She joined the study because she wants her two daughters and six granddaughters to have more information than she had, and she's disappointed it has ended early. "Are they really going to get all the answers they need?" she wonders.

Alving and other officials say yes and that another year of follow-up would not have changed their conclusions. "If you're driving a car and you come to a cliff, do you keep driving and go over the edge?" Alving asks. "This trial was clearly headed to a boundary." Jacques Rossouw, WHI's project officer, believes strokes were the critical issue. "Stroke is extremely serious. This was a trial to show benefit, and benefit was predicated on a reduction in heart attack. If there is none, and with an increased risk of stroke, then it's important." Though no firm statistics are yet available on the number or the severity of unexpected strokes, WHI officials say there

were about as many as in the earlier trial—or eight extra strokes per 10,000 women. That translates to about 6,800 excess strokes per year.

The most intriguing question raised but not answered in the trial is whether estrogen increases breast cancer risk as much as combined HRT. WHI officials say there appeared to be no increase in breast cancer in the seven years of the trial. But some investigators aren't so sure. Stanford's Stefanick believes the different characteristics of the women in the two studies—weight and age, for example—might be obscuring the results. For example, several separate studies have shown that hormones increase breast cancer risk more for thin women as compared with overweight women, presumably because heavier women make more natural estrogen in their fat cells. So the effect of added estrogen in pill form may be less noticeable in terms of increasing breast cancer risk. Says Rossouw: "We're hypothesizing now; this is not known. But it's also possible that the body's own estrogen is a more powerful cancer producer than estrogen pills." He speculates further: "The result may be a 'tamoxifenlike effect.' That's how tamoxifen works to retard breast cancer—it binds to the receptors and blocks the body's own estrogen." Investigators will analyze the results in a variety of ways to consider the weight of participants. "It's also possible," Rossouw adds, "that we haven't gone long enough to find the breast cancers."

The good news from the study is that women's bones clearly benefit from hormone therapy.

Then why stop now? Elizabeth Barrett-Connor, a member of the safety monitoring board, believes the answer lies, in part, with the wrath expressed by physicians and drug manufacturers when the earlier HRT study was stopped. "For WHI 1," says Barrett-Connor, professor and chair of the Department of Family and Preventive Medicine, at the University of California-San Diego School of Medicine, "participants were told, a paper was done, physicians were blind-sided, but you could answer the questions." In an attempt to avoid physicians' angry reaction, everyone has been told the study is stopping, but

there is no paper and no way to answer the many questions raised. "I expect many of the main purveyors of hormones will like this better," Barrett-Connor adds, "because they have more opportunity to discuss and debate unhampered by the real numbers."

Even when the real numbers are released in April, they'll be preliminary. New interpretations of the earlier HRT trial, published since the July 2002 cancellation, have changed investigators' view about HRT's impact on breast and colon cancer. There was, for instance, a 24 percent increase in breast cancer in women taking combination HRT, compared with those on the placebo. Nearly twice as many women on HRT had abnormal mammograms; increased breast density caused by HRT may explain that difference. What's newly discovered is that the cancers in women on HRT were larger, more advanced, and more likely to involve lymph nodes, leading to speculation that HRT use might result in a less favorable breast cancer prognosis.

Similarly, scientists are revising their interpretations of colon cancer results. One clear benefit seems to be a 44 percent reduction in colorectal cancers, the second leading cause of cancer death in the United States. However, Rowan Chlebowski, a WHI investigator from the Harbor-UCLA Research and Education Institute, recently found that the cancers in the hormone group were more serious: Many involved the lymph nodes—a sign that the cancer had already spread. "Though the numbers are small, these represent terminal cancer," says Chlebowski. While fewer cancers were diagnosed in the HRT group, slightly more women died of them than in the placebo group. In fact, both types of cancers were strikingly similar in HRT users, Chlebowski adds. "The data are consistent with a delay in diagnosis of two of the three most common cancers in postmenopausal women—colon and breast cancer." The final analysis of the results from both trials may not be available for several years.

Last week, Stanford researchers told Mary Lazarus she was among the WHI participants taking estrogen, not the placebo. She feels sad that the trial is over, and just a little nervous waiting for the results. "Still," she says, "I'm glad I did it. I always knew there were risks."

Sex, Drugs & Rock'n'Roll

The Damage Done: A HEALTH REPORT

By Sue Woodman

DO YOU EVER WONDER IF YOUR DAILY HUNT for your glasses has anything to do with those magic mushrooms you took in 1971? Or whether the painful years of infertility you endured could be linked to the stranger you went home with after a party one night when you were 22?

For most of us, the days of multiple sex partners, fistfuls of drugs and cranking Led Zeppelin up to maximum decibels are long gone. Today, we try to at least exercise and take vitamins and, most of the time, feel we're holding our own against mortality.

So what became of the dire predictions that drugs would demolish our brain cells, that changing sexual partners would harm us and that rock music would blow out our eardrums?

We're not the only ones wondering. Across the country—in universities and hospitals, in cancer labs and neurobiology centers—medical and social scientists are examining the alleged fallout of sex, drugs and rock 'n' roll on our brains, organs and well-being.

The results are complex, sometimes influenced as much by politics as by science. The short answer: If you did it then but don't do it now, you're probably fine. "The human body is amazing in its ability to heal over time," says Richard Seymour, managing editor of the *Journal of Psychoactive Drugs*. The longer answer, though, is often not as optimistic. Below is the latest information on the potential lingering effects of your crazy, hazy youth.

sex: The sexual revolution brought some important gains, notably the birth of the women's health movement, with its emphasis on sexual, as well as reproductive, well-being. But that freedom came at

a price. Baby boomers have lived through numerous medical disasters as a result of their sexual habits—including injuries and pelvic inflammation from contraceptives such as the Dalkon Shield IUD and from epidemics of sexually transmitted diseases (STDs). Many of these STDs have contributed to serious illnesses that are surfacing only now.

For example, women who contracted the human papillomavirus (HPV) are at higher risk for developing cervical cancer, which strikes some 12,800 women a year. This disease often develops when women are between the ages of 40 and 60, and HPV is now recognized as its leading cause, says Dr. Richard Rothenberg, a physician at Emory University School of Medicine in Atlanta. Fortunately, an annual Pap smear can detect abnormal cervical cells before they become malignant.

It's been a long, strange trip... What have we done to our bodies?

Experts strongly suspect that the rise in chlamydia, a common bacterial STD, may have contributed to the increase in couples who suffered fertility problems in the 1980s.

"Women were also postponing having children at that time [and fertility declines with age], so there were other causes," says Dr. Ward Cates, president of Family Health International, a nonprofit health research and information organization in North Carolina. "But we know that there was suddenly a time in the mid-eighties when visits to infertility specialists went

up. A lot of women in their thirties were trying to get pregnant and couldn't."

Far worse, many physicians believe that the powerful infertility drugs women took may have increased their risk of ovarian cancer. Fertility drugs cause ovulation, and the more a woman ovulates, the greater her risk of developing cancerous cellular changes in her reproductive organs, according to the National Cancer Institute. The drugs also raise certain hormone levels that may heighten the cancer risk. The data are still inconclusive, but there is evidence that women who used fertility drugs but didn't conceive have an increased chance of ovarian cancer. (Women who became pregnant show no higher incidence of the disease.)

"I have come to believe there's a link (between fertility drugs and ovarian cancer), though in my circles, it's not politically correct to say so," concludes Dr. Mitchell Essig, a New York City gynecologist and infertility specialist. If you underwent infertility treatment, inform your doctor and be vigilant about having regular, thorough gynecological examinations.

drugs: Marijuana, LSD, speed, cocaine, mescaline, mushrooms, Quaaludes... they made us high, they changed our perception, they blew our minds. But did they do lasting harm?

It's difficult to say, because all drug studies are to some degree political. Many are funded by parties with their own axes to grind, such as pharmaceutical companies or the National Institute on Drug Abuse. Other studies were conducted on animals or very small groups, which makes them unreliable. But certain conclusions have emerged.

HEROIN: If you experimented with heroin in your youth, get a blood test to make sure you're not carrying a potentially deadly souvenir: hepatitis C.

About four million Americans—many of them over 45—are estimated to be harboring this sometimes-fatal virus. The symptoms, which include lethargy, jaundice and abdominal pain, may take up to three decades to appear. As many as 70 percent of cases result in chronic liver disease, and nearly one in four of those patients will develop cirrhosis.

Hepatitis C can be spread through sex, but its main transmission routes are syringes shared during IV-drug use. Blood transfusions were also a culprit until a new screening test finally flagged tainted blood in 1992. A staggering 90 percent of IV-drug users may have contracted hepatitis C—even if they shot heroin infrequently. "Most don't know they have it," says Seymour. "I fear that within the next decade, this disease will outstrip AIDS as a public health crisis."

LSD: In the four decades since LSD appeared on the street, between 1 and 1.5 million "teens, Deadheads and hippies" have tried it, estimates Seymour. While some people saw God on acid, others glimpsed madness.

There's disagreement about how long the effects of LSD may linger. A 1993 study, published in the journal *Addiction*, reported that hallucinogen persisting perceptual disorder (HPPD) could occur for as long as five years after using the drugs. But Seymour claims that he's seen almost no lasting problems from psychedelic-drug use as the first generation to try them reaches 60 and beyond. "Most middle-aged people seem to have left the experience behind long ago," he says. Of course, see your doctor if you have any symptoms oddly akin to those vibrantly colored journeys of yesteryear.

COCAINE: For a few reckless years starting in the late 1970s, cocaine became the drug of choice: chic, sharp and addictive. Today, our generation seems to be over that love affair. According to the 1998 National Household Survey on Drug Abuse, cocaine use has dropped by 90 percent since its peak in 1985.

The immediate risks of snorting coke, such as a stroke or heart attack, are well-known. But new studies suggest that some of cocaine's effects on the brain may be irreversible and lead to chronic problems later on.

For many, speed was the first drug—and probably the most dangerous.

"Cocaine causes long-term, possibly irreversible, alterations in brain blood flow," says Dr. Jonathan Levin, an assistant professor at Harvard Medical School, who has been studying cocaine's effect on blood flow and brain function for almost a decade. Brain scans of cocaine users show distinct areas where blood flow is diminished, and this may be related to the problems associated with long-term cocaine use: memory loss, shortened attention span, sleep disorders and depression, among others.

Does this brain damage repair itself in the years after you stop sniffing cocaine? "Abstinence does repair some of the abnormalities, but it's not clear to what extent," says Levin. Luckily, researchers haven't found any concrete proof that casual cocaine users who did a few lines at parties 20 years ago caused lasting harm to their brains.

SPEED: For many, speed was the first drug—the one they started taking as students simply to pull a few all-nighters—and new findings show it was likely the most dangerous. Methamphetamine, or speed, has become fashionable again among young drug takers, so there's been a glut of new research on the substance. Frighteningly, it shows that speed might be more destructive to the brain than heroin or cocaine.

In a series of studies at the government's Brookhaven National Laboratory, the lead investigator, Dr. Nora Volkow, found that speed causes "significant changes" in the brain's dopamine transporters, and abusers still experienced reduced cognitive abilities, memory loss and slowed motor function one year after use.

"The drug's assault on the brain's dopamine [system] makes things slow down, just as aging makes things slow down," says Volkow. "Effectively, it accelerates the aging process of the brain."

Are the effects permanent? "We don't yet know, but we're doing the studies to find out," says Volkow. There is speculation that having used methamphetamine may predispose people to neuro-degenerative diseases like Parkinson's. So if you spent junior year whirling at 80 mph, share this news with your physician.

MARIJUANA: Marijuana is one of the most studied substances in science, yet the verdict on whether it's harmful or not is still quite inconclusive.

While one set of scientists is bent on proving marijuana's medical benefits (research suggests that the substance can stimulate appetite and relieve chronic pain), another is documenting its health risks. The studies pile up on both sides, but the jury is still out—especially on the long-term effects of smoking pot.

On the optimistic side, a study from the Biological Psychiatry Laboratory at McLean Hospital in Belmont, Massachusetts, found that when long-term marijuana tokers stopped toking—even after years of continued use—their mental acuity returned in full force. "In a full battery of neuro-psychological tests, our preliminary data showed that while smoking, all these activities were impaired," explains substance-abuse researcher Dr. Amanda Gruber. "But twenty-eight days later, the long-term smokers did as well on all the tests as non-smokers. There seemed to be no irreversible effects."

On the gloomy side, a study done by Dr. Zhang Zuofeng of UCLA's Jonsson Cancer Center found that past marijuana smoking could sharply increase the risk of developing head and neck cancers. Zhang puts the risk at 2.6 times higher for former occasional pot smokers than for nonsmokers, and 4.9 times greater for those who smoked more than once a day.

"In the sixties, we had very high numbers of people in their twenties smoking [marijuana]," says Zhang. "Our study suggests those people are just now getting to the ages at which they will get head and neck cancers."

And perhaps lung cancer, too. At the UCLA School of Medicine, Dr. Donald Tashkin is midway through a 2,400-person, five-year study investigating marijuana's long-term link to lung cancer.

"Can the microscopic, premalignant changes smoking [marijuana] causes in the lung be repaired? Is a former smoker's lung-cancer risk eventually eliminated?" asks Tashkin. "I suspect the answer will be no, not completely."

Importantly, those of us who still indulge should know that smoking pot causes a sharp increase in heart rate, and that could be dangerous for people over 50 with other health problems. In fact, one recent study found that people who smoke marijuana have a five times greater risk of heart attack during the first hour after use—the same degree of cardiac risk brought on by strenuous exercise. The short-term risk is considerable, especially for patients with other risk factors, such as high blood pressure or elevated cholesterol, says researcher Dr. Murray Mittleman, director of cardiovascular epidemiology at Boston's Beth Israel Deaconess Medical Center.

rock 'n roll: You can almost hear Ted Nugent's mother saying, "I told you so." Unfortunately, Ted can't. He's nearly deaf in one ear, the archetypal victim of noise-induced hearing loss.

Yes, all that loud music damaged our eardrums. "We are beginning to see a lot of high-frequency hearing loss in forty- and fifty-year-olds," says Dr. Kenneth Einhorn, an Abington, Pennsylvania, otolaryngologist who treats many musicians for degrees of deafness. "Years ago, we didn't see these kinds of hearing problems till people entered their sixties or seventies." Noise-induced hearing loss happens gradually, as loud sounds blast the delicate cells of the inner ear and cause cumulative, irreparable damage.

After one loud concert, there may be a muffled quality to the ambient sound. After a few years of concerts, the muffle might not go away. By age 45, there may be some permanent high-frequency hearing loss—the kind that causes you to miss parts of conversations, particularly when there's competing background noise. Some people also develop tinnitus, or ringing in the ears.

There's no cure, but you can slow the damage and protect what hearing remains. Wear earplugs during any noisy activities, such as mowing the lawn, running an electric saw—or listening to loud music, recommends Einhorn.

If your hearing has been damaged, consider getting a hearing aid. Don't think they're just for fogies; Bill Clinton wears one. The latest models now use digital sound, a refinement that has noticeably improved their quality.

WHAT SHOULD WE MAKE OF ALL THIS INformation? Listed together, it makes for sobering reading. What it means, the professionals tell us, is that if we're still

tempted to go home with strangers or to roll a joint when the kids are out, we shouldn't. There may be consequences we don't expect.

Although there's little we can do about the past, the most important prevention for the future, say medical researchers, is to give up (or limit) the two drugs we may have kept using all along: nicotine and alcohol. "These kill more people than all the illegal substances combined, particularly with prolonged use," says Seymour. Consider that about 434,000 people die of tobacco-related disease every year, and more than 100,000 are killed by alcohol.

Still, there's plenty of room for optimism. Sex and drug-taking—to the extent they went on in the '60s and '70s—are now just a distant memory to the boomer generation, says Rothenberg. "In fact, given all the healthy habits the baby-boomer generation has adopted, it's likely they'll achieve unparalleled longevity."

So forget the past, deal with the present and stop worrying. After all, Keith Richards is still alive and—despite any rumors to the contrary—doing remarkably well.

WHAT PROBLEM?

A lack of sexual desire is no stranger among us. It is the most common sexual condition in America—some 25 percent of us suffer from it. Gerald Weeks, Ph.D., and Jeffrey Winters offer methods for overcoming this vexing problem.

Gerald Weeks, Ph.D., and Jeffery Winters

KELLY SEEMED TO HAVE IT ALL. A LOVING MOTHER of three and a public-relations executive in Manhattan, she had a handsome and charming partner who was a successful entrepreneur. They jetted off for vacations in the Caribbean and dined in the finest restaurants. But their relationship floundered in one intractable area.

"After a while," Kelly says, "he just stopped wanting to have sex. He'd go months without even touching me."

It's a subject that's full of shame: low sex drive. When your partner has no interest in sex despite your best efforts, it's easy to become perplexed. And without guidance, partners may characterize the problem in ways that can destroy the relationship.

In a society saturated with sexual imagery, it seems strange that some people have no desire for sex. But it is a startlingly common problem. Millions of people suffer from a condition known as hypoactive sexual desire (HSD)—

about 25 percent of all Americans, by one estimate, or a third of women and a fifth of men. Sex researchers and therapists now recognize it as the most common sexual problem.

In recent years, experts have turned their attention to the causes of HSD, and sex therapists are working on strategies to treat it. Although there is a 50 percent positive outcome in treatment, many of those who have HSD don't seek help. This is usually because they don't realize it's a problem, other issues in the relationship seem more important or they feel ashamed.

Many couples in conflict may have an underlying problem with sexual desire. When desire fades in one partner, other things start to fall apart.

How little is too little?

For Pam, happily married and in her forties, her once healthy sexual desire simply disappeared about six months ago. "I

FOR MEN ONLY

It's a paradox: Men are generally characterized as being ready, willing and able for sex at just about any moment of the day or night. But recent surveys show that up to 20 percent of men report little or no sexual desire. And the stereotype of the horny male makes it difficult for men with HSD to get to a healthy level of desire. Instead of getting stuck in a self-perpetuating loop of comparing one's own desire to the stereotype, men can try these techniques:

• LINKING INTIMACY AND SEX
There are plenty of men who boldly—and coldly—go from one conquest to the next. For them, sex is just sex. But many men don't feel this way. In fact, quite a few need to work their way up from zero.

One way to get going is to link sex with intimacy. A walk on a quiet beach or caressing in front of a fireplace can eventually lead to lovemaking. Even more important is sharing a feeling of closeness and providing genuine emotional support. Satisfying a partner in this way can build a sense of accomplishment—and trust—that can help lead to increased desire.

• DON'T LOOK OVER YOUR SHOULDER
Sexy clothing, dim lighting and suggestive play should get men in the mood. But rather than turn men with HSD on, the extra attention can backfire. Trying to force your partner into the mood can result in anxiety and frustration for both of you.

Sometimes the best way for men to get around this block is to look for the underlying problem. Going slowly, without pressure, and getting professional help can point you toward a solution.

• BANISH PESSIMISM
After a while, one may wonder if desire will ever return. And sometimes, heartfelt attempts at change—even through therapy—can lead nowhere.

Don't give up. Getting past HSD often takes months, and sometimes years. A sex therapist may be needed to help guide a couple in building intimacy. And it takes work to deal with the issues that have suppressed desire. But this sort of work can result in a stronger overall relationship—and lead to desires and pleasures long forgotten.

don't know what has happened to my sexual appetite," she says, "but it is like someone turned it off at the switch." She and her husband still have sex, maybe once every few weeks, but she does it out of obligation, not enthusiasm.

"I used to enjoy sex," Pam says. "Now there's a vital part of me that's missing."

Ordinary people aren't in a constant state of sexual desire. Everyday occurrences—fatigue, job stress, even the common cold—can drive away urges for lovemaking. Usually, however, spending romantic time with a partner, having sexual thoughts or seeing stimulating images can lead to arousal and the return of a healthy sex drive.

Yet for some people, desire never returns—or was never there to begin with. Frequently, even healthy sexual fantasies are virtually nonexistent in some people who suffer from HSD.

Just how little sex is too little? Sometimes, when a partner complains of not having enough sex, his problem may actually be an unusually *high* sex drive. Experts agree that there is no daily minimum requirement of sexual activity. In a recent British survey, published in the *Journal of Sex and Marital Therapy*, 24 percent of couples reported having no sex in the previous three months. And the classic study, Sex in America, found that one-third of couples had sex just a few times a year. Although the studies report frequency of sex, not desire, it's likely that one partner in these couples has HSD.

One tiny pill

Four years ago, another sexual problem—erectile dysfunction—received a sudden burst of attention when a medical "cure" hit the shelves. Before Viagra came along, men with physically based problems suffered impotence in silence, and without much hope. Now many couples enjoy a renewed reservoir of passion.

Obviously, any pill that relieves hypoactive sexual desire would be wildly popular. Unfortunately, the causes of HSD seem to be complex and varied; some sufferers might be treated with a simple pill, but most will likely need therapy—not chemistry.

One common source of reduced desire is the use of antidepressants known as selective serotonin reuptake inhibitors. SSRIs have been found to all but eliminate desire in some patients. Antidepressants such as Prozac and Zoloft are among the most widely prescribed drugs for treating depression. Yet one distressing side effect is a drop in sex drive. Some studies indicate that as many as 50 percent of people on SSRIs suffer from a markedly reduced sex drive.

Researchers believe that SSRIs quash the libido by flooding the bloodstream with serotonin, a chemical that signals satiety. "The more you bathe people in serotonin, the less they need to be sexual," says Joseph Marzucco, MSPAC, a sex therapist practicing in Portland, Oregon. "SSRIs can just devastate sexual desire."

Fortunately, researchers are studying antidepressants that act through other channels. Bupropion hydrochloride, which enhances the brain's production of the neurotransmitters dopamine and norepinephrine, has received extra attention as a substitute for SSRIs. Early studies suggest that it may actually increase sexual desire in test subjects. A study reported last year in the *Journal of Sex and Marital Therapy* found that nearly one-third of participants who took bupropion reported more desire, arousal and fantasy.

It's all in your head

Physiological problems can also lead to a loss of sexual desire. Men with abnormal pituitary glands can overproduce the hormone prolactin, which usually turns off the sex drive.

FOR WOMEN ONLY

Some women blame their hormones; others fault their upbringing. But for women struggling with HSD, it's hard not to blame themselves. They shouldn't. Desire can't be turned on with a switch. For women who find themselves without desire, guilt from themselves or their partners can often make things worse. Instead of playing the blame game, try these solutions:

• **WORK ON THE RELATIONSHIP**
Sex therapists agree that the level of a woman's sexual desire is often determined by how comfortable she is in her relationship. If she isn't sure about what her partner thinks of her—or how much she can trust him—the level of desire may plummet. Underlying problems with intimacy—such as fear of losing control or being controlled, rejection and conflicts leading to resentment—can suppress desire.

Sometimes, experts suggest spending more time together and away from the roles of everyday life. Try, for example, a sight-seeing outing, a bicycle ride or just dinner and a movie. When both partners can get out of their routines, they may well rediscover the joys of spending time together. Simple steps like these can help restore confidence in a relationship.

• **BROADEN THE DEFINITION OF SEX**
When it comes to sex, intercourse is the entire focus for many men. Unfortunately, too many women buy into this idea, as well. And for women with HSD, this intercourse-or-nothing outlook can create real barriers.

How about a full-body massage? Or a good foot rub? There are many ways partners can please each other without the pressure of having intercourse. And once a woman gets a taste for these pleasures, it can build into a desire for more traditional physical sex.

• **IT'S OK TO FANTASIZE**
To some women, fantasizing about sex with someone other than their partner is a betrayal. But fantasy and behavior aren't the same things. Experts agree that a healthy fantasy life is a way to build up sexual desire. So go ahead: close your eyes and dream of Brad Pitt.

• **CREATE A SEXUAL ENVIRONMENT**
Instead of waiting to stumble over sexual desire, women with HSD can work to create a more sexual mental environment. Take time to think about sex, how to build up a better sex life, or even to plan naughty sexual encounters with your partner. Often, a little proactive thinking will prime the pump of desire, leading to a more receptive state later.

Addicted to Sex

If you think the media is sex obsessed, take note: Even psychologists have a decidedly pro-sex bias. For proof, look no further than the "bible" of the psychological profession, the *Diagnostic and Statistical Manual of Mental Disorders*, or DSM.

Psychologists use the definitions in the DSM as a means of diagnosing—and treating—mental health problems. The DSM provides a three-part clinical definition for hypoactive sexual desire:

❤ **Persistently or recurrently deficient (or absent) sexual fantasies and desire for sexual activity. The judgment of deficiency or absence is made by the clinician, taking into account factors that affect sexual functioning, such as age and the context of the person's life.**

❤ **The disturbance causes marked distress or interpersonal difficulty.**

❤ **The sexual dysfunction is not better accounted for by another disorder (except another sexual dysfunction) and is not due exclusively to the direct physiological effects of a substance (a drug or medication) or a general medical condition.**

If having little or no sexual desire is a problem, what about wanting too much sex? The term "sexual addiction" was coined a few years back to describe people with an obsessive sex drive. Yet according to the DSM, wanting too much sex isn't a problem. No diagnosis for sexual addiction is described in its pages.

That doesn't jibe with the experience of mental health professionals, who see people coming into their offices displaying symptoms of out-of-control sexual desire. And according to Robin Cato, executive director of the National Council on Sexual Addiction and Compulsivity (NCSAC) in Atlanta, the lack of DSM acknowledgement hinders attempts to help such patients. "Without a DSM listing, few insurance companies are going to pay for treatment," Cato notes.

Not all professionals are enthusiastic about the movement to make sex addiction a disorder; some dismiss the effort as financially motivated. Michael Ross, Ph.D., a professor of public health at the University of Texas and the past president of the Society for the Scientific Study of Sexuality, doubts that the evidence is all in. "Sexual addiction," says Ross, "does not meet the criteria for a classic addiction."

As reported in a recent issue of the *International Journal of Impotence Research*, tests of a drug that blocks prolactin found it increased the libido in healthy males.

In women, some experts believe that one cause of weak sexual desire is, ironically, low testosterone levels. Normally associated with brawny, deep-voiced men, testosterone is a hormone with a definite masculine identity. But women also make small amounts of it in their ovaries, and it plays an important role in their sexual lives. Without a healthy level of testosterone in the blood, some researchers believe, women are unable to properly respond to sexual stimuli. Furthermore, there is anecdotal evidence that testosterone supplements can restore the sex drive in women.

Rosemary Basson, M.D., of the Vancouver Hospital and Health Sciences Center in British Columbia, however, cautions that too little is known about the role testosterone plays in women. "We don't even know how much testosterone is normal," Basson says. "The tests designed for men can't pick up the levels found in women."

In one study suggesting that HSD is more *psychological* than physiological, Basson and her colleagues tested the effects of Viagra on women who reported arousal problems. Basson found that while the drug generally produced the physical signals of sexual arousal, many women reported that they still didn't feel turned on.

Indeed, many psychologists and sex therapists believe that most patients with HSD have sound bodies and troubled relationships. The clinical experience of Weeks has shown that two factors identified in a relationship can, over time, devastate the sex drive: chronically suppressed anger toward the partner and a lack—or loss—of control over the relationship. And once these issues threaten a healthy sex drive, lack of intimacy can aggravate the problems further. Without help, these issues can balloon until the relationship itself is seriously damaged. And, consequently, HSD becomes further entrenched.

Lacking the desire for desire

Although HSD is one of the most difficult to address of all sexual problems, it can be treated successfully. The key is to find a highly qualified sex and marital therapist who has experience in dealing with it. Unfortunately, while HSD is the most common problem that sex therapists see, millions of cases go untreated.

Some people who lack desire are just too embarrassed to seek help, especially men. Others are so focused on immediate concerns—such as a stressful job or a family crisis—that they put off dealing with the loss of a healthy libido. Still others have become so used to having no sex drive that they no longer miss it; they lack the desire for desire. These people represent the most severe cases—the hardest to treat.

Some people who don't get treatment find ways to adjust. "Thank goodness my husband is so patient and caring," Pam says. "He tries to spark interest, but when it is not ignited he'll settle for cuddling and caressing."

Other relationships can't survive the strain. After a year, Kelly and her boyfriend broke up. "I couldn't convince him that it was a problem," she says, "but it was."

Gerald Weeks, Ph.D., A.B.S., is a professor of counseling at the University of Nevada in Las Vegas and a board certified sex therapist of the American Board of Sexology.

Jeffrey Winters, formerly with Discover magazine, is a science writer based in New York.

When Sex Hurts

If lovemaking is more agony than ecstasy, the problem may be medical. Now there's help.

By Lisa Collier Cool

Thanks to recent advances, doctors have more effective treatments than ever for sexual pain. But zeroing in on the right diagnosis may be tricky, says Susan McSherry, M.D., who is affiliated with Tulane Medical School, in New Orleans. "If the first treatment doesn't help, keep working with your doctor. Painful sex isn't something you have to grit your teeth and tolerate. It's usually very treatable." Below are some common problems—and solutions.

Infections

Vaginal infections (collectively known as vaginitis) are so common that more than 75 percent of women can expect to develop at least one during their lifetime. The usual culprits are bacteria (bacterial vaginosis), yeast, and *Trichomonas* microorganisms, which are responsible for trichomoniasis, a sexually transmitted infection.

Symptoms With some infections, you may have an unpleasant-smelling discharge, painful urination, and, in some cases, lower abdominal discomfort—plus itching and burning of the vagina and outer labia. But with other forms of vaginitis, there may be no special symptoms, says Erica V. Breneman, M.D., an obstetrician-gynecologist at Kaiser Permanente in Oakland, California.

During sex The irritation may worsen when you're having intercourse or afterward.

Diagnosis If itching is your main symptom and you have been diagnosed with a yeast infection in the past, try an over-the-counter medication. But if the problem doesn't clear up in a few days, see a gynecologist; left untreated, some forms of vaginitis can lead to more serious problems, including infertility. Your doctor will do a pelvic exam and examine your vaginal fluid for microorganisms.

Treatment Depending on the cause, antibiotics, antifungal drugs, or medicated vaginal creams or suppositories. (For some infections, both partners need to be treated.) Symptoms should clear up—and sex should be comfortable—within several days.

Endometriosis

This disorder occurs when cells from the uterine lining (the endometrium) migrate to other parts of the abdomen, then swell and bleed during your period but aren't discharged as the uterine lining is. Over time, this misplaced tissue often causes chronic inflammation, scars, and weblike adhesions, most commonly on the ovaries or fallopian tubes, on the outer surface of the uterus, or on the internal area between your vagina and rectum.

Symptoms Pain in the abdomen or lower back, severe menstrual cramps, fatigue, diarrhea, and/or painful bowel movements during your period.

During sex Often there is deep, burning pain in the pelvis, abdomen, or lower back.

Diagnosis In a procedure called laparoscopy, a gynecologist examines your pelvic organs using a lighted tube inserted through a small incision in your abdomen. Small lesions can usually be removed during the same procedure.

Treatment For mild or moderate endometriosis, pain medication may be enough. But if you have severe cramping, or if the condition is interfering with your ability to become pregnant, or in order to suppress further growth of the lesions, you may need surgery or hormone treatment that temporarily stops your period. Neither of these is a cure, but two thirds of women improve after surgery; for the hormone treatment, the rate is a little more than half.

As for sex, you may find it's more comfortable during the week or two after your period rather than later in your cycle. And choosing a position that avoids deep penetration—side by side, for example, or with the woman on top—may help too.

> **"Painful sex isn't something you have to grit your teeth and tolerate," says one expert.**

Fibroids

An estimated 20 to 30 percent of American women are affected by these noncancerous masses of muscle and fibrous tissue that grow inside the uterus (or, occasionally, outside). No one knows why some women are more prone, but a report from the National Institute of Child Health and Development shows that women who have had two or more children are far less likely to develop fibroids than those who have never given birth.

Symptoms Some women are never bothered by their fibroids. But others may have heavy and painful periods, midmonth bleeding, a feeling of fullness in the lower abdomen, frequent urination, constipation, bloating, and lower back pain.

During sex Your husband's thrusting can set off deep pelvic pain, due to pressure on your uterus.

Diagnosis A routine pelvic exam. If a fibroid is detected, your doctor may use ultrasound or magnetic resonance imaging to check its size and location.

Treatment For mild or occasional pelvic pain—including during sex—ibuprofen or other analgesics may be enough. If your fibroids need to be treated, there are several surgical approaches, as well as a new nonsurgical technique called fibroid embolization.

Interstitial cystitis (IC)

Unlike "regular" cystitis, which is caused by a bacterial infection, the cause of IC is a mystery. This chronic inflammation of the bladder wall strikes women almost exclusively.

Symptoms Very frequent urination (up to 30 times a day) and/or burning and pressure before urination; chronic lower abdominal pain that may intensify before your period.

During sex Intercourse frequently triggers painful flare-ups, "like a severe headache all over your pelvis," says Dr. McSherry. Some women also have vaginal spasms, lower back pain, or pain that radiates down the thighs.

Diagnosis First, your doctor will rule out other causes. Then she'll perform a test called cystoscopy—in which the bladder is filled with fluid and examined for tiny hemorrhages (a telltale sign of IC).

Treatment Elmiron is the only oral medication specifically approved for IC. But many other drugs are available to relieve symptoms: Some women are helped by certain antidepressants that have pain-blocking effects (such as Elavil) or anti-inflammatory drugs that are inserted into the bladder. The good news is that 85 percent of patients can be successfully treated with one or more of these therapies, says Dr. McSherry. As for sex, women may find it's more comfortable side by side and when they're fully aroused.

Vaginal dryness

The most common reason for this annoying (though not medically serious) problem is the drop in estrogen that takes place at menopause or during perimenopause—the three to six years before your periods actually stop. Some women also experience a decrease in lubrication after having a baby or while breast-feeding. Allergies, too, can trigger dryness. Soap is probably the biggest offender, but laundry detergent, fabric softeners, bubble bath, vagi-

---

A Mysterious Disorder

Imagine pain so piercing you can't even tolerate pantyhose rubbing against your genitals, much less sex. That's what vulvodynia can feel like, say sufferers, who may seek help from doctor after doctor, only to be dismissed as hypochondriacs. Part of the problem is that everything usually looks normal; women have no symptoms beyond persistent pain in the vulva, the skin folds around the vagina. (In a few cases, however, there may be inflammation.)

Experts don't know for sure what causes vulvodynia, though they theorize that nerve injury may play a role. Interestingly, over-the-counter products can trigger the condition in women who are pre-disposed, says Howard Glazer, Ph.D., associate professor in the department of obstetrics and gynecology at Cornell University Medical Center in New York City and codirector of the New York Center for Vulvovaginal Pain. "Some 85 percent of my patients tell me they treated what they thought was a yeast infection with an OTC cream or douche—and then developed pain that never went away." It may be they're reacting to an irritant in the cream, Glazer suggests.

To diagnose the condition, your doctor may do what's called a Q-Tip Test, in which a cotton swab is used to gently check the vulva and the vaginal entrance for areas of pain and hypersensitivity. You may be able to relieve symptoms with medication (antidepressants, nerve blocks, or anticonvulsant drugs that also combat pain) or with biofeedback. In severe cases, surgery to remove the affected tissue may help.

---

nal-hygiene products, and spermicidal creams or foams can all be culprits as well.

Symptoms Chafing, irritation, and itching. At menopause, falling estrogen levels also cause the walls of your vagina to become thinner and less elastic.

During sex Friction may leave you quite sore. Discomfort may occur only at penetration or during thrusting.

Diagnosis Fairly self-evident, but check with your doctor if you suspect an allergy.

Treatment Over-the-counter lubricants, such as Replens or Astroglide. At menopause, talk to your gynecologist about hormone replacement therapy or estrogen cream. For allergic dryness, try using mild liquid bath soaps and fragrance-free or hypoallergenic brands of laundry and cosmetic products. Try different brands of spermicides until you find a nonirritating one. And ask your doctor about taking antihistamines: That might be wise until you figure out what you are allergic to.

Pelvic congestion syndrome (PCS)

There's some controversy about this syndrome: Not all doctors are convinced that it is a cause of pain during sex. Those who believe it is say that the disorder is triggered by varicose veins in the pelvis, a condition similar to varicose veins in the legs (and, indeed, about half the women with PCS also have the leg problem). In both cases, valves that normally keep the blood moving forward become leaky, allowing blood to flow backward and pool. As a result of the pressure, veins become large and bulgy. Most women develop the disorder after pregnancy, says Luis Navarro, M.D., director of The Vein Treatment Center, in New York City.

Symptoms Aching, heaviness, pressure, or throbbing in the pelvis; sometimes visibly protruding veins in the genital area.

During sex The discomfort intensifies during or after intercourse (as well as before or during your menstrual period).

Diagnosis Several noninvasive tests, including the recently developed venography. During this procedure, a thin catheter is used to inject special dye into the pelvic veins, allowing the doctor to map blood flow with X rays.

Treatment Tiny metal coils or a gluelike liquid are used to block off the affected area. The procedure has a success rate of 80 to 90 percent, says Dr. Navarro. But it can take a couple of weeks for symptoms to clear up.

The Rise of the Gay Family

More and more American children are growing up with same-sex parents

By Dan Gilgoff

"We were afraid people out here would be skeptical of us," says Sheri Ciancia, sipping a glass of iced tea outside the four-bedroom house she and her partner bought last fall in Tomball, Texas, a half-hour's drive from Houston. "Afraid they wouldn't let their kids play with ours."

"But we've got to take chances," adds Stephanie Caraway, Ciancia's partner of seven years, sitting next to her on their concrete patio as their 8-year-old daughter, Madison, attempts to break her own record for consecutive bounces on a pogo stick. "We're not going to live in fear."

A trio of neighborhood boys pedal their bikes up the driveway, say hello to the moms, and ask Madison if they can use her bike ramp. The boys cruise up and down the ramp's shallow slopes while Madison continues bouncing, the picture of suburban serenity. Despite their misgivings about relocating from Houston to this tidy subdivision, the family has yet to encounter hostility from their neighbors. "We have to give straight people more credit," Caraway says with a wry smile. "I'm working on that."

Tomball—its roads lined with single-room Baptist churches and the occasional sprawling worship complex, known to some locals as "Jesus malls" —may seem an unlikely magnet for gay couples raising kids. A year before Caraway and Ciancia moved here, activists in the neighboring county got a popular children's book that allegedly "tries to minimize or even negate that homosexuality is a problem" temporarily removed from county libraries. So imagine Caraway's and Ciancia's surprise when, shortly after moving in, their daughter met another pair of moms rollerblading down their block: a lesbian couple who had moved into the neighborhood with their kids just a few months earlier.

Growing. Gay families have arrived in suburban America, in small-town America, in Bible Belt America—in all corners of the country. According to the latest census data, there are now more than 160,000 families with two gay parents and roughly a quarter of a million children spread across some 96 percent of U.S. counties. That's not counting the kids being raised by single gay parents, whose numbers are likely much higher—upwards of a million, by most estimates, though such households aren't tracked.

This week, the commonwealth of Massachusetts will recharge the gay-marriage debate by becoming the first state to offer marriage licenses to same-sex couples. The move has raised the ire of conservatives who believe gay marriage tears at the fabric of society—and earned support from progressives who think gay men and lesbians deserve the same rights as heterosexuals. But the controversy is not simply over the bond between two men or two women; it's about the very nature of the American family.

Gay parents say their families are much like those led by their straight counterparts. "I just say I have two moms," says Madison, explaining how she tells friends about her parents (whom she refers to as "Mom" and "Mamma Sheri"). "They're no different from other parents except that they're two girls. It's not like comparing two parents with two trees. It's comparing two parents with two other parents."

Many of today's gay parents, who grew up with few gay-parent role models, say their efforts have helped introduce a culture of family to the gay community. "In the straight community, adoption is a secondary choice," says Rob Calhoun, 35, who adopted a newborn daughter with his partner 20 months ago. "But in the gay community, it's like, 'Wow, you've achieved the ultimate American dream.' "

The dream has not been without cost, though. Gay parents and their kids in many parts of the country frequently meet with friction from the outside world, in the form of scornful family members, insensitive classmates, and laws that treat same-sex parents differently from straight parents. In general, Americans are split on the subject. A national poll this winter found that 45 percent believe gays should have the right to adopt; 47 percent do not.

Many traditional-marriage advocates argue that marriage is first and foremost about procreation. "It is the reason for marriage," Pennsylvania Sen. Rick Santorum said last summer. "Marriage is not about affirming somebody's love for somebody else. It's about uniting together to be open to children." Other critics call gay and lesbian couples who are raising kids—whether from previous marriages, adoption, or artificial insemination—dangerously self-centered. "It's putting adult desires above the interest of children," says Bill Maier, psychologist in residence at Focus on the Family and coauthor of the forthcoming *Marriage on Trial: The Case Against Same-Sex Marriage and Parenting.* "For the first time in history, we're talking about intentionally creating permanently motherless and fatherless families."

Evidence? Three decades of social science research has supplied some ammunition for both sides of the gay-parent debate. Many researchers say that while children do best with two parents, the stability of the parents' relationship is much more important than their gender. The American Psychological Association, the American Academy of Pediatrics, the National Association of Social Workers, and the American Bar Association have all re-

Gay Nuptials in the Bay State

Planning a wedding is tough under pretty much any circumstances, but for thousands of gay and lesbian couples in Massachusetts hoping to marry this week, the path to the altar has been littered with lawsuits, constitutional amendments, and other legal bric-a-brac.

When the Massachusetts high court sanctioned same-sex marriage last November, it gave the state six months to brings laws into line. Opponents of the ruling used that time to attempt to block the measure, first by crafting a civil-union plan like Vermont's, then, when that failed, initiating an amendment to the state's constitution that would define marriage as solely between a man and woman. This amendment passed the legislature once by must take another pass in the 2005–6 session before going to the voters, in the fall of 2006. Gov. Mitt Romney asked for a stay on the gay-marriage decision until the 2006 vote, but the state's attorney general refused.

Wedding bells. So barring an 11th-hour appeal, Massachusetts will probably be issuing same-sex marriage licenses this week. Marriages performed in Oregon, California, New Mexico, and New York are still clouded by litigation. For his part, President Bush is backing an amendment to the U.S. Constitution that would limit marriage to heterosexual couples, but it's apt to be a tough sell.

Romney, meanwhile, has cited an obscure 1913 miscegenation law to make marriages for out-of-state couples, who would not be legally recongnized in their home states, illegal. Defiant clerks in Provincetown, Worcester, and Somerville say they will nevertheless marry all comers, despite the governor's threat of legal action. "I think there're still statutes against witches in the books," says Worcester Mayor Timothy Murray. "Why don't we enforce those?" –*Caroline Hsu*

families through adoption, artificial insemination, or surrogacy may offer some advantages over straight parents. "In the lesbian and gay community, parents are a self-selecting group whose motivation for parenthood is high," says Charlotte Patterson, a psychologist and researcher at the University of Virginia. But studies on the subject have so far examined relatively few children (fewer than 600, by some counts) and virtually no kids of gay dads.

One study coauthored by Stacey and widely cited by both supporters and opponents of gay parenting found that children of lesbians are more likely to consider homosexual relationships themselves (though no more likely to identify as homosexuals as adults) and less likely to exhibit gender-stereotyped behavior. "If we could break down some of society's gender stereotypes, that would be a good thing," says Ellen Perrin, professor of pediatrics at the Floating Hospital for Children at Tufts-New England Medical Center. Focus on the Family's Maier disagrees: "They don't have rigid gender stereotypes? That's gender identity confusion."

While the debate continues, the number of kids with gay parents keeps growing. According to Gary Gates, an Urban Institute demographer, 1 in 3 lesbian couples was raising children in 2000, up from 1 in 5 in 1990, while the number of male couples raising kids jumped from 1 in 20 to 1 in 5 during the same period. The uptick is partly due to changes in the census itself, which in 1990 tabulated most same-sex couples that identified themselves as married on census forms as straight married couples. In the 2000 census, though, those couples were tabulated as gay and lesbian partners. But the leap in such couples with children is large enough to suggest a real spike. And because gay and lesbian couples are sometimes reluctant to identify themselves as such on census forms, actual figures could be much higher.

Moving in. What's perhaps most surprising is that gay- and lesbian-headed families are settling in some of the most culturally conservative parts of the country. According to the *Gay and Lesbian Atlas* published earlier this month by the Urban Institute, Alaska, Arizona, Georgia, Louisiana, and New Mexico are among the 10 states with the largest number of gay families—along with more historically gay-friendly New York, California, and Vermont. States where gay and lesbian couples are most likely to have children (relative to the state's total number of gay couples) are Mississippi, South Dakota,

Alaska, South Carolina, and Louisiana, in that order. "Same-sex couples who live in areas where all couples are more likely to have children" may simply be more likely to have children themselves, according to the atlas. And couples with children—regardless of their sexual orientation—are looking for good schools, safe streets, and outdoor green space. "It's gay couples who don't have kids whose behavior tends to be different: They live in more-distressed areas of cities, with higher crime and more racial diversity," says Gates. "But a large portion of gay people own their homes, live in the suburbs, and are raising two children."

Most of these children are the products of previous heterosexual relationships. Madison, for one, is Caraway's daughter by a former boyfriend. Caraway says the pregnancy forced her to come to terms with her homosexuality; she started dating Ciancia soon after her daughter's birth. "If you stay in a relationship but you're not in love or committed to the person, children sense that," says Caraway, now 31. "What kind of message does that send?"

But as these children enter middle and high school, their peers are more likely to inquire about their parents' sexuality—and not always politely. The Tufts-New England Medical Center's Perrin, who authored the American Academy of Pediatrics' policy on gay parenting, says that children of same-sex parents "get stigmatized because of who their parents are. It's the biggest problem they face by far." Just like many gays and lesbians themselves, children of homosexuals speak of "coming out" as a long and often difficult ordeal. "You are, on a day-to-day basis, choosing if you're out or if you're going to be hiding the whole truth," says Abigail Garner, author of the recently released *Families Like Mine*, about children of homosexuals. "Is she your mom's roommate or your aunt or your mom's friend?"

During middle school and part of high school, A. J. Costa, now a freshman at Texas Lutheran University outside San Antonio, kept his mother's relationship with a live-in partner secret. He grew close to his mom's partner, even preferred the arrangement to his mom's previous marriage, which ended when he was 7, but never invited friends to the house. "I didn't want anyone to make fun of me," says Costa. "Nobody was going to mess with my family."

Costa's fears were reinforced by some classmates who did find out and referred to his moms as "dykes." But in the summer

leased statements condoning gay parenting. "Not a single study has found a difference [between children of gay and straight parents] that you can construe as harmful," says Judith Stacey, a professor of sociology, gender, and sexuality at New York University and a gay-rights advocate.

Stacey and other researchers even suggest that gay and lesbian parents who form before his junior year in high school, Costa visited Provincetown, Mass., for "Family Week," an annual gathering of gay parents and their children. "I couldn't get over how many families there were, all like mine," he recalls. "I realized that it wasn't about whether I have two gay *moms*. It was that I have two moms. It was getting past the fact that they're gay."

Support. In recent years, support networks for children of gay parents and for parents themselves have expanded dramatically. Children of Lesbians and Gays Everywhere, or COLAGE, has chapters in 28 states. The Family Pride Coalition, whose dozens of local affiliate organizations attract gay parents who want their kids to meet other children of gays and lesbians, has doubled its member and volunteer base in the past five years, to 17,000. Vacation companies like Olivia, founded 30 years ago for lesbian travelers, now offer packages specifically for gays and lesbians with children, and R Family Vacations, underwritten by former talk-show host Rosie O'Donnell, will launch its inaugural cruise this summer. Tanya Voss, a 36-year-old college professor in Austin who, with her partner, has two young boys through artificial insemination, plans to attend the first Family Pride Coalition weekend at Disney World next month. Kids need environments where "they don't have to explain their families," she says, "a safe place where they could just be."

Still, neither COLAGE nor Family Pride Coalition has affiliate groups in Mississippi, South Dakota, or Alaska, the states where gay and lesbian couples are most likely to have kids. ("The way you manage in a more hostile environment,"

says Gates, "is to go about your business and not draw much attention to yourself.") Many such states also present the highest legal hurdles for those families. Roughly two thirds of children with same-sex parents live in states where second-parent or joint adoptions—which allow the partner of a child's biological or adoptive parent to adopt that child without stripping the first parent of his or her rights, much like stepparent adoption—has been granted only in certain counties or not at all.

Gay families are settling in some of the most conservative parts of the country.

Absent such arrangements, a biological or adoptive parent's partner could be powerless to authorize emergency medical treatment or denied custody if the other parent dies. When Voss and her partner were planning to have their first child, they decided Voss wouldn't carry the baby because her parents—who disapprove of Voss's homosexuality—would have likely claimed custody in the event that their daughter died during childbirth.

Gay-rights advocates argue that it's often children who end up suffering from laws restricting gay parenting—and same-sex marriage. If a parent without a legal relationship with his or her partner's child dies, a 10-year-old child whose nonlegal parent was earning $60,000 at the time of death, for example, would forgo nearly $140,000 in Social Security survivor benefits paid to children of married couples, according to the Urban Institute and the Human Rights Campaign. That's on top of the more than $100,000 in Social Security paid to a widow—but not a gay partner—whose spouse earned $60,000. And without laws recognizing them as legitimate parents, nonlegal parents are unlikely to be required to pay child support if they leave their partner.

Recently, some states have further restricted adoption. Earlier this year, a federal appeals court upheld Florida's ban on homosexuals' adopting children, the only one of its kind in the nation. Arkansas now bans gay foster parenting, Mississippi bans same-sex couples from adopting, and Utah bans adoptions by all unmarried couples. "State legislatures that opposed gay marriage are going to push to replicate what Florida has done," says lawyer John Mayoue, author of *Balancing Competing Interests in Family Law*. "We'll see more of this as part of the backlash against gay marriage."

Even so, more gay couples—especially male couples—are adopting than ever before. A study last year found that 60 percent of adoption agencies accept applications from homosexuals, up from just a few a decade ago. The 2000 census showed that 26 percent of gay male couples with children designate a stay-at-home parent, compared with 25 percent of straight parents. "When you have children, whether you're gay or straight, you spend lots of time wondering how good a job you're doing for your kids; you lose sleep over it," says Mark Brown, 49, whose partner stays home with their two young adopted kids. "It doesn't leave much time to worry about how we're being perceived by straight society."

WHY ARE WE GAY?

Everybody has an idea: It's **genetics**—we're born that way. It's our mothers and **testosterone** in the womb. It's the **environment** as we were growing up. One thing we know for sure: The possible explanations raise as many questions as they answer, particularly: What would happen if we found the one true answer? and, Would we change if we could?

By Mubarak Dahir

Mark Stoner pins it on the clarinet.

Ever since Stoner, a 41-year-old creative director for an advertising agency in Lancaster, Pa., realized that three out of four of his childhood friends who played the clarinet grew up to be gay, he has taken note of who among his adult gay friends once played the instrument. What he calls an "exhaustive but unscientific" survey covering two decades indicates that "there is an extremely high correlation between playing the clarinet and being gay," he says.

> "THE QUESTION OF WHETHER OR NOT GAYNESS IS IMMUTABLE IS RATHER CRUCIAL IN THE POLITICAL ARENA. THE AMERICAN PUBLIC WILL HAVE A DIFFERENT ATTITUDE TOWARD GAY RIGHTS DEPENDING ON WHETHER THEY BELIEVE BEING GAY IS A MATTER OF CHOICE OR NOT."
> —*Neuroscientist Simon LeVay, who found differences in the brain*

"My theory is that most boys want to play the trumpet," the former woodwind player says, only partly in jest. "But the more sensitive boys wind up with the clarinet, and we're the ones who turn out gay."

Stoner's theory, of course, is offered tongue-in-cheek. But in the past decade or so, researchers from disparate fields spanning genetics, audiology, and behavioral science have amassed bits and pieces of evidence that they believe indicate what may determine sexual orientation. If they're right, our sexual orientation may well be fixed long before any maestro blows his first note.

But despite some compelling studies that indicate that the propensity to be gay or lesbian is determined before birth—either genetically or through biological processes in the womb—most researchers today agree a complex combination of genetics, biology, and environmental influences work together to make the determination. Just how much is predetermined by the forces of genes and how much is shaped by influences such as society and culture remain unclear—and hotly debated. So too does the corollary question of whether sexual orientation is somehow an innate trait and thus fixed for life or whether it is malleable and thus changeable over time.

More than scientific curiosity hangs in the balance. For years the gay and lesbian political establishment has leaned, at least to some degree, on the argument that sexual orientation is inborn and permanent and thus should not be a basis for discrimination. The tactic has proved incredibly successful. Polls repeatedly indicate that Americans who believe sexual orientation is either genetic or biological are much more likely to support gay and lesbian civil rights than those who believe it is determined primarily by environmental influences.

In a Gallup Poll conducted in May, half of those surveyed said they believe homosexuality is genetic, and half said it is environmental. In a 1977 Gallup Poll, respondents pointed to the environment over genetics by more than a 4-to-1 ratio. The poll calls this shift in perception "one of the more significant changes in American public opinion on gay and lesbian issues." It is clearly accompanied by increasing tolerance toward gays and lesbians. In May, 52% of Gallup respondents said homosexuality is an "acceptable alternative lifestyle," compared with 38% in 1977. And a majority, 54%, agreed that "homosexual relations between consenting adults should be legal," compared with 43% in 1977.

"The question of whether or not gayness is immutable is rather crucial in the political arena," says Simon LeVay, a neuroscientist who in 1991 found structural differences between the brains of gay men and heterosexual men. "The American public will have a different attitude toward gay rights depending on whether they believe being gay is a matter of choice or not. You can argue all you want that it shouldn't be that way, but that's the fact. If science can show sexual orientation is a deep aspect of a person's being, there is potential for immense good. But it does mean the science gets politicized."

ALL THE SCIENCE SO FAR

Here's what researchers have reported in their search for the "cause"

- Lesbians' ring fingers tend to be longer than their index fingers, whereas straight women's ring fingers tend to be the same length as their index fingers.

- Boys who show "pervasive and persistently" effeminate behavior have about a 75% chance of growing up gay.

- A person with a gay identical twin is at least 10 times more likely to be gay than a person without one.

- There is about a 2% chance that a firstborn male will grow up gay. That chance grows to at least 6% for males with four or more older brothers.

- Gay men and lesbians are more likely to be left-handed.

- Gay men have smaller hypothalamuses than straight men.

- A man is more likely to be gay if there are gay men on his mother's side of the family.

- Lesbians' inner ears tend to react to sounds more like men's inner ears than like straight women's.

- Gay men have more testosterone and larger genitalia than straight men.

IS IT GENETIC?

NICK VELASQUEZ

Stats: Student, 21, California native
Gay relatives: "My dad was gay. He died of AIDS in 1991 at 34 years old. Also on my dad's side I have two distant cousins, both lesbian."
Why are you gay? "I identify as bisexual, actually. I think it's very limiting, the notion that people can't love both [sexes], that it is one way or the other—it's on a continuum. I've always felt different, that there was something that separated me from other people, a different outlook on life; even when I was so young, [it was] in a nonsexual way."

DEBORAH REECE

Stats: Security guard and student, 45, California native

Gay relatives: "I have a gay grandmother, a bisexual aunt, and at least two gay nephews. Half my family is gay!"
Why are you gay? "That's the million-dollar question. And if I knew the answer, I'd be a millionaire! I am who I am. I've known since I was 4. It's natural to me. My mother told me [I was gay]. She used to tell me, 'Don't bother with those guys.'"

DANNY LEMOS

Stats: TV writer, 44, California native
Gay relatives: "Three gay brothers, including my twin, who died of AIDS."
Why are you gay? "Destiny. Some people are meant to be doctors, artists. I was meant to be gay, out, expressive. I served as a role model, especially to my younger brothers. If there's a God,

I think he picks it. If it's science, that's what picks it. I've never had a moment where I didn't know who I was."

KATE NIELSEN

Stats: Writer, 41, Colorado native
Gay relatives: None
Why are you gay? "I think you're born into it, just like some people are born left-handed. It's just what you're dealt. I was 6, I went to see *The Sound of Music*, and I wanted to be Christopher Plummer because I wanted to be with Julie Andrews."

Politics aside, scientists insist there is commanding research to show that sexual orientation is largely influenced by genetics. "There's no debate on that from any reasonable scientist. The evidence for it stands fast," says Dean Hamer, a molecular biologist at the National Insti-

tutes of Health and an early pioneer in research linking sexual orientation to genes. In 1993, Hamer was the first to report finding a specific slice of DNA that could be linked to homosexuality.

He first studied the family histories of 114 gay men and discovered that many

male relatives on the mother's side of the family were also gay. Since men always inherit an X chromosome from their mothers, the study suggested a genetic link between the X chromosome and homosexuality. Hamer then scrutinized the DNA for 40 pairs of gay brothers and found that

ADVOCATE READERS WEIGH IN

We asked out online visitors to tell us *their* stories about why they're gay.
Here are some of their responses.

GENETICS

No doubt about it in my family: God made us the way we are—genetically. I suspect that my grandfather was gay for many reasons. His second son, my uncle, came out to the entire family at my parents' 50th wedding anniversary party—he was 70 at the time! His son, my cousin, is gay. I am gay. Pretty sound evidence, considering we were all born in different decades, in different places, and were raised in totally different environments.

W.Z., Indianapolis, Ind.

I don't have a history of abuse, and I didn't just wake up one morning and decide to be lesbian. Also, I don't think it was anything my mom did while she was pregnant with me, as she often laments. I am this way. I must have been born this way. When I was growing up, The *Dukes of Hazard* was popular. I watched it every night, religiously. Daisy stirred something in me that I couldn't explain. I was 8 or 9 then.

T.M., Indiana

I am sure I was born gay. I used to steal dolls and jump ropes from girls then hide them, knowing that I would get into *big* trouble if I didn't like "boy things." Luckily I learned to "pass for a boy," so I didn't get bullied too often, but I did bear witness to the horrors bestowed upon more fey-type males.

A.S., via the Internet

Clearly genetic. No straight person I know can tell me the date, time, and even when they "decided" they were straight—so

this notion of "choice" is pure crap. It can't be a gift—it would be one that most people would return. But to where and to whom? Is there a customer service line for this? It's not a "choice" and it is not a "lifestyle"—it's a genetic "orientation." It was an initially unwelcome visitor... now [it] gives me comfort as well as challenges me every day.

E.B., Chicago, Ill.

ENVIRONMENT

I was raised in the archetypal situation for being a gay man: with a chronically overbearing, fiercely possessive mother; a weak, quiet, completely uncommunicative father; and a thorough disinterest in violent sports! I, like many, many thousands of other gay men of my generation (I was born in 1950, in a tiny town), went through absolute hell growing up "hiding." Growing up "gay" (never liked that word—there's nothing "gay" about being gay!) nearly destroyed my life! Frankly, I wish to God (or whoever or whatever is out there) that I had *never* been homosexual!

M.D., San Francisco, Calif.

I think genes are passed on with neutral sexual orientation. To me, homosexuality or heterosexuality is totally due to the environment in which we are raised. In a nutshell, I believe a male who stays bonded with his mother is usually homosexual. A female who bonds more strongly with the father is usually homosexual. A male and a female who bond about equally with the mother and the father are more likely to be bisexual.

My mother died when I was 8 months old. My father remarried

when I was 1 year old. His new wife did not want him to have much to do with his first children. I had five older brothers and three older sisters. My brothers did not want to have much to do with me. My three sisters adored me, so I spent most of my time with them. The sisters painted my deceased mother as being almost a saint. I think I naturally identified with my sisters' values and the values of my mother, which they told me about in detail. This included their sexual orientation.

We all inherit certain physical characteristics from our parents and we can inherit certain abstract characteristics such as temperament. I do not think that these genetically inherited qualities lead to homosexuality.

J.D., via the Internet

GOD

I personally believe I am gay because God made me such. I believe it is a gift and that he has a special reason for creating me as a lesbian. It doesn't matter if I was created this way biologically or if circumstances in my life molded me; this is who I am meant to be. I am proud to be a lesbian and at peace.

D.S., Poland, Ohio

I embrace the gift God gave me. I believe God chose each and every gay, lesbian, bi, and transgendered individual to teach others about love, tolerance, and acceptance. So I remind all my gay brothers and sisters: Don't worry. God did not make a mistake. He has a plan and a reason for your existence.

A.G., Oxnard, Calif.

Before I met Mary-love and fell in love with her, I never told myself I wanted to be a lesbian. The thought never crossed my mind. After a few bad relationships with guys, I guess falling in love with Mary-love after two years and four months of a friendship was bound to happen—it was a destiny I believe God gave to me.

E.D., via the Internet

IT'S A CHOICE

Although I have been married and have two sons, I was a late bloomer and decided in my late 20s or early 30s that being a lesbian was OK and that, for me, it is a choice.

J.L., via the Internet

As a graduate clinician in speech-language pathology, I find it difficult to deny that there is a genetic propensity to homosexuality, just as there is to stuttering. However, the choice to act upon the drive is entirely a symbol of our humanity. The degree to which we embrace our genetic predisposition is the degree to which we marry our understanding of our physical self and our identity.

T.A., Boston. Mass.

It is always a choice whether to be completely honest with yourself and admit you are not in the majority and are attracted to the same sex. I wasn't able to admit this to myself until a few weeks before my 28th birthday. The *choice* is to live your life as best as you can. The question "Why are you gay or lesbian?" is a small part of a much bigger question: "Why are you You?"

C.F., Louisville, Ky.

33 of them shared a specific region on a portion of the X chromosome.

His work supported earlier evidence pointing to a genetic link to homosexuality.

In 1991, J. Michael Bailey, a psychology professor at Northwestern University, and Richard Pillard, a psychiatrist at Boston University School of Medicine, examined

a group of gay men, 56 of whom had an identical twin, 54 of whom had a fraternal twin brother, and 57 of whom had a brother by adoption. Among those with an identical twin, in 52% of the cases the twin was also gay. Among fraternal twin bothers, in 22% of cases both twins were gay. Just 11% of those who had a brother by adoption reported that the brother was gay. Another study by Bailey and Pillard found similar patterns in lesbians.

WAS IT OUR PARENTS?

SUSAN DOST

Stats: Owner of an assisted-living company, 36, Michigan native
Gay relatives: "There seems to be a lineage of women in my family who end up 'single.'"
Why are you gay? "I believe that is the way the universe intended for me [to be]. I don't think I have a choice in the way I am. I think it's biological."

HAINES WILKERSON

Stats: Magazine creative director, 46, California native
Gay relatives: "One, but not out."
Why are you gay? "I didn't have any choice in the matter whatsoever. It's completely genetic. Environment modifies a gay person's behavior, but it doesn't cause it. I tried to impose straight attributes for my life. They never stuck."

CHUCK KIM

Stats: Reporter and comic book writer, 29, New York native
Gay relatives: None
Why are you gay? "I just remember always wanting to be around guys. I think being gay is a combination of environment and genetics—something that may act as a catalyst, activating that potential."

CLAUDIA SANCHEZ

Stats: Educator, personal chef, 26, California native
Gay relatives: None
Why are you gay? "All my physical and emotional attractions have been to women. It wasn't really a choice, just something I've always had. Men just never attracted me. Being a lesbian is my reality."

Overall, a person with a gay identical twin is at least 10 times more likely to be gay. A man with a gay brother is anywhere from three to seven times more likely to also be gay. And a woman with a lesbian sister is anywhere from four to eight times more likely to also be lesbian. "All this shows that sexual orientation is largely genetic," Pillard says.

Hamer says genes provide about 50% of the influence on sexual orientation. Pillard wouldn't give a fixed percentage, although he said he believes it is "substantially" greater than 50%. Other scientists have estimated the genetic contribution could be as high as 70%.

However strong the influence of genes, it is not 100%. "We're never going to find the 'gay gene'" Hamer says. "There's no switch that turns it on or off. It's not that simple."

He an other researchers agree that the remaining influences are a complex mixture of biological developments and environmental stimuli. But how much power each wields is as yet unknown.

Evidence is mounting, however, for the argument that much of the remaining influence comes from prenatal biological phenomena. LeVay, for example, found a size difference between gay men's and straight men's hypothalamuses—a part of the brain believed to affect sexual behavior. His "hunch," he says, is that gay men's brains develop differently than straight men's because they are exposed to higher levels of testosterone during pregnancy.

"There's a growing evidence to support the idea that biological and developmental factors before birth exert a strong influence on sexual orientation," LeVay says.

A host of biological indicators of homosexuality boost the theory. For example, research from the University of Liverpool in England has shown that gay men and lesbians are more likely than straights to be left-handed and that lesbians have hand patterns that resemble a man's more than a straight female's. Dennis McFadden, a scientist at the University of Texas at Austin, has reported that lesbians' auditory systems seem to develop somewhere between what is typical for heterosexual men and women. According to studies done by

Marc Breedlove, a psychologist at the University of California, Berkeley, there is a direct correlation between the lengths of some fingers of the hand and gayness. An what gay man doesn't relish the study that found that gay men tend to be better endowed than their straight counterparts?

BY CHOICE?

JOHN STRAUSS

Stats: Retired motion picture music editor, 81, New York native
Gay relatives: None
Why are you gay? "Because I'm gay. I was an overprotected child, a sissy boy, and felt uncomfortable with my surroundings. My mother was very protective. My first awareness that I had a sexuality at all was when I was 12 or 13. It developed in an instance when I saw my roommate at camp undressed, and there was a voice in my head that said, *Oh, my God, I'm gay*. Only we didn't call it that at the time; we called it *homosexual*."

TONY ROMAN

Stats: CyberCenter coordinator, Los Angeles Gay and Lesbian Center, 56, New York native
Gay relatives: "I had a gay cousin, who died of AIDS."
Why are you gay? "Nature and God just made me that way. At first I blamed my upbringing for it. I was raised by my mom and stepdad; my father died when I was young. It was a strict Catholic upbringing, [which] had a lot to do with the guilt and suppressing these feelings. I have no kind words for churches. I did a lot of drinking. After I sobered up, I realized I had no one to blame. I am who I am."
—*Profiles reported by Alexander Cho*

The common thread in many of these findings is the belief that differences in prenatal development are responsible for the variances in anatomy—and in sexual orientation as well. Like LeVay, Breedlove attributes his finding of finger-length differences between gay and straight men to the level of fetal exposure to testosterone. "There is a growing body

WHY ARE WE GAY?

JESSICA MENDIETA

Stats: hairdresser, 31, Ohio native
Gay relatives: "I have a gay nephew and at least four gay cousins."
Why are you gay? "I was born gay. I was always attracted to women. My best friends all through junior high and high school were all women. I had my first lover when I was 19. When I met her it was like, *Bang! I definitely love women.*"

JOSHUA EWING

Stats: Student, 18, California native
Gay relatives: None
Why are you gay? "I think it's most definitely genetics. I grew up with my mom and step-dad, and in high school moved in with my biological father. My dad thinks it's a choice, but I knew all along that I wasn't like the other boys, chasing girls. I was doing it, but more to fit in, to conceal my true identity of being homosexual. There are people out there who say they choose, and that's OK. But I didn't have a choice. Everyone is different."

MICHAEL KING

Stats: Editor-designer, 28, West Virginia native
Gay relatives: "I don't know of any concretely, but there are a few that I suspect."
Why are you gay? "It's just who I am. I grew up in the Bible Belt; I played football. I am the perfect example of why environment *doesn't* cause you to be gay, because being gay in West Virginia is not even an option."

LIONEL FRIEDMAN

Stats: Retired from the entertainment industry, 69, Missouri native
Gay relatives: "My younger brother is gay."
Why are you gay? "It's always been there. I just like men. I absolutely feel like I was born with it. I came out at a very young age, 13. My dad was very supportive. My mother wasn't."

ALEXANDER CHO

Stats: Intern at *The Advocate*, 20, California native
Gay relatives: None

Why are you gay? "I have no clue. I grew up in a conventional home, and [being gay] has been with me as long as I can remember, so I'd probably say I was born with it. It was certainly not a choice, although I did choose to suppress it for a long time. I was filled with a lot of self-hate when I realized [I was gay], and it's something that I'm just now beginning the process of getting over."

MERCEDES SALAS

Stats: Waitress, 24, native of the Dominican Republic
Gay relatives: "I have two bisexual cousins, both female."
Why are you gay? "I just feel it. I feel no sexual attraction to men. Instead, I feel attraction to women. Even when I didn't know the concept, the feeling was always there. It was at age 16, when I was reading about it, I came to know that people were 'gay.' Women weren't as badly treated [as gay men], so that made me feel more comfortable asking questions."

of research to support the theory that different hormone levels can cause the brain to differentiate one way or the other—to be straight or gay," LeVay adds.

"THERE IS A SMALL MINORITY OF PEOPLE IN WHICH SEXUAL ORIENTATION IS MALLEABLE. IT WOULD SEEM THAT REPARATIVE THERAPY IS SOMETIMES SUCCESSFUL. I TALKED TO 200 PEOPLE ON THE PHONE. SOME MAY BE EXAGGERATING THEIR CHANGES, BUT I CAN'T BELIEVE THE WHOLE THING IS JUST MADE UP."

—*Psychiatrist Robert Spitzer, who found that gay people can change their sexual orientation if they are "highly motivated"*

But it remains murky just how much and just how strongly these biological factors shape sexual orientation. "I honestly can't be sure how to interpret the differences I found in brain structure." LeVay says.

Which leaves open the final, and most controversial, possibility: How much is sexual orientation determined by a person's environment?

Even the most ardent geneticists and biologists aren't willing to discount a role for external stimuli. "I certainly wouldn't rule out that life experiences can play a role in sexual orientation." LeVay says.

Historically, determining the "causes" of homosexuality was left entirely to the domain of psychology, which attempted to explain homosexuality with theories of mental maladjustment. Perhaps ironically, today it is often psychologists and psychiatrists who argue most arduously against the environmental influence on gayness.

"I've spent 30 years studying psychology, and I don't see any environmental differences that affect a person's sexual orientation," says Richard Isay, a psychiatry professor at Cornell University and author of the book *Becoming Gay*.

Psychiatrist Richard Pillard agrees. "I strongly believe that at birth the wiring in the brain tells us if we are gay or straight," he says.

Isay says that "all the tired old postulations"—that homosexuality is caused by, for instance, an overprotective mother, a distant father, or a sexual molestation or trauma in childhood—have been "completely discredited" by the mental health profession. What the environment affects, he says, is "how you express your sexuality. Very, very few mental health professionals hold on to the notion that environment molds sexual orientation, and there's just no real evidence to support that."

However, numerous researchers point to what LeVay categorizes as the "oodles of data" that sexuality appears to be more fluid in women than in men, suggesting that, for some people at least, sexual orientation may not be genetically or bio-

COMMENTARIES: "WHY?" IS THE WRONG QUESTION

BEING GAY OR LESBIAN IS A BLESSING, SAYS SPIRITUAL WRITER **CHRISTIAN DE LA HUERTA**. THE BEST USE OF THAT GIFT IS NOT TO SEEK ITS CAUSE OR TRY TO CHANGE IT BUT TO USE IT TO FIND OUR TRUE PURPOSE

Part of me would be fascinated to know what makes me gay. My earliest sexual fantasies—before I knew what sex was—were always about men. Interestingly, my earliest romantic fantasies—those involving kissing, holding hands, etc.—were about women. The heterosexist cultural conditioning had already begun.

Though we may never know for sure, I suspect that gayness results from a combination of genetic and environmental factors. Ultimately, however, does it really matter? Nature or nurture, genetics or the environment, choice or not, so what? Knowing what makes us gay might be interesting, might help take the discussion out of religious and moral arenas, but it won't change who we are or the fact that we are here and always have been.

Clearly, evolution, in its mysterious and inexorable wisdom, would long ago have handled the situation if queer folk did not serve some kind of purpose. It may be more useful, then, to ask a different question: What are we going to do with the reality of our existence? If, in fact, we serve a purpose, what might that be? What contributions do we make? How do we make a difference in the world?

In contrast to what "ex-gay" ad campaigns would have us believe, far from needing to "recover" from homosexuality in order to have spiritual grace, it appears that throughout history and across different cultures queer people have not only been spiritually inclined but have actually been respected and revered for assuming roles of spiritual leadership. Many enact those same roles today. Mediators, scouts of consciousness, keepers of beauty, healers, teachers, caregivers, sacred clowns, shamans, priests—these are roles to which we have gravitated, for which we have exhibited a propensity, and which we have filled in disproportionate numbers.

Our outsider status gives us a special sense of perspective—our ability to see the forest *and* the trees. Because we stand outside the mainstream in one area, we are not as rigidly bound by its rules in other areas. Although this may be stressful and cause pain, loneliness, and alienation at some points in our lives, it also creates the opportunity to live by our own rules. We are privy to a more honest process of enlightenment than blind acceptance of tired rules handed down to us by past generations.

Countless people have suppressed their sexual feelings—with varying degrees of success and failure—throughout history and continue to do so. But modifying or suppressing sexual behavior is one thing; changing a person's fundamental orientation is quite another. Far from being an effort to be more "natural," the attempt to change such a fundamental characteristic is an *affront* to what is natural.

One year after I came out to my father, a Catholic psychiatrist, I understood what is often meant by *choice*. After kindly reassuring me that I would always be his son and that he and my mother would always love me, my father proceeded to advise that I choose another lifestyle. He said that it is a very difficult life, that he knew because he had treated many homosexuals, even "curing" some. What my father didn't know, however, is that at least two of those he'd "cured" I'd slept with postcure. I know because after we did our thing, they asked if I was related to so-and-so. When I answered that he was my father, they said "Oh, I used to go to him."

Sexuality, like everything else, including matter, is a form of energy. Though it can be transmuted, energy cannot be destroyed. What is suppressed in one place will inevitably surface elsewhere. And when the suppressed energy of sexuality reemerges elsewhere, it too often does so in ugly and unhealthy forms.

For me, repressing such an intrinsic part of myself was no longer an option. It's been a very long and arduous journey, but I have come to such a profound place of acceptance that I actually live in a state of gratitude for being gay.

I look forward to the day when sexual orientation will be a nonissue, and perhaps all the energy now spent on trying to figure out why we're here could be redirected toward maximizing our unique potential. More and more people are beginning to realize that queers add value to our collective human existence, and given the desperate state of our world, we need all the help we can get—whatever the source.

Being gay is an advantage. It is a gift, a blessing, a privilege. In many ways it frees us up to discover who we really are. And who we are goes far beyond our sexual practices or the people with whom we tend to make romantic and emotional connections.

Had there been a way to alter my sexual orientation when I was growing up—and barely surviving the long, existential depression of my adolescence—what would I have done? I don't know, but now the answer is clear. To even consider the possibility of changing is ludicrous to me. Sure, life is still much easier for heteros. I still experience self-consciousness—truth be told, fear—in certain situations. Recently, at a national park, the guy I was with reached out and held my hand while a group of tourists approached. I felt tension. I felt fear. I pulled my hand away.

But would I change? Not a chance! I love being who I am and what I am. I love being gay. I love the sense of perspective, the freedom from societal rules, the generally more fun and open outlook on life. These blessings don't tell me *why* I'm gay, but they make me understand that "Why?" is not a question I need to ask.

De la Huerta is the founder of QSpirit and the author of Coming Out Spiritually *and* Coming Out Spiritually: The Next Step.

logically predetermined but heavily influenced by factors such as culture, customs, politics, and religion.

It's no secret why the long-standing debate over environmental influences is so critical and so contentious: If environmental stimuli can "make" us gay, can't other stimuli then "make" us straight?

COMMENTARIES "WHY?" IS THE WRONG QUESTION: (CONTINUED)

AS A GAY RIGHTS BATTLE CRY, "IT'S NOT OUR FAULT" SHORTCHANGES OUR HUMANITY, ARGUES **REBECCA ISAACS**. WHAT'S MORE, THE FLUIDITY OF SEXUALITY MAKES HARD-AND-FAST DEFINITIONS POOR POLITICAL TOOLS

Whatever we know about the origins of sexual orientation, we know that it is a complex and fascinating topic that will remain unresolved and controversial for the foreseeable future. Many discussions of sexual orientation's causes have subtext of the search for responsibility, even blame. But we need to attach blame only if we accept our opponents' premise that homosexuality is bad. The major point for me as we continue this discussion of the interplay between nature and nurture is that we need to affirm a basic premise: *Gay is good*. As a parent of a 6-year-old daughter, imparting a sense of pride in her family is critical to her well-being. Vanessa, my partner of 11 years, and I want Rachel to know that the most important value of our family is that we love and care for each other. She has learned from an early age about the importance of validating and believing in herself and her family.

From my perspective, the question is not so much "Where does homosexuality come from?" but "Why are we so concerned about knowing the 'cause'?" In the political arena, as in our daily lives, we need to assert the validity of our sexuality and our humanity as lesbian, gay, bisexual, and transgendered people *without* the need for caveats or explanations. After all, there is little discussion about the origins of *hetero*sexuality.

It's ironic that while heterosexuality is so entrenched and unquestioned, the right wing continues to paint marriage and heterosexuality as being in a constant state of instability and crisis, with alternative sexualities as a principal threat. Right-wing ideology puts forward the premise that homosexuality is an enticing disease that people will catch if exposed, that it's a choice or temporary mental condition that must be overcome by counseling, prayer, coercion, abstinence, repression or electroshock therapy.

The counterassertion, that sexual orientation is a fixed and immutable characteristic, has also long been a part of the legal and political arguments we make for equal rights. If sexual orientation is fixed, the argument goes, then we are not responsible for being gay and are therefore worthy of protection from discrimination. Yet a definitive answer to "Why are we gay?"—even if it were found—would not resolve our quest for equal rights, because those who would block our rights would continue to oppose us on other grounds.

I think that most people extrapolate a universal homosexual-origin story from their own personal experience. If they remember feeling different, feeling attraction to the same sex at an early age, they tend to think that sexual orientation is fixed from birth. Yet many people, women in particular, experience sexual orientation as more fluid than fixed. We need to be open to the range of personal, scientific, and social science theories that analyze sexuality in all its manifestations. Sexual orientation is not fixed in the same way for all people.

We know, for example, that there is a range to when people identify their sexual orientation. Many recognize same-sex attraction from an early age, but others come out later in life, in a particular context, with a particular person. Because we must embrace these differences, it also becomes more difficult to embrace a unified theory of sexuality's origins.

It is very hard to know what sexuality would look like freed from the dominance of heterosexuality. What if there were no stigma attached to being gay, lesbian, or bisexual? What if being gay didn't correlate to isolation, violence, rejection, and limited horizons for many teens? What if the strong arm of normative heterosexuality didn't force all of us into a separate and unequal box? What if sexual orientation truly were a part of each person's journey of self-discovery?

In my own experience I came to lesbianism through feminism, both personally and politically. Ti-Grace Atkinson said, "Feminism is the theory, lesbianism is the practice." I truly believed that, and I was in college in the 1970s at a time and in an environment where the heavy curtain of heterosexuality was momentarily lifted. My friends and I came out during that time of openness. Life after the lesbian nirvana, when we left our created community, was not so open. The pressures of dominant structures like heterosexual marriage reappeared. Today, some of us are still lesbians, some became straight-identified, and some identify as bisexual. I don't believe we each followed our one true, essential path or that there was only one path for each of us. A confluence of societal and personal experiences shaped our identities. Explaining that away with a scientific theory of sexual orientation seems unnecessary and indeed impossible.

I really do believe that for many people, sexuality involves acting on a range of feelings, behaviors, and opportunities. And I also believe that in a society that exacts a toll on people open to same-sex desire, options are more limited than they should be. We have learned from the bisexual movement that there is a range of sexual orientations and that desire is much more complicated than the identity categories we have set up. We box ourselves into a corner when we let others set the agenda and narrow the possibilities of expression.

Those who oppose our equal status politically and socially do so to deny our validity as human beings. Proving a biological or genetic basis will now sway them from that goal. The burden of equal treatment is on a society that discriminates, not on those who experience discrimination, coercion, and physical violence. We must show that the toll on a society that tolerates homophobia is great, that all of us suffer when any one group is targeted for discrimination and harassment. Each of us has a unique origin story that must be embraced. Our rights and freedoms depend not on what causes our sexuality but on our common humanity.

Isaacs is a director of policy and public affairs at the Los Angeles Gay and Lesbian Center.

The latest firebomb thrown into this discussion is the now highly contested report by Columbia University psychiatrist Robert Spitzer, who in May disclosed results of a study in which he claimed that 66% of the gay male partic-

It's all about choices

notes from a blond bruce vilanch

You can't blame straight people for being confused. Not only do we want to get married, have children, and serve in the military—three things they would cheerfully be rid of, given the chance—but just when they have decided that we are fundamentally OK, a doctor comes along on CNN and tells them that a lot of us would rather be straight. And it wasn't even Dr. Laura. His name is Spitzer, and he's gotten some mileage recently out of a survey he did that seemed to say it is easy for gays to convert. His subjects turned out mostly to be the product of "ex-gay" ministries, so his entire study would appear to be statistically flawed, but that didn't stop the networks from pouncing on him as catnip for the evening news.

Hot on the heels of this pronouncement, the folks at the Gallup Poll revealed that, at long last, a majority of Americans seem to accept homosexuality as "an alternative lifestyle" and don't register any major disapproval of us per se, even though we appear to register it about ourselves. Gallup probably didn't use the same phone book as Spitzer.

But straight people, who want to know as much about us as they want to know about plumbing, can be forgiven for shaking their heads in disbelief. If a straight majority thinks homosexuality is OK, why are homosexuals turning away from it? If homosexuality is as wicked as it is painted, why are so many gay people at KFC buying the family pack? Why do so many gay men spend so much time making women look pretty? How can people decide their sexuality anyway, and at so many different times of life? Is the closet we come out of stacked full of discarded ballots with dimpled chads from previous votes when we decided *not* to come out?

Just get me a beer and the remote and let somebody else work on it.

THAT'S WHEN YOU BEGIN TO UNDERSTAND WHAT CHOICE IS ABOUT. IT'S DENIAL. WE COME OUT WHEN WE ARE FINISHED DENYING OUR TRUE NATURES.

Part of the confusion stems from the notion of choice, of choosing to be gay. Since one thing science won't agree on is the genetic explanation of sexuality and since people keep tromping onto *Jenny* and *Jerry* and *Oprah* and *Ricki* to announce they have decided they are gay, it's difficult for the unknowing to dismiss the idea of choice.

It always amazes me when people who see me on *Hollywood Squares* ask me if I am really gay, as casually as they ask if I'm really blond. Why would I make this up? I like being blond because I like the look, but that's not why I'm gay. "Well," they say, "it works so well for you. It's your shtick, you know, like Dean Martin was drunk." But guess what? Dean Martin *was* drunk. I drank with Dean Martin. He didn't knock back a pitcher of lemonade before he staggered onto the stage. It was part of who he was. Cheech and Chong didn't hire a roomful of stoners and take notes. Besides, if I were going to choose a comic shtick, why would I choose one that would leave me open to so much potential hostility? Couldn't I just be a jovial fat guy?

The fact that sexuality is a part of who you are has been a very difficult concept for Americans to swallow, from Kinsey on down. Even prominent black civil rights leaders have had a difficult time when we try to position ourselves as an oppressed minority like theirs. We have a choice, they say. They have to be black, but we can be invisible. And that's when you begin to understand what choice is about. It's denial. We come out when we are finished denying our true natures. When we have had enough of paying the emotional price of passing for, I don't know, call it white. No one suddenly chooses to be gay. Even Anne Heche, at the height of her whirlwind ride on the gay roller coaster, didn't claim to be a lesbian. She just claimed to be in love.

No one chooses to be gay. But they do choose to be straight. They are comfortable enough in their lives, if not in their skin. They choose not to jeopardize their lives and instead do damage to their souls. Eventually, the gnawing within becomes too painful, and they can't stand it. They no longer have a choice. And that, the right wing will tell you, is when we choose to be gay. But we know different. It's when we choose to be free.

ipants and 44% of the lesbians who were "highly motivated" could change not just their sexual behavior but their sexual orientation. The study has come under harsh criticism from psychologists and psychiatrists for its methodology, particularly for relying on data provided solely by phone-interviewed subjects recruited primarily from religiously biased "ex-gay" organizations.

"There's no question in my mind that what Spitzer reported was not a change in sexual orientation but simply a change in sexual behavior," Isay says.

But Spitzer is sticking to his guns. While he admits that "the kinds of changes my subjects reported are highly unlikely to be available to the vast majority" of gay men and lesbians, "there is a small minority of people in which sexual orientation is malleable." He estimates that perhaps 3% of gays and lesbians can change their sexual orientation. "It would seem that reparative therapy is sometimes successful," he says. He brushes aside questions about his methodology of relying too heavily on the self-reporting of obviously self-interested parties. "I talked to 200 people on the phone. Some may be exaggerating [their changes], but I can't believe the whole thing is just made up."

Spitzer, who was among those who worked to get homosexuality removed as a mental disorder from the American Psychiatric Association in 1973 and who has long been a supporter of gay rights, says his work has come under attack "because it challenges both the mental health professionals and the gay activists on their party line. I would hope my work causes people in both camps to rethink their dogma."

Spitzer also acknowledges that his research is being "twisted by the Christian right" for political purposes and says that was never the intention of his work. But science, he says, "will always be manipulated by people on both sides of the political debate."

Spitzer's study notwithstanding, gay and lesbian activists applaud the mounting scientific evidence regarding the origins of sexual orientation. But even though most results would likely be considered favorable to the gay and lesbian political agenda, activists remain cautious about basing too much political strategy on scientific findings.

"We welcome research that helps us understand who we are," says David Smith, a spokesman for the Human Rights Campaign, a gay lobbying group based in Washington, D.C. "And we've seen a growing body of evidence to indicate there are genetic and biological in-

fluences on sexual orientation. But we believe the studies shouldn't have a bearing on public policy. Gay, lesbian, bisexual, and transgendered people should have equal rights regardless of the origins of sexual orientation."

And Shannon Minter, a senior staff attorney at the National Center for Lesbian Rights in San Francisco, is "skeptical that science can ever fully answer the questions to something as humanly complex as sexual orientation. Sure, it's interesting and worth studying, but I'd be careful about jumping to too many conclusions either way."

Mark Stoner shares Minter's ambivalence about finding "the answer" and her wariness that human sexuality can be easily tabulated and measured in the lab.

"It's interesting cocktail chatter, but I don't particularly care what made me

gay," says Stoner, who has two older brothers and thus may be a personal example of one theory that links having older brothers with higher levels of prenatal testosterone and thus a greater chance of being gay. "I don't think we'll ever be able to boil it down to a finite set of variables. It's probably genetic and biological and environmental and cultural and social and a whole lot more that we can't squeeze into comfortable definitions. There are always going to be exceptions to whatever rules the scientists discover."

As if to underscore his point, Stoner adds a footnote to his clarinet theory: "Over all the years of doing my survey, I did find one gay trumpet player."

Dahir, who writes for a number of publications, played the clarinet from age 8 to 17.

'Dr. Sex'

A human-sexuality expert creates controversy with a new book on gay men and transsexuals

By ROBIN WILSON

J. MICHAEL BAILEY clicks on an audio recording of four men: Two are gay and two are straight. Can the audience guess which ones are gay just by listening to their voices? asks Mr. Bailey, a professor of psychology at Northwestern University.

When the majority of those in the Stanford University lecture hall decide that a man with hissy s's and precise articulation is gay, the professor pronounces them correct. The lesson: You can determine a man's sexual orientation after simply listening to him talk for 20 seconds.

Sound like science?

It is billed that way in *The Man Who Would Be Queen: The Science of Gender-Bending and Transsexualism*, a new book aimed at a popular audience and published by the prestigious National Academies Press. Mr. Bailey, who spoke at Stanford as part of a book tour that has also taken him to Emory University and the University of California at Los Angeles, is already widely known for his studies linking sexual orientation to genes. (His research on twins is mentioned in most introductory psychology texts.)

But his latest work has created a bigger buzz than most scholars hope to enjoy in their entire careers. Not only does he identify a set of interests and behaviors he says can be used to tell whether a man is gay, he ties homosexuality to transsexualism. The book is receiving praise and damnation in equal measures, and the controversy is quickly making the author one of the most talked-about sex and gender researchers in academe.

Steven Pinker, a prominent psychologist at the Massachusetts Institute of Technology who is about to move to Harvard, wrote in a comment for the cover that the book "illuminates the mysteries of sexual orientation and identity," deeming it "the best book yet" on the subject. In an interview, he says Mr. Bailey has "opened up a whole new field by asking new questions about sexual preference."

Other scholars and activists have blasted the book for reinforcing inaccurate stereotypes. It has come under the harshest attack for challenging the common medical diagnosis of "gender-identity disorder," which is used in treating people who want to change their sex. Men who want a sex change to become women have long been thought of by psychiatrists as "women trapped in men's bodies." But Mr. Bailey writes that men who want sex-change operations are either extremely gay or are sexual fetishists.

The contention has infuriated activists and scholars who are transsexual. They have produced reams of strident online commentary about Mr. Bailey's book. One Web site calls the book "junk science" and likens it to Nazi propaganda.

Daniel I.H. Linzer, dean of the college of arts and sciences at Northwestern, says Mr. Bailey's work is "having an impact on the field. ... The most we can hope to do as scholars is stimulate additional thinking and work. ... That's a wonderful recognition of the impact Mike is having now."

Mr. Bailey, chairman of the psychology department at Northwestern, teaches "Human Sexuality," one of the most popular classes on the campus, with up to 600 undergraduate students each year. Some of those students have dubbed him "Dr. Sex" or "the Sex Professor." Despite the draw he has on the campus, many of the descriptions of Mr. Bailey and his new book that have appeared on Web sites and in interviews have been ugly. "Cocky," "insensitive," "lurid," "condescending," and "mean-spirited" are just some of the designations used.

ACADEMIC NERD

It is hard to imagine that all this venom has been inspired by the soft-spoken 45-year-old, who has barely a trace of his native Texas drawl. If anything, Mr. Bailey is an academic nerd who is just growing into his reputation as a provocateur. He doesn't mind exposing what he considers sexual myths, no matter how much the results might offend people. And he argues that he is "very pro gay," while acknowledging that "the research I do isn't." While he counts female transsexuals among his friends, he says some "have their feelings hurt" when he contends their sex changes were motivated by erotic fantasies, not gender-identity problems. But he adds, "I can't be a slave to sensitivity."

He majored in mathematics at Washington University in St. Louis, married his college sweetheart, and worked as a high-school teacher for a couple of years until he enrolled in graduate school at the University of Texas at Austin in 1982. He decided against an advanced degree in mathematics because, he says, he knew he wasn't in the same league as some of the top math students at the university. Besides, says the man who now studies transsexuals, "two of them were very strange."

Instead, he pursued an interest in Freudian psychology that was piqued by an undergraduate history course on the topic. "Freud was into all this dark and sexy stuff with the unconscious and how people's motives are usually hidden," says Mr. Bailey. "I thought, 'I can become a psychoanalyst.'"

But at Texas he quickly grew annoyed with the clinical-psychology program. "The people doing it were not really researchers. They were more like an authoritarian cult: Believe this or else," he says. He was more attracted to scholars who were "being hard-headed and asking questions," and even considering unpopular possibilities, like a link between IQ and genes.

Mr. Bailey focused his dissertation on what was then a little-studied subject: the biological causes of homosexuality. The project ran directly counter to Freud's explanation, which is that gay men are the result of overbearing mothers.

The dissertation kicked off an important area of research, which Mr. Bailey continued after landing an assistant professorship at Northwestern in 1989. Two years later, he was a co-author of an article in the *Archives of General Psychiatry* based on a study of brothers that found a genetic component to homosexuality. The research found that 52 percent of the identical twins of homosexual men were also gay, compared with only 22 percent of the fraternal twins and 9.2 percent of the brothers who were not twins.

Mr. Bailey makes a point in his book and in his off-campus lectures of telling people he is straight. He divorced in 1996, and has two all-American looking teenagers, who excel at swimming, wrestling, and academics. What's it like to have a sex researcher for a dad? The kids know all about their father's work, although Mr. Bailey has been known to cover his 16-year-old daughter's ears when discussing his research. If the kids visit his office, though, they're bound to see some of the dozens of sex-related videotapes he uses for his research or in class, including *The Sexual Brain, Men, Sex, and Rape*, and a three-part series: *Sex: A Lifelong Pleasure*.

Mr. Bailey says his divorce, not his research on sexuality, has influenced his choice in clothing. Now, instead of a white dress shirt and khaki pants, he wears tight-fitting knit shirts, a black-leather jacket, and plenty of Ralph Lauren Safari cologne. After Northwestern gave him the raise three years ago, the professor bought himself a car that stands out as well—a black BMW 325i.

Still, Mr. Bailey is not a social magnet. He has an awkward, bouncy walk and a reserved, sometimes brusque manner. But he is well liked, not always the case for a department chairman. "He's the kind of person you go to when you have a problem," says David H. Uttal, an associate professor of psychology.

Mr. Bailey lives in an apartment on the edge of Boys' Town, Chicago's historic gay district, and frequents gay bars on Halsted Street, both for research and for fun. "It is very interesting and vibrant and kind of wild," he says.

He recalls one time in 1995 when he took students to a gay bar called Vortex, where he was doing research. He was interested in drag queens, surmising that they were a link between gay men and transsexuals. "There was gay porn on video monitors, and here I was with these 21-year-old sorority girls," he recalls.

'POLITICALLY INCORRECT'

Four rooms constitute Mr. Bailey's sex lab in Northwestern's Swift Hall. In one room, a graduate student plays videotapes of men and women talking and asks visitors to rate the subjects' voices and body language on a scale from masculine to feminine. It is the kind of research that backs up Mr. Bailey's claim that gay men are more effeminate than straight men, and confirms, he says, that snap judgments about sexual orientation are often correct.

In another small room, graduate students monitor Mr. Bailey's most sexually explicit project. Subjects are left alone to watch pornographic videos on a small television in a darkened room where gauges measure their arousal. The subjects also report their own responses by operating an electronic lever.

The arousal study is supported by a $100,000 federal grant from the National Institute of Child Health and Human Development, and the results are to be published soon in the journal *Psychological Science*. Mr. Bailey found that while straight men are aroused by women and gay men are aroused by men, women—whether heterosexual or lesbian—are bisexual in their arousal, attracted to both men and women.

Mr. Bailey likes to call himself "politically incorrect," and takes positions that run contrary to conventional wisdom. For example, acting as an expert witness in a 1999 case in Illinois, he supported a child molester who requested a reduced jail sentence after agreeing to be castrated.

"People for emotional reasons were saying stuff that simply wasn't true, like castration won't work because rape and child molestation are crimes of violence, not crimes of sex," says Mr. Bailey. "Although this may have been violent to the victims and wasn't sexually enjoyable, that doesn't mean it wasn't for the rapist." He wrote an article with another psychologist on the subject for the *Northwestern University Law Review*, citing others' research on how castration reduces sex drive.

Mr. Bailey also believes AIDS-education campaigns are misguided. "Middle-class, straight kids at Northwestern who are having sex with other middle-class, straight kids at Northwestern have a close to zero chance of getting AIDS," he says. "They are being over-worried about AIDS. If people feel there's little difference between gay or straight and getting AIDS, gay men are going to underestimate the risk."

Those are hot topics in the professor's human-sexuality course. But the most popular part of the course actually takes place outside the lecture hall. Mr. Bailey invites transsexuals and gay men to speak after class, and gives undergraduates free rein in asking questions.

Students have requested tips on oral sex and wondered what the gay men think about monogamy. Mr. Bailey says he's never received any flak from Northwestern, either about his course or about his research. In fact, when the University of Pennsylvania offered him a full professorship in 2000, Northwestern matched the offer, giving him a $28,000 raise, to $92,000 a year.

That doesn't mean everyone on the campus agrees with his work. "He is looking to the body for truth, as opposed to social and cultural frameworks," says Lane Fenrich, a senior lecturer in the history department who teaches gay and lesbian history and the history of the AIDS epidemic. "It's in many ways no different from the way in which people were trying to look for the alleged basis of racial differences in people's bodies."

GAY FEMININITY

It was during his visits to gay bars near his home that Mr. Bailey began to refine his research on gay men's femininity, and came to the conclusion that homosexuality and transsexuality are part of the same continuum.

Gay men have more feminine traits than straight men, he writes, including their interests in fashion and show tunes and their choice of occupations, including florist, waiter, and hair stylist. If a man is feminine, says Mr. Bailey, it is a key sign that he is gay. And if a man is gay, Mr. Bailey says he can tell a lot about what that man's childhood was like. He "played with dolls and loathed football" and "his best friends were girls," he writes in the book.

In fact, writes Mr. Bailey, some gay men are so feminine that they want to become women. He calls men who have sex changes for that reason "homosexual transsexuals." These people are typically very sexy and convincing as women, as well as extremely likely to work as escorts, or as waitresses, receptionists, and manicurists, he writes. They have trouble settling down with a mate because, like gay men, he says, they enjoy casual sex with several partners.

The other type of transsexual is completely different, asserts Mr. Bailey. These men who want to become women were not particularly feminine as little boys and aren't particularly female-looking after a sex change.

As men, they may have cross-dressed, or masturbated to fantasies of themselves as women, and they typically have "sex reassignment" surgery much later in life than do the first type.

Using categories defined in work by other sex researchers, Mr. Bailey labels this type of transsexual "autogynephilic," which means they are sexually stimulated by the act of making their male bodies female.

Mr. Bailey realizes that most transsexuals won't like his characterization. In fact, he says, some are so unwilling to face their motivations that they "lie," falling back instead on the more accepted "I'm a woman in a man's body" narrative. But, he says, their protests don't negate his theory.

Some prominent gay scientists argue that Mr. Bailey's book candidly tackles subjects that have been taboo among gay men.

"If you go back a decade or two, people would be much more defensive and stridently deny the existence of 'gaydar,' and emphasize that gay people are just like straight people," says Simon LeVay, a neuroscientist who has published several books on sexuality. "Well, we're not. There's more to being gay than who you're sexually attracted to."

But Niko Besnier, a visiting professor of anthropology at the University of California at Los Angeles, believes "there is a real homophobic agenda" underneath Mr. Bailey's pronouncements. "You cannot judge whether a voice sounds masculine or feminine," says Mr. Besnier. "I can sound much more feminine if I start talking about interior decorating, even if I don't change my voice."

Mr. Besnier says there are all kinds of gay men, from the "feminine, willowy type to the butch, leather daddy." He was one of about a dozen gay and transsexual people who showed up at Mr. Bailey's lecture at UCLA this month. While most of them asked respectful questions after the professor's talk, some harshly criticized Mr. Bailey.

The same group persuaded a bookstore in West Hollywood that caters to gay customers to cancel a reading by Mr. Bailey and stop selling *The Man Who Would Be Queen*.

'AS VARIED AS ANY GALS'

No one is more outraged by Mr. Bailey's book than transsexual activists and scholars who believe he has mischaracterized them. One Web site, tsroadmap.com, posted photos of the professor's teenage son and daughter, with black bars over their eyes and sexually explicit captions underneath. "Bailey's book is one of the most insidiously vicious pieces of 'transphobia' ever to come out of academia," Andrea James, a transsexual woman, wrote on the Web site, where she labeled Mr. Bailey's book a "bigoted treatise."

Mr. Bailey says he isn't intimidated by tsroadmap, and he accuses Ms. James of "throwing a tantrum and calling me and my family names." (Ms. James recently removed the photographs.)

Lynn Conway, a professor emeritus of electrical engineering and computer science at the University of Michigan at Ann Arbor, says Mr. Bailey is threatening to overturn 40 years of mainstream scientific thought that says men who want to become women are suffering from "gender-identity disorder."

"This book seems like a lurid and reactionary attempt to strip us of our hard-won female gender and of our social and legal rights, too, by relabeling us as either homosexual men or male sexual fetishists," says Ms. Conway. She had a sex-change operation 35 years ago and describes herself as a "nice married gal" who lives in rural Michigan with her husband Charlie, whom she has been with for 15 years.

Ms. Conway and other transsexuals say Mr. Bailey never bothered to talk to them, even though many learned about his project and offered their views. Instead, they charge, he focused on the handful of transsexuals he met in Chicago's gay bars.

"He knows, what, nine gals?" asks Ms. Conway. "I've known hundreds of post-op women, and they're all over the boat. There is no generalization. They are as varied as any gals are."

Joan Roughgarden, a professor of biology at Stanford University who had a sex-change operation in 1998, was so angry about Mr. Bailey's book that she wrote a letter to the National Academies Press. "In academia, we've lived on this Noah's ark of inclusion, and we're sailing along on calm waters when all of the sudden we hit this big rock, and that rock is a psychologist," she said in an interview. Mr. Bailey's research method was simple, says Ms. Roughgarden. He calls all transsexuals he finds attractive "homosexual transsexuals," and all the rest "autogynephilic."

Mr. Bailey's work on transsexuals, unlike his scientific research on gay men, is anecdotal, and his book doesn't cite any figures to back up his claims. In his defense, he says he "went every place I could think of that I'd find a decent chance of finding transsexuals" to talk to and observe. That often meant gay bars near his home, like the Circuit nightclub.

Mr. Bailey, who bites his cuticles and shifts in his seat during a dinner one evening with his children and a reporter, seems more comfortable later on at the Circuit. He mixes easily among the transsexual women he knows, and buys a round of drinks. Most of the women are what Mr. Bailey would call "homosexual transsexuals," and unlike their academic counterparts, they count Mr. Bailey as their savior.

As a psychologist, he has written letters they needed to get sex-reassignment surgery, and he has paid attention to them in ways most people don't.

"Not too many people talk about this, but he's bringing it into the light," says Veronica, a 31-year-old transsexual woman from Ecuador who just got married and doesn't want her last name used. A real-estate agent, she wears her black hair pulled back in a tight ponytail, and her slight build and smooth face would never betray her origin as a man.

Anjelica Kieltyka, a 52-year-old transsexual woman, was the "poster girl" for Mr. Bailey's writings on autogynephilia. At least on the surface, her appearance matches Mr. Bailey's classification to a T: her thinning, bleached-blonde hair is tucked up under a brown tweed beret, and her towering frame and broad shoulders give her an androgynous look.

But Ms. Kieltyka says the professor twisted her story to suit his theory. "I was a male with a sexual-identity disorder," not someone who is living out a sexual fantasy, she says.

At midnight a show begins on the dance floor. The place is packed, and smoke fills the air as the performers sing and dance to Latin music.

Mr. Bailey and his guests crane their necks to see, putting his theories to the test by wondering aloud whether the performers' voices, looks, and movements betray their identity as gay, straight, or transsexual.

When the show ends an hour later, the professor and his friends head for the dance floor—where he seems to come alive.

UNIT 3
Interpersonal Relationships

Unit Selections

Key Points to Consider

- What makes male-female intimacy difficult to achieve? Have you learned any lessons about yourself and the opposite sex "the hard way"?

- Do we as a society focus too little or too much on sexual mechanics—sexual parts and acts? List at least six adjectives you find synonymous with great sex.

- Which do you think is harder—finding a partner or keeping a relationship strong? Why?

- Have you ever felt smothered or too-tightly bound in a relationship? Why do you think some people clutch and fear letting go (despite the often quoted advice that with birds or humans letting go is the only way to truly have something)?

- Do you know anyone who spends what you consider to be an excessive amount of time visiting internet sites associated with meeting people and/or sex? What are your observations of them and the impact on their life and relationships?

 **Links: www.dushkin.com/online/**
These sites are annotated in the World Wide Web pages.

American Psychological Association
http://www.apa.org/topics/homepage.html
Bonobos Sex and Society
http://songweaver.com/info/bonobos.html
The Celibate FAQ
http://www.glandscape.com/celibate.html
Go Ask Alice
http://www.goaskalice.columbia.edu

Most people are familiar with the term "sexual relationship." It denotes an important dimension of sexuality—interpersonal sexuality or sexual interactions occurring between two (and sometimes more) individuals. This unit focuses attention on these types of relationships.

No woman is an island. No man is an island. Interpersonal contact forms the basis for self-esteem and meaningful living. Conversely, isolation results in loneliness and depression for most human beings. People seek and cultivate friendships for the warmth, affection, supportiveness, and sense of trust and loyalty that such relationships can provide.

Long-term friendships may develop into intimate relationships. The qualifying word in the previous sentence is "may." Today many people, single as well as married, yearn for close or emotionally intimate interpersonal relationships but fail to find them. Despite developments in communication and technology that past generations could never fathom, discovering how and where to find potential friends, partners, lovers, and soul mates is reported to be more difficult today than in times past. Fear of rejection causes some to avoid interpersonal relationships, others to present a false front or illusory self that they think is more acceptable or socially desirable. This sets the stage for a game

of intimacy that is counterproductive to genuine intimacy. For others, a major dilemma may exist—the problem of balancing closeness with the preservation of individual identity in a manner that satisfies the need for both personal and interpersonal growth and integrity. In either case, partners in a relationship should be advised that the development of interpersonal awareness (the mutual recognition and knowledge of others as they really are) rests upon trust and self-disclosure—letting the other person know who you really are and how you truly feel. In American society this has never been easy, and today some fear it may be more difficult than ever.

These considerations regarding interpersonal relationships apply equally well to achieving meaningful and satisfying sexual relationships. Three basic ingredients lay the foundation for quality sexual interaction: self-awareness, understanding and acceptance of the partner's needs and desires, and mutual efforts to accommodate both partners' needs and desires. Without these, misunderstandings may arise, bringing anxiety, frustration, dissatisfaction, and/or resentment into the relationship. There may also be a heightened risk of contracting AIDS or another STD (sexually transmitted disease), experiencing an unplanned pregnancy, or experiencing sexual dysfunction by one or both partners. On the other hand, experience and research show that ongoing attention to these three ingredients by intimate partners contributes not only to sexual responsibility, but also to true emotional and sexual intimacy and a longer and happier life.

As might already be apparent, there is much more to quality sexual relationships than our popular culture recognizes. Such relationships are not established by means of sexual techniques or beautiful/handsome features. Rather, it is the quality of the interaction that makes sex a celebration of our humanity and sexuality. A person-oriented (as opposed to genitally oriented) sexual awareness, coupled with a whole-body/mind sexuality and an open, relaxed, even playful, attitude toward exploration make for joy and pleasure in sexuality.

The subsection, *Establishing Sexual Relationships,* fittingly opens with "Great Expectations," an article that warns readers that unrealistic expectations about relationships or a partner will interfere with the initiation and development of meaningful relationships.

The first article in the subsection, *Responsible Quality Sexual Relationships,* focuses on sex within marriage. "The Viagra Dialogues" is a short, but powerful article that covers what Viagra and its successors in the erectile dysfunction treatment arena do and don't do to enhance sexual and emotional intimacy. Finally, "Secret Lives of Wives" comprehensively covers the history and current patterns of marital infidelity by wives.

Great Expectations

By: Polly Shulman

Summary: Has the quest to find the perfect soul mate done more harm than good? Psychologists provide insight into how the never-ending search for ideal love can keep you from enjoying a marriage or a healthy relationship that you already have.

Q: How do you turn a good relationship sour?

A: Pursue your inalienable right to happiness, hot sex, true love and that soul mate who must be out there somewhere.

Marriage is dead! The twin vises of church and law have relaxed their grip on matrimony. We've been liberated from the grim obligation to stay in a poisonous or abusive marriage for the sake of the kids or for appearances. The divorce rate has stayed constant at nearly 50 percent for the last two decades. The ease with which we enter and dissolve unions makes marriage seem like a prime-time spectator sport, whether it's Britney Spears in Vegas or bimbos chasing after the Bachelor.

Long live the new marriage! We once prized the institution for the practical pairing of a cash-producing father and a home-building mother. Now we want it all—a partner who reflects our taste and status, who sees us for who we are, who loves us for all the "right" reasons, who helps us become the person we want to be. We've done away with a rigid social order, adopting instead an even more onerous obligation: the mandate to find a perfect match. Anything short of this ideal prompts us to ask: Is this all there is? Am I as happy as I should be? Could there be somebody out there who's better for me? As often as not, we answer yes to that last question and fall victim to our own great expectations.

Nothing has produced more unhappiness than the concept of the soul mate.

That somebody is, of course, our soul mate, the man or woman who will counter our weaknesses, amplify our strengths and provide the unflagging support and respect that is the essence of a contemporary relationship. The reality is that few marriages or partnerships consistently live up to this ideal. The result is a commitment limbo, in which we care deeply for our partner but keep one stealthy foot out the door of our hearts. In so doing, we subject the relationship to constant review: Would I be happier, smarter, a better person with someone else? It's a painful modern quandary. "Nothing has produced more unhappiness than the concept of the soul mate," says Atlanta psychiatrist Frank Pittman.

Consider Jeremy, a social worker who married a businesswoman in his early twenties. He met another woman, a psychologist, at age 29, and after two agonizing years, left his wife for her. But it didn't work out—after four years of cohabitation, and her escalating pleas to marry, he walked out on her, as well. Jeremy now realizes that the relationship with his wife was solid and workable but thinks he couldn't have seen that 10 years ago, when he left her. "There was always someone better around the corner—and the safety and security of marriage morphed into boredom and stasis. The allure of willing and exciting females was too hard to resist," he admits. Now 42 and still single, Jeremy acknowledges, "I hurt others, and I hurt myself."

Like Jeremy, many of us either dodge the decision to commit or commit without fully relinquishing the right to keep looking—opting for an arrangement psychotherapist Terrence Real terms "stable ambiguity." "You park on the border of the relationship, so you're in it but not of it," he says. There are a million ways to do that: You can be in a relationship but not be sure it's really the right one, have an eye open for a better deal or something on the side, choose someone impossible or far away.

Yet commitment and marriage offer real physical and financial rewards. Touting the benefits of marriage may sound like conservative policy rhetoric, but nonpartisan sociological research backs it up: Committed partners have it all over singles, at least on average. Married people are more financially stable, according to Linda Waite, a sociologist at the University of Chicago and a coauthor of The Case for Marriage: Why Married People are Happier, Healthier and Better Off. Both married men and married women have more assets on average than singles; for women, the differential is huge.

We're in commitment limbo: We care deeply for our partner but keep one stealthy foot out the door of our heart.

The benefits go beyond the piggy bank. Married people, particularly men, tend to live longer than people who aren't married. Couples also live better: When people expect to stay together, says Waite, they pool their resources, increasing their individual standard of living. They also pool their expertise—in cooking, say, or financial management. In general, women improve men's health by putting a stop to stupid bachelor tricks and bugging their husbands to exercise and eat their vegetables. Plus, people who aren't comparing their partners to someone else in bed have less trouble performing and are more emotionally satisfied with sex. The relationship doesn't have to be wonderful for life to get better, says Waite: The statistics hold true for mediocre marriages as well as for passionate ones.

The pragmatic benefits of partnership used to be foremost in our minds. The idea of marriage as a vehicle for self-fulfillment and happiness is relatively new, says Paul Amato, professor of sociology, demography and family studies at Penn State University. Surveys of high school and college students 50 or 60 years ago found that most wanted to get married in order to have children or own a home. Now, most report that they plan to get married for love. This increased emphasis on emotional fulfillment within marriage leaves couples ill-prepared for the realities they will probably face.

Because the early phase of a relationship is marked by excitement and idealization, "many romantic, passionate couples expect to have that excitement forever," says Barry McCarthy, a clinical psychologist and coauthor—with his wife, Emily McCarthy—of Getting It Right the First Time: How to Build a Healthy Marriage. Longing for the charged energy of the early days, people look elsewhere or split up.

Flagging passion is often interpreted as the death knell of a relationship. You begin to wonder whether you're really right for each other after all. You're comfortable together, but you don't really connect the way you used to. Wouldn't it be more honest—and braver—to just admit that it's not working and call it off? "People are made to feel that remaining in a marriage that doesn't make you blissfully happy is an act of existential cowardice," says Joshua Coleman, a San Francisco psychologist.

Coleman says that the constant cultural pressure to have it all—a great sex life, a wonderful family—has made people ashamed of their less-than-perfect relationships and question whether such unions are worth hanging on to. Feelings of dissatisfaction or disappointment are natural, but they can seem intolerable when standards are sky-high. "It's a recent historical event that people expect to get so much from individual partners," says Coleman, author of Imperfect Harmony, in which he advises couples in lackluster marriages to stick it out—especially if they have kids. "There's an enormous amount of pressure on marriages to live up to an unrealistic ideal."

Michaela, 28, was drawn to Bernardo, 30, in part because of their differences: She'd grown up in European boarding schools, he fought his way out of a New York City ghetto. "Our backgrounds made us more interesting to each other," says Michaela. "I was a spoiled brat, and he'd been supporting himself from the age of 14, which I admired." Their first two years of marriage were rewarding, but their fights took a toll. "I felt that because he hadn't grown up in a normal family, he didn't grasp basic issues of courtesy and accountability," says Michaela. They were temperamental opposites: He was a screamer, and she was a sulker. She recalls, "After we fought, I needed to be drawn out of my corner, but he took that to mean that I was a cold bitch." Michaela reluctantly concluded that the two were incompatible.

In a society hell-bent on individual achievement and autonomy, working on a difficult relationship may get short shrift.

In fact, argue psychologists and marital advocates, there's no such thing as true compatibility.

"Marriage is a disagreement machine," says Diane Sollee, founder of the Coalition for Marriage, Family and Couples Education. "All couples disagree about all the same things. We have a highly romanticized notion that if we were with the right person, we wouldn't fight." Discord springs eternal over money, kids, sex and leisure time, but psychologist John Gottman has shown that long-term, happily married couples disagree about these things just as much as couples who divorce.

"There is a mythology of 'the wrong person,'" agrees Pittman. "All marriages are incompatible. All marriages are between people from different families, people who have a different view of things. The magic is to develop binocular vision, to see life through your partner's eyes as well as through your own."

The realization that we're not going to get everything we want from a partner is not just sobering, it's downright miserable. But it is also a necessary step in building a mature relationship, according to Real, who has written about the subject in How Can I Get Through to You: Closing the Intimacy Gap Between Men and Women. "The paradox of intimacy is that our ability to stay close rests on our ability to tolerate solitude inside a relationship," he says. "A central aspect of grown-up love is grief. All of us long for—and think we deserve—perfection." We can hardly be blamed for striving for bliss and self-fulfillment in our romantic lives—our inalienable right to the pursuit of happiness is guaranteed in the first blueprint of American society.

This same respect for our own needs spurred the divorce-law reforms of the 1960s and 1970s. During that era, "The culture shifted to emphasize individual satisfaction, and marriage was part of that," explains Paul Amato, who has followed more than 2,000 families for 20 years in a long-term study of marriage and divorce. Amato says that this shift did some good by freeing people from abusive and intolerable marriages. But it had an unintended side effect: encouraging people to abandon relationships that may be worth salvaging. In a society hell-bent on individual achievement and autonomy, working on a difficult relationship may get short shrift, says psychiatrist Peter Kramer, author of Should You Leave?

We get the divorce rate that we deserve as a culture, says Peter Kramer.

"So much of what we learn has to do with the self, the ego, rather than giving over the self to things like a relationship," Kramer says. In our competitive world, we're rewarded for our individual achievements rather than for how we help others. We value independence over cooperation, and sacrifices for values like loyalty and continuity seem foolish. "I think we get the divorce rate that we deserve as a culture."

The steadfast focus on our own potential may turn a partner into an accessory in the quest for self-actualization, says Maggie Robbins, a therapist in New York City. "We think that this person should reflect the beauty and perfection that is the inner me—or, more often, that this person should compensate for the yuckiness and mess that is the inner me," says Robbins. "This is what makes you tell your wife, 'Lose some weight—you're making me look bad,' not 'Lose some weight, you're at risk for diabetes.'"

Michaela was consistently embarrassed by Bernardo's behavior when they were among friends. "He'd become sullen and withdrawn—he had a shifty way of looking off to the side when he didn't want to talk. I felt like it reflected badly on me," she admits. Michaela left him and is now dating a wealthy entrepreneur. "I just thought there had to be someone else out there for me."

The urge to find a soul mate is not fueled just by notions of romantic manifest destiny. Trends in the workforce and in the media create a sense of limitless romantic possibility. According to Scott South, a demographer at SUNY-Albany, proximity to potential partners has a powerful effect on relationships. South and his colleagues found higher divorce rates among people living in communities or working in professions where they encounter lots of potential partners—people who match them in age, race and education level. "These results hold true not just for unhappy marriages but also for happy ones," says South.

The temptations aren't always living, breathing people. According to research by psychologists Sara Gutierres and Douglas Kenrick, both of Arizona State University, we find reasonably attractive people less appealing when we've just seen a hunk or a hottie—and we're bombarded daily by images of gorgeous models and actors. When we watch Lord of the Rings, Viggo Mortensen's kingly mien and Liv Tyler's elfin charm can make our husbands and wives look all too schlumpy.

Kramer sees a similar pull in the narratives that surround us. "The number of stories that tell us about other lives we could lead—in magazine articles, television shows, books—has increased enormously. We have an enormous reservoir of possibilities," says Kramer.

And these possibilities can drive us to despair. Too many choices have been shown to stymie consumers, and an array of alternative mates is no exception. In an era when marriages were difficult to dissolve, couples rated their marriages as more satisfying than do today's couples, for whom divorce is a clear option, according to the National Opinion Research Center at the University of Chicago.

While we expect marriage to be "happily ever after," the truth is that for most people, neither marriage nor divorce seem to have a decisive impact on happiness. Although Waite's research shows that married people are happier than their single counterparts, other studies have found that after a couple years of marriage, people are just about as happy (or unhappy) as they were before settling down. And assuming that marriage will automatically provide contentment is itself a surefire recipe for misery.

"Marriage is not supposed to make you happy. It is supposed to make you married," says Pittman. "When you are all the way in your marriage, you are free to do useful things, become a better person." A committed relationship allows you to drop pretenses and seductions, expose your weaknesses, be yourself—and know that you will be loved, warts and all. "A real relationship is the collision of my humanity and yours, in all its joy and limitations," says Real. "How partners handle that collision is what determines the quality of their relationship."

Such a down-to-earth view of marriage is hardly romantic, but that doesn't mean it's not profound: An authentic relationship with another person, says Pittman, is "one of the first steps toward connecting with the human condition—which is necessary if you're going to become fulfilled as a human being." If we accept these humble terms, the quest for a soul mate might just be a noble pursuit after all.

Polly Shulman is a freelance writer in New York City.

From Psychology Today Magazine, March/April 2004, pp. 33–34, 37–38, 41–42. Copyright © 2004 by Sussex Publishers, Inc. Reprinted by permission.

LOOKING FOR

Ms.
Potato Head

Men in their 30s and 40s still hoping to marry well (or at all) face a woman shortage that will only get worse in the coming years. So shouldn't these longtime bachelors take the plunge when they have a chance? What's holding them back? A single guy tries to explain how hard it can be to put all the pieces together

BY SHANE TRITSCH

My buddies and I are quite the trendsetters. And it's not because we wear snazzy clothes or drive fancy cars or frequent the latest Chicago hot boîtes (though we do all those things). We're trendy because we belong to the fastest-growing segment of the U.S. population—the "never married," whose ranks have swelled more than twofold in just the past 15 years, according to recent census data. By my reckoning, we're in the only demographic group defined by what we have failed to do. Call us the Great Unwedded.

Of course, being so au courant has its drawbacks. For one thing, without wives to go home to, my single pals and I probably spend too much time hanging out in smoky bars, at peril to our livers and lungs. No wonder studies suggest we're not as healthy or happy as married folks, who live longer, have more sex, make more money, and have less trouble finding a handy Scrabble partner than single people do. Nor do married people have to live with the burden of feeling 50 percent whole in a society that values contractually joined sets of better halves. We are the halve nots.

To a man my single friends and I, most of us in our late 30s and early 40s, would like to become a little less cutting edge—we really do hope to get married and start families someday. But now we have word from a respected source that our hopes may be dimmer than we had thought. In December, *The Wall Street Journal* reported that two phenomena—a sharp falloff in birthrates from 1955 to 1973 and the tendency of men to marry women a few years their junior—were conspiring to produce a heap of frustration for thirty- and fortysomething bachelors still hoping to get hitched. Because birthrates plunged by 40 percent as the baby boom went bust, single men born toward the end of the boom, which officially ended in 1964, now find themselves fishing in a steadily shrinking pool of marital prospects. Already there is a surplus of 80,000 single men in their 30s for every million single women that age; by 2010, the *Journal* noted, men in their late 30s and early 40s will outnumber women five to ten years younger by two to one. Looks like it's time to sell those water heater stocks—demand for cold showers is about to soar.

I never planned on this lingering twilight of bachelorhood. If you had asked me 20 years ago if I'd be happily married by now, with kids, I surely would have said yes. So what went wrong?

The thing is, my friends and I didn't need some highfalutin rag to tell us what we've known in our lonely hearts for years. We see it whenever we're out and about in Chicago. What we've found is the opposite of the old Beach Boys song—there're two guys for every girl. Or so it often seems in the precincts we haunt: a spinning carousel of postwork happy hours, charity soirees, coed sports league games, after-hours museum mixers, and cocktail parties thrown by friends and friends of friends. It's not that there aren't any women crossing our paths. It's just that Ms. Right never seems to be among them. And so we remain stuck, like figures on a Grecian urn, forever in pursuit of some woman who is just out of reach.

In a way, news of the "new biological clock," as the *Journal* dubbed it, comes as a great relief to my buddies and me. Now when our married friends or nosy relatives or women we've just met want to know why we haven't married, we can deflect scrutiny from ourselves by blaming the burgeoning "woman shortage."

Of course, we wouldn't need such excuses if we weren't feeling the sharp point of the question. It may be OK, after all, to be young and single, but if you manage to push the envelope of adolescence all the way to the cusp of middle age, it starts to get a little awkward, as if you're letting everyone down—your married friends, your family, society, yourself. Sometime in my mid-30s—I'm 41 now—I noticed that women I dated were starting to ask me why I had never married. At least, that's how they politely worded it. Of course, what they really meant was: "What on earth is wrong with you?"

Like my other single friends, I never planned on this lingering twilight of bachelorhood. If you had asked me 20 years ago if I'd be happily married by now, with kids, I surely would have said yes. So what went wrong? The usual stuff: The timing was bad. The differences were irreconcilable. The chemistry fizzled. A few good ones got away, as did a lot of nice ones I liked but didn't love.

And it hasn't always been up to me, I'm humbled to report. Women have their own mysterious agendas, as my experiences of the past year painfully demonstrate. There was Mary (I've changed the names), a head-turning brunette Ph.D. candidate who was fascinated with the diabolical workings of the criminal mind. We bonded at a party last summer while discussing an article I had just written about a scam artist, and we started dating—until one day a few months later, when she stopped returning my calls. She said in an e-mail that she wanted to avoid any attachments that would complicate her leaving Chicago when she finished school. Then there was Cathy. Smart, alluring, funny, she worked in broadcasting. After a few good dates, I called her one day at work to see if she wanted to have dinner. She said she was busy but would call right back. She didn't call. The woman who cuts my hair fixed me up with Anne, an attractive blond graphic designer who wore fashionable clothes and had an easy laugh. We had fun at the van Gogh–Gauguin exhibition and enjoyed wide-ranging conversations on several dinner dates. One day I called to see if she wanted to explore taquerías in Pilsen or see a movie. I got her answering machine. I never heard back from her. I could offer other examples, but the point is this: It's rough out there, folks.

No doubt some people will look at me and my single friends and dismiss our solo act as merely the tired dance of narcissism—we must be so in love with ourselves that we just can't make room for someone else. Or, like Peter Pan, we're having so much fun we simply refuse to grow up. Or maybe, after so many years of going it alone, we are ill equipped for the negotiations, compromises, and accommodations of a shared existence.

I have to admit that a life of unfettered freedom and self-indulgence does have its charms. The toilet seat can stay up for days at a stretch. Belching in the privacy of your own home means never having to say, "Excuse me." And money that could have gone into Junior's college fund can instead be put toward designer clothes or fast cars or fabulous vacations. The problem is that none of these perks ultimately satisfies the heart. When I see an elderly couple holding hands like teenagers, or a young couple pushing a baby stroller, or one of my married friends reading a bedtime story to his daughter, suddenly a life unnourished by significant otherdom begins to seem a bit barren.

In late March, my friends and I—five educated, success-ful, unreformed bachelors in all—took one of those fabulous getaways that have made us the envy of our more responsibility-bound friends. For four days of spring skiing in Aspen, we had no jobs, no commitments, no one to answer to. But we didn't exactly sit around congratulating ourselves for leading such untethered lives. Over dinner one night at one of Aspen's froufrou restaurants, in fact, round about our second bottle of silky Châteauneuf-du-Pape, we began talking about just the opposite: our frustrated attempts to find lasting attachment back home in Chicago.

"You take this one's beauty and that one's intelligence and that other one's sense of humor and try to assemble it all in one person," says one bachelor. "The bar keeps getting raised higher."

What we concluded was that there had to be a better way. "The crux of the issue is that the system is very inefficient," says Rick (again I've changed the names), a business consultant. "There are probably a lot of really compatible, attractive women out there whom we never meet." In an efficient market, supply and demand should get along famously. But the dating world, alas, is not an efficient market. It's a system straight out of Soviet central planning, with shortages cropping up here and surpluses piling up there. Privation and dissatisfaction abound, for men *and* women. Where, oh, where is Adam Smith's invisible hand to smooth out the imbalances?

It could be that we simply aren't looking in the right places. Singles bars in this, the city that gave birth to them, might have been fine when we were in our 20s. But as we've gotten older, their usefulness to us has dwindled right along with the number of age-appropriate women who still frequent them. Of course, that hasn't stopped my friends and me from gathering at our favorite watering holes once in a while. The beer is always cold. It's a good bet a ballgame will be on the tube. And one never knows—some enchanted evening, one of us might meet a stranger who will turn out to be the one.

"The chances [of that happening] are extremely low," says George, an information technology manager. "But they're greater than zero. If you just go home and watch television, your chances are zero."

Knowing that the women of our dreams most likely are not hanging out at bars, we have tried to diversify our acquaintance-making opportunities—through work, friends, church, coed sports leagues, black-tie balls, winetastings, and the like. I even know a guy who has picked up women on the Kennedy Expressway at 65 miles an hour—now, that's what I call speed dating. He drives alongside until he catches their attention, then gestures for them to pull off at the nearest exit. Mostly these objects of his auto eroticism stare back as if he had just skipped out of the asylum, but now and then one will actually pull off and swap business cards with him.

What none of us has done is file a personal ad or join a dating service or—the hot trend among twentysomethings—put a profile on the Internet. Maybe we just think that any of those approaches is an admission of failure, a cry for help, the equivalent, for a guy, of being lost and having to ask for directions. But maybe those of us who aren't in serious relationships should give some of those methods a try, because right now "we're not meeting quality women," says Paul, a real estate developer. "We know they're there in Chicago, but we're not finding them."

As comforting as it would be to blame the crummy system for our romantic disappointments, if you catch one of us in a deeply reflective moment, we might be willing to acknowledge that maybe some infinitesimal degree of fault rests within ourselves. Most of us at some point or another have squirmed as the "C" word—as in "commitmentphobe"—was unsheathed and waved at us. And though our first impulse is to deny the accusation, if we're really honest we'll admit that, yes, we're terrified of making, and possibly botching, the biggest decision we'll ever face: choosing a life partner, the future mother of our children. "There's fear of making a mistake," says George. "You become less willing to take that chance."

It doesn't help, of course, that we are surrounded by cautionary tales. Nearly half of all marriages end in divorce, and plenty of couples that stay together wind up miserable anyway—or cheat on each other. The high attrition rate raises questions about the wisdom of making a lifelong commitment to anyone. Maybe human beings, yearning for variety, simply aren't wired to be with the same person till death them do part. As George indelicately puts it, "How many times can you eat chicken before you find yourself craving a steak?"

And so we never seem to settle, engaging instead in an endless game of relationship surfing. "It's like having control of the TV clicker," says George, who has gone out with more than a dozen women in the past year. "No matter how good the show you're watching, you want to know what's on the other channel."

Obviously we have not made our task any easier by being so picky about what we want. "I think all of us are agreeable to getting married to the right person," says Paul. "The key is finding the right person, someone who's not just attractive but also intelligent and personable. As you get older, you have a better understanding of what you like and you're less willing to compromise. We're being more selective." Meanwhile, as our requirements continue to expand, our options continue to shrink.

"Maybe we're looking for Ms. Potato Head," offers George. "You know—someone who combines the best qualities of all the women you've ever dated: You take this one's beauty and that one's intelligence and that other one's sense of humor and try to assemble it all in one person. The bar keeps getting raised higher and higher as we get older. Maybe our expectations are unrealistic."

Maybe women do the same thing. "There are unrealistic expectations on both sides," says Rick, who points out that it's no longer enough for a man simply to be a provider, as it often was in our parents' day. Most women nowadays are perfectly capable of fending for themselves financially, thanks very much, so they want more from a man—a best friend, a soul mate, someone sensitive but not wimpy, self-assured but not self-absorbed, successful professionally but also able to connect emotionally. Oh, and it can't hurt if he has the style of Sinatra and the virility of a New York firefighter. And, if the images of male beauty gracing the covers of men's magazines are a gauge, a set of six-pack abs might also help.

At the froufrou restaurant, the plates are cleared and Sandra, a stunning brunette from Copenhagen, serves us a round of 20-year-old tawny, then joins the conversation, offering up her version of what women seek in men. "Even though we want to be strong, independent women of the 21st century," she says in her scrumptious Danish accent, "we still fight with our old-fashioned ways—that part of us that also wants to be treated like a princess and swept away by a prince in his castle."

It sure sounds pretty, but it illustrates the essential problem. Women are doing it. Men are doing it. We're all waiting for our Prince Charming or fairy-tale princess—or Ms. Potato Head, as the case may be—and we won't settle for anything less.

Maybe the real problem, for those of us who wish to leave the ranks of the never married, isn't so new at all.

Maybe it is merely an old lesson that must be relearned by new generations—just as the occasional Dutch tulip mania or dot-com stock bubble reminds the naïve, after the collapse, that in real life stupendous riches cannot be conjured from thin air.

Maybe we're in the midst of a bubble economy in romance. Our culture is so saturated with silly love songs and Hollywood endings in which the hunky guy always gets the dream girl that people's romantic expectations have become absurdly inflated. What's needed is an Alan Greenspan to throw cold water on all that irrational exuberance, someone to annoy us into accepting the fact that the perfect princess exists only in fairy tales. And that shiny castle inhabited by a prince? It's made of sand.

Maybe entering a relationship is really more like moving into a nice house. Everything is wonderful in the beginning, but then the roof starts to leak. And one day you notice the floors are sagging, the paint is peeling, and the furnace is losing heat. Upkeep is required. It's mundane, unglamorous stuff—and a lot of hard work. But for all its quirks and flaws, the place grows on you, and you reach a point where you wouldn't trade it for anything, and so you do the hard work. You keep it together, the cracks tightly caulked, the furnace cranking out heat.

Of course, learning to think this way would require a radical tempering of expectations. That's not nearly as exciting as believing in a fairy tale. But it could be the start of a hot new trend.

How to Tell Your Potential Lover about Your Chronic STD

by Dr. Jeff Gardere

Dating, getting to know someone intimately, or discovering a potential life partner can be exciting and oh so fun! But what most folks forget is that along with reaching out and touching another human being comes an awful lot of responsibility.

So often you hear people talk about protecting themselves when it comes to the dating game. Women will complain that they are afraid of early physical intimacy because they want to "protect" their hearts. Men will brag about how they are double bagging it (two condoms) because they want to "protect" their penises!

But the sad fact of the matter is that while everyone is seeking to "protect" themselves in one way or another, not enough thought is given to being responsible for the well being and protection of those we come in contact with sexually, especially when it comes to physical illness; sexually transmitted diseases (STD's).

The gifts that keep on giving... bad news

Now I know you're probably thinking, "Oh no Dr. Jeff, please, not another lesson on dating and the dangers of disease!" Besides, a quick visit to the old Doc and some antibiotics will fix the problem lickety-split, right?

Wrong. I'm not talking about the old garden variety STD's like chlamydia, syphilis, and gonorrhea, which are curable through medicine (though some strains of STD's now resist antibiotics). No, I'm discussing the newfangled, modern, chronic STD's that are for the most part incurable, can be dangerous, and depending on the disease, even terminal!

That's right; these are the gifts that keep on giving. I'm talking about genital herpes, genital warts, the variations of hepatitis (A, which is transmitted by fecal matter; B, which is passed through sex; and C, which is transmitted less through sex and more through infected blood). And HIV.

Both hepatitis and of course HIV can cause severe illness and even death. Though these STD's can be managed and placed into remission through medical treatment and healthy living, they always remain and live in their human host.

So that's why we have to go there! That's why we must change our mindset in the dating game from just protecting our own selves from the dangers of STD's, to also being responsible enough to protect our potential lovers from our chronic and transmittable diseases.

The mental torment of unsafe sex practices

I cannot tell you how many of my patients have fallen into deep clinical depressions after having been infected with an incurable STD, sometimes on the first sexual contact! On the flip side, I have also worked with patients who are wracked by guilt and depression because they accidentally but carelessly infected a lover (who had no idea that sexual disease was present) through unsafe sex practices.

I am sure that there are sill some disbelievers amongst you who may think that I am exaggerating the potential danger of contracting these STD's. The Center for Disease Control has reported 793,026 cases of AIDS in the US as of June 2001. According to a recent *Newsweek* magazine, over 3 million Americans are infected with Hepatitis C. Results of a recent nationally representative study show 45 million people infected with herpes nationwide. And according to the American Social Health Association, 20 million Americans have human papilloma virus, better know as genital warts.

So there is definitely a more than average profitability that if you are reading this article, you may meet or already be dating someone with one of these chronic diseases, especially herpes or warts, and you might not even know it!

Most STD's transfer by accident, not intentionally

Now this is not to say that people who have chronic STD's are dangers to society who are looking to infect their lovers. Like Anne Frank, I believe that all people are basically good in nature. I can tell you from my clinical experience that I have never had one patient intentionally pass on an STD. It has always been due to accidental and careless exposure. This is especially true to people who are carriers of herpes or warts.

What STD's are like

Unlike HIV and hepatitis, which can be catastrophic to the emotional and physical system, herpes and warts are initially considered to be nothing more than major inconveniences to living. After some time of adjustment they then become very minor to human and sexual functioning. Here's why:

The initial herpes outbreak (the cluster of sores on the genitalia) is usually very painful, and scary as hell. Warts, though not usually painful, can be very unsightly on the genitalia. Both viruses can also cause secondary but treatable problems such as itching and discharge in women.

The psychological effect to anyone with these viruses can be quite upsetting. But after some time, (it varies from individual to individual) the infected person comes to several realizations; it is not a terminal disease, it can be managed, and there can be extremely long periods of time without re-occurrence, especially when a healthy and less stressful lifestyle is adopted.

Add to the mix, effective anti-viral medications that suppress many future herpes outbreaks and the effectiveness of laser surgery to removes warts, and voila, having these STD's becomes part of day-to-day functioning, normally forgotten, especially when in remission.

It's easy to get careless with the manageable STD's

But therein lies the problem. Because these STD's are so easily managed medically and do not carry the stigma of HIV for example, it is easy to become much more complacent and therefore more careless in transmitting them to others.

Then there are folks who are in remission from herpes or warts and therefore feel no reason to have to reveal their secret until absolutely necessary—or sometimes not at all. Many of them take anti-virals for herpes and are fooled into thinking they are virus free when symptoms are not present.

The truth is that even without obvious symptoms, or even while on medications, you could still be shedding the virus and transmitting the disease. The same thing goes for warts. Just because you do not see warts on your genitalia, it may not mean that you are symptom free. They can be sub-clinical or not easily visible to the naked eye, but still present and infectious. What's more, with females, the herpes lesions or warts can be inside the vagina and not visible unless there is a pelvic examination and or a biopsy.

Even invisible STD's are contagious

All of this to say, when it comes to carrying an STD—any STD—and having sex, you can never be totally sure that you are 100 percent safe from passing it on to a lover, no matter how symptom free you think you are. That's why it is essential to be truthful with a partner or potential lover at some point about your condition. Otherwise, you risk unwittingly infecting them, disrupting their lives and you have to live with that guilt for the rest of your life!

So let's get to the heart of the matter as to when and how you should discuss your STD in a relationship with someone you like, love or lust!

Come to terms with your own STD

First and foremost, you must come to terms with your having a chronic STD. Unless you work through it, your self-esteem will be destroyed and you will never be comfortable discussing it with anyone you are attracted to or with whom you are involved. And if you can't deal with it on your own, then get some professional help. Short-term counseling can be very helpful. With my patients who are struggling with this, usually two to three sessions provide enough time and intervention for a healthy adjustment.

The most important realization you must make—whether in therapy, on your own, or even through an informal support group of friends with the same problem—is that *you are not the disease* and *the disease does not define you*. The disease is a small part of you that *can* be managed. Of course for HIV and hepatitis, this psychological and spiritual process takes more time, but can be achieved with hard work.

Timing

The issue of when to tell is strictly a personal choice. But any physician will advise that you should inform your partner of your medical condition before any intimate or sexual contact outside of kissing. The exception is HIV: If there are bleeding gums or sores in the mouth, than you should discuss your status even before any deep kissing.

Also, as a psychologist who has treated many people for issues of living with STD's, it is my opinion that, if you are in the dating game, it is not necessary to share your medical status until there is a conscious decision to take the relationship from an acquaintance or superficial friendship to a more serious track that may lead to emotional and or physical intimacy. I have had patients, however, due to the seriousness of having HIV or hepatitis, for example, who will make their medical status known to friends and potential lovers right away, not just for health reasons, but to establish immediately who is willing to support and walk the long road of survival with them.

How to talk about it

Again, professional interventions are very helpful in explaining your medical status to a love interest. Many of my patients with chronic STD's have invited their potential partners to a therapy session to discuss the issues and that has worked fabulously. All feelings, anxieties and fears are discussed in a therapeutic manner. Others will arrange for the same forum with a family physician to discuss all the implications, treatment and safe sex options.

"I know many of you are probably thinking, 'Let my potential lover know about my STD before our first sexual encounter?! Be real, Dr. Jeff, are you trying to destroy my love life?!'"

If you'd rather keep the shrinks out of it and handle it on your own, I would suggest a quiet place where you can have privacy. The place should be conducive to dialogue, questions, and lots of talking. Maybe a long walk in the park, at the beach, or sitting on a park bench can be the right setting for creating a tranquil environment where thoughtful decisions can be made.

Provide as much clinical and printed information as you can about the STD. After presenting your information, then just listen as much as possible. Don't try to strong-arm a decision or get resolve in one meeting. Instead, have a series of talks about the matter at different times. Give them time to explore their feelings, concerns and even fears.

Honesty is the best policy

I know many of you are probably thinking, "Let my potential lover know about my STD before our first sexual

encounter?! Be real, Dr. Jeff, are you trying to destroy my love life?!"

Actually, by taking my advice, I am going to help you make it better! There are many more benefits than drawbacks to being honest about your STD with someone with whom you really want to pursue a relationship. The reality is that anyone who walks away from you after you tell them about your STD would not have worked out anyway. They would not have the emotional strength to support and engage with you in a healthy physical and sexual relationship. But for those souls who are willing to stay and work it out, you can make decisions together about dealing with the STD and growing the relationship together. That partner will also be very appreciative that they were given full disclosure and the opportunity to participate equally in safeguarding themselves as much as possible from disease.

Again, from the many cases I have worked with in my practice, I can assure you that the difference between getting a chronic STD from a partner who you did not know had it versus the one who explained the possible risks from the beginning is quite different and much more positive.

The magical commitment honesty can bring

In a strange but very beautiful and romantic way, sharing this intimate information with your potential lover early in the relationship puts you both on the fast track to communication, honesty, responsibility for one another and even commitment. Think about it; no one should be willing to expose themselves to the possibility of contracting a chronic STD from a partner unless they are committed and willing to make a go at sharing their life with that individual. Then, magically the STD is no longer an issue in the relationship.

The bottom line is living with a chronic STD need not be a physical and emotional burden to any romance. If you handle it honestly and positively at the beginning of a potential romance, it will soon become insignificant. Instead you will have more time and energy for developing a healthy and loving relationship together.

Hey baby, the truth shall set you free!

Dr. Jeff Gardere is a clinical psychologist and author of the book, *Smart Parenting for African Americans*. He appears frequently on TV news and talk shows as well as radio. He can be reached at *myprofessionaladvice.com.*

THE NEW
Flirting Game

*IT MAY BE AN AGES-OLD, BIOLOGICALLY-DRIVEN ACTIVITY,
BUT TODAY IT'S ALSO PLAYED WITH ARTFUL SELF-AWARENESS
AND EVEN CONSCIOUS CALCULATION.*

By Deborah A. Lott

To hear the evolutionary determinists tell it, we human beings flirt to propagate our genes and to display our genetic worth. Men are constitutionally predisposed to flirt with the healthiest, most fertile women, recognizable by their biologically correct waist-hip ratios. Women favor the guys with dominant demeanors, throbbing muscles and the most resources to invest in them and their offspring.

Looked at up close, human psychology is more diverse and perverse than the evolutionary determinists would have it. We flirt as thinking individuals in a particular culture at a particular time. Yes, we may express a repertoire of hardwired nonverbal expressions and behaviors—staring eyes, flashing brows, opened palms—that resemble those of other animals, but unlike other animals, we also flirt with conscious calculation. We have been known to practice our techniques in front of the mirror. In other words, flirting

among human beings is culturally modulated as well as biologically driven, as much art as instinct.

In our culture today, it's clear that we do not always choose as the object of our desire those people the evolutionists might deem the most biologically desirable. After all, many young women today find the pale, androgynous, scarcely muscled yet emotionally expressive Leonardo DiCaprio more appealing than the burly Tarzans (Arnold Schwartzenegger, Bruce Willis, etc.) of action movies. Woody Allen may look nerdy but he's had no trouble winning women—and that's not just because he has material resources, but because humor is also a precious cultural commodity. Though she has no breasts or hips to speak of, Ally McBeal still attracts because there's ample evidence of a quick and quirky mind.

In short, we flirt with the intent of assessing potential lifetime partners, we flirt to have easy, no-strings-

attached sex, and we flirt when we are not looking for either. We flirt because, most simply, flirtation can be a liberating form of play, a game with suspense and ambiguities that brings joys of its own. As Philadelphia-based social psychologist Tim Perper says, "Some flirters appear to want to prolong the interaction because it's pleasurable and erotic in its own right, regardless of where it might lead."

Here are some of the ways the game is currently being played.

TAKING The Lead

When it comes to flirting today, women aren't waiting around for men to make the advances. They're taking the lead. Psychologist Monica Moore, Ph.D. of Webster University in St. Louis, Missouri, has spent more than 2000 hours observing women's flirting maneuvers in restaurants, singles bars and at parties. According to her findings, women give non-verbal cues that get a flirtation rolling fully two-thirds of the time. A man may think he's making the first move because he is the one to literally move from wherever he is to the woman's side, but usually he has been summoned.

By the standards set out by evolutionary psychologists, the women who attract the most men would most likely be those with the most symmetrical features or the best hip-to-waist ratios. Not so, says Moore. In her studies, the women who draw the most response are the ones who send the most signals. "Those who performed more than 35 displays per hour elicited greater than four approaches per hour," she notes, "and the more variety the woman used in her techniques, the more likely she was to be successful."

SEXUAL Semaphores

Moore tallied a total of 52 different nonverbal courtship behaviors used by women, including glancing, gazing (short and sustained), primping, preening, smiling, lip licking, pouting, giggling, laughing and nodding, as if to nonverbally indicate, "Yes! yes!" A woman would often begin with a room-encompassing glance, in actuality a casing-the-joint scan to seek out prospects. When she'd zeroed in on a target she'd exhibit the short darting glance—looking at a man, quickly looking away, looking back and then away again. There was something shy and indirect in this initial eye contact.

But women countered their shy moves with other, more aggressive and overt tactics. Those who liked to live dangerously took a round robin approach, alternately flirting with several different men at once until one responded in an unequivocal fashion. A few women hiked their skirts up to bring more leg into a particular man's field of vision. When they inadvertently drew the attention of other admirers, they quickly

pulled their skirts down. If a man failed to get the message, a woman might parade, walking across the room towards him, hips swaying, breasts pushed out, head held high.

WHO'S Submissive?

Moore observed some of the same nonverbal behaviors that Eibl-Eibesfeldt and other ethologists had deemed universal among women: the eyebrow flash (an exaggerated raising of the eyebrows of both eyes, followed by a rapid lowering), the coy smile (a tilting of the head downward, with partial averting of the eyes and, at the end, covering of the mouth), and the exposed neck (turning the head so that the side of the neck is bared).

Who determined that baring the neck is a sign of female submissiveness? It may have a lot more to do with the neck being an erogenous zone.

But while many ethologists interpret these signs as conveying female submissiveness, Moore has an altogether different take. "If these behaviors serve to orchestrate courtship, which they do, then how can they be anything but powerful?" she observes. "Who determined that to cover your mouth is a submissive gesture? Baring the neck may have a lot more to do with the neck being an erogenous zone than its being a submissive posture." Though women in Moore's sample used the coy smile, they also maintained direct eye contact for long periods and smiled fully and unabashedly.

Like Moore, Perper believes that ethologists have overemphasized certain behaviors and misinterpreted them as signifying either dominance or submission. For instance, says Perper, among flirting American heterosexual men and women as well as homosexual men,

the coy smile is less frequent than direct eye contact and sustained smiling. He suggests that some cultures may use the coy smile more than others, and that it is not always a sign of deference.

In watching a flirtatious couple, Perper finds that a male will perform gestures and movements that an ethologist might consider dominant, such as sticking out his chest and strutting around, but he'll also give signs that could be read as submissive, such as bowing his head lower than the woman's. The woman may also do both. "She may drop her head, turn slightly, bare her neck, but then she'll lift her eyes and lean forward with her breasts held out, and that doesn't look submissive at all," Perper notes.

Men involved in these encounters, says Perper, don't describe themselves as "feeling powerful." In fact, he and Moore agree, neither party wholly dominates in a flirtation. Instead, there is a subtle, rhythmical and playful back and forth that culminates in a kind of physical synchronization between two people. She turns, he turns; she picks up her drink, he picks up his drink.

Men are able to recite in enormous detail what they do once they are in bed with a woman, but it is women who remember each and every step in the flirtation game that got them there.

Still, by escalating and de-escalating the flirtation's progression, the woman controls the pace. To slow down a flirtation, a woman might orient her body away slightly or cross her arms across her chest, or avoid meeting the man's eyes. To stop the dance in its tracks, she can yawn, frown, sneer, shake her head from side to side as if to say "No," pocket her hands, hold her trunk rigidly, avoid the man's gaze, stare over his head, or resume flirting with other men. If a man is really dense, she might hold a strand of hair up to her eyes as if to examine her split ends or even pick her teeth.

PLANNING It Out

Do women make these moves consciously? You bet. "I do these things *incidentally* but not *accidentally*," one adept female flirter told Perper. She wanted her movements and gestures to look fluid and spontaneous but they were at least partly planned. In general, says Perper, women are more aware than are men of exactly what they do, why they do it and the effect it has. A man might simply say that he saw a woman he was attracted to and struck up a conversation; a woman would remember all the steps in the flirtation dance. "Men can tell you in enormous detail what they do once they are in bed with a woman," declares Perper. But it is the women who know how they got there.

LEARNING The Steps

If flirting today is often a conscious activity, it is also a learned one. Women pick up the moves early. In observations of 100 girls between the ages of 13 and 16 at shopping malls, ice skating rinks and other places adolescents congregate, Moore found the teens exhibiting 31 of the 52 courtship signals deployed by adult women. (The only signals missing were those at the more overt end of the spectrum, such as actual caressing.) Overall, the teens' gestures looked less natural than ones made by mature females: they laughed more boisterously and preened more obviously, and their moves were broader and rougher.

The girls clearly modeled their behavior on the leader of the pack. When the alpha female stroked her hair or swayed her hips, her companions copied quickly. "You never see this in adult women," says Moore. "Indeed, women go to great lengths to stand out from their female companions."

Compared with adults, the teens signaled less frequently—7.6 signs per hour per girl, as opposed to 44.6 per woman—but their maneuvers, though clumsy, were equally effective at attracting the objects of their desire, in this case, teen boys.

BEYOND The Straight and Narrow

Flirting's basic purpose may be to lure males and females into procreating, but it's also an activity indulged in by gays as well as straights. How do flirting rituals compare?

Marny Hall, a San Francisco-area psychologist who's been an observer and participant in lesbian courtship, recalls that in the 1950s, gay women adhered to rigid gender-role models. Butches did what men were supposed to do: held their bodies tight, lit cigarettes with a dominating flourish, bought drinks, opened doors and otherwise demonstrated strength and gallantry. "Butches would swagger and wear chinos and stand around with one hip cocked and be bold in their gazes," she observes. "Femmes would sashay and wiggle their hips and use indirect feminine wiles."

Beginning in the late 1960s, such fixed role-playing began to dissolve. Lesbians meeting in consciousness-raising groups rejected gender assumptions. It was considered sexually attractive, says Hall, to "put yourself out without artifice, without deception." In the 90s, however, the butch-femme distinction has returned.

But with a difference. Today's lesbians have a sense of irony and wit about the whole charade that would do Mae West proud. "A butch today might flirt by saying to a femme, 'Can I borrow your lipstick? I'm trying to liberate the woman within,'" she says with a laugh. "The gender roles are more scrambled, with 'dominant femmes' and 'soft butches.' There's more plurality and less polarization."

Male homosexuals also exhibit a wide range of flirting behaviors. In his studies, Perper has observed two gay men locked in a stalemate of sustained eye contact for 45 minutes before either made the next move. At the other end of the spectrum, he's seen gay dyads go through the entire flirtation cycle—"gaze, approach, talk, turn, touch, synchronize"—and be out the door on the way to one or the other's abode within two minutes.

In San Francisco, gay men are learning the flirting repertoire used by straight women.

The advent of AIDS and the greater societal acceptance of long-term gay attachments are changing flirtation rituals in the gay community. A sign of the times may be a courtship and dating course currently offered at Harvey Milk Institute in San Francisco. It instructs gay men in the repertoire of gestures long used by straight women seeking partners—ways of slowing down the flirtation, forestalling physical contact and assessing the other's suitability as a long-term mate. In short, it teaches homosexuals how to employ what the ethologists call a "long-term strategy."

FLIRTING Bi-Ways

When you're a crossdresser, all possibilities are open to you," says a male heterosexual who goes by the name Stephanie Montana when in female garb. In feminine persona, says Montana, "I can be more vulnerable, more animated and use more intermittent eye contact."

On one occasion Montana discovered what women seem to learn early on. A man was flirting with her, and, giddy with the attention, Montana sustained eye contact for a bit too long, gave too many overt sexual signals. In response, the man started acting in a proprietary fashion, frightening Montana with "those voracious male stares." Montana had learned the courtship signals but not the rejection repertoire. She didn't yet know how to put on the brakes.

Bisexuals have access to the entire panoply of male and female gestures. Loree Thomas of Seattle, who refers to herself as a bisexual non-op transsexual (born male, she is taking female hormones and living as a woman, but will not have a sex-change operation), has flirted *four* ways: dressed as a man interacting with men or with women, and dressed as a woman in encounters with women or men.

As a man flirting with a woman, Thomas found it most effective to maintain eye contact, smile, lean close, talk in a low voice and offer sincere compliments about the woman's best features. Man to man, says Thomas, the progression to direct physical contact accelerates. As

a woman with a woman, Thomas' flirting has been "more shy, less direct than a man would be." As a woman with a man, she's played the stereotypical female role, "asking the man questions about himself, and listening as if totally fascinated." In all cases, eye contact and smiling are universal flirtation currency.

What the experience of cross-dressers reinforces is the degree to which all flirtation is a game, a careful charade that involves some degree of deception and role-playing. Evolutionists talk about this deception in terms of men's tendency to exaggerate their wealth, success and access to resources, and women's strategic use of cosmetics and clothing to enhance their physical allure.

Some of the exhilaration of flirting, of course, lies in what is hidden, the tension between what is felt and what is revealed. Flirting pairs volley back and forth, putting out am-

biguous signals, neither willing to disclose more than the other, neither wanting to appear more desirous to the other.

To observers like Moore and Perper, flirtation often seems to most resemble the antics of children on the playground or even perhaps the ritual peek-a-boo that babies play with their caregivers. Flirters jostle, tease and tickle, even sometimes stick out a tongue at their partner or reach around from behind to cover up their eyes. As Daniel Stern, researcher, psychiatrist, and author of *The Interpersonal World of the Infant* (Karnac, 1998), has pointed out, the two groups in our culture that engage in the most sustained eye contact are mothers and infants, and lovers.

And thus in a way, the cycle of flirting takes us full circle. If flirting sets us off on the road to producing babies, it also whisks us back to the pleasures of infancy.

PASSION FLOWERS

Five extraordinary women consider the many ways in which passion has marked their lives

Be who you are and who you will be
learn to cherish that boisterous Black Angel that drives you
up one day and down another
protecting the place where your power rises running like hot blood

AUDRE LORDE

SWEET STILLNESS

By Diane McKinney-Whetstone

There is a certain shade of pink that is a bold mix of brown and red and cream. This color stops me whenever I see it, whether it's in a string of the sky at dawn or a luxurious cashmere shawl or most recently, to my husband and children's near horror, on my living-room walls. Everything about me responds to this color with a rush of movement inside that feels like thunder getting ready to roll—without the sound though, just the deep, deep sensation. Except I now know that what I'm actually feeling is a rush of stillness about to descend. And after years of spinning my wheels in the mud, I've come to realize that, for me, much passion resides in stillness.

I spent decades skirting that simple truth. I once believed that motion heaped upon motion was an indicator of how passionate I was, that I needed to be in a perpetual state of expending frenetic energy, kicking up much dust around me to prove that I was passionate about my relationships with family and friends, work, community, wherever my interests took me. But instead of experiencing the intensity of burning passion, I mostly ended up striking matches in the wind, garnering more fatigue than passion because I hadn't given

myself the necessary prerequisite of having my fire lit.

For me passion is a collective response, the climactic mix of intellect and desire, mind and body that can often feel erotic, except that to relegate it only to the sexual realm misses the point. Those things we respond to with a gush of intense feeling are often fickle, impulsive. But they can still lead us to sources of contentment that become our mainstays when passion's onslaught has come and gone.

I wasn't even aware that I was about to change my life the first time I peeled myself from the warmth of my bed one predawn morning almost a decade ago and pushed through the darkness to make it downstairs without waking anybody else in the house. I just knew that everything about me from my very core responded to the velvety stillness of that morning. I wrapped myself in a flannel robe and stared out the window to witness the silent blending of night into day, and there was that perfect mix of pink edging across the back of the sky. In that moment, maybe for the first time ever, I was dripping with stillness on the inside too, meditative. And the stillness transformed me. I became open. I gathered the confidence from my response

to this new absence of movement to begin to do the very thing my perpetual motion had prevented me from doing. Finally the match was lit, and I was on fire. Finally I began to do what I believed I was really meant to do, spurred on by my response to the stillness. That morning I began to write. And I wrote using all of me, using all those deep, deep sensations.

Most of my passionate responses are not as transforming. There's the first touch of chocolate-covered coconut against the tip of my tongue, the fringed lamp shade I spotted at a thrift store that is perfect against my pink living-room walls; there's the feel of a good pen between my fingers, or the rare times I've done a truly charitable thing and managed to keep it to myself. All give me that sensation of thunder about to roll, though I know that instead a stillness will descend, because for me there is so much passion in stillness, getting me ready to feel.

Diane McKinney-Whetstone is the author of three novels. Her most recent is **Blues Dancing***.*

THE KISS

By Shay Youngblood

As kisses go, it was one of the longest and most illuminating. I sat on the front porch of Miss Stanley's house (where I rented a room) at dusk behind the hedge of thick shrubbery outside her bedroom window, kissing a boy I'd just met.

This is how it started. It was the first week of sophomore year, the first day of my work-study job in the college library. He was a good-looking premed student, with honey-colored eyes and a sweet smile. I'd helped him find a book. He offered to walk me home. I couldn't invite him into my room, so we sat on the front porch. We talked for a long time, whispering so our voices wouldn't carry, about where we were born and what our majors were, our favorite books, music and what foods we liked to eat. He said something that made me laugh from deep down inside, and because I was shy about the small gap in the middle of my smile, I brought my hand up to my mouth. He reached for the hand covering my mouth and stroked it, brought it up to his face and closed his eyes. He tasted the inside of my wrist as if he were hungry. I was barely breathing. He, however, took a deep breath and rubbed his face into my hand as if it were a velvet glove. This hand dance made me shiver, though it was a warm, early fall evening in the South. It was the first time so much attention had been paid to my hand. He massaged my palms, stroked each finger firmly between his thumb and forefinger. He looked into my eyes not speaking, stroking my hands as if to soothe me. As my hands relaxed, so went my arms, my shoulders—my whole body became a puddle, a lake, a river.

Night was falling around us. With his fingers he studied my face slowly, gingerly, thoroughly, as if he were having a final exam in anatomy. He wrapped his arms around me and pushed his face into my neck, planting deep kisses as if roses would grow. I was a little afraid. *What if Miss Stanley looks out her window? What if he thinks I'm fast? What if...* I pushed away every doubt or fear as quickly as it came. I let myself go, never imagining how far he would take me. He knew I was ready. He leaned in toward me and pressed his dense, buttery lips to my yielding mouth. The instant we touched there was a powerful current that connected us. My mouth was moist and receptive. At first we were waltzing—one, two, three, one, two, three—but then our passion transformed into a fiery flamenco. We kissed nonstop for an hour and 15 minutes.

This sweet, delicious pleasure was what I've come to know as a soul kiss. The entire 75 minutes were not totally focused on the sensory experience. By the time the streetlights came on, my mind began to drift. I started to think about how coming to Atlanta was a new beginning for me. I had grown up in a public-housing project and was the first person in my immediate family to graduate from high school. It had taken all my family's meager resources, a government-sponsored grant, an academic scholarship and a work-study job in the school's library to make it possible for me to attend college. I wanted to be a television journalist or an entertainment lawyer. All the desire I felt for a full, rich and happy future I put into that kiss. All my hopes for a better life had me married to this unsuspecting premed student who would be a doctor in private practice within ten years. I would be the mother of his children, and we'd live in a house in the suburbs and spend vacations in the Caribbean. I kissed him as if all my happiness were contained in that moment in the porch swing. I kissed him as if all I had was this single moment of joy. If Miss Stanley hadn't come to the front door and cleared her throat, we might still be kissing. My lips raw, my body tingling, I could still feel his hands on my face hours later as I drifted to sleep, into dreams in which I was invincible.

I did not see much of my young man in the days following our big kiss. He was absorbed with his studies, and I became interested in pursuing more creative passions. By the end of the semester I had discovered the power of poetry, other kinds of kisses, new passions that would come to consume me and make me feel as fearless as I did when I chose the longest kiss.

Author and playwright Shay Youngblood's most recent novel is Black Girl in Paris. *She lives in New York*.

JAGGED EDGES

By dream hampton

My love for him is wide. My soul reached out and chose him. It holds on even when I want to be free. When we come together, it is all the things I'm told are dangerous to seek. It's perfect. Every moment is a dream. It transcends who we are, the other lovers we might know. It's all things made possible. It's utterly distracting. When we make love, it feels as if he is trying to disappear inside me, as if he wants to climb inside and make me his home. When we collaborate, I can see our future, a full life of love and art and purpose. Our conversations are marked by both kindness and a deep desire to understand.

Our connectedness feels many lifetimes old, and easy. When we part, and we do, for years at a time, I have private conversations with him in my mind. I need to know if he thinks my absurd thoughts might be brilliant. I want to know if he read the same book I did, if he knows to see the movie I just loved. Walking down the street I find myself laughing aloud at some quirky observation he made nearly 18 months before. I imagine him in his apartment with his imported vinyl, or on his farm with his children. I conjure in my mind his long fingers, his light touch, his comfort with silence, his bizarre sense of humor. I keep him near me in this parallel reality because to banish him altogether would be for me a virtual death. Loving him, I've learned my passion is a boundless place, impossible to map or contain.

Unchecked, I worry: Is my passion no different than romantic obsession? Is this lover, unable to totally commit no matter how complete our love, merely living proof of my own woundedness? Can my passion weather his moodiness? I am afraid that my hunger for him is matched only by his for other women. And now I understand blues women who cut their men. Or burned them with grits. But because I know this man, because I have held his heart in my hands, I find it impossible to truly judge or be angry with him. I'm disappointed, certainly, at the reckless way he sometimes moves through life. But no more so than I am with the many ways I have betrayed and hurt the ones I truly love.

He calls my love a pretty pressure, and concedes to failure before he even gives us a chance. I accuse him of cowardice, because crippling a giant love like ours is a way to do less living. So I punish him with my absence, create distance between the nape of my neck and his kisses, as if wind could be bottled. I don't want passion that is measured by fits. I don't want to be so damn Billie. I try so hard to get it right. I try, as my therapist friends recommend, to "disentangle," and where I can manage, I do. I visualize the mature, whole relationships I'm told to want. I even make attempts at them, but it is our love, burdened by the irreversible pain we have caused each other, that occupies, as if in protest, the seat of my heart. This stormy love, this makes-me-feel-alive love, this private, nameless love, this hold-on-my-soul love.

---

dream hampton leads an enviably romantic life in Harlem.

THE TROUBLE WITH PASSION

By Jeannine Amber

Even when I was a kid, I was always a little *extra*. Like when I was in fourth grade and found out that my teacher, Mrs. Murakami, was returning to school after having her baby. I was so happy when I told my mother that I started to cry. Not many 8-year-olds shed tears of joy, but I couldn't help myself. No more than I could hold back from overturning the pitcher of orange juice on the kitchen table because my baby-sitter was getting on my last nerve. Or sobbing in my room for hours because my father was mad at me. Or beating my little brother over the head with the remote because I didn't like his program selection. Even as a young girl my emotions ran high, and my responses were immediate, often violent, and with complete disregard for the consequences. I was a passionate child.

As a teenager it only got worse. There were months of inconsolable sadness and reckless sex punctuated by books and telephones and ashtrays being slammed into my bedroom wall. But by then I had convinced myself it was okay, because by acting on every impulse I was simply being true to myself. I possessed a certain integrity, I was sure, that other, more repressed girls lacked.

And despite my having no particular artistic talent, I considered myself kin of every passionate painter, poet and writer. We were all loose cannons, wildly intense and, I thought, far more special than everybody else. *I can't help it*, I told myself, *if I feel too much*. On those grounds alone, I reasoned, my behavior would be absolved. So after my boyfriend suddenly got up and walked out in the middle of one of my teary monologues, I opened the kitchen cupboard and smashed every single dish in his house. And when a motorcycle-riding boy from school sent me love notes in envelopes filled with tiny dried flowers and feathers, I gave him my heart, never mind that he had a girlfriend and a baby on the way.

That's how I lived for years. From temper tantrum to love affair to broken heart to utter joy to complete collapse. But I didn't have a problem living my life guided by impulse. The problem, to paraphrase Jean Paul Sartre, was other people.

Had I been a man, it would have been different. I might have been considered sexy or a rebel or a go-getter or frightening or even powerful. And the girls would whisper, "Oh, he's so *passionate*" and try to get a date. But as a woman I was labeled crazy. *Cra-zy*. As in not sane. As in out of her mind. And crazy was one of the nicer words.

As far as I can tell, people use *crazy* as a catchall for any impassioned behavior that makes them uncomfortable: too much crying, too much yelling, too much flying off the handle, too much falling in love too quickly or carrying on with more exuberance than others think the occasion requires. Sometimes, even the ones who know me the best can barely stand it. After one particularly emotive episode, my best friend locked herself in the bathroom and then didn't speak to me for months.

I've tried to accommodate people's sensitivities, and change. I've been to half a dozen therapists, including one who charged me $175 an hour to tell me that I'm "too impulsive." I've been prescribed various "mood regulators," one of which flattened me out so much that I couldn't cry even when something really, really sad happened. I've tried to fake it, spending the whole day at work with a smile plastered on my face only to burst into tears the minute I stepped into a cab just from the sheer exhaustion of it.

But none of this really worked. And besides, who was I really doing it for anyway? Coworkers I never liked to begin with? Men who (in my view) were too uptight for words? After years of trying to temper my impassioned responses to life, I've decided that the best approach is to simply surround myself with people who feel the world as I do: men who cry over a failed relationship, women who yell when something isn't going their way. Every one of these passionate, emotional, slightly bruised and damaged souls exists on the wrong side of appropriate behavior, where no one is in a position to judge. Instead, we grant each other immunity for the hysterical 3:00 A.M. phone call, listen patiently to every last detail of some painful interaction, celebrate with great fanfare any happy occasion. But sometimes I wonder what it would be like on the other side, where life is calm and emotions are kept in check. Boring, I imagine. And to me *that* would be crazy.

Jeannine Amber is a contributing writer for ESSENCE.

I PASS ON

By Edwidge Danticat

I have often heard people say that they have a passion for life. I always wonder, if we can have such a passion for life, then why can't our life itself be our passion: the routine melody of our breath; the thump of our beating hearts; the swing of our steps; what Maya Angelou brilliantly calls our "phenomenal woman-ness"; our abilities to think, create, make decisions for ourselves and even to choose what to let go of as much as what to hold on to.

I have had to sacrifice many destructive passions to make room for other positive and lasting ones. Indeed, when I unscramble the word *Pass-I-On*, I find, among other phrases, "I pass on." Thus my passions have as much to do with the things I let go as well as those I maintain in my life.

Most days I pass on my favorite Haitian coconut-and-peanut confections in order to maintain something of a waistline. I pass on meat and shellfish, which my body in its own wisdom violently rejects in order to keep some of the density in the fragile bones I have had since adolescence. I pass on body- and spirit-breaking relationships in order to know what it is like to truly and honestly love other human beings. Unlike years ago when I pursued the friendship of people who disliked me hoping to win them over, I now concentrate my energies on the people *I* love. I would rather hear my infant niece and nephew singsong baby talk, than sit and listen to someone tear me or others down.

I pass on crippling perfectionism and simply try to do the best I can in every situation. I pass on procrastination and try to accomplish my tasks, plain and difficult ones alike, one step at a time. I pass on parties and social calls and nights out in order to write in solitude, because I find myself more at ease in imaginary landscapes. I pass on saying things I don't mean, so at least I can trust my own voice.

I never fret too much about what I am forsaking, however, because somewhere on the other side is something fundamentally life-enhancing and instructive. Even if I am momentarily leaving a true passion behind, I know that another path will return me there, for authentic passions must, and will, stand the test of time. And if I am blessed, my passion will ignite such a flame that I will ultimately, in some direct or indirect way, pass it on to others. And they, too, will do what they can and give what they have and make their own passions a loving task.

Award-winning author Edwidge Danticat's most recent novel is **The Farming of Bones**.

save your relationship

A breakthrough therapy to find love again

Couples therapy is growing in popularity, but few approaches have proven reliably beneficial. Emotionally Focused Couples Therapy, or EFT, is one that has. This groundbreaking theory of adult love is highly successful, and there is plenty of research to back it up. Here, EFT expert **Susan Johnson,** *Ed.D., maps out the nine-step process for rekindling love.*

It was Mitchell Irving's affair that finally led him and his wife, Karen, to my office for couples counseling. But the betrayal was merely a symptom of a deeper problem in their 19-year marriage. "He felt like he wasn't getting his emotional needs met at home," says Karen, 45, a mystery-novel writer in Ottawa, Canada. "Maybe that's because he was never here! He was a complete workaholic and didn't come home until midnight every night—for years." When Karen told Mitchell she wanted to spend more time together, he would pull out his calendar and say, "How's lunch next Thursday?" "It would be funny if it weren't so sad," Karen says. "I felt neglected and abandoned, and over time, I withdrew emotionally. Between his not being there in person and my not being there in spirit, we just stopped being able to get close."

The Irvings were perfect candidates for EFT, a short-term approach to marital counseling that seeks to re-create a sense of connection between partners. Unlike the traditional cognitive-behavioral approach, which focuses predominantly on teaching communication skills, EFT hinges on getting partners to recognize that they're both emotionally dependent upon the other for love, comfort, support and protection, much like a child depends on a parent. In my sessions with couples, we get straight to the heart of the matter: the need for emotional security in the relationship. Because without that security, asking troubled couples to trust and confide in each other is like asking people who are standing at the edge of a cliff and staring down a 2,000-foot drop to use their skills of listening and empathy—they can't, because they're too busy feeling afraid.

While a doctoral student at York University in Toronto, I began working with British psychologist Les Greenberg, Ph.D., in designing EFT based on attachment theory, which was developed 50 years ago by psychiatrist John Bowlby. Through his

worldwide observations, Bowlby concluded that everyone has an innate yearning for trust and security, or attachment. Children need to feel attached to a parent; adults need to feel attached to another adult, usually a romantic partner. And when those we're attached to can't respond to our needs—maybe one partner is emotionally unavailable—we become anxious and fearful or numb and distant, which sets up dangerous patterns of interaction.

The Irvings' situation is a case in point. Their toxic behavioral pattern, one of the most common, involves a wife who criticizes and becomes contemptuous toward her husband, while he distances himself and stonewalls his wife. "I would tell Mitchell, 'I need you to be around more,' and I meant, 'I miss you,'" Karen explains. "But because of the irritation in my voice, he would hear, 'I am disappointed in you,' and he'd stay away."

(Step 1)

Mary: He doesn't care about anything but work. He has a love affair with his computer. I've had enough.

Harry: You are so difficult. I try to talk to you and all I get is how I can never do anything right.

Patterns like this, which may eventually superimpose themselves onto every element of the relationship, often create a slippery slope to divorce. Recent research by relationship guru John Gottman, Ph.D., author of The Seven Principles for Making Marriage Work, confirms that it's often emotional distance—not conflict—that determines whether a relationship will flourish or begin to disintegrate. After all, every couple fights, but as long as partners can connect emotionally, their relationship should remain healthy. This same notion was also recently supported by Sandra Murray, Ph.D., a psychology professor at the University at Buffalo, State University of New York. Murray's study, just published in the Journal of Personality and Social Psychology, found that partners who feel well-regarded by their mates better handle the occasional hurts that occur in their relationships. So rather than pulling away or lashing out in defense, a confident partner instead draws the offending mate closer to protect the relationship's solidity.

The goal of EFT, therefore, is to help partners feel securely connected by fostering feelings of safety, accessibility and responsiveness. Once in this safe haven, partners are more capable of handling difficult feelings. They more easily process information, deal with ambiguity and see the other's perspective. They also send clearer messages and are better at collaborative problem solving and being assertive. In truth, most distressed couples already have good communication skills—they get along very nicely with other loved ones and coworkers—they just can't apply those skills in their relationship. But if they have a solid emotional connection, if they feel loved and soothed, they'll naturally use the skills they already possess.

Although it's easy for some to dismiss the idea of emotional dependence as antiquated—particularly for women in this post-feminist era—there's no arguing with EFT's success rates. Between 70 and 75 percent of couples report being happy with each other again after undergoing EFT, compared with only 35 percent among those who try cognitive-behavioral counseling. The number of people who experience "significant improvement" is above 90 percent. The dropout rate? Negligible.

(Step 2)

Harry: The more I move away, the madder she gets.

Mary: Right. I feel you've gone off, like, to another land, so yes, I bang on the door louder and louder, trying to get your attention.

So how does EFT go about rebuilding intimacy? It's a nine-step treatment that can take anywhere from 8 to 20 sessions (30, in very complex cases). The first four steps involve helping partners recognize that the problem is not their individual personalities per se, but the negative cycle of communication in which they're stuck. In the next three steps, the therapist works with couples to promote sharing, soothing and bonding, before helping the couple incorporate those acts into everyday life in the last two steps. This final process of showing couples how to keep their connection alive can help prevent relapse.

To better understand how EFT works, it's instructive to see it in action. Take the story of Mary and Harry, married seven years, with one child. Both are managers by profession and very

competent, so when they showed up at my office they expressed that they were puzzled by their inability to "manage" their marriage. They said they had lost a sense of intimacy and were no longer making love. In addition, Mary had discovered what she described as "very friendly" e-mails to her husband from a female colleague of his. Although Harry wasn't having an affair—yet—Mary was distraught at the thought of her husband sharing more with this woman than he was with her. Both spouses were thinking about splitting up. But the key snippets of conversations, taken from our sessions together, demonstrate how EFT helped restore their connection.

Step 1. Partners lay their problems out on the table

Describing a recent fight in detail often helps partners begin to identify core problems. Most couples fight about pragmatic issues—doing laundry or paying bills, for instance—but it's the emotional needs underlying these tiffs that need attention. The following conversation between Mary and Harry illustrates their negative pattern of communication as the two argue about Harry's typical reaction to his wife's frequent mood swings: As she complains and criticizes, he gets defensive and withdraws.

Mary: He doesn't care about anything but work. He has a love affair with his computer. I've had enough. I don't even know who he is anymore. [*To Harry*] You never reach for me! Am I supposed to do all the work in this relationship?

Harry: You are so difficult. I try to talk to you, and all I get is how I can never do anything right. It's always the same: You're angry, and you lecture me a thousand times a day, so I guess I do go downstairs to my computer. I get a bit of peace that way.

Step 2. Partners recognize the cycle that's keeping them emotionally distant and try to identify the needs and fears fueling that cycle

As couples more carefully explore the underlying source of their arguments, they begin to realize that the enemy is not the partner but the unhealthy behaviors in their relationship. In this step, I encourage couples to use non-evaluative language to uncover any fears they might have—of rejection, say, or failure—which are driving the relationship dynamic. In the following exchange, note how Harry and Mary are beginning to explore each other's motivations.

Harry [*to me*]: Yes, I do turn away from her, I guess. I try to move away from the message that I'm a big disappointment—that's what I hear—and the more I move away, the madder she gets. Maybe she feels like she is losing me.

Mary: Right. I feel you've gone off, like, to another land. So yes, I bang on the door louder and louder, trying to get your attention, trying to tell you we need to do something.

Step 3. Partners articulate the emotions behind their behavior

At this point, my role is to help both partners understand and clearly explain what's driving their behaviors, while ensuring that the other is also gaining an accurate understanding. Below, Mary realizes that she's not really angry with Harry but frantic to gain his affection. Harry realizes that he withdraws not because he doesn't want to be with Mary but because he doesn't want to be criticized or face his fear that their marriage is in danger.

Mary: I start to feel really desperate. That's what you don't hear. If I can't get you to respond, well...[*she throws up her hands in a show of defeat*].

Harry: I shut down just to get away from the message that I am so disappointing for you. I can't let it in; it's upsetting. In a way, it's terrifying, so I move away and hope you will calm down.

Step 4. Partners realize they're both hurting and that neither is to blame

As the couple begins to see the negative dynamic as the source of their problems, they become more aware of their own needs for attachment, as well as those of their partner. Armed with empathy, partners can now approach their problems with a less combative mind-set. In the following exchange, Mary and Harry begin to see the cycle as a common enemy and discover new hope for the future.

Mary: The more desperate I get, the more I push; and the more scared you get, the more you shut down.

Harry: [*Nods and smiles*] That's it.

Mary: This thing we're doing, it's got us by the throat.

Harry: Maybe it's that we both get scared. I never knew you were so scared of losing me. I never knew you needed me that much.

Mary: Maybe we can step out of this, if we try it together.

(Step 6)

Harry: I never saw how small you felt. I guess you were screaming for me when I saw you screaming at me.

Mary: I didn't think I was getting through to you. I feel awful when you tell me that you were hurting so much that you'd freeze up inside.

Step 5. Partners identify and admit their emotional hurts and fears

At this stage of EFT, my role becomes even more integral in the couple's progress. Their honesty makes them feel increasingly vulnerable, and my job is to encourage and support them and to help them remain responsive to each other. In this exchange, Harry and Mary risk expressing their deepest feelings.

Harry: I don't know how to tell you how deep the pit is that I go into when I hear that I have failed, that I can't make it with you. I freeze. I shut down.

Mary: I never saw that you were hurting. I guess I saw you as calm and in control, almost indifferent, like you didn't need me at all, and that is the loneliest feeling in the world. There is no "us." I am alone, small. I feel like a fool.

Step 6. Partners begin to, acknowledge and accept the others feeling and their own new responses to those feelings

After years of believing a partner's behavior indicates one thing, it's difficult to accept that it actually means another. In step six, couples learn to trust these newly revealed motivations and, in turn, experience new reactions to these motivations. Note how Harry and Mary now listen to each other and exhibit mutual compassion.

Harry: I never saw how small you felt. I guess you were screaming *for* me when I saw you screaming *at* me. I don't want you to feel small and alone.

Mary: I didn't think I was getting through to you. I feel awful when you tell me that you'd freeze up inside. I guess I was having an impact. I was trying to get you to let me in.

TRY EFT AT HOME

If you and your partner have felt alone, alienated and unable to soothe and support each other for a period of months, you might consider trying Emotionally Focused Couples Therapy on your own. Begin by thinking of a recent argument you've had with your partner and try to detect a pattern of behavior governing it. Don't look to assign blame; just examine the steps in your relationship dance and how those steps cue you and your partner to keep circling around in distress.

Now, allow yourself to be vulnerable for a moment and recognize the fears that might be driving those patterns, such as the fear of being rejected, of being a failure, of being unlovable or abandoned. If you've uncovered any anxieties, try to express them to your partner and ask him or her to reciprocate.

Once you've both shared your fears, rephrase them in terms of what you need from your partner emotionally, if, for instance, you said, "I'm afraid that when you don't return my calls at work it's because you think I'm bugging you, like I'm a nagging wife," you might rephrase that worry and instead say, "I need you to call me back when I leave messages at your office. That shows me that you love me and care about what I have to say." Work together with your partner to incorporate any changes that might help bring you closer in your daily lives.

Trying EFT on your own might be enough to heal your relationship, but you may also find that a professional can help in providing necessary insight. To find an EFT-trained therapist in your area, e-mail the Ottawa Couple & Family Institute at ofci@magma.ca, or contact the American Association of Marriage and Family Therapy by calling (703) 838-9808, or going to www.aamft.org.

CelebrityCounsel

Actors Delta Burke and Gerald "Mac" McRaney were devastated by Delta's depression. Here, they share how couples therapy strengthened their marriage.

Delta Burke

How did depression play into your relationship? When I met Mac we were swept up in our romance, so he didn't know it was anything more than the blues. When I was officially diagnosed, Mac tried to learn along with me what needed to be done. **What happened as you progressed?** Each year I got a little bit better, but Mac was super protective. As I got stronger, it was an adjustment to our relationship. Mac didn't know when he should let me handle things. **How did you confront this problem?** Mac came to therapy with me. The first time, I didn't realize how angry I was. At one point, I started screaming, "I hate you!" He walked out, and I thought. 'There goes my marriage.' But then he came back. **How did couples therapy help?** When we weren't communicating right, Mac's booming voice scared me; I would shut down. The therapist worked with us on recognizing our patterns, it was hard, but it helped us communicate better. **How is your relationship today?** Now we're safe with each other. Everybody goes through scary ups and downs in a relationship. To know that we're really there for each other is wonderful.

Gerald "Mac" McRaney

How did Delta's depression affect you? You know how everybody thinks the entire universe spins around them? At least, I do. Naturally I assumed that I'd done something to disappoint her, that I caused it. **What was your response to her isolation?** I got really protective of her. She was frightened of the press, so I wouldn't let anyone remotely connected to the press near her. **Did this affect you emotionally?** Yes, it got me down because I felt so badly for her, I recall getting frustrated. **Did you ever consider giving up?** No. **You simply loved her too much?** Yup. **Was couples counseling helpful?** Very. I learned that you need a break from time to time; you've got to recharge your batteries. Otherwise you're no good to anybody. **What made you realize this?** The constant reassurance that there was nothing I could do to fix the problem. All I could do was be her husband. **So, you're happy today?** Oh, my God, yes. Just the other night I had to let her know how important she is to me and how glad I am that I'm sharing life with her. **She's a lucky lady.** I'm a terribly lucky man.

Step 7. Partners are drawn together through the expression of their emotional needs

At this stage, partners are willingly available to each other, so when talking about their vulnerabilities, they're able to assure each other and soothe hurt feelings. This becomes the most emotional part of the therapeutic process as couples like Harry and Mary create a new, bonding cycle that begins to replace the old, destructive one.

Harry: I want you to give me a chance to learn how to be close to you. I can't deal with being labeled a failure. I want to let you in—I want to be close—but I need to feel safe, like you are going to give me the benefit of the doubt.

Mary: It's scary to feel lonely when you turn away. I need reassurance. If I tell you "I need some holding, some 'us' time," I want to know that you'll be there. I want to feel safe again, [In response, Harry holds her tightly.]

Step 8. Partners create new solutions to their problems

In step eight, partners share the new story of their relationship and how hard they worked to rewrite it together. Processing this experience and viewing their history in a different light allows couples to find newer, healthier ways of approaching pragmatic problems. Here we see Harry—who once ran and hid from the relationship—actively create more opportunities to bond with Mary.

Harry: We can have time together in the evening, after the kids are in bed. Let's make coffee and sit together, and if you trust me a little, I'll make us a schedule for nights out. It makes me feel good to know you need time with me.

Step 9. Partners consolidate their new positions and cycles of behavior

After months of work, it's vital that the couple continues to remember what first got them off track and how they found their way back. Without reassessing this process, maintaining this new cycle will lose importance and ultimately lead to a relapse. As Harry and Mary reflect on their therapy experience, both clearly see how they first became distressed and what they did to repair the relationship.

Harry: It was when I got promoted that it all started. I needed to prove myself to everybody. I did get immersed in work, but now when I hear that tone in your voice I remember how much you need me, and I want to reassure you: I am here, Mary. I know we can do this now. We're learning to trust each other again. It's like we are finding the "us" we had when we got married. We still fight sometimes, but these close times make all the difference.

For the right people, EFT can work magic. In fewer than four months, it brought Karen and Mitchell Irving back from the brink of divorce. "We discovered that our marriage was built on these ludicrous underlying assumptions," Karen says now. "Mitchell had this sense of entitlement and believed I should be there for him no matter what. I, coming from a dysfunctional family, believed I wasn't worthy of more consideration than that. When we realized how off our perceptions were, we giggled about it."

More important than the levity these revelations brought were the changes that grew out of them. Mitchell cut back on his office hours and is enjoying spending more time with Karen. And they don't feel childish, as they had before, when asking each other for "close time." "We've learned not to sacrifice intimacy for independence," Karen concludes. "One of the greatest joys of marriage is discovering how much we need each other."

Sadly, for some couples it may be too late. EFT is not designed for people who have tried unsuccessfully to reconnect for so long that they've already mourned the lost relationship and become completely detached. It's also not appropriate for abusive relationships. But if, despite your obstacles, you still desire to make your relationship work, I encourage you to see an EFT-trained therapist.

LEARN MORE ABOUT IT

The Seven Principles for Making Marriage Work John Gottman, Ph.D. (Three Rivers Press, 2000)

Creating Connection: The Practice of Emotionally Focused Marital Therapy Susan M. Johnson, Ed.D. (Routledge, 1996)
www.emotionfocusedtherapy.org
www.ocfi.ca

Susan Johnson, Ed.D., is the main proponent of Emotionally Focused Couples Therapy and a licensed clinical psychologist, professor of psychology at the University of Ottawa in Canada, visiting professor at Alliant University in San Diego and director of the Ottawa Couple & Family Institute.

Aviva Patz is a freelance writer in Upper Montclair, New Jersey, and a former editor at *Psychology Today*.

How to rediscover desire

The *last* thing you want to do is discuss your love life with a stranger.
But sex therapists can help you reconnect with your spouse in bed—and in life.

By Michael Castleman

alan and Diane had what is known as a desire discrepancy: In other words, he wanted to make love twice as often as she did. The couple had been married 12 years and had two sons when they first consulted a sex therapist. For the next 18 months, Alan and Diane, both 41, discussed their sex life—and a lot of other things. It turned out that their problem involved more than different sexual appetites. Diane came from a family with fundamentalist religious beliefs and was raised to view sex—especially oral sex—as dirty. The couple also discussed Alan's desire for more cuddling and hand holding, and Diane's tendency to criticize her husband's abilities as a wage earner.

After Alan and Diane aired these concerns, they came to understand each other better—and to realize the impact marital problems were having on their sex life. In the end, Diane still didn't want sex as often as Alan did, but it became less of an issue between them. They learned how to enjoy each other

more, and to enjoy their sex life more as well.

"Good sex is one of life's greatest pleasures," says sex therapist Dennis Sugrue, Ph.D., a clinical associate professor of psychiatry at the University of Michigan Medical School in Ann Arbor and president of the American Association of Sex Educators, Counselors, and Therapists. "If you're not enjoying it as much as you'd like, there's no reason to feel inadequate, embarrassed, ashamed, or resentful of your partner. That's where sex therapy can help. It not only improves the quality of your sex, but it also deepens the trust, security, and intimacy in your relationship."

Yet sex therapy, which was created by William Masters, M.D., and Virginia Johnson in the 1960s, has been vastly misunderstood. Over the years, misconceptions have included the idea that patients have intercourse in front of their therapists or are asked to make love with someone other than their spouse (a surrogate). Neither was true of legitimate sex therapy then—and it's not true now.

Sex therapy is basically talk therapy, during which couples sit down with a qualified professional to discuss problems that are primarily sexual in nature. Although marriage counselors and sex therapists are both psychotherapists, sex therapists have additional training. "Couples counseling often deals with issues of communication and control, but it may not deal with sex at all," says Janet Hyde, Ph.D., a professor of psychology and women's studies at the University of Wisconsin in Madison and current president of the Society for the Scientific Study of Sex. "However, when couples consult a sex therapist, sex is definitely on the agenda."

The process

Sex therapy usually takes four to six months of weekly, one-hour sessions. Depending on where couples live, each session costs between $75 and $175 per hour. Some health insurers will cover it, though they may place limits on the

talking sex... and solutions

Escaping stress

Larry, 37, and Janet, 34, had been married seven years when they decided to consult Allen Elkin, Ph.D., a certified sex therapist and director of the Stress Management and Counseling Center in New York City. They were arguing over Larry's lack of interest in sex, which was causing him to have performance problems. Larry had begun avoiding intimacy altogether—to his wife's dismay. The first thing Elkin did was get Larry to see that job stress was playing a major role in his sexual difficulties.

Next Elkin focused on Janet, who felt so rejected by Larry's lack of attention that she frequently lashed out at him. She was convinced that her husband found her unattractive. At Elkin's prompting, Larry reassured his wife. Once Janet realized that Larry's problem wasn't about her, she was able to be less angry and demanding—and to help her husband more.

Larry then learned breathing and muscle-relaxation techniques to relieve his physical tension. Elkin helped him identify his stress triggers, so Larry could catch himself before having an anxiety attack, and they discussed how Larry could function better on the job.

Elkin finally addressed the couple's sex problems directly. He advised them to do sensate focus, in which each partner massages the other, revealing how they like to be touched. Larry had to learn to concentrate on the process and not on his overall performance. Now, five months later, the couple has gone from having sex once every two months to once a week.

More tender time

Suki Hanfling, MSW, AASECT-certified sex therapist, and founder and director of the McLean Hospital Human Sexuality Program in Belmont, Massachusetts, first started seeing Steven, 42, and Catherine, 40, about five months ago. Catherine didn't enjoy the way Steven made love but was convinced that he was the "expert" in such matters and something must be wrong with her. During their ten years of marriage, she never spoke up about her desires or preferences. When her anger and discomfort grew unbearable, she started avoiding her husband's advances.

Steven, wounded by her withdrawal, began sulking and cooling off to her as well. Hanfling identified the problem quickly: Steven didn't realize how important romance and connection could be in a relationship. Catherine wanted tender time with her husband, in bed and out.

But Catherine also had to learn to communicate. After working on this in a separate session, she was able to discuss her preferences more easily with her husband. Then Hanfling addressed some practical matters: Because making love right before bedtime could be rushed, she advised the couple to save sex for mornings or weekends. Husband and wife decided to send their four-year-old daughter to her grandparents every other Saturday night so they could enjoy each other's company. And Steven learned to approach Catherine in a softer, less demanding way that made her feel less pressured. This change also allowed for more cuddling—which both of them had been missing. By the end of their therapy, the couple was back on track, having sex regularly.

Less pressure

Jack and Pamela had been married for 23 years and had a healthy sex life. Then Jack, 56, started having difficulty ejaculating. The couple went to see Norman S. Fertel, M.D., an AASECT-certified sex therapist in Brooklyn. Dr. Fertel first sent Jack for a urology exam to make sure the condition wasn't caused by an enlarged prostate or other medical problem.

After the tests came back normal, Dr. Fertel sat down with Pamela, 45, and Jack and explained that aging causes delayed ejaculation and that older men need more stimulation to get aroused. Then he talked the couple through their relationship history, helping them rediscover what attracted them to each other, identify what had changed over the years, and pinpoint what kept them close.

Once Pamela understood the physical component of Jack's problem and heard him tell her why he still loved her, she immediately felt better. Jack, realizing his problem was common, felt less pressure. Dr. Fertel then suggested a few techniques they could try to vary their routine. Pamela and Jack both learned not to worry if everything didn't always go as planned, and their sex life began to improve.

number of sessions. (See "Finding a Qualified Therapist.")

Most therapists use the first session to ease their clients into the process, because so many feel uncomfortable talking about sex. They start by reviewing the couples' medical histories. "Sexuality can be affected by chronic illness, medications, substance abuse, and de-

pression," explains Michael Plaut, Ph.D., an associate professor of psychiatry at the University of Maryland School of Medicine in Baltimore and president of the Society for Sex Therapy and Research, "so we need to understand if outside factors are involved." Next, they discuss the clients' family backgrounds and their relationship history.

Usually toward the end of the initial meeting, the questions begin to center around sex. Therapists ask the basics. Why are you here? How long has the problem been going on? When does it occur? How are each of you reacting? "Then I make it clear," Plaut says, "that I have no agenda for what the sexual relationship 'ought' to be in terms of what they do together, when they do it, or how often. That's up to them. I see my job as helping them work out a sexual relationship they can both live with comfortably."

Subsequent sessions focus on the sexual and nonsexual issues that factor into the relationship. "Couples often come in resenting each other," says Louanne Cole Weston, Ph.D., a sex therapist in Fair Oaks, California. "They don't see the other person's perspective. I try to help them make peace with each other."

Unlike most couples counseling, sex therapy involves various types of homework. In addition to reading, assignments may include practicing sensual, but nonsexual, intimacy—for example, hugging more often, cuddling, or trading massages. "Sensual massage without genital contact," Sugrue says, "can be a great way for couples to rediscover the power of touch without getting caught up in performance concerns."

Adds Weston, "If I'm dealing with a man who has premature ejaculation or a woman who can't have orgasms, then the homework involves some type of self-stimulation."

Weston recently worked with Ted, 37, and his wife, Susan, a 33-year-old teacher who had never had an orgasm. The therapy not only involved Susan's problem but also her guilt about faking

---

finding a qualified therapist

•Ask your family doctor or gynecologist for a recommendation.

•Call local or state psychological or social work organizations for referrals. (Don't pick the sex therapist closest to you only because it's convenient.)

•Write to the American Association of Sex Educators, Counselors, and Therapists, P.O. Box 238, Mount Vernon, IA 52314-0238. If you include a self-addressed, stamped, business-size envelope, the organization will send a list of AASECT-certified sex therapists in your area. Some of the therapists are listed on the organization's Web site: www.aasect.org.

•Interview all the candidates by phone, and ask about their experience dealing with your problem, their credentials, their approach, when you might arrange sessions, and fees. Then select the one with whom you feel the best rapport.

•Don't be afraid to change therapists if the one you've chosen isn't meeting your needs.

---

orgasms with Ted and his anger about her deception. After a lot of discussion, experimentation, and support from Ted, Susan learned how to have orgasms.

The proof

Studies support the effectiveness of sex therapy. Researchers at the University of Pennsylvania School of Medicine in Philadelphia tracked 365 married couples who sought sex therapy for a variety of problems. Sixty-five perfect reported that their problem was resolved. Those who *didn't* find the therapy effective usually had an illness that impaired sexual functioning.

"Although husbands and wives occasionally seek individual sex therapy, it is most helpful in a cooperative relationship where both people are equally committed to working together," Plaut says.

Sex is perfectly natural, but often not naturally perfect. "You have to pay attention to your own pleasure, while simultaneously paying attention to the other person's," Weston explains. "Some people don't pay enough attention to themselves. Some don't pay enough to the other. But with a little time and energy, sex therapy can help couples in loving relationships overcome their problems and enjoy themselves again."

The Viagra Dialogues

By Deborah Pike Olsen

This drug can put the bloom back in sex—but it can also cause relationship problems. Hear what real-life couples have to say about "vitamin V."

It's 16 years later, but Gary Haub and his wife, Carolyn Acton, still remember how devastating it was when he couldn't make love to her. "I didn't feel like touching her," Gary, now 53, recalls. "I felt like less than a man."

Gary and Carolyn, who live in Irving, Texas, drew apart. "When I hugged Gary, I'd worry that he'd think I wanted more, so I stopped being affectionate," says Carolyn, also 53. Like many women, she blamed herself. "I had put on weight with each of our three children, so I feared Gary no longer found me attractive," adds Carolyn. "Because I wasn't working, I was afraid I was boring." Carolyn became depressed, then angry: "I remember thinking, I'm still the same woman you married."

Finally Gary saw a urologist, who diagnosed erectile dysfunction (ED), a condition caused by aging as well as by certain medical problems. Penile injections helped, but were uncomfortable. Then, in 1998, Viagra appeared. Gary and Carolyn were so pleased with the pill, he has taken it ever since: "I don't know if we'd still be married if Viagra hadn't come along," Gary says bluntly.

Hailed as "vitamin V," Viagra created a stir when it was introduced. Since then, it's helped to repair countless marriages. But many men also use it recreationally—even as an aphrodisiac. "Viagra has evolved into more of a social drug," says Martin Resnick, M.D., chairman of the department of urology at Case Western Reserve University School of Medicine, in Cleveland. "It's being targeted toward men who simply want to perform better." In early TV commercials, the long-married, 70-something former senator Bob Dole extolled the virtues of Viagra. Now virile young athletes do the endorsements. All this makes some wives worry that Viagra will prompt their husbands to cheat—or expect sex on demand. Yet other women are urging the men in their lives to try it.

With two similar drugs (see "Viagra Wannabes") poised to debut this year, Viagra and the hotly debated issues surrounding it are bound to make news again in a major way.

Bring on the Viagra!

At a recent all-girls lunch in Dallas, Viagra was the prime topic of conversation. One woman in her 50s confided that the drug had saved her ten-year marriage. "Sex was a strong part of our relationship," she said. So when her husband could no longer perform, she became concerned: "We needed to connect physically as well as emotionally." And she worried about the impact ED was having on her husband's ego. Finally about a year ago, he tried Viagra, and she declared at the lunch, "I'm very appreciative!"

Women have even started to take the initiative when it comes to Viagra, asking their husband's doctor for a prescription. Domeena Renshaw, M.D., director of the Sexual Dysfunction Clinic at Loyola University in Chicago, recalls a woman in her 60s asking what the drug tasted like—because she wanted to slip a tablet into her husband's hot chocolate!

On Viagra, "he thinks he's Tarzan," says one wife, "but I'm not sure I'm Jane."

Men can be secretive as well. One woman tells of finding a packet of Viagra tucked in her husband's un-

In the works: Viagra wanna-bes

Two Viagra-like drugs—Cialis and Levitra—are scheduled to debut this year, pending FDA approval. There is obviously a market: Erectile dysfunction affects an estimated 20 million to 30 million men in the United States. Like Viagra, the new drugs increase blood flow to the penis, triggering an erection in 30 minutes to an hour—or less. But the makers of Cialis and Levitra maintain that their drugs will allow men to have erections over longer periods of time than Viagra does. All three medications can trigger side effects, which may include headaches, facial flush, upset stomach, nasal congestion, or a bluish tinge to the vision. And all are off-limits to men who take a nitrate medicine for heart disease.

Viagra has also been prescribed for women with arousal problems, but it is not approved by the FDA for this purpose—which means no one knows for sure if it's safe and effective. But a new topical medicine for women, called Alista, is in the pipeline. It's designed to increase blood flow to the genital area.

derwear drawer, with one pill missing. When she asked him about it, he confessed he had used it recently but wanted his wife to think his erection had been "natural."

Not tonight, dear

Of course, some women are less than thrilled with Viagra. Typically, when a man obtains a prescription, he hasn't been intimate with his wife for at least 18 months. During that time, the dynamics of their relationship may have changed for all sorts of reasons. If a woman is postmenopausal, intercourse may be painful. If her husband hasn't shown affection in years she could have adapted to their more platonic relationship. Or perhaps she craved affection, and when her husband didn't respond, she became resentful or insecure. Suddenly, Viagra enters the bedroom—and her middle-aged husband starts acting like a young stud. If he doesn't engage in foreplay, "a woman may feel she's being treated like a receptacle," says Jean Koehler, Ph.D., president of the American Association of Sex Educators, Counselors, and Therapists. And she may fear that if she doesn't respond, her husband will leave her. Dr. Renshaw tells of a woman who called her shortly after Viagra became available. "She said, 'We stopped having sex 20 years ago, and he just came home with Viagra. I'm 65, and I'm not interested in intercourse. But I have to say yes: If he doesn't do it with me, he'll do if with someone else.'"

Even couples who enjoy lovemaking, Viagra-style, may disagree on how much is enough. When Alfred Pariser, a 63-year-old consultant in Rancho Mirage, California, became impotent after prostate cancer surgery seven years ago, he participated in a study of Viagra and has been taking it ever since. "I felt awful about not being able to have sex with my wife," he says. "Intercourse is one of the great parts of marriage."

His wife, Cheryl, agrees—to a point. "Thank God there's Viagra," she sighs. "Alfred would go nuts if he couldn't have an erection." Still, she says, there are times when "he wants sex more than I do. He thinks he's Tarzan, but I'm not sure I'm Jane."

A cautionary tale

Experts insist that Viagra by itself can't solve underlying problems in a relationship. "Sex is about more than erections," says psychologist Eileen Palace, Ph.D., director of the Center for Sexual Health in New Orleans. "Viagra doesn't address the way couples feel about each other." And if a man isn't attracted to his partner, he still may not be able to get an erection with Viagra.

Even if the sparks are flying, Viagra can interfere with spontaneity: The drug must be taken 30 minutes to an hour before intercourse. What's more it doesn't come cheap: Viagra costs about $10 per tablet. "Sometimes I'll take a pill, and Cheryl will change her mind about sex," says Alfred Pariser. "Or we'll fall asleep."

Still, when used properly, Viagra can be liberating. For the Parisers, the drug has been a gift. Says Alfred: "Viagra helped us recapture the intimacy we'd lost."

THE SECRET LIVES OF WIVES

By Lorraine Ali and Lisa Miller

Why they stray: With the work place and the Internet, overscheduled lives and inattentive husbands—it's no wonder more American women are looking for comfort in the arms of another man

WHEN GROUPS OF WOMEN get together, especially if they're mothers and have been married for more than six or seven years, and especially if there's alcohol involved, the conversation is usually the same. They talk about the kids and work—how stressed they are, how busy and bone tired. They gripe about their husbands and, if they're being perfectly honest and the wine kicks in, they talk about the disappointments in their marriages. Not long ago, over lunch in Los Angeles, this conversation took a surprising turn, when Erin, who is in her early 40s and has been married for more than a decade, spilled it. She was seeing someone else. Actually, more than one person. It started with an old friend, whom she began meeting every several months for long dinners and some heavy petting. Then she began giving herself permission to flirt with, kiss—well, actually, make out with—men she met on business trips. She understands it's a "Clintonian" distinction, but she won't have sex with anyone except her husband, whom she loves. But she also loves

the unexpected thrill of meeting someone new. "Do you remember?" She pauses. "I don't know how long you've been married, but do you remember the kiss that would just launch a thousand kisses?"

I DO, I DO
NOT EVERY BRIDE IS WILLING TO FORSAKE ALL OTHERS

Erin started seeing other men when she went back to work after her youngest child entered preschool. All of a sudden she was *out there*. Wearing great clothes, meeting new people, alive for the first time in years to the idea that she was interesting beyond her contributions at PTA meetings. Veronica, on the other hand, fell in love with a man who was not her husband while she was safely at home in the Dallas suburbs looking after her two children. Hers is the more familiar story: isolated and lonely, married to an airline pilot, Veronica, now 35, took up with a wealthy businessman she met at a Dallas nightclub. Her lover gave her everything her husband didn't:

compliments, Tiffany jewelry, flowers and love notes. It was, in fact, the flowers that did her in. Veronica's lover sent a bouquet to her home one afternoon, her husband answered the door and, in one made-for-Hollywood moment, the marriage was over. Now remarried (to a new man), Veronica says she and her friends half-jokingly talk about starting a Web site for married women who want to date. "I think there might be a market in it," she says. There is. Wives who want extramarital sex—or are just dreaming about it—can find what they seek on Yahoo!, MSN or AOL.

BLIND EYE
FEW HUSBANDS SUSPECT THEIR WIVES CHEAT

Much has changed since Emma Bovary chose suicide with arsenic over living her life branded an adulteress—humiliated, impoverished and stripped of her romantic ideals. In the past, U.S. laws used to punish women who cheated; in a divorce, an unfaithful wife could lose everything, even the property she owned before marriage. Newer laws have been designed to protect these women. The reality is this: American women today have more opportunity to fool around than ever; when they do fool around, they're more likely to tell their friends about it, and those friends are more likely to lend them a sympathetic ear. They probably use technology to facilitate their affairs, and if they get caught, they're almost as likely to wind up in a wing chair in a marriage counselor's office as in divorce court. Finally, if they do separate from their husbands, women, especially if they're college educated, are better able to make a go of it—pay the bills, keep at least partial custody of the children, remarry if they want to—than their philandering foremothers. "It was just so ruinous for a woman to be caught in adultery in past times, you had to be really driven or motivated to do it," says Peter D. Kramer, clinical professor of psychiatry at Brown University and author of "Should You Leave?" "Now you can get away with it, there's a social role that fits you."

Just how many married women have had sex with people who are not their husbands? It's hard to say for sure, because people lie to pollsters when they talk about sex, and studies vary wildly. (Men, not surprisingly, amplify their sexual experience, while women diminish it.) Couples therapists estimate that among their clientele, the number is close to 30 to 40 percent, compared with 50 percent of men, and the gap is almost certainly closing. In 1991, the National Opinion Research Center at the University of Chicago asked married women if they'd ever had sex outside their marriage, and 10 percent said yes. When the same pollsters asked the same question in 2002, the "yes" responses rose to 15 percent, while the number of men stayed flat at about 22 percent. The best interpretation of the data: the cheating rate for women is approaching that of men, says Tom Smith, author of the NORC's reports

on sexual behavior. When Michele Weiner-Davis, a marriage counselor and founder of the Divorce Busting Center in Woodstock, Ill., started practicing 20 years ago, just 10 percent of the infidelity she knew of was committed by women. Now, she believes, it's closer to 50 percent. "Women have suddenly begun to give themselves the same permission to step over the boundary the way that men have."

A rise in female infidelity, though titillating, does not do much to clarify the paradoxes in American culture surrounding sex. Taboos about female sexuality are falling away; together, Dr. Phil and "Sex and the City" have made every imaginable sex act fodder for cocktail-party conversation. At the same time, Americans developed a lower tolerance for infidelity: 80 percent of Americans say infidelity is "always wrong," according to the NORC, up from 70 percent in 1970. Popular opinion is on to something: infidelity can be devastating. If discovered, it can upend a marriage and create chaos in a family. Nevertheless, in America, as in other parts of the world, a double standard continues to thrive: boys will be boys, but girls are supposed to be good. Even though women are narrowing the gap, men still do the bulk of the domestic damage. "Bill Clinton, who we're all loving on TV—he's a charmer. The poor, weak, wandering guy is kind of a cultural norm," says Elizabeth Berger, a psychiatrist in Elkins Park, Pa., and author of "Raising Children With Character." A weak or wandering mother is a scarier image, she adds.

What would she do without her cell phone or computer? 'I can't even imagine,' Amanda says.

Popular culture has always been full of unfaithful wives, but even today's fictional cheaters share something that sets them apart from the tragic Anna Karenina or the calculating Mrs. Robinson. Their actions may cause their lives to unravel, but the new philanderers aren't victims.

When, on the HBO series "The Sopranos," Carmela finally took a lover after putting up with her mob-boss husband's extracurricular antics for years, audiences cheered. (Her lover was a cad in the end, but the dalliance gave Carmela a secret source of strength.) Sarah, the heroine of this year's best-selling novel "Little Children," falls in love with a handsome stay-at-home dad she meets at the playground; the affair doesn't last, but it gives her the impetus she needs to leave her husband, a weaselly man with a fetish for the underpants of a swinger he met online. And with her role in the 2002 movie "Unfaithful," Diane Lane created an iconic new image of a sexually adventurous wife. Beautiful and well dressed, Connie Sumner has what looks like a perfect life, and she fools around not because she's miserable but simply because she can (a decision that soon makes her life a lot less perfect).

"Women always say 'thank you' for that role, and at first I wasn't sure how to take that," says Lane, who adds that the character was capable of far more denial than she could ever be. "I mean, she was cheating and lying. Then I realized it was because she wasn't a victim. She made a choice to have an affair. It's not something you often see."

Where do married women find their boyfriends? At work, mostly. Nearly 60 percent of American women work outside the home, up from about 40 percent in 1964. Quite simply, women intersect with more people during the day than they used to. They go to more meetings, take more business trips and, presumably, participate more in flirtatious water-cooler chatter. If infidelity is an odds game, then the odds are better now than they used to be that a woman will accidentally bump into someone during the workday who, at least momentarily, interests her more than her husband does. There's a more subtle point embedded in here as well: women and men bring their best selves to work, leaving their bad behavior and marital resentments at home with their dirty sweatpants. At work, "we dress nicely. We think before we speak. We're poised," says Elana Katz, a therapist in private practice and a divorce mediator at the Ackerman Institute for the Family in New York City. "And many people spend more time out in the world than with their families. I think sometimes people have the idea that [an affair] will protect the marriage." They get a self-esteem boost during work hours and don't rock the boat at home. "In some paradoxical sense this may be a respite, a little break from the marriage."

"I wasn't out there looking for someone else," says Jodie, 34, a marketing professional in Texas and mother of two. (NEWSWEEK talked at length to more than a dozen women who cheated, and none of them wanted her real name used.) Her continuing affair with a co-worker started innocently enough. She liked his company. "We would go to lunch together and gradually it started feeling like we were dating." At Christmas, Jodie asked her husband of 10 years to join her at the office party, and when he declined, the co-worker stepped in. "We just had so much fun together and we laughed together and it just grew and grew and grew until . . . he kissed me. And I loved it."

'He tells me my skin is soft,' says Marisol. 'I know it sounds stupid, but it makes me feel sexy again.'

It's not just opportunity that fuels the impulse to be unfaithful; it's money and power as well. American women are better educated than they've ever been. A quarter of them earn more money than their husbands. A paycheck and a 401(k) don't guarantee that a woman will stray, but if she does, they minimize the fallout both for her and for her children. The feminist Gloria Steinem once said, "Most women are one man away from welfare," but she recently amplified her views to NEWSWEEK: "Being able to support

oneself allows one to choose a marriage out of love and not just economic dependence. It also allows one to risk that marriage." In other words, as women grow more powerful, they're more likely to feel, as men traditionally have, that they deserve a little bit of nooky at the end (or in the middle) of a long, busy day.

And like their fathers before them, these powerful women are learning to savor the attentions of a companion who is physically attractive but not as rich, successful—or as old—as they are. In his practice in Palo Alto, Calif., family therapist Marty Klein sees a rise in sexual activity between middle-aged women and younger men. "Forty-year-old women have more of a sense of entitlement to their sexuality than they did before the 'Hite Report,' the feminist movement and 'Sex and the City'," he says. A story currently circulating in Manhattan underscores his point. It seems that a group of 6-year-old girls from an elite private school were at a birthday party, and the conversation turned to their mommies' trainers. As the proud mothers listened nearby, one youngster piped up: "My mommy has a trainer, and every time he comes over, they take a nap." The wicked laughter this story elicits illustrates at least what is dreamed of, if not actually consummated.

The road to infidelity is paved with unmet expectations about sex, love and marriage. A woman who is 40 today grew up during the permissive 1970s and went to college when the dangers of AIDS were just beginning to dawn. She was sexually experienced before she was married and waited five years longer than her mother to settle down. She lives in a culture that constantly flaunts the possibility of great sex and fitness well after menopause. "Great Lovers Are Made, Not Born!" read the ads for sex videos in her favorite magazines; "What if the only night sweats you had came from a good workout?" ask the ads for estrogen therapy.

COVER-UP
WORKING WOMEN SAY HIDING FLINGS IS A CINCH

At the same time, she's so busy she feels constantly out of breath. If she's a professional, she's working more hours than her counterpart of 20 years ago—and trying to rush home in time to give the baby a bath. If she's a stay-at-home mom, she's driving the kids to more classes, more games, more playdates than her mother did, not to mention trying to live up to society's demands of perfect-momhood: Buy organic! Be supportive, not permissive! Lose five pounds! Her husband isn't a bad guy, but he's busier than ever, too, working harder just to stay afloat. And (this is practically unmentionable) therapists say they're seeing more cases of depressed male libido. It turns out he's too tired and stressed to have sex. An affair is a logical outcome of this scenario, therapists say: women think they should be having great sex and romantic dates decades into their marriage, and at the same time, they're pragmatic enough to see how impossible that is. Couples begin to live parallel lives, instead of intersecting ones, and that's when the loneliness and resentment set in.

Marisol can't remember the last time her husband paid her a compliment. That's why the 39-year-old grandmother, who was pregnant and married at 15, looks forward to meeting with her boyfriend of five years during lunch breaks and after work. "There is so much passion between us," she says. "He tells me my skin is soft and that my hair smells good. I know it sounds stupid, but that stuff matters. It makes me feel sexy again."

Ironically, the realities of the overprogrammed life make it easier, not harder, to fool around. When days are planned to the minute, it's a cinch to pencil in a midday tryst—and remember to wear the lace-edged underwear—at least compared with trying to stay awake and in the mood through "Law & Order." And as any

WAYWARD WIVES 101

Throughout history, women, both real and imagined, have shown that when it comes to infidelity, it's not solely a man's world. Here's a crash course.

Bathsheba
CIRCA 100 B.C.
Spotted bathing by a voyeuristic King David, the married Bathsheba obliges his demands for a royal romp. Pregnant with David's child, Bathsheba stands by as he murders her husband; the child conceived with the king dies.

Guinevere
FIFTH OR SIXTH CENTURY
Though accounts of the myth vary, one fact is almost indisputable: Guinevere, betrothed to King Arthur, fell for Sir Lancelot. In some versions, their first kiss ignited their undying love. In others, they united during a rescue.

Catherine the Great
EIGHTEENTH CENTURY
She needed to produce an heir to the Russian throne but her husband (and cousin), Peter III, was impotent, sterile and mad. Somehow, though, she conceived five children.

Hester Prynne
'THE SCARLET LETTER' (1850)
Assuming her husband is lost at sea, Hester takes up with the town's Puritanical preacher. After giving birth to his child Pearl, Hester is forced to sew her guilt onto her garment.

Emma Bovary
'MADAM BOVARY' (1857)
The 19th century's material girl, Emma is more interested in couture and cash than in her husband. But the debts and suspicions mount, and rather than swallow her pride, she swallows arsenic.

Anna Karenina
'ANNA KARENINA' (1878)
Vronsky loves Anna. Anna loves Vronsky. Anna is married. What to do? She begins seeing Vronsky, and seeks divorce from her husband to no avail. Trapped, she throws herself under a train.

Ingrid Bergman
1949
The cold war started, but this Swedish star's affair with director Roberto Rossellini had Americans steaming mad. After leaving her family, she retreated into a seven-year acting hiatus.

Elizabeth Taylor
1963
Talk about a serial spouse. While filming the 1963 movie "Cleopatra," Taylor—then with hubby number four, Eddie Fisher—fell for her costar Richard Burton. She ran off with Burton soon after.

Mrs. Robinson
'THE GRADUATE' (1967)
A restless housewife, Mrs. Robinson (Anne Bancroft) seduces Ben (Dustin Hoffman) shortly after his college graduation. When he begins dating her daughter, the middle-aged ice queen exacts revenge by sabotaging their relationship.

Francesca Johnson
'THE BRIDGES OF MADISON COUNTY' (1995)
A lonely Iowa farm wife (Meryl Streep) plays tour guide to a rugged National Geographic photographer (Clint Eastwood). They begin looking at bridges but have eyes only for each other.

Camilla Parker Bowles
1994
Rumors of an illicit affair began to circulate as Prince Charles's highly publicized marriage to Diana became strained. Two weeks ago he added Camilla to his financial accounts.

Connie Sumner
'UNFAITHFUL' (2002)
Connie (Diane Lane) is a well-to-do Weschester mother and wife until she literally collides with a sensual, 28-year-old French bookseller on the street. The steamy affair leads to a murder of passion.

Carmela Soprano
'THE SOPRANOS' (2004)
Ever-faithful while husband Tony slept around, Carmela finally had sex with her son's guidance counselor this past season. A.J. wound up with a passing grade in English, and Carmela reunited with Tony.

---

guileless teenager knows, nothing obscures your whereabouts better than an Internet connection and a reliable cell phone. Amanda's husband has no idea she has six e-mail addresses, in addition to an account specifically for messages from her boyfriend Ron. Amanda, a customer-service rep in L.A., uses e-mail to flirt with Ron, then turns to her instant messenger or cell phone when it comes to setting up a rendezvous. "Text messaging is safer than e-mailing," says Amanda, 36, who's been married for eight years. What would she do without her mobile or computer? "No cell phone? I can't even imagine."

Along with its 4 million porn sites, the Internet has exploded with sites specifically for people who want to cheat on their spouses—sites like "Married and Flirting" at Yahoo, "a chat room dedicated to those who

are married but curious, bored or both!!" These sites contain all the predictable pornographic overtures, but also such poignant notes as this: "Ok, I know it is late almost 11:30 my time and I am still up on this pitiful Friday night. Hubby STILL at work."

Online romances have a special appeal for married women. For one thing, you don't have to leave the house. "You can come home from work, be exhausted, take a shower, have wet, dripping hair, have something fast to eat and then, if you're feeling lonely, you can go on the Internet," says Rona Subotnik, a marriage and family therapist in Palm Desert, Calif. On the Web, women can browse and flirt without being explicit about their intentions—if they even know what their intentions are. Clicking past porn, women

prefer to visit sites that dovetail with their interests, such as chess, bridge or knitting, explains Peggy Vaughan, author of "The Monogamy Myth" and host of dearpeggy.com, a Web site for people with unfaithful spouses. "They find somebody else who seems to think like they do, and then they gradually move from that to an instant message, and then they wake up one day and they cannot believe it happened to them," says Vaughan. Last year Vaughan did a survey of a thousand people who visited her Web site, and 70 percent of the respondents were women. Her results, though not scientific, are remarkable: 79 percent said they were not looking for love online. More than half said they met their online lover in person, and about half said the relationship culminated in sex. Sixty percent said their spouses had no idea.

John LaSage was shocked to come home one day and find his wife of 24 years had disappeared. No note, no phone call, nothing. He'd bought her a computer four months previously, he says, and he knew something was wrong: she'd stay up until 3 or 4 a.m., browsing online. She told him she was doing research for a romance novel she was writing, he says, and after her disappearance, he hacked into the computer to investigate. "She had set up a chat room that was called . . . gosh . . . 'Smooth Legs.' And so guys would come in there and flirt with her. I have transcripts. I can't tell you how excruciating it was to read the e-mails from people supposedly speaking with my wife, but she wasn't talking like my wife. That was just weird." Two weeks later he discovered she had left the country, he says. "I wasn't the perfect husband. I would have done a lot of things differently, but I never got the chance," says LaSage, who has since founded an online support group (chatcheaters.com) for people with spouses who stray.

In 1643 Mary Latham, who was 18 years old and married, was hanged in Massachusetts with her lover James Britton. Since then, adultery has been a crime in many states. A woman accused of adultery could, in divorce court, lose her home, her income and her children. All that changed in the 1970s, when most states adopted "no fault" and "equitable distribution" divorce laws, in which nearly all the assets accrued to either partner during the marriage belong to the marriage and, in a divorce settlement, are split evenly. And unless a woman (or man) has been flagrantly or inappropriately sexual in front of the children, or has, in the frenzy of an affair, neglected them, infidelity does not legally affect settlements or custody. In researching her book "The Price of Motherhood," journalist Ann Crittenden found, however, that an implicit bias against female adultery still prevails in the country's pre-

dominantly male courtrooms—and that when it came to settlements, that bias was costly to women. "There may be no fault as grounds, but fault has not left the system," she says.

Unearthing infidelity is shattering to any spouse. Men can be as traumatized as women by such a revelation; they can also be more surprised. David, 39, a government worker in Washington, D.C., discovered his wife was cheating the day she told him she wanted a divorce. "Never in a million years did I think it was possible." He found out later that his wife had started seeing someone at work, someone David knew fairly well because the two couples often met socially. Once the reality set in, he couldn't get images of his wife and the other man out of his head. Beset by nightmares, he started taking antidepressants. "I felt shame for what had happened, like I couldn't keep a person happy enough to stay with me." Now, eight months later, David is beginning to date again. His divorce should be final this month.

Just over half of all cases of female infidelity end in divorce, says Susan Shapiro Barash, a professor of gender studies at Marymount Manhattan College and author of "A Passion for More: Wives Reveal the Affairs That Make or Break Their Marriages." But that number may be shrinking. The conservative-marriage movement, as well as recent books like Judith Wallerstein's "The Unexpected Legacy of Divorce," have created a backlash against separation and raised consciousness about the seriousness of its effects on children. Therapists who see the overworked professional set say they've noticed an interesting trend: people who have children and marry late in life tend to be less interested in cheating than their contemporaries who married earlier—and more willing to work it out when a woman (or man) does stray. These women have spent a lot of time alone, and they're wise to the benefits of companionship. They've also waited a

long time to have families and have a realistic sense of what's at stake. "I think people try to stay together," says Alvin Mesnikoff, a psychiatrist with a private practice in New York. In spite of the temptations, "women want a relationship, and they're willing to work hard at it."

Divorce or no, how do responsible parents protect the hearts of their children when they're in the midst of heartbreak themselves? Therapists say kids don't care whether it's Mom or Dad who fools around—all they care about is knowing they're safe and that their lives will remain stable. It's difficult, but parents who are dealing with a revelation of infidelity need to protect young kids from the facts of the case, as well as from their own anger. "There are very few things I will be absolute about, and this is one of them," says Katz. "Everything [children] ask for is not something they want. And if they ask, you should say, 'Yes, you're right. Things are tense around here, but this is between Mom and me'."

Explaining infidelity to older children is somewhat more complicated. If a 15-year-old turns to his mom and asks, "How long has this been going on?" a truthful answer may be in order, says Berger, the Elkins Park psychiatrist. And if he asks, "How could this happen?" "It may be reasonable for Mom to say, 'You don't understand, dear, that Dad has been cheating on me'," Berger says. Sometimes correcting the record is all right. "There's nothing gained by one parent being a martyr to the other parent's mistreatment." What parents need to avoid at all costs is to wrap the children into the drama by treating them as confidants.

Nadine grew up in a small, Midwestern town, and when she was 13 years old, her mother cheated on her father, moved to a town two hours away and married the other man. "There weren't any fights, nothing crazy," says Nadine, who at 28 lives in a big city and works in finance. "We sat down at Christmas. We discussed that Mother was leaving; it was nothing we had done." She and her siblings continued to live with her father; her mother went to school conferences and games as she had always done. Her parents remained, as she puts it, "best friends." But Nadine's teenage years were difficult. She never warmed up to the new man. She felt abandoned.

'Do you remember that kiss?' Erin asks. 'The kiss that would just launch a thousand kisses?'

In retrospect, Nadine understands what pushed her mother to be unfaithful. Beautiful and intelligent, her mother was stifled by her life's low horizons, and her father, a stand-up guy, was probably a little bit boring. The new man promised travel, wealth and adventure; her father was the kind of guy who'd say, "Why go around the world? You'll get plane-sick." And although she and her mother have made a kind of peace—"I got tired of making her

cry," she says—she thinks the affair eroded any kind of trust she has in marriage or love. She can't stay in long relationships. "Ever since I could date, all I could think was, 'I will never, ever, ever do what my mom did.' I will never have a man take care of me. I have been called an ice princess in the past. I feel in some way my mom sold out and kind of fell for something."

Who said being married and raising kids was easy? The good news is that the wounds inflicted on a family by a woman's infidelity are not always critical. Therapists say couples often can—and do—get past it. Sometimes the husband sees it as a wake-up call and renews his efforts to be attentive. Sometimes, especially if neither party is too angry, too defensive or too far out the door, the couple can use it as an opportunity to air grievances and soothe old hurts. Sometimes the woman sees the dalliance for what it is, a fling,

and takes it with her to the grave. In her study of good marriages, Wallerstein found that an affair did not necessarily damage family life—especially if it fell into the category of a "one-night stand." "In good marriages this doesn't dominate the landscape, and the kids don't know," she says. She remembers interviewing a 30-year-old man, who said that when he was 9, his mother had an affair, but his father assured him that they would stay together. The man said: "I learned from my father that anything worth having is worth fighting for." When lunch is over and the wine wears off, most women will admit that if they were the prize in a fantasy duel between an imperfect but loving husband and a handsome stranger, they'd root for the husband every time.

With Vanessa Juarez, Holly Peterson, Karen Springen, Claire Sulmers, William Lee Adams, and Raina Kelley.

UNIT 4

Reproduction

Unit Selections

Key Points to Consider

- In your opinion, what are the most important characteristics of a contraceptive? Why?

- Under what circumstances might a person not use contraception and risk an unintentional pregnancy?

- Should contraceptive responsibilities be assigned to one gender or be shared between men and women? Defend your answer.

- In the situation of an unplanned pregnancy, what should be the role of the female and the male with respect to decision making? What if they do not agree?

- If you discovered you or your partner were infertile, what technologies or options would you consider or pursue? Are there any you would not, and if so, why?

- Have you found a fairly comfortable way to talk about contraception and/or pregnancy risk and prevention with your partner? If so, what is it? If not, what do you do?

 **Links: www.dushkin.com/online/**
These sites are annotated in the World Wide Web pages.

Ask NOAH About Pregnancy: Fertility & Infertility
http://www.noah-health.org/english/pregnancy/fertility.html
Childbirth.Org
http://www.childbirth.org
Planned Parenthood
http://www.plannedparenthood.org

While human reproduction is as old as humanity, many aspects of it are changing in today's society. Not only have new technologies of conception and childbirth affected the *how* of reproduction, but personal, social, and cultural forces have also affected the *who,* the *when,* and the *when not.* Abortion remains a fiercely debated topic as well as the legislative efforts for and against it abound. Unplanned pregnancies and parenthood in the United States and worldwide continue to present significant, sometimes devastating, problems for parents, children, families, and society.

In light of the change of attitude toward sex for pleasure, birth control has become a matter of prime importance. Even in our age of sexual enlightenment, some individuals, possibly in the height of passion, fail to correlate "having sex" with pregnancy. In addition, even in our age of astounding medical technology, there is no 100 percent effective, safe, or aesthetically acceptable method of birth control. Before sex can become safe as well as enjoyable, people must receive thorough and accurate information regarding conception and contraception, birth, and birth control. However, we have learned that information about, or even access to, birth control is not enough. We still have some distance to go to make every child one who is planned for and wanted.

Despite the relative simplicity of the above assertion, abortion and birth control remain emotionally charged issues in American society. While opinion surveys indicate that most of the public supports family planning and abortion, at least in some circumstances, there are certain individuals and groups strongly opposed to some forms of birth control and to abortion. Voices for and against birth control and abortion—traditional and newer methods—remain passionate, and face-offs from academic debate to protests and violence continue. Supreme Court, legislative, and private efforts to restrict the right or access to abortion or the availability of birth control methods continue while others have mandated freer access to abortion and reproductive choice and have restricted the activities of anti-abortion demonstrators. Voices on both sides are raised in emotional and political debate between "we must never go back to the old days" (of illegal and unsafe back-alley abortions) and "the baby has no choice."

The nature, and scope of the questions raised about the new technologies of reproduction from contraception and abortion through treatments for infertility, known as "assisted reproduction," to the possibility of human cloning, have become very complex and far-reaching. Medical, religious, political, and legal experts, as well as concerned everyday people, are debating basic definitions of human life as well as the rights and responsibilities not only of men, women, and society, but of eggs, sperm donors, and surrogates. The very foundations of our pluralistic society are being challenged. We will have to await the outcome.

Access Denied

Growing numbers of doctors and pharmacists across the country are refusing to prescribe or dispense birth control pills. Here's why

By Caroline Bollinger

In April, Julee Lacey, 33, a Fort Worth, TX, mother of two, went to her local CVS drugstore for a last-minute Pill refill. She had been getting her prescription filled there for a year, so she was astonished when the pharmacist told her, "I personally don't believe in birth control and therefore I'm not going to fill your prescription." Lacey, an elementary school teacher, was shocked. "The pharmacist had no idea why I was even taking the Pill. I might have needed it for a medical condition."

Melissa Kelley,* 35, was just as stunned when her gynecologist told her she would not renew her prescription for birth control pills last fall.

"She told me she couldn't in good faith prescribe the Pill anymore," says Kelley, who lives with her husband and son in Allentown, PA. Then the gynecologist told Kelley she wouldn't be able to get a new prescription from her family doctor, either. "She said my primary care physician was the one who helped her make the decision."

Lacey's pharmacist and Kelley's doctors are among hundreds, perhaps thousands, of physicians and pharmacists who now adhere to a controversial belief that birth control pills and other forms of hormonal contraception-including the skin patch, the vaginal ring, and progesterone injections cause tens of thousands of "silent" abortions every year. Consequently, they are refusing to prescribe or dispense them.

Scenarios like these—virtually unheard-of 10 years ago—are happening with increasing frequency. However, until this spring, the issue received little attention outside the antiabortion community. It wasn't high on the agendas of reproductive rights advocates, who have been preoccupied with defending abortion rights and emergency contraception. But when Lacey's story was picked up by a Texas

TV station and later made the national news, Planned Parenthood Federation of America and others took notice.

Limiting access to the Pill, these groups now say, threatens a basic aspect of women's health care. An estimated 12 million American women use hormonal contraceptives, the most popular form of birth control in the United States after sterilization. The Pill is also widely prescribed by gynecologists and family doctors for other uses, such as clearing up acne, shrinking fibroids, reducing ovarian cancer risk, and controlling endometriosis.

"Where will this all stop?" asks Lacey. "And what if these pharmacists decide they suddenly don't believe in a new lifesaving medicine? I don't think pharmacists should be in a position to decide these things."

A Matter of Belief

The members of the antiabortion group Pharmacists for Life International say they have every right to make that kind of decision. "Our job is to enhance life," explains the organization's president, pharmacist Karen Brauer, RPh, who first refused to fill prescriptions for some types of birth control pills in 1989. "We shouldn't have to dispense a medication that we think takes lives."

Anti-Pill doctors and pharmacists base their stand on the fact that the Pill isn't perfect: Although it is designed to suppress ovulation and prevent fertilization, both can—and do—occur in rare cases. About 1 woman in every 1,000 who take the Pill exactly as directed becomes pregnant in a given year. But while mainstream experts say ovulation happens only 2 to 3% of the time and fertilization is rare, anti-Pill groups claim both happen frequently. They say most of these fertilized eggs—in their view, nascent human lives—are unable to attach to the hormonally altered uterine lining. Instead of implanting and growing, they slough

---

*Not her real name

The Post-Fertilization Effect: Fact or Fiction?

Manufactures of oral contraceptives have long claimed that the Pill provides three lines of defense against pregnancy: It prevents ovulation (most of the time), blocks sperm by thickening cervical mucus, and, should all else fail, theoretically reduces the chances that a fertilized egg will implant in the uterus by hormonally altering the uterine lining.

But does this so-called post-fertilization effect really happen? Truth is, nobody knows. "There is no evidence that the Pill's effect on the uterine lining interferes with implantation or has a post-fertilization effect," says contraception expert Felicia Stewart, MD, codirector of the Center for Reproductive Health Research and Policy in San Francisco. "Documenting it would be a very difficult research task."

David Grimes, MD, a clinical professor in obstetrics and gynecology at the University of North Carolina School of Medicine, says the Pill and other hormonal contraceptives work primarily by preventing ovulation.

Consensus comes from a surprising source. "The post-fertilization effect was purely a speculation that became truth by repetition," says Joe DeCook, MD, a retired OB/GYN and vice president of the American Association of Pro-Life Obstetrics and Gynecologists. "In our group the feelings are split. We say it should be each doctor's own decision, because there is no proof."

Further clouding the issue is the fact that even among women trying to become pregnant—women obviously not taking the Pill—fertilized eggs fail to implant 40 to 60% of the time. They're eliminated when a woman menstruates.

off. This theoretical action, which scientists can't confirm, is called the post-fertilization effect.

At the heart of the debate between anti-Pill forces and mainstream medicine lies a profound difference of opinion about when pregnancy *and* life begin. The long-standing medical definition of pregnancy, held by the American College of Obstetricians and Gynecologists, is that it starts not when an egg is fertilized, but when the fertilized egg implants in the uterine lining.

This distinction is practical: A pregnancy test won't show a positive result before implantation. "It can't be an abortion before there is a pregnancy," points out David Grimes, MD, a clinical professor in obstetrics and gynecology at the University of North Carolina School of Medicine and one of the country's leading contraception experts.

But anti-Pill doctors and pharmacists say life begins sooner, at fertilization. Sloughing off a fertilized egg, in their view, is a "chemical abortion."

> "Imagine a pharmacist asking a customer whether his Viagra prescription is to enhance sexual performance in his marriage or in an extramarital affair"

"How many women know that if they become pregnant after breakthrough ovulation, these 'contraceptives' will almost always kill any son or daughter they've conceived?" asks the anti-Pill organization Pro-Life America on the group's Web site, ProLife.com.

Surprisingly, there's no science to back the theory that birth control pills really do discourage implantation. This claim, made by contraceptive manufacturers for decades, has never been proven, Grimes says. Even the American Association of Pro-Life Obstetricians and Gynecologists agrees that it's just speculation. {See "The Post-Fertilization Effect: Fact or Fiction?")

Under the Radar

In the past decade or so, the "hormonal birth control equals abortion" view has quietly grown roots in the antiabortion underground. It's spread from doctor to doctor, through local newsletters, in books with titles such as *Does the Birth Control Pill Cause Abortions?* (written by Randy Alcorn, an Oregon based antiabortion pastor and author}, and through lobbying groups that have encouraged lawmakers in Arkansas, South Dakota, and most recently Mississippi to enact "conscience clauses." These legislative provisions protect health care professionals—in this case, pharmacists—who refuse to provide services they oppose on moral, ethical, or legal grounds. At press time, similar legislation had been introduced in 11 more states.

An Internet search turns up thousands of Web sites containing articles with titles such as "The Pill Kills Babies," "Are Contraception and Abortion Siamese Twins?" and "The Dirty Little Secrets about the Birth Control Pill." Hundreds of physicians and pharmacists have pledged not to provide hormonal birth control. Among them: 450 doctors affiliated with the Dayton, OH-based natural family planning group One More Soul; some members of the 2,500 doctors in the Holland, MI-based American Association of Pro-Life Obstetricians and Gynecologists; and a growing number of the 1,500-member Web-based Pharmacists for Life International, says Brauer.

Not even anti-Pill groups know how many doctors and druggists are involved. And while the total is still a small percentage of the nation's 117,500 family physicians and OB/GYNs and 173,000 pharmacists, they are making their presence felt in women's lives and among law and policy makers on both the state and national levels. Their influence is far-reaching and disproportionate to their size—a quiet version of the public shock waves produced by the nation's relatively small number of antiabortion activists.

"Refusing women access to the Pill is a very disturbing trend," says Gloria Feldt, president of Planned Parenthood Federation of America. "The war on choice is not just about abortion anymore. It's about our right to birth control."

There's no science to back the theory that birth control pills really do discourage implantation

Morality versus Public Health

Anti-Pill doctors and pharmacists across the country say the issue isn't about a woman's right to hormonal contraceptives, but about their right to act according to their beliefs. "I feel chemical contraceptives have the potential to harm an embryo," says Mary Martin, MD, an OB/GYN in private practice in Midwest City, OK. "And I decided, based on moral and ethical grounds, that I simply could no longer prescribe them." She stopped writing prescriptions for hormonal birth control in 1999. OB/GYN Arthur Stehly, of Escondido, CA, who hasn't prescribed contraceptives since 1989, says he feels the same way: "I function better and I sleep better at night knowing I'm not giving the Pill."

But at what point does personal belief undermine public health? If more women lose access to hormonal contraceptives, rates of unintended pregnancy and abortions will rise in the United States, predicts Beth Jordan, MD, medical director of the Washington, DC-based Feminist Majority Foundation, an advocacy and research group.

What's more, oral contraceptives aren't only used to prevent pregnancy. The Pill may cut the risk of ovarian cancer by up to 80% and is used by women at high genetic risk for this hard-to-detect and usually fatal cancer. "There are easily more than 20 noncontraceptive uses for the Pill in common practice," says Giovannina Anthony, MD, an attending physician of obstetrics and gynecology at Beth Israel Medical Center in New York City. "This drug saves women from surgery for gynecological conditions like endometriosis, fibroids, and severe bleeding and pain."

Most women's doctors agree that contraceptives are an important tool of good medical care. "I have a hard time with people who market themselves as women's health care physicians but who won't prescribe such a basic part of women's health care," says Anne Drapkin Lyerly, MD, a reproductive rights ethicist and an assistant professor of obstetrics and gynecology at Duke University Medical Center. "We're seeing a growing trend among pharmacists and medical practitioners who consider it acceptable to impose their morality on women's bodies. I don't think moral aspects should be a concern. Imagine a pharmacist asking a customer whether his Viagra prescription is to enhance sexual performance in his marriage or in an extramarital affair. Never!"

Katie Williams's Story

Last winter, 24-year-old Katie Williams encountered a doctor who refused to give her a prescription for the Pill, even though she'd already been taking it for 5 years—originally to relieve extremely painful menstrual cramps. Williams, who had just moved to Milwaukee for a job with an insurance company, realized she was nearly out of Pills. Her roommate recommended the physician who had written a Pill prescription for her a year before: Cynthia Jones-Nosacek, MD, a board certified family doctor with St. Mary's Medical Clinic, a Catholic medical center in Milwaukee. Williams made the appointment, explaining she needed a routine annual exam and a new prescription.

But when she arrived at the office, recalls Williams, "the doctor's assistant told me 'the doctor doesn't write prescriptions for the Pill.' I was totally floored. I just stared at her."

Williams opted to take her chances and see the doctor anyway, thinking the assistant must have been confused. After the doctor finished her exam, Williams asked for her script, explaining she'd been taking the Pill for several years. "The doctor told me she doesn't believe in oral contraceptives and does believe in natural family planning," Williams claims. "I told her 'that's ridiculous.'" Angry, Williams stormed out of the doctor's office.

In an interview, Jones-Nosacek, who has been in practice for 21 years, says she stopped prescribing the Pill after discovering a paper written by Salt Lake City family doctor Joseph B. Stanford, MD, an assistant professor of family and preventive medicine at the University of Utah and a recent Bush appointee to the FDA's Reproductive Health Drugs Advisory Committee. "The paper talked about the Pill's post-fertilization effect," says Jones-Nosacek. "After reading it and several other books and papers, I realized I could no longer justify prescribing the Pill."

The Debate over Emergency Contraception

Taken within 72 hours of unprotected intercourse, emergency contraception (EC)—pills containing high doses of estrogen and progestin, the same hormones found in some birth control pills—is 89% effective in preventing pregnancy. Unlike RU-486 (mifepristone) and surgical abortions, EC doesn't work once a woman is pregnant. But many antiabortion groups maintain EC is akin to abortion because it could prevent an egg from implanting. Many pharmacies nationwide, including Wal-Mart, are refusing to dispense it for that reason.

In December 2003, two FDA advisory committees recommended that an emergency contraceptive called Plan B be sold without a prescription, citing scientific evidence that EC is "safer than aspirin." But in May, the FDA declined to give the drug over-the-counter status, saying that teens younger than 16 wouldn't be able to understand the drug's directions. Women's rights groups say the FDA bowed to political pressure from social conservatives.

"We fervently hope that this shameful episode in FDA history will pass and that respect for scientific evidence will prevail once again at the FDA," says Vivian Dickerson, MD, president of the American College of Obstetricians and Gynecologists.

Abortion rights groups claim that EC has the potential to prevent 800,000 abortions each year.

Although Jones-Nosacek says she may have lost patients over her stand, she thinks most are happy to hear her opinion. "I think most women feel life begins at fertilization," she says. "When they find out the Pill has a potential post-fertilization effect, they're surprised, and some rethink their decision."

As for Williams, she got her prescription that day. Desperate—new to her job, she couldn't afford to take off another day without pay—she asked for help from an employee in Jones-Nosacek's office, who told her there was an OB/GYN in the same building. Williams went there directly and asked one of the doctor's assistants to relay her story to the gynecologist. This new doctor wrote her a prescription, no questions asked. "The doctor's assistant was shocked," says Williams. "She couldn't believe any doctor would refuse to give the Pill to somebody who had already been taking it successfully."

Friends in High Places

Planned Parenthood's Feldt believes anti-Pill groups, like the larger antiabortion movement that spawned them, have been emboldened by the Bush administration's antiabortion policies and appointees. "Pro-life groups know they have friends in high places," she says. In his first budget to Congress, President Bush stripped out a provision that required insurance companies participating in the Federal Employees Health Benefits Program to cover contraceptives. He has also withheld funding for international family planning; signed the Partial-Birth Abortion Ban Act of 2003, which critics say could result in making even second-trimester abortions illegal; and signed the Unborn Victims of Violence Act, which gives a fertilized egg, embryo, or fetus separate legal status if harmed during a violent crime. (Abortion rights groups say that giving a fetus separate legal rights from the pregnant woman opens the door to prosecuting anyone involved in an abortion.)

> ## "The vast majority of people in this country believe access to birth control is a basic right"

Bush also appointed three antiabortion doctors to the FDA Reproductive Health Drugs Advisory Committee: W. David Hager, MD, Susan Crockett, MD, and Stanford. When their committee and the FDA's Nonprescription Drugs Advisory Committee met jointly last December, the group voted 23 to 4 in favor of giving over-the-counter status to emergency contraceptives. Dissenters included Hager, Crockett, and Stanford. In May, the FDA decided not to grant the drug OTC status. (See "The Debate over Emergency Contraception.")

While Hager and Crockett have gone on record saying they do not believe standard birth control pills cause abor-

---

> ### What's Natural Family Planning?
>
> The natural family planning method (NFP) advocated by Milwaukee physician Cynthia Jones-Nosacek, MD, and other anti-Pill doctors involves avoiding intercourse during the most fertile days of a woman's cycle. Success depends on accurately pinpointing those days by using one or more techniques: tracking changes in cervical mucus, charting the rise and fall in body temperature, using a fertility monitor, and/or relying on the rhythm method, in which a woman and her partner don't have intercourse on certain days in the middle of her cycle. With typical use, the failure rate for NFP can be as high as 25%; for the pill, it's 6 to 8%.

tions, their colleague Stanford says he has never prescribed them. "I found out in medical school that they may prevent fertilized eggs from implanting, and I decided then that I wasn't ever going to prescribe them," he says. A paper of Stanford's, published in the February 2000 issue of *Archives of Family Medicine*, in which he discusses the post-fertilization effect of the Pill, is often cited by anti-Pill groups.

Federal and state legislators are quietly adopting similar views. US Senator Rick Santorum (R-PA), for example, does not support use of the Pill to prevent pregnancy, his staffers told *Prevention*. In March 2003, during a debate on the Senate floor that touched on emergency contraception, Santorum said, "I will not be supportive of covering medications that would lead to a fertilized egg not [being] implanted in the uterus. I believe life begins at conception. I would not support drugs that would prevent a conceived embryo [from being] implanted."

Problems at the Drugstore

Though three states have conscience clauses for pharmacists, there is no such legal provision in Texas, where the CVS druggist refused to fill Julee Lacey's prescription.

The night it happened, Lacey says, she was shocked and responded, "Are you sure? I've had this filled here many times before." But the pharmacist was emphatic. "I just couldn't believe what I was hearing," recalls Lacey. "It was a school night, and I knew I had to put my kids to bed and get organized for work the next morning. I didn't want to run all over town for my Pills." Lacey and her husband complained to the assistant store manager that night and the district manager the next day. Finally, the pharmacy supervisor called and said he would have Lacey's prescription delivered that day. "He apologized and said he was unaware of the pharmacist's moral objections to the Pill. Apparently it was a new belief," says Lacey. (A CVS corporate spokesperson contacted by *Prevention* confirmed Lacey's story. None of the employees has ever been named.)

Pharmacists in other states have refused as well. In 2002, a Kmart pharmacist in Stout, WI, allegedly denied Pills to a student from the local campus of the University of Wisconsin. The state department of regulation and licensing filed a complaint against the pharmacist; at press time a hearing on the matter had not yet taken place.

In 1996, Brauer says, she was fired from a Kmart pharmacy in Delhi, OH, after she refused to sign an agreement to dispense all lawfully prescribed medications regardless of her feelings or beliefs. (She filed suit against Kmart, but since the discount chain is in bankruptcy proceedings, it has never been settled.) "We've known for a long time that birth control pills are abortifacients," she says. "Now it's finally catching on."

Public Opinion

While abortion continues to be a divisive public issue, contraception is not. In fact, 95% of American women use some form of birth control during their childbearing years.

This is no silent majority. When a woman is denied the Pill and the incident becomes public, it triggers a loud response. Case in point: After Lacey's story appeared in the *Dallas Morning News*, there was an enormous outpouring of letters from readers appalled by the pharmacist's actions. "This was a huge issue in our area, and we're a conservative community," says Emily Snooks, director of media relations and communications at Planned Parenthood of North Texas. "People here are still talking about it, simply because the vast majority of people in this country believe access to birth control is a basic right."

But what will you do if, like Kelley, Williams, and Lacey, you encounter a doctor who tells you no or a pharmacist who won't honor your prescription? "If your gynecologist won't prescribe the Pill, find a new doctor—and tell all your friends what has occurred," says Vanessa Cullins, vice president for medical affairs, Planned Parenthood Federation of America in New York City. The same goes for pharmacists who refuse to fill your prescription. The best defense against this grassroots movement, Cullins notes, is another one—in opposition.

Caroline Bollinger is *Prevention*'s fitness editor.

What's New in Contraception?

UNDERSTANDING THE OPTIONS

Kristen Kennedy, Ph.D., and Paul Insel, Ph.D.

SINCE THE FOURTH CENTURY B.C., HUMANS HAVE USED anything from crocodile dung to lemon juice to seaweeds—to suspend the unwanted union of sperm and egg. While we've certainly come a long way since the days of lemon juice, the search for the ideal contraceptive continues—and it is, indeed, a much needed exploration. Consider that 50% of all pregnancies are unplanned, and that the U.S. boasts one of the highest teen pregnancies rates of all industrialized nations. These facts alone point to some problems with our current options for and the effectiveness of birth control methods, not to mention the lack of reliable, comprehensive information available to people looking for answers. Add to this the many unreliable representations of sexuality and sexual responsibility broadcast in popular culture as well as our general difficulty discussing sexual matters in a frank and honest way, and the need for consistent and careful information about birth control is clear.

The advent of HIV and AIDS in both the cultural and medical worlds opened some dialogue about—among many other things—the limits of contraceptives that do not protect against STDs as well as the need for ones that do. However, confusion still surrounds newer methods, how they work, and how effective they really are. In addition, the recent FDA approval of the emergency contraceptive Preven has raised questions about how this method differs from RU-486, which has also received tentative approval in the U.S. In response, we want to report on some of the newer methods available, how they work, and their effectiveness. Of course, any discussion of contraception can only be partial when it excludes the parties who are considering their options. Ultimately, you have to decide which choices are best for you, your body, your wallet, and your values.

With an estimated 925,000 daily occurrences of curable STD transmission and 550,000 daily pregnancies worldwide, a con-traceptive that offers protection against both STDs and pregnancy would be optimal. At the moment, the most effective option to prevent STDs is still the latex male condom, but even this method doesn't protect against everything. Condoms must be applied before sexual intercourse occurs and only act as a barrier over the areas the condom covers. Norplant implants, male sterilization or vasectomy, and Depo-Provera injections are the three leading, and most reliable, ways to prevent pregnancy. Any of these methods in combination with condom use are the best ways to prevent pregnancy as well as the transmission of STDs. What's interesting, however, about hormonal therapies—therapies that use hormones to suppress ovulation—like Norplant and Depo-Provera—is that while they are the most effective at preventing pregnancy, less than 2% of women worldwide use them.

Consider that 50% of all pregnancies are unplanned, and that the U.S. boasts one of the highest teen pregnancy rates of all industrialized nations.

The most widely used hormonal method is, of course, the oral contraceptive or the pill. The pill works quite effectively to prevent pregnancy if it's taken properly: that's every day, at the same time. It suppresses ovulation by mimicking the hormonal behavior of pregnancy. During pregnancy, the body secretes progesterone and estrogen in amounts high enough to prevent pregnancy. The pill imitates this hormonal effect. Fertility is not affected by the pill either. Its health benefits include a decrease in benign breast disease, iron-deficiency anemia, PID or pelvic inflammatory disease, ectopic pregnancy, endometrial cancer, and ovarian cancer. For healthy, young, non-smoking women, the pill does not present any higher risk of stroke or heart attack.

The Norplant Implant and Depo-Provera

MANY OF US KNOW VERY LITTLE ABOUT THESE OTHER, LESS popular hormonal methods. We might hear about them in magazines or on the news, but have little direct experience with the method and how it works. Take, for example, the Norplant implant, which looks a little bit like an acupuncture kit. Norplant implant is made up of six flexible, match-stick-sized capsules, each containing progestin, a synthetic progesterone, which is released in steady doses for up to 5 years. The capsules are placed under the skin, usually on the inside of a woman's upper arm. The insertion procedure takes about 15 minutes under a local anesthetic and requires only a small incision. Similar to the birth control pill, Norplant works by inhibiting ovulation. Unlike the pill, however, Norplant does not use estrogens to do so. Its other contraceptive effects include thickening of the cervical mucus, which inhibits the movement of sperm, and protecting against pelvic inflammatory disease.

Like Norplant, Depo-Provera works by releasing a steady dose of progestin which prevents ovulation. Unlike Norplant, Depo-Provera injections are given every 12 weeks, rather than a one-time insertion. None of the hormonal methods alone protect against STD and HIV infection and both Depo-Provera and Norplant can have similar side effects: irregular menstrual periods, headaches, weight gain, breast tenderness, and acne, not unlike those side effects associated with oral contraceptives. Norplant, in particular, has also received some negative press since lawsuits claimed the manufacturer did not disclose difficulties with capsule removal and warnings about side effects. Nevertheless, for women who are not able to take oral contraceptives—and the estrogen that comes with them—injection and implant methods may be viable options.

Preven Emergency Contraception

DERIVED FROM THE BIRTH CONTROL PILL, THE PREVEN Emergency Contraception Kit was approved by the FDA in 1998 for use as emergency contraception. The Kit contains four pills and a pregnancy test. If a woman fears she might be pregnant shortly after unprotected sex, say when a birth control method has failed, she takes two of the pills within 72 hours of last intercourse. The second two pills follow 12 hours later. Preven works just like the birth control pill by preventing ovulation, and a doctor must prescribe it. Side effects include nausea, vomiting, and breast tenderness. While there is some debate about how emergency contraception works and how it differs from an abortifacient, Preven is not the same as the so-

called "abortion pill." Preven can only prevent pregnancy, it is not designed to end one.

RU-486

THE LATEST NEWS ON THE LEGALITY AND APPROVAL OF RU-486 is that the FDA has given tentative approval for the drug to be marketed in the U.S. However, legal, political, and manufacturing difficulties have delayed its introduction. RU-486 or Mifepristone works in two doses. The first works by preventing uterine absorption of progesterone, which in turn causes the uterine lining and any fertilized egg to shed. Progesterone is a necessary hormone for pregnancy, so when RU-486 prevents it from working the way it should, the uterus sheds its lining, just like it does during a menstrual period. Two days after the first dose of the drug, a woman takes a second drug, a prostaglandin that induces contractions.

RU-486 has a 95% success rate, and has been approved for use in the first 7 weeks of pregnancy. The downside of this method is that it generally takes longer than surgical abortion—anywhere from 4 to 24 hours. Mild side effects include abdominal pain, nausea, and vomiting, while more serious side-effects include vaginal bleeding, which generally lasts longer than that associated with surgical abortion.

Sterilization

IN ADDITION TO ORAL AND INJECTION CONTRACEPTIVE, BARRIER methods such as the diaphragm, the cervical cap, and the female condom are also available, but have higher failure rates. More permanent solutions to the question of contraception is, of course, sterilization. Surprisingly, sterilization is the most popular contraceptive choice in both the U.S. and the world. For men, a vasectomy is easier, less costly, and can be performed in a doctor's office. For women, sterilization presents more risks of complication and infection than vasectomy, but the risks are quite low. Tubal sterilization for women involves blocking or cutting the fallopian tubes, a process that prevents the egg from reaching the uterus. Hysterectomy also results in sterilization, but it is not a recommended or preferred method of contraception. Most hysterectomies are performed only in the presence of disease or damage to the uterus.

New Methods

RESEARCHERS ARE CURRENTLY TESTING IMPROVEMENTS AND new designs for both male and female contraception. Most of this work involves improving upon or developing variations of existing contraceptives. Some of those in the works include the following.

Biodegradable Implants Like Norplant, these progestin-filled implants reside under the skin, providing uninterrupted, long-term contraception. Unlike Norplant, they dissolve over time rather than requiring surgical removal.

Vaginal Ring Similar to the ring of a diaphragm, the vaginal ring emits progestin and estrogen which prevent ovulation and is worn internally for three weeks at a time. After three weeks, the ring is removed and a menstrual period begins. Another ring can then be inserted.

Contraceptives for Men Weekly injections of the hormone testosterone enanthate have proven to prevent pregnancy. However, weekly injection is hardly an advantage of this method. Researchers hope to develop a pill or implant for men.

Hormone Injection A solution containing tiny clusters of molecules, each filled with hormones, is injected into the body. Over several months, doses of hormones are released at a steady level. This method is being studied for use by both men and women.

Contraceptive Immunization By sensitizing them to their own sperm or egg cells, a man or woman would produce antibodies that inactivate the sperm or egg cells as if they were a disease. One immunocontraceptive currently under study targets just the protein covering of the egg cell, which would prevent sperm from penetrating the egg without affecting normal egg development.

Reversible sterilization Current methods of sterilization are 50–70% reversible, but researchers would like to make the process more reliable. Techniques such as injecting liquid silicone into the fallopian tubes where it forms a plug, and placing various type of clips on the vas deferens to block sperm flow are two ideas currently in the works.

Prostaglandins These are chemicals that exist naturally in the body and that stimulate muscle contractions, like cramping. Via pill or tampon, prostaglandins induce a menstrual period, regardless of whether conception has occurred.

Evolving approaches to contraception insure that more—and hopefully better—options remain in the future. At the moment, that future promises a steady increase in world population, especially in developing countries. There as well as here, issues of access, affordability, culture, and religion are but a few factors that affect contraceptive use. Medicine can only provide the means of controlling when or if conception will occur. Ultimately, the decision about which method is right for you comes from having the most timely and helpful information at hand.

Paul Insel is Clinical Associate Professor of Psychiatry and Behavioral Sciences at Stanford University School of Medicine. Kristen Kennedy is Managing Editor of HEALTHLINE *and* SICKBAY TODAY.

From *Healthline*, April 2000, pp. 6-8. © 2000 by Healthline. Reprinted by permission.

Barren

COMING TO TERMS WITH A LOST DREAM

by DEBORAH DERRICKSON KOSSMANN

WHEN I WAS 5, I listed several things I wanted to be when I grew up: teacher, archaeologist (my mother had wanted to be that and had explained what it was), author, and mother. I have always thought of myself as an archaeologist of sorts, dusting off bones from my clients' emotional digs, figuring out how they fit together to make an understandable history. I teach graduate students. I write. But I have not become a mother. What does it mean to be barren, unable to grow anything in the land that is the body?

Infertility is about the body. One's identity becomes defined by what the body does or does not do. During my first miscarriage, I experienced slow, aching cramps and the punch of the uterus as if it were saying, "No, not now, not time." There was no happy announcement of pregnancy, only the feeling of sadness when the bleeding came. By the time we learned I was pregnant, it was already over.

The second pregnancy began with more Clomid, a medication we were using to stimulate ovulation, and a new set of medical procedures, including a test called a hysterosalpingogram. No one understands why some women unexpectedly get preg-

nant after having this test. Perhaps a slight blockage exists, perhaps the dye they use is like Liquid-Plumr. Envision pipes opening up as the gunky stuff drains away. During the test, I lay on the table with the sheet covering my bottom half, the nurse and the doctor directing me: "Here you relax.... Here you breathe.... We'll see your uterus above on that screen." I had to turn my head from the hard table to see it. But first I focused on an image: blue dye being threaded into me, the shock of its entry almost like sexual intrusion. Not rape; I wanted this, didn't I? The goal was to find the blocked places, to make my body a host that could grow things. The dye entered and my body fought back. Above me, my uterus floated, distinct, not looking like those pictures in biology books. Mine is elongated, a shapely part of me, like a pink heart. Tubes stretched out from it. Momentarily fascinated, I ignored the physical discomfort as I looked inside myself.

The test took place two weeks before my nephew, Michael (my sister's third child), was born. My husband and I visited the hospital, bringing my sister Chinese food—greasy egg rolls, noodles in sauce. She was tired, but happy. She tried

not to be too happy, mindful of our struggles with infertility, as she gave Michael to me to hold. Looking back, I wonder if my uterus at that moment opened and if somehow that muscle inside me relaxed, allowing my egg to roll downward and inside. I picture the egg, cartoonlike, smiling.

The night after Michael's birth, we conceived. My husband dreamed that night of a blond boy in a bucket. He told me the next morning we were pregnant, but I didn't believe him. And then, suddenly, we were. It was Christmastime and I was tired, green, and hungry. I told people early: I couldn't contain our news. For a long time after the first miscarriage, we'd waited to try and get pregnant, and we'd waited through more cycles on the medication. Now, I read things about babies. I imagined ourselves dividing over and over inside me. We had a nickname for it. We called it "Pea." I stayed green and tired and full of indigestion. My temperature stayed up. My breasts began to hurt all the time and grow larger. My husband noted this outward sign. He began to buy books about finances, investments. He was worrying about building our nest with enough twigs and sticks to weave securely for the egg—the blond boy in the bucket.

On Super Bowl Sunday, we returned from brunch with friends and some part of me felt different. Several days earlier, I'd finally stopped taking my temperature, believing at last my hormone levels would remain high. Then it appeared: a rusty red spot as I wiped myself. I started to panic. I went to the bathroom every hour. Each time, it was still there, another drop. It was a stop sign, red light, a flashing siren light on the top of a police car telling us to pull over, stop driving. I called the doctor—not *my* doctor, but the doctor on call. He sounded irritated. He was probably watching the game, eating snack foods, and drinking beer. I told him what was happening. "Call tomorrow for an ultrasound appointment," he said. "There's nothing to do today."

Should I rest, lie down?

"You can do that if you want," he said. "It probably won't matter."

In the hours that followed, I thought about my wedding day when my sister was several months pregnant with my second niece, Maddie. Right after the reception, she began bleeding. Her doctor put her on bed-rest for more than a month. We still shiver to think of Maddie's not being; we were so close to losing her. After the phone call to the doctor, I lay in bed and cried because I knew what was happening. My uterus was clenching, not to hold on, but to let go. It was like a star falling. You don't exactly see the trajectory, only the brief light and the memory that once it was reality, if only for the briefest breath. I lay flat and very still. Sometimes, when I was a child with a fever, I'd look at the corners of my bedroom ceiling and imagine walking on it like it was the floor. What a strange possibility if the whole world could be upside-down! In the suspended shadows, I'd hang in the wrong direction and try to experience that fevered moment before the world swung back.

The next morning, when I called for the ultrasound appointment,

they told me to drink fluids. I drank, ten, twenty, thirty ounces. I was still drinking on the way to the hospital. I was still bleeding. "Many women spot early in their pregnancies. I've read this and it could be true," I told my husband. "My sister bled and it was bright red and Maddie is here now. It could be true, couldn't it?" My husband nodded a little distractedly and held my hand. It was as if he'd already begun dissembling the nest, knocking twigs everywhere.

I stripped off all my clothes and put on my **blue** *gown and bracelet. My husband sat with me. It was a funeral of* **waiting.**

At the hospital, the technician ran the probe over my abdomen. "You didn't drink enough. Go drink more," she said accusingly. I was sitting in a room with pamphlets about sexually transmitted diseases and bladder infections, and I was drowning myself with water. I felt myself float like a balloon, and still the technician said it was not enough water. She said with annoyance now, "We can't read it this way. We'll do a transvaginal. Now go urinate." I peed and peed and peed. Then she brought out the condom-covered probe, which I helped her put inside me. It reminded me of a stick shift on one of those driving video games. She stared at the incomprehensible screen that was turned slightly away from me. My husband seemed not to notice the weirdly pornographic quality to the whole interaction. "I can't see," the technician said, "I'll be right back." But I knew already what I knew—that something had happened. The radiologist came in and said, "I'm sorry. It stopped growing a week or so ago." She compared the size of the yolk with the technicians' developmental chart and moved the probe around again inside me. I began to cry then, just wanted to get up and go somewhere like those ani-

mals that howl and howl, deep in the forest.

But first we had to walk back to the obstetrician's office. My doctor was almost tearful at the news. The nurse-practitioner was actually crying. She asked me, "Do you want to wait? Or we can do a dilation and evacuation (D&E) and see if we can get a tissue sample. Then we can maybe figure out what happened. You don't have to wait and then bleed. You can know it's finished." I could barely think because I was that animal howling, but I made the D&E appointment for the next day. I knew that was better: I couldn't stand to wait.

The next day, we checked into the hospital. I told the admissions person the reason for our visit and cried. I told the doctor doing the surgery what had happened when she asked, and I cried again. I stripped off all my clothes and put on the blue gown and bracelet. My husband sat with me. He held my rings because I was not allowed to wear them into surgery. It was a funeral of waiting.

After they came to take me into surgery, he waited in the other room like those old movies where they show the father pacing the waiting area during the baby's delivery. I was still sobbing when they wheeled me into the operating room. The surgical team put my feet up into high stirrups. The anesthesiologist said something that I didn't hear because it was suddenly dark. My obstetrician had cautioned, "Don't worry about whatever you say or do during the procedure." Afterward, when I woke up after the surgery, a nurse was hovering over me, my face was wet, and my hands held a ball of damp tissues. I knew I'd said and done things I couldn't remember as they carefully cleaned out that beautiful elongated space inside me that must have clenched its muscled will against the intrusion, the loss, and the flowing out.

After the second miscarriage, we both took the nest apart. A friend once told me about some misguided birds that had built a nest by her front door inside a large flowerpot. One of the eggs—a finch egg, she thinks—was accidentally knocked out and broken. Thinking about that story, I wondered if the bird missed the shattered egg. After the D&E, I stayed home for a few days in the dark house in stunned silence. I read two murder mysteries in 24 hours. I slept. But mostly, I just sat quietly and took painkillers for the cramps. It was raining outside, a winter rain, the hard, cold kind. I sat in my living room for almost three hours before I noticed that it was raining *inside* the house, a steady drip in the entranceway. I put a pot under it and sat some more. My husband didn't know what to do. He held me, but as is the way with wild animals, I'd found a cave and remained in it.

We visited a high-risk specialist who told us nothing we hadn't figured out already. She offered us a different medication, the possibility of a study. We both underwent full panels of genetic testing and filled vials of blood in the lab. The results of the D&E testing came back. The obstetrician showed us the numbers and pronounced them "normal." He told me they couldn't be sure if they'd obtained the right tissue. It was so early in the pregnancy that the tissue they used may have been from the embryo or my own body. He was gentle and encouraging about trying again. He said, "If you want to, and whenever you feel ready." There seemed to be no answers for what was termed "secondary infertility." After all, I'd finally been able to get pregnant when on medication, hadn't I?

When I visited my sister during this time, I didn't hold my nephew. He was exactly nine months ahead of the child I was missing. My husband and I decided to try again and spent more months on drugs and off drugs with no conception. The anniversary of the first miscarriage passed. Then the anniversary of the due date of the second miscarriage approached. I tried to speak to my husband from the cave. "It's a harder time than I expected," I said, "The

28th will be difficult." He said he understood. The 28th passed, and he said nothing. On the 29th, I climbed out of my cave and tried to beat some conversation out of him. Where had he gone? He no longer guarded the cave, no longer grieved as I did. "I want our old life back," he said. He said he didn't really want children, maybe never did. Men and women grieve differently, the literature claims. I wanted to rip at his seeming indifference with unforgiving claws.

We talked to resolve our differences. But in order to have children, we needed to agree to proceed with the medical process we'd been going through. And then we needed to decide at what level we'd stop treatment. Imagine two posturing like a bull and a matador. After several conversations like this, our battle became scripted. One wave of the cape and we were off. We began to avoid the ring. We began to avoid sex. Once when we were scheduled to have sex—neither of us called these times making love at this point—my husband turned to me and said in a businesslike voice, "Okay, let's pretend we're in a lab and they're forcing us." We took turns elaborating this scenario so much that our laughter rang over the bed and bounced back to us until we could make love.

How can I explain what the infertility journey does to a sex life? First, there's fun, the joy of trying to make something. Then, there's the fear of making something you will lose. Then, there's the stress of having to make something on a schedule and the fact that hoping at all becomes so painful. The pain is like a small, deep cut that won't heal.

When the third miscarriage happened, we barely talked. I knew the pregnancy was over three days before the bleeding started. I was now so attuned to my body that I almost swore I could feel when the egg released. I tried to control what I could. I kept my butt elevated for 20 minutes after sex, even though it was futile. But I told myself maybe it would matter and at least I could do some-

thing. When the bleeding for the miscarriage began, I cried in the bathroom at the community mental health center where I worked, big heaving sobs that I tried to stifle, since I told myself the patients used the same bathroom, and I didn't want to upset or have to comfort them. I was glad I'd had the D&E last time, since each change of pads and tampons now made me wonder, Was this life? Was *this*?

In the infertility specialist's office, the new doctor, a reproductive endocrinologist, sat across from me. He said, "You seem stressed by your situation," and asked if I wanted to see their psychologist. This would have been funny at any other time, since I'm a psychologist married to a psychologist, and had already been seeing a psychologist on and off during the whole ordeal. This new doctor seemed to believe that, because I was starting anew with him, the past three years and three miscarriages didn't count. "Here are new vitamins and new blood work and more medication," he said. I wasn't very hopeful, but I took the medication and felt myself ovulate days before I was supposed to. I took the ovulation test at work between patients and brought it home to my husband, because I didn't even trust myself to read its results right any more. He thought I'd ovulated, too. He said this carefully, since I was wild with hormones. When I called the doctor panicked and afraid we'd missed another opportunity to get pregnant, the doctor said I couldn't have ovulated. We scheduled time to have sex as soon as the doctor's office called back because we knew it was the "right" time. We lay on the yellow, sun-warmed afternoon bed and tried to make a baby. We didn't.

Time to Stop

At the next doctor's visit, when he told us we could try stronger drugs or in vitro fertilization (though there were still no known reasons for the miscarriages) and when he said the words "let's take another blood test," I knew. I knew, just as I knew when it was time to break up with somebody or change jobs, that it was time to stop. I told my husband on the way home. I didn't say it directly, however. I told him (half in the cave) that I was getting rid of all the over-sized clothes and borrowed maternity outfits I'd been keeping. Once home, I angrily cleaned out closets and drawers. I was getting rid of the clothes that no longer fit me or were no longer about who I was or wanted to be.

That night and for the whole week following, as my husband and I climbed into bed, we listened to a confused mockingbird singing in the dark, just outside our window. He was looking for a mate, looking to make a bird family. He was singing at the wrong time, but what a song of trills and warbles and fakery! He sang as if his life depended upon finding his mate. The week after his glorious midnight performances brought only silence. In all that darkness, could he have found something?

I began working out every day at the gym and lost all the weight I'd gained, reclaiming my body. I began writing poetry again, stories and words about grief. I quit my 30-hour-a-week administrative job at the community mental heath center. I remembered that I once liked my husband as a friend and that, while neither of us was perfect dealing with our infertility or each other, as a couple, we'd survived.

I suddenly felt tears push at the back of my eyelids as the **thought** *welled up that I would never make a cake like this for my daughter.*

Bodily scars linger. I have bigger breasts from the pregnancies and, possibly, some other physical effects from the medications I took. I strug-

gle with my feelings about what it means to be female and not give birth. I recently walked into a hair salon where four pregnant women and one woman with an infant sat. It reminded me in an instant that I'm different from other women: I won't hold a child that looks like my husband and me.

But there are also moments of solace. My husband jokingly holds our favorite cat up next to his cheek and grins. "See the resemblance?" he asks. A few months ago, I attended the opening of an art exhibit held by a young woman who'd been one of my first long-term psychotherapy clients. She made textured and original ceramic pieces symbolizing parts of her personality, and she'd wanted me to see them. (They were too big to bring to my office.) She stood next to me with shining eyes and excitement at the fulfillment of making something, and I recognized that I'd helped in this. The years we'd worked together had created something in her that, in turn, created something else, healthy and full of her life energy.

I'm an aunt. In some cultures this is an important and respected position—someone who doesn't have her own children, but loves others' children as if they were her own. My first niece, Sarah, is 8 years old, as old as my relationship with my husband. We attended her birthday party and watched as she blew out the candles on the orange, pumpkin-shaped cake that my sister had crafted. My family sang "Happy Birthday" in all different keys to her happy face. I suddenly felt tears push at the back of my eyelids as the thought welled up that I'd never make a cake like this for my daughter.

My 5-year-old niece, Maddie, was pleased that I hung her artwork on my kitchen door. "Aunt Debbie," she asked holding a small fistful of tiny yellow flowers she'd bunched up with tape borrowed from my drawer, "Can you hang these up? These are for you." I looked at the small wilted weeds,

the same yellow as her hair and her ruffled dress. She was smiling at me and I was acutely aware of the ache her gifts sometimes caused. She was not my own child, yet my love for her touched the emptiness inside me.

My nephew Michael was talking. He said, "Aunt Bebbie." When I visited my sister, he played a new game with me, jumping off the coffee table into my arms over and over, sure that I'd catch him. And I did, every time, though each time he flew into the air and I held him, I remembered what had slipped from my grasp.

How long does it take to give birth to oneself as a childless woman? A year after we'd stopped all the procedures and the medications, given up the idea of trying, and continued along our changed life path, I suddenly became pregnant. On a television show, a surprise situation like ours should have turned out fine. It didn't. I had another early miscarriage. For a while after this, I halfheartedly entertained thoughts about adoption. This was fantasy, a way to imagine a life that ran parallel to this one, in some other universe. That alternative life included a little boy or girl running through our backyard, playing pretend under the peach tree. I began to realize that I'd always be barren if I continued to hold onto the idea that a child should be in me and produced by me. If I believed this idea, planted in me when I was a child myself, I'd always have only a weed-filled field, scrub trees, and emptiness. Here, in this infertile place, I kept the grief about "Pea" and the other lost embryos, along with the fantasies about what might have been.

A second-floor room in our house had been painted bright yellow before we'd moved in, six years ago. I said it would make a great baby's room. Each morning, it filled with sunshine, and several contented cats stretched out in its warm spots. A few weeks ago, my husband suggested moving my home office from the corner of the basement into the yellow room. To take my creativity upstairs meant reorganizing the whole house—moving heavy furniture to different rooms, carrying what seemed like endless numbers of books from bookshelf to bookshelf, opening boxes, tossing files I hadn't looked at in a wile, cleaning out old pictures, and deciding what I should take with me. In the middle of the chaos, my husband leaned over my shoulder as I ordered office furniture online. He joked in a low inviting voice, "Come upstairs, out of the cave, write happy things in the yellow room."

Once I moved into the yellow room, I could see from my windows the neighbors' houses and their children running between the fenced backyards. In our own yard, the peach tree, planted from a dried pit, is now mature enough to begin bearing juicy fruit itself. Inside my new room, I see lots of photographs of my husband and me with our nieces and nephew, snapshots of our friends and family, and pictures of the places the two of us have visited together. High on a bookshelf, almost out of reach, sits a small, closed box, a gift from my husband's aunt, from the days before the second miscarriage. Inside, protected in white tissue paper, nestles a pair of green, hand-knit baby booties.

Deborah Derrickson Kossmann, Psy.D., is a clinical psychologist in private practice and also works in a multidisciplinary medical oncology practice. She is a journalist, essayist, and poet. Address: 1709 Langhorne-Newton Rd., Suite 2, Langhorne, PA 19047. E-mails to the author may be sent to drskoss@aol.com.

A form of this article originally appeared in "Families, Systems & Health", 18, No. 4, Winter 2000, pp. 479-484. From *Psychotherapy Networker*, July/August 2002, pp. 40-45, 58. © 2002 by Deborah Derrickson Kossmann. All rights reserved.

UNDER THE RADAR

Thirty years after *Roe v. Wade*, the White House is pressing its case against
ABORTION delicately. An inside look at the strategy

By Karen Tumulty and Viveca Novak

GEORGE W. BUSH'S FIRST WORKDAY was also the day that tens of thousands of antiabortion activists gathered in Washington for their annual protest against the landmark Supreme Court decision guaranteeing a woman's right to abortion. So new was the Bush team on Jan. 22, 2001, that most officials hadn't yet been issued their White House telephone extensions. Kansas Senator Sam Brownback frantically dialed cell-phone numbers from the rally's stage beneath the Washington Monument. When he finally reached Tim Goeglein of the Office of Public Liaison, Brownback put his request for a show of support bluntly: "If you're going to take this position, now's the time to announce." Less than an hour later, it was Brownback's cell phone that rang. In his first reversal of Clinton Administration policy, the new President—who had downplayed abortion during his campaign—said he would block federal money from international family-planning organizations that offer or counsel abortion. The crowd roared when Brownback delivered the news.

Two years later, as the 30th anniversary of *Roe v. Wade* is marked this week, the antiabortion movement finds itself at a moment of both possibility and tension. Some think Bush

has lived up to the promise of that early victory. "He's been a star," says Republican Congressman Chris Smith of New Jersey, one of the House's leading abortion foes. But others say the President is in danger of squandering what they see as the biggest opportunity abortion opponents have had since *Roe* to severely restrict—maybe even ban—abortion. "He has tremendous political capital, and I wish he had said more to America and not just to us," says Gary Bauer, a conservative activist who ran against Bush for the G.O.P. nomination. "They've made a calculation: take action, but with the least discomfort to other portions of the coalition—some of the more moderate suburban women who don't react to this with the same enthusiasm I might."

Abortion is on the decline in this country, no matter how you measure it: in total numbers, the rate at which women choose abortion or the percentage of pregnancies that end in abortion. Between 1990 and 2000, the number of abortions dropped 18%, from an estimated 1.6 million a year to 1.3 million, according to the Alan Guttmacher Institute, a nonprofit research organization that both sides of the debate rely on for data. Twelve years ago, about 27 women out of every 1,000 of childbearing age had

KEY DECISIONS UNDER THE BUSH ADMINISTRATION

Some ignited controversy and major headlines; others slipped under the radar

• Made "unborn children" eligible for coverage under the Children's Health Insurance Program as part of an effort to establish the fetus as a person

• Nominated strongly antiabortion advocates such as Attorney General John Ashcroft to high-level positions

• Filed lower-court brief supporting Ohio's ban on "partial birth" abortions

• Nixed taxpayer funding for additional stem cells to be extracted from embryos and used to research cures for diseases

• Reimposed global gag rule barring international organizations receiving U.S. funds from providing abortion services

• Revised government website to include suggestion of a link between abortion and breast cancer, which is not yet proved

had an abortion; by 2000, the number fell to just over 21. And whereas 28% of those who found themselves pregnant in 1990 had an abortion,

TIME/CNN POLL

- Would you describe yourself as being more pro-choice—supporting a woman's right to have an abortion—or more pro-life—protecting the rights of the unborn children?

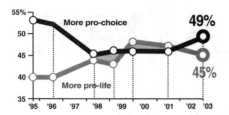

the number dropped below 25% two years ago.

Meanwhile, there are fewer and fewer doctors willing to perform the procedure. The number of physicians providing abortion is down to 1,800 nationally, from nearly 2,400 in 1992, and 87% of U.S. counties have none at all, according to the Guttmacher Institute. Another indicator: this month the National Abortion and Reproductive Rights Action League, the abortion-rights movement's leading organization, officially changed its name for the fourth time, to NARAL Pro-Choice America, dropping the word abortion and adopting the acronym instead.

With Congress and the White House in G.O.P. hands, abortion foes will push this year to get a ban on the late-term procedure they call partial-birth abortion passed (as it has been twice already) and signed into law (President Bill Clinton vetoed it both times). But G.O.P. strategists concede it is unlikely that other measures—like a bill to make it a separate crime to injure a fetus during an attack on a pregnant woman or legislation making it illegal to evade state parent-notification laws by taking a minor across state lines—will become priorities for the President or get through the closely divided Senate. "If all they can muster is the elimination of one abortion method, that's a loss," says former antiabortion lobbyist Teresa Wagner, editor of a new book of essays about the movement. "It's a catastrophic loss."

"God willing, the human-life amendment will someday become the law of the land."

—REPRESENTATIVE CHRIS SMITH, New Jersey

For its broader goals, the anti-abortion movement still can't make the political math work. The Senate has a Republican majority, but at least 53 Senators are on record as favoring *Roe*. And the public is not prepared to see it overturned. In the latest TIME/CNN poll, 55% of respondents said they support a woman's right to have an abortion in the first three months of pregnancy.

At the same time, 60% of those polled said it has become too easy to obtain an abortion, which helps explain why opponents have been so effective in nibbling at the edges of the abortion question. Ever since a 1992 Supreme Court decision, *Planned Parenthood v. Casey*, opened the door for states to impose greater limits on the right to an abortion, activists have taken up the fight state by state, measure by measure. In the past seven years, 335 new restrictions have been put on the books around the country, according to NARAL. Most common are parent-notification laws, required waiting periods, and state-mandated lectures and literature about fetal development and alternatives to abortion such as adoption. In Alabama, women have to get sonograms before they can end their pregnancies. While a few states such as California have liberalized their laws, the trend is very much in the other direction.

As Bauer noted, the White House strategy seems to be to push many of its abortion actions under the radar, where they will not be noticed by moderate women voters. True, Bush made headlines with his nomination of the staunchly evangelical, anti-abortion John Ashcroft for Attorney General and the decision not to provide taxpayer funds to develop additional fetal-stem-cell lines for medical research. But other moves barely made a ripple by comparison. A year ago, the Administration filed a brief supporting Ohio's partial-birth-abortion ban in an appellate court (not waiting, as it normally would, for the case to hit the Supreme Court). A few months later, it quietly removed from a government website information saying that abortions do not increase the risk of breast cancer. (A replacement fact sheet suggests a possible link, though major studies turn up no evidence for one.) Last March the Administration made fetuses eligible for the Children's Health Insurance Program, keying off the antiabortion groups' strategy of establishing "fetal rights" as a way of eventually undermining *Roe*. And just three weeks ago, the State Department sent a cable to its Agency for International Development (AID) offices worldwide urging them to ensure that U.S. funds weren't going to groups that provide abortion services—and suggesting that the AID offices surf the websites of funded groups as a way of checking.

Bush has also issued avowals that he will veto appropriations bills when the Senate has threatened to repeal existing restrictions on abortions. As recently as last Friday, he warned Congress that if a catchall spending bill under consideration omits even one existing curtailment of federal funds for abortion, his advisers would recommend a veto. "It's a mistake to underrate his focus," says Democratic Congresswoman Zoe Lofgren, an abortion-rights advocate who has found herself on the losing side of the abortion wars. "They are persistent, and they are insistent."

The partial-birth ban, if enacted, would be the biggest federal anti-abortion initiative since the mid-1970s, when the government banned use of federal funds to provide abortions for poor women. But it is certain to face a legal challenge, and has lost in the courts before. In 2000 the Supreme Court knocked down all state partial-birth bans because they defined the procedure in ways that also included the most common type of second-trimester abortion and offered no exception to preserve a woman's health or life.

Court rulings like that have raised the stakes in what promises to be the real test of Bush's antiabortion agenda: his Supreme Court nominations. What keeps *Roe* standing is the razor-thin five-vote majority that has stood by the decision. If Bush replaces anti-*Roe* Chief Justice William Rehnquist (rumored to be retiring this year) with another like him, it won't change the calculus, though abortion will still loom huge in confirmation hearings. But when it's Sandra Day O'Connor's turn to go or that of any of the others who have upheld *Roe*, the stakes will be enormous. If *Roe* is overturned, NARAL predicts that 12 states are likely to ban abortion in all or most circumstances, and five others might.

With so much at stake, NARAL is spending $2.5 million this year on print and television ads, unprecedented for the group in a year with no presidential elections. On Tuesday night, every contender for the 2004 Democratic nomination is expected to appear at a NARAL dinner in Washington. And to make sure that abortion foes are not the only ones making a show of force in Washington, a big march is planned for before the presidential election.

So for now, 30 years after *Roe*, abortion has become a war of small skirmishes—but with both sides on high alert. "I think that this Administration and Congress are weaving a pernicious web of anti-choice initiatives that taken together strangle reproductive rights," says Gloria Feldt, president of the Planned Parenthood Federation of America. And that's one point on which the two sides can agree. "God willing, the human-life amendment [which would ban abortion in all cases except to save the mother's life] will someday become the law of the land," says Congressman Smith. "But meanwhile we are using every modest and incremental approach possible."

Which Babies?

Dilemmas of Genetic Testing

Shelley Burtt

What sort of life is worth living? Advances in medical technology have given Socrates' question a new, more poignant meaning. For the first time in history, we have the means to will the disappearance of those born disabled at the same time that we have the resources to enable these children to live better and longer lives than was ever possible before. How will we respond to these new cross-cutting possibilities? Genetic testing gives us the tools to choose in advance against certain sorts of lives. How are these tools to be used? What sort of lives are worth living?

As a bereaved parent of a child with Down syndrome, I am painfully aware that the life my son led for two and a half joyous years is a life that many individuals would cut short before it began. Although genetic testing is often presented as a service designed to reassure parents that their children-to-be are without congenital abnormalities, the practice in fact functions to prescreen "defective" fetuses for abortion. The assumption of most health care providers in the United States is that the successful diagnosis of a genetic anomaly provides an opportunity to "cure" a pathological condition. Once the arrival of a normally healthy baby is in doubt, the decision to abort is seen as rational and the opportunity to do so as fortunate.

For an anxious parent, genetic testing accompanied by the possibility of therapeutic abortion appears to enhance individual freedom by providing an additional measure of control over one's reproductive choices. But this perspective represents a woefully limited understanding of what it might mean to live as or with a person whose genetic makeup differs markedly from the general population and in a way that will to some extent impair his functioning. I'd like instead to explore what reasons we might have to resist the conclusion that a diagnosis of genetic abnormality is in itself a good reason to terminate a pregnancy and what cultural resources might be required to encourage this resistance.

My husband and I first welcomed Declan into our lives on a hot summer morning in July 1993. We had just come from the midwives' office where I had refused the genetic test (AFP) that screens for neural tube defects and would almost certainly have alerted us to our son's chromosomal abnormalities. Sitting on a bench outside Central Park, we asked ourselves, "What if there were a disability? What use would we make of the information the test promised to provide? Although we come from different religious traditions (my husband is Jewish; I am Christian), we shared the view that the decision to create another human being was not conditional on the sort of human being that child turned out to be. For both of us, the child I was carrying was best understood as a gift we were being asked to care for, not a good we had the responsibility or right to examine for defects before accepting. With a blissfully innocent optimism, or perhaps an eerie prescience, we affirmed that day that we would love this child for who he was, whatever that turned out to be.

Not every couple will willingly go through a pregnancy in ignorance of their fetus's health or future prospects, especially when the tests for a variety of disabling conditions are so readily available. What we can insist on, however, is a clear-eyed recognition of how genetic testing actually functions in our society and a greater commitment on the part of medical practitioners and prospective parents to fully reflect on the knowledge it provides. Whether or not to carry on with a pregnancy at all, let alone one which will result in the birth of a child with either moderate or profound disabilities, ought to be a decision made carefully and thoughtfully by the prospective parents of that child, not by strangers, legislators, or disability rights activists. But what does a good decision in these circumstances look like?

For many bioethicists, the watchword when it comes to difficult decision-making is individual autonomy. The role of the medical practitioner is not to prescribe a course of action but to provide the necessary information for the patient to decide what he or she truly wants to do. Yet, when a fetus is diagnosed as disabled or "defective" in some way, few parents are offered a truly informed choice about their options, as medical providers are rarely neutral when it comes to choosing between bringing an abnormal fetus to term or ending the pregnancy and "trying again." Because genetic abnormality is defined not as one characteristic with which a human being might be challenged but as a treatable medical problem, few parents faced with a positive diagnosis are invited to think beyond the now troubled pregnancy to the joy and rewards as well as the heartache and challenge that accepting and raising a child with special needs can bring.

More than this: to offer a therapeutic abortion as a "cure" for the diagnosed disability is deeply disingenuous. We do not cure cystic fibrosis and Down syndrome by ensuring that fetuses caring this trait do not come to term; we simply destroy the affected entity. The service health care providers offer in this regard is more truthfully characterized as a form of eugenics, either medical (if driven by physicians' preferences) or personal (if driven by parents'). Physicians genuinely committed to patient autonomy in the context of genetic testing would not prejudge the worth or desirability of bearing a child whose genetic makeup was in some way abnormal. Instead, they would seek to ensure that parents truly understood what it meant to care for a child with special needs. This would mean, at a minimum, encouraging parents to inform themselves about the diagnosed condition, giving them the opportunity to speak to pediatricians familiar with the problem, and enabling them to meet with families already caring for children with this condition.

Those who believe that the practice of genetic testing followed by selective abortion is an acceptable way of ensuring the birth of a healthy child often argue that the desire to parent a certain sort of child is not morally blameworthy. We can wish to be parents without wishing to be parents of a child with Fragile X syndrome or Tay-Sachs disease. Yet few who make this argument are willing to probe how our reproductive desires are constructed or at what point our desires become sufficiently self-reflective to be valid guides to action. On what basis do parents feel themselves "not ready" to parent a child with unexpectedly special needs? The picture they hold of a child's disabling trait and the effect it will have on the child and the family's life as a whole may be grounded in a volatile combination of fear and ignorance, not in some acquaintance with the actual life experiences of individuals already engaged in this task or deep reflection on the nature and purpose of parenting. It also seems likely that we cannot accurately assess in advance what challenges we are ready for. It is difficult to predict how we might grow and change in the face of seemingly adverse circumstances.

Certain parents might feel they cannot responsibly continue a pregnancy in which an abnormality has been diagnosed because they lack the financial or emotional resources to care for such a child. But this assessment is not made in a vacuum. What we feel we can manage depends in part on the level of social and political support families with disabled children can expect to receive, support which in turn depends on the degree to which such lives are valued or appreciated by our community.

The weight it is appropriate to give to parental desires in a reproductive context can perhaps be clarified by considering the internationally prevalent practice of sex-selective abortions. Parents around the world currently use the information derived from prenatal sonograms to advance their desire for a son by aborting female fetuses, a practice about which many physicians and most ethicists have grave moral reservations. Here, where parental desires are already considered suspect, the cultural construction of these desires and the appropriateness of resisting their expression is readily acknowledged. It is held to be an important part of making the world more just to change those cultural scripts which led parents to prefer a son over a daughter so strongly that they will end a pregnancy rather than have a girl. We need to think critically and courageously about why a similar revaluation of social attitudes towards congenital disabilities is not also considered necessary.

I believe it is possible for some parents, after profound and prayerful reflection, to make the difficult decision that, all things considered, it is best for a child that it never be born. Incapacitating physical or mental deformity or the certainty of a life destroyed by a wasting disease are conditions which might conceivably, but not necessarily, call forth such a conclusion. But a judgement of this sort cannot be made with any fairness when speaking of disabilities such as spina bifida or Down syndrome where the quality of life available to the afflicted person is relatively high. A commitment to truly informed choice would ensure that we do not dismiss the possibility of caring for children burdened by disease or disability without an effort to appreciate and understand their possible lives.

But we need more than a commitment to truly informed choice if we are to create a world in which the birth of a disabled child is not thought of primarily as a stroke of bad luck, readily avoidable by more aggressive prenatal testing. The lives of those whose capacities fall outside the normal range must be personally and socially recognized as independently valuable, not only worth living in themselves but worth living with.

As the parent of a disabled child, I have experienced first hand the transformed perspective on life possible when one is given the opportunity to live with those who confound our routine expectations, who have too much or too little of a range of expected human traits, who experience life in a way that much remain opaque to the majority of normally functional human beings. What my parents' generation would have called Declan's "mental retardation," we termed his "developmental disabilities." But what was neither retarded nor disabled was a infectious enthusiasm for life which illuminated any interaction with him, an ability to give and receive love that was uncomplicated by the egoism, self-awareness, or self-consciousness of a "typical" child. Parenting this child forced us to reconsider our conception of what qualities and capacities made life worth living; the joy my son clearly took in life and the joy he gave us compelled such a re-evaluation.

But it is not enough to catalog the ways in which life with "them" is valuable for what it brings "us." The respect due to all persons by virtue of their humanity is not dependent on possessing only that sort of genetic makeup which guarantees normal human functioning. Our religious and political traditions teach that each human life has independent and intrinsic value. What would the consequences be of taking this truth seriously when we contemplated becoming parents?

Such a commitment would have to call forth a profound re-assessment of the place of human will in the creation of human life. Both the cause of human freedom and of human equality have been admirably served by the ability, achieved only in this century, to choose to become parents. But we in the industrialized world now teeter on the brink of being able to choose what sort of children we want to become parents of. To some this capacity to control our destiny as parents is an almost unadulterated positive. One of the advantages of scientific progress is supposed to be the ability it gives humans to control their lives. Some make the point that being a good parent is hard enough without the additional burdens of severe or moderate disabilities to cope with. Other argue that it is cruel to bring a child into the world who will always be different, for whom the normal trials of life will be magnified hundreds of times. Why not, then, embrace the opportunity offered by advances in prenatal testing to discard those reproductive efforts we will experience as "disappointing," less than perfect, abnormal, or unhealthy? The most important reason is that sorting the results of the human reproductive process in this way ranks human beings according to their capacity to please their creators, fulfill their parents' dreams, or contribute to social productivity. This willingness to sit in judgement over the sorts of persons deserving a place in our moral communities closes down rather than enlarges the scope of human freedom. The ability to control one's destiny that science supposedly promotes turns out to be conditional on being the right sort of person.

As my younger sisters became pregnant in the wake of Declan's death, I hoped right along with them for a niece or nephew free from illness, defect, or developmental challenges. The question is not whether it is right to desire a "normal" child, but how one ought to respond when genetic testing reveals that desire has been thwarted. To take steps at that point to abort the fetus and "try again" is not just to decide against being pregnant or in favor of "controlling one's life." It is to decide in advance and for another that a certain sort of life (a female one, a physically handicapped one, a mentally retarded one) is not worth living. The moral scope and impact of this decision appears to me far more troubling than a decision for or against parenthood based solely on a positive pregnancy test. Postponing an abortion decision until one knows what sort of child has been created places relative weights on human beings: some are more worthy of living, of being cared for, of being cherished, than others.

Having cared, however briefly, for a special needs child, I do not belittle the level of care and commitment called forth by the opportunity to parent a child or adult with moderate to severe disabilities. But I remain deeply skeptical that the best response to these challenges is the one currently favored by the Western medical establishment: to treat congenital imperfections as we do infectious diseases and to seek their cure by their eradication. Rather we need, through a genuine encounter with those whose identities are shaped but never fully encompassed by their bodies' imperfections, to rethink our willingness not only to live with the disabled but to live with unchosen obligations. Our cultural assumptions to the contrary, living a good and rich life does not require and is not identical with complete control of its circumstances. In fact, the aspiration for such "freedom" dishonors a fundamental aspect of the human condition. To those willing to recognize the essential humanity of every possible child, sometimes to choose not to know—or not to act on what we do know—will be the best choice of all.

Shelley Burtt has taught at Yale University and the London School of Economics and Political Science. She is the author of Virtue Transformed *(Cambridge, 1992).*

From *Tikkun*, Vol. 16, No. 1, pp. 45-47. Reprinted with permission of the Institute for Labor & Mental Health.

Sex Without Sex? Keeping
Passion Alive

Marjorie Osterhout

Ask a hundred pregnant women if they enjoy sex and you'll hear a hundred different answers. Some have a romp 'em, stomp 'em good time, living it up in their underbelly bikini panties and enjoying the extra endowment nature bestows on their breasts. At the other end of the spectrum you'll find tired, moody, queasy women with a body pillow down the middle of the bed—a hurdle too high for even the most determined lover. And in between are the rest of us: sometimes interested and sometimes not, sometimes feeling sexy and sometimes feeling more like a bloated whale.

It's normal during pregnancy to feel less interested in sex at times. Some pregnant women or their partners may be worried about hurting the baby, even with reassurance from a doctor. For others, intercourse may be uncomfortable, especially in the later stages of pregnancy. Many women feel insecure about their new body shape or just plain old not in the mood. And raging hormones, exhaustion, tender breasts and morning sickness also play a role.

Finding Middle Ground

The key to a satisfying sex life is to communicate about what you each need, want and hope for sexually. This is true throughout life, including during pregnancy. Regardless of how much you do (or don't) want intercourse, sex is not an all-or-nothing deal. Even though there's a watermelon between you and your partner, there's room to be innovative when it comes to physical intimacy. Creative foreplay can be fun and sexy, and it doesn't necessarily need to end in a "touchdown."

Consider the options. Most pregnant women would give almost anything for a good foot rub or back massage. And we're not talking a 1-minute quickie, either: unpack the massage oils, turn down the lights and get horizontal. Don't be shy about telling your partner exactly what aches and what feels good. If you use oil or lotion, stick to stretch-mark creams or specially formulated pregnancy massage oils. Many general massage oils contain essential oils, which can be harmful for pregnant women (especially during the first trimester).

Later in pregnancy, it's safe to use essential oils that are considered soothing as opposed to stimulating (with your healthcare provider's approval). When in doubt, use oils that are derived from flowers rather than herbs. Safe bets include lavender, bitter orange, or ylang ylang. When massaging essential oils into your skin, dilute them first in a "carrier oil" (such as almond oil), not-too-hot bath water or lotion. To scent the air, put four to six drops in a bowl of hot water or a diffuser. You can also put a couple of drops on a cotton ball and place it under your pillow.

Oral sex can be a fun and safe alternative to intercourse, but tell your partner not to blow air forcefully into your vagina. Blowing hard could cause an air embolism, where air enters your blood-stream and is potentially dangerous for both mother and baby. Normal breathing shouldn't interfere, though, so enjoy!

Showering together is another way to enjoy physical intimacy without the pressure to have sex. Offer to wash if he'll dry, break out the expensive body wash and take your time. Warm water is powerfully relaxing, and showering together is a great way to be intimate and prepare for a good night's sleep.

Even something as simple as sleeping naked (or almost naked) with your partner can promote togetherness. Skin-on-skin contact is comforting and intimate, and the best part is that it lasts all night long. If you can't sleep comfortably without wearing a bra or support belt, that's okay. Naked legs tangled together can be just as nice. Kissing, caressing and holding each other can be very satisfying, too, especially if you are feeling anxious or stressed.

Sometimes sex drives are lopsided and one person wants sex more than the other—a lot more. In general, partners should respect each other's sexual desire (or lack thereof). But if your partner is about to implode from sexual frustration and you have the energy to stay awake for a few more minutes, go for it. Your hands and mouth are powerful ways to satisfy your partner, and it's okay to have an occasional one-sided romp.

When No Means No

Dr. Valerie Davis Raskin is a clinical associate professor of psychiatry at the University of Chicago Pritzker School of Medicine and author of *Great Sex for Moms: Ten Steps to Nurturing Passion While Raising Kids*. According to Dr. Raskin, it's not necessarily important for pregnant couples to maintain their physical connection. But, she says, it is important to maintain a "loving, intimate connection. Sex is one way couples do that, but temporary breaks in physical intimacy do not necessarily cause a problem in the long run. The key is that both partners feel respected and 'heard' when it comes to negotiating sexuality around childbearing (or any other time)."

If your partner is about to implode from sexual frustration and you have the energy to stay awake for a few more minutes, go for it.

If you and your partner are concerned about having sex for health reasons, ask your medical caregiver whether or not it's safe. Since orgasm and semen can cause mild contractions, many caregivers advise against intercourse if you have any of the following conditions:

- A higher-than-average risk for miscarriage
- A history of premature labor or birth
- Unexplained vaginal bleeding or discharge
- Abdominal cramping
- Leaking amniotic fluid
- An incompetent cervix
- A dilated cervix
- Placenta previa
- A multiple pregnancy
- Your water has broken
- Any sexually transmitted disease, including unhealed herpes lesions in you or your partner

If physical intimacy of any kind is too uncomfortable for you, remember to practice small kindnesses that can keep you and your partner connected emotionally. Cooking dinner and arranging for a fantastic date may not seem like grand gestures, but small things make a difference. Send your partner a sweet email, browse baby-name books together or go shopping together for baby items. And don't forget to express your love and thanks for kindnesses received.

About the author: Marjorie Osterhout is a freelance writer in Seattle.

A Tale of Two Mothers

Two mothers. Three babies. One thoroughly modern tie:
Samantha Wood was hired to be Pam Guagenti's surrogate–
and the pair have been great friends ever since

BY CYNTHIA HANSON

It was 10:30 in the morning, and life hectic as usual for Pam Guagenti, of Torrance, California; with a phone between her ear and a shoulder, she was carrying a wailing Kyle, one of her 3-month-old twins, while chasing son Chase, a rambunctious toddler who had just managed to remove half his clothes. When Pam's friend Samantha Wood, 34, and her sons Aidan, 7, and Kail, 4, walked in on the chaos, Pam was relieved. "So glad you're here," she said. "Could you give the baby his bottle?"

Later, the two moms found some calmer moments to chat. "They keep sending you this stuff when you have a baby," Samantha said at one point, fishing baby-formula coupons out of her purse and handing them to Pam. Pam happily accepted—she hadn't been receiving any coupons herself. In fact, Pam had never even been pregnant: Samantha had given birth to all three of Pam's children.

Samantha was hired to be a surrogate—an "oven," as Samantha herself likes to say—to carry embryos created by Pam and her husband, Gary. Such parenthood partnerships, known as "gestational" surrogacies (as opposed to ones in which the surrogate contributes her egg *and* carries the baby), are booming, and not just for well-to-do celebrities like Joan Lunden: In the U.S. over the past two decades, an estimated 20,000 babies have come into the world through surrogacy. In 2000 alone, 1,210 babies were born of gestational surrogacies, double the number in 1997.

But while technology has made pregnancy by proxy a rather routine miracle, the process still has the potential to be an emotional and psychological nightmare—making Pam and Samantha's relationship the most astonishing part of it all. "I went into this figuring the couple would send me pictures of the child once a year," says Samantha, holding baby Kyle in her arms. Adds Pam, laughing, "I wanted a baby, not a friendship! But when I met Sam, I knew she'd be more than just a surrogate." Indeed, their experience spawned a special bond neither woman could have ever imagined, and has made the whole experience more meaningful for both of them.

The Baby Bill

How the costs of having a surrogate child add up for prospective parents*:

Agency fee:	$12,000
IVF procedures:	$13,000
Insurance policy:	$200
Medical screenings:	$5,000
Pregnancy care:	$5,000
Freezing/storing eggs:	$920
Lawyer's fee	$6,000
Surrogate's fee	$17,000
Total:	**$59,120**

*All costs are approximate.

From Heartbreak to Hope

Pam Guagenti's journey began in 1989, when she was 16 and living in Phoenix. Her mother, concerned that her youngest daughter had not started to menstruate, took Pam to a gynecologist. A pelvic exam revealed that Pam had been born without a uterus, a rare condition called Rokitansky syndrome. It meant she'd never be able to bear children.

"I was upset, but I didn't want to discuss it with anyone— not my doctor, my mother, my three older sisters or the counselor my mother wanted me to see," Pam recalls. "Everybody kept saying, 'You can adopt.' There's nothing wrong with adoption, but I didn't want to hear about it then." An ultrasound revealed that Pam had two ovaries—which gave her hope that she might someday have kids. "I knew about surrogacy from a TV movie," she says, "so even though it was controversial, I knew it was an option."

In 1994, while at Arizona State University, Pam met Gary Guagenti, a business major. She fell fast for his easygoing charm, and after only two weeks of dating, she felt close enough to him to bring up her condition. He was sympathetic, supportive and undeterred. He told her, "I'm not falling in love with you for what you can give me, but for who you are."

The couple wed in April 1998, then put their family plans on hold to concentrate on their jobs, hers as a kindergarten teacher and his as the owner of a Snap-on Tools franchise. In August 1999, they consulted Bill Yee, M.D., a fertility specialist. "I was very determined to have a baby of my own, somehow," says Pam. If her ovaries produced eggs, Dr. Yee explained, an embryo could be created with Gary's sperm. An ultrasound confirmed that Pam did indeed ovulate. "It's possible for you to have children," Dr. Yee told an elated Pam. "The next step is to find a surrogate."

Searching for a Soul Mom

Of the 10 surrogacy agencies they contacted, the Guagentis were most impressed with Building Families Through Surrogacy, in Lake Forest, California, and its director, Carol Weathers. A former accountant, Weathers, 39, started the agency in 1991 after watching a co-worker struggle with infertility, which affects an estimated 6 million couples nationwide. Since then, 105 surrogates in her program have delivered a total of 152 babies.

Most of her clientele are middle-class couples who are willing to pay a hefty price for a chance at biological parenthood—about $60,000, of which the surrogate receives $17,000. Each contract signed is for one pregnancy; should a surrogate fail to get pregnant, she does not receive any funds. Many clients foot the bill by taking out loans, as the Guagentis did.

Most surrogates in Weathers' program are about 30 years old, married and working; all are natural mothers of their own children, so they are known to have carried a pregnancy successfully. Everyone must pass a rigorous screening process that includes a home visit, a criminal background check and filling out a 587-point questionnaire to gauge emotional health. The Guagentis had to undergo similar psychological testing.

The prospective parents seal the partnership by signing an agency contract and a separate agreement with the surrogate; the specifics on these agreements can vary, but all need to be ironclad, since there aren't many laws governing surrogacy. And the surrogate must agree to relinquish all rights to the baby at birth.

The Guagentis were told they might have to wait up to six months to be paired with a surrogate. But three months after signing the contract, Samantha Wood, a part-time nurse in Poway, California, spotted an ad for Building Families Through Surrogacy in a parenting magazine and contacted Weathers. For years, she had toyed with the idea of becoming a surrogate, having watched a friend struggle with infertility. "I couldn't imagine being told that I was unable to have children," says Samantha. "I knew I'd be a good candidate: I have a 'fixer' personality. And I enjoy being pregnant—even giving birth." After many lengthy discussions, she persuaded her husband, Tristan, a Navy medical dive technician, to let her proceed. In December, Samantha passed the psychological screening and Weathers matched her with Pam, who lived two hours away. The pair seemed to be a good fit: They shared similar middle-class upbringings and family values and both had gregarious personalities.

Soon after, the Guagentis and Woods met for the first time for dinner at a steakhouse. The couples talked for five hours about everything from their families to their careers. Finally, Gary turned to Tristan and asked, "I assume you're supportive, but how do you really feel about Samantha's becoming a surrogate mother?"

Tristan put down his fork. "When she told me she wanted to do this, I was so touched I almost cried," he said. Samantha was stunned. "You never told me that," she said, touching his arm.

Then Pam spoke up. "Why do *you* want to become a surrogate?" she asked Samantha.

"I want to help someone who can't have a baby the traditional way," Samantha responded.

Pam ventured her next question tentatively: "If you deliver a baby girl, would you want to keep her?"

"I wouldn't want your daughter," Samantha replied, smiling. "If I want a baby girl, I'll try for one with my husband."

Pam's eyes filled with tears. "I don't know why I'm crying," she said.

"Because you're going to have a baby," said Samantha. And with that, their adventure in baby-making began.

The Conception Connection

The odds for a successful journey through the technical part of the process were in the women's favor: Pam, then 27, was young enough to produce healthy eggs, and Samantha had a history of normal pregnancies and deliveries. In February 2000, the women went to Gabriel Garza, M.D., and Arthur L. Wisot, M.D., of a fertility practice called Reproductive Partners, which has performed more than 40 successful procedures with surrogates in the last five years. Pam received hormone injections to stimulate her ovaries and Samantha got doses of estrogen to prepare her uterus to accept an embryo. Of the 11 eggs retrieved from Pam, eight were fertilized with Gary's sperm. Dr. Wisot transferred two embryos to Samantha, in the hope that one would implant (each embryo has about a 20 percent chance of becoming a fetus). The remaining eggs were frozen. A blood test in April revealed the best possible news: Samantha was pregnant. "We were both at the doctor's office when we found out, and we were screaming and crying and hugging each other," says Pam. The Guagentis decided to keep the sex of the child a surprise. "We'd used enough technology already," says Pam.

Throughout the pregnancy, the women kept in touch by phone, and each month Pam accompanied Samantha to her prenatal checkups and to visit with the midwife they chose to deliver the baby at the hospital. "I didn't want to miss anything," says Pam, who resigned from teaching at the end of the school year. "Since I always wondered how it would feel to have a baby moving inside of me, Samantha called when the baby kicked for the first time and described the sensation." Pam kept a scrapbook with pictures of a pregnant Samantha so, she says, "I could show my child this wacko thing his parents did!"

Samantha says she found Pam supportive, but not suffocating. "She never called to see if I was eating my vegetables. She was very protective, though, to the point where she almost hired a housekeeper for me." And the baby turned out not to be their only bond. Over lunches and trips to the mall, Pam and Samantha discussed their vacation plans, even their marriages. "If I'd met Pam under different circumstances," says Samantha, "I definitely would have chosen her as a friend."

Unlike other close friends, though, the women sometimes found themselves defending their relationship. "I'd be out to dinner and strangers would ask, 'When is your baby due?' And I'd say, 'It's not mine, I'm a surrogate' and they'd say 'Oh, you make a lot of money doing that,'" says Samantha. "I'd just laugh it off. I wasn't about to get into an argument." Seventeen thousand dollars is definitely a tidy sum, Samantha concedes, "but surrogacy is a huge commitment—on my part, my husband's part, my children's part. And pregnancy is hard on your body. There are easier ways to make money."

Pam faced her own struggles. She occasionally grieved because she wasn't the one carrying her child. "Once in the

supermarket," she recalls, "there was a very pregnant lady people were gushing over and I felt like saying, 'Well, I'm eight-and-a-half months pregnant, too.' But they wouldn't have understood."

On December 26, 2000, the Guagentis' phone rang at 3:15 A.M. "I think I'm in labor," Samantha blurted. Everyone raced to the hospital, and the Guagentis, Tristan and Carol Weathers joined Samantha in the birthing room. Gary stood by Samantha's head, feeling somewhat awkward, as Pam held one of Samantha's legs and Tristan the other. Calmly and without pain medication, Samantha delivered Chase Maxwell, 9 pounds, 21 inches. As they'd planned, the midwife placed Chase on Samantha's stomach, Gary cut the umbilical cord and Samantha passed him to Pam's open arms.

THE VIRTUAL WOMB

Will the miracles of medicine make surrogacy obsolete?

Women like Pam Guagenti may soon have more options in their quest to become mothers. Medical science has already introduced uterus transplants: In April 2000 a Saudi Arabian woman received another woman's uterus. Even though the transplant ultimately failed, scientists say that it was a milestone in the treatment of infertility.

Now even more remarkable developments are under way. According to news reports, scientists in Japan have created an artificial womb capable of incubating a goat fetus for up to three weeks. Similar work is happening in the U.S. as well. Hung-Ching Liu of the Center for Reproductive Medicine and Infertility at New York's Cornell Medical Center has already gotten mouse embryos to survive for up to two weeks in an artificial environment. Liu and fellow researchers are also working on techniques to grow human endometrial tissue, with the hope that they will someday be able to use it to repair damaged uteruses.

While researchers like Liu believe their work creating artificial wombs will offer women who can't have a baby new hope, others are concerned. "This might seem like a feminist career woman's dream," satirized columnist Tony Blankley in the conservative *Washington Times*. "Not only can she avoid the messy part of conception, but she needn't miss a day of work due to pregnancy." Adds Jeremy Rifkin, writing in the liberal *Guardian*, "What kind of child will we produce from a liquid medium inside a plastic box?" Given the recent advances in reproductive technology, it may not be long until we find out.

—*Leslie Laurence*

But Wait—Is Surrogacy *Ethical*?

We asked prominent ethicists: Is it morally okay for one woman to carry the baby of another?
—*Anne Cassidy*

"Helping infertile couples have babies is a highly ethical thing to do—and surrogacy is a piece of that. As long as everyone understands going in what his and her rights and obligations are, it can be a good way to help people have a family who couldn't otherwise."
—*Arthur Caplan, Ph.D., professor and director of the Center for Bioethics at the University of Pennsylvania, in Philadelphia*

"When a woman hires another woman to carry her baby for her, it reduces pregnancy to a 'job' and women to vessels. It also makes us forget about the relationship between a mother and her fetus. The fetus is connected to her—it is the flesh of her flesh—no matter what the genetic tie."
—*Barbara Katz Rothman, Ph.D., professor of sociology at City University of New York*

"Look at your baby," Samantha said, beaming at the Guagentis. Weathers snapped a picture of that moment—a moment, the women agree, that perfectly captures their surrogacy experience. "Most women who've just pushed out a 9-pounder will look at the baby, but my bond was with Pam, and so in the picture I'm looking at her," says Samantha. "Short of the birth of my own two children, it was the most special moment of my life." The image also captured Tristan rubbing his wife's back, looking fairly pleased himself.

As Pam cuddled Chase, marveling at how his almond-shaped eyes looked just like Gary's, she felt overcome with affection and respect for Samantha. "I didn't feel jealous," recalls Pam. "I was in awe of her selflessness and willingness to give us the greatest gift that anyone ever could."

Overcome with joy at being parents after so long, the Guagentis also had the happy knowledge that they wouldn't have to stop now that they were a little family of three. Earlier, after having discussed it with her husband, Samantha made them an offer they couldn't refuse: "I'll do it again whenever you're ready."

More Great Expectations

Over the next months, Pam and Samantha kept in touch, swapping photos and tales of motherhood. "Pam called all the time for baby advice," recalls Samantha. "I'd originally assumed I'd be paired with someone who'd been trying to get pregnant for years; I never thought I'd be the older woman in the relationship." Occasionally, their families got together for barbecues.

In the summer of 2001, when Chase was 7 months old, the Guagentis decided to accept Samantha's offer. In January 2002, their remaining three embryos (frozen from the first round of treatments) were transferred into Samantha's uterus. She didn't become pregnant. The women were disappointed, but determined. On an increased dosage of ovarian stimulation medication, Pam produced 29 eggs, and 25 developed into embryos. Dr. Wisot placed two in Samantha's uterus. Two weeks later, Samantha was pregnant and this time, the ultrasound detected two heartbeats. Pam and Gary were ecstatic.

The second pregnancy progressed smoothly and on November 12, 2002, Samantha gave birth with the Guagentis and Tristan again by her side. First to arrive was Ella, weighing 6 pounds, 6 ounces and 19 inches. Kyle followed at 6 pounds, 1 ounce, also 19 inches. Pam started bawling. As for Samantha, "I was relieved that the babies were healthy, and I was very tired!" A month later, they got together at Pam's house for a baby shower; Samantha made a cross-stitched sampler for the twins and gave Pam a charm bracelet with three booties and a heart.

The women still talk on the phone once a month and see each other as much as their jam-packed family lives will allow. Samantha says she always gets choked up seeing Pam's kids. "When I look at them, I know they're not mine.

WOULD YOU DO IT?

Here are your candid responses to a recent LHJ.com poll:

Is it ethical for a woman to carry another couple's biological child?

55%	Yes, even if the parties aren't related
24%	Yes, if it's being done for a family member
21%	No

Would you ever become a surrogate mother?

41%	No
17%	Yes, for my sister
17%	Yes, for a stranger
13%	Yes, for a friend
12%	Yes, for another close relative

Typically, a surrogate mother is paid $10,000 to $20,000. For you to be a surrogate mother, how much money would you have to be offered?

40%	No amount of money would be enough
20%	$10,000 to $20,000
5%	at least $50,000
5%	at least $100,000

But I do have a connection, in the way I imagine foster mothers must feel. After I had Chase, Pam's mother told me, 'You're family now.' I'm not just the surrogate."

During the women's last visit, Samantha's 4-year-old fell in love with baby Ella. "Kail was calling her 'My girlfriend.' He said he wanted to marry her," says Samantha, laughing. "I looked at Gary and said, 'That would be weird me giving birth to my own daughter-in-law!'"

Pam plans to have her kids call Samantha by her first name; as soon as they are old enough to understand, she'll explain Samantha's relationship to them. But she knows she'll never be able to put into words the gratitude she feels in her heart. "My sister has three kids, and every time she got pregnant, I'd look at her and think, When is it going to be my turn?" says Pam. "Thanks to Samantha, I got my turn."

UNIT 5

Sexuality Through the Lifecycle

Unit Selections

Key Points to Consider

- Do you remember trying to get answers about your body, sex, or similar topics as a young child? How did your parents respond? How did you feel? Do you hope your children will ask you questions about sex? Why or why not? Which topics or questions do you expect will be hardest for you to handle and answer?

- How do you view sex and sexuality at your age? In what ways is it different from when you were younger? How do you perceive the changes—positively, negatively, not sure—and to what do you attribute them? Are there things you feel you have missed? What are they?

- Close your eyes and imagine a couple having a pleasurable sexual interlude. When you are finished, open your eyes. How old were they? If they were younger than middle age, can you replay your vision with middle-aged or older people? Why or why not? How does this relate to your expectations regarding your own romantic and/or sexual life a few decades from now?

- Do you ever think about your parents as sexual people? Your grandparents? Was considering these two questions upsetting for you? Embarrassing? Explain your answers as best you can.

 **Links: www.dushkin.com/online/**
These sites are annotated in the World Wide Web pages.

American Association of Retired Persons (AARP)
http://www.aarp.org
National Institute on Aging (NIA)
http://www.nih.gov/nia/
Teacher Talk
http://education.indiana.edu/cas/tt/tthmpg.html
World Association for Sexology
http://www.tc.umn.edu/nlhome/m201/colem001/was/wasindex.htm

Individual sexual development is a lifelong process that begins prior to birth and continues until death. Contrary to once popular notions of this process, there are no latent periods in childhood or old age during which the individual is nonsexual or noncognizant of sexuality. The growing process of a sexual being does, however, reveal qualitative differences through various life stages. This section devotes attention to these stages of the life cycle and their relation to sexuality.

As children gain self-awareness, they naturally explore their own bodies, masturbate, display curiosity about the bodies of the opposite sex, and show interest in the bodies of mature individuals such as their parents. Exploration and curiosity are important and healthy aspects of human development. Yet it is often difficult for adults (who live in a society that is not comfortable with sexuality in general) to avoid making their children feel ashamed of being sexual or showing interest in sexuality. When adults impose their ambivalence upon a child's innocuous explorations into sexuality, fail to communicate with children about this real and important aspect of human life, or behave toward children in sexually inappropriate ways, distortion of an indispensable and formative stage of development occurs. This often leaves profound emotional scars that hinder full acceptance of self and sexuality later in the child's life.

Adolescence, the social stage accompanying puberty and the transition to adulthood, proves to be a very stressful period of life for many individuals as they attempt to develop an adult identity and forge relationships with others. Because of the physiological capacity of adolescents for reproduction, sexuality tends to be heavily censured by parents and society at this stage of life. However, prevailing societal messages are powerful, conflicting, and confusing: "Just Say No" . . . "Just Do It"; billboards and magazine ads using adolescent bodies provocatively and partially undressed; "romance" novels, television shows, MTV, movies with torrid sex scenes; seductive teenage "boy" and "girl" singers and bands; and Internet chat rooms. In addition, individual and societal attitudes place tremendous emphasis on sexual attractiveness (especially for females) and sexual competency (especially for males). These physical, emotional, and cultural pressures combine to create confusion and anxiety in adolescents and young adults about whether they are okay and normal. Information and assurances from adults can alleviate these stresses and facilitate positive and responsible sexual maturity if there is mutual trust and willingness in both generations.

Sexuality finally becomes socially acceptable in adulthood, at least within marriage. Yet routine, boredom, stress, pressures, the pace of life, work, or parenting responsibilities, and/or lack of communication can exact heavy tolls on the quantity and quality of sexual interaction. Sexual misinformation, myths, and unanswered questions, especially about emotional and/or physiological changes in sexual arousal/response or functioning, can also undermine or hinder intimacy and sexual interaction in the middle years.

Sexuality in the later years of life has also been socially and culturally stigmatized because of the prevailing misconception that only young, attractive, or married people are sexual. Such an attitude has contributed significantly to the apparent decline in sexual interest and activity as one grows older. However, as population demographics have shifted and the baby boomer generation has aged, these beliefs and attitudes have begun to change. Physiological changes in the aging process are not, in and of themselves, detrimental to sexual expression. A life history of experiences, good health, and growth can make sexual expression in the later years a most rewarding and fulfilling experience, and today's aging population is becoming more vocal in letting their children and grandchildren know that as we age we don't grow out of sex, but that, in fact, like fine wine, it can get better with age.

The first article in the *Youth and Their Sexuality* section looks at the effects parental dating can have on children and explains their developmental needs. The next articles address trends and a variety of issues and perspectives on pre-teen and teenage sexual behavior.

The articles in the *Sexuality in the Adult Years* subsection look realistically at lifelong sexuality and sexual satisfaction as natural, desirable, but, at times, hard to manage life goals in today's world. "Sex In The '90s" will put to rest entirely the myth that only the young are interested in sex.

The sexual revolution hits junior high

The kids are doing more than baring bellies: They're shocking adults with their anything-goes behavior

Kim Painter
Special for USA TODAY

Picture the mating rites of middle-schoolers. Perhaps you imagine hand-holding and first kisses, girls trying out eye shadow, boys sneaking a peek at vulgar men's magazines.

Now look again, through the eyes of increasingly concerned educators and experts:

• Researchers in Washington, D.C., recently started a program to prevent early sexual activity. They planned to offer it to seventh-graders, but after a pilot study decided to target fifth-graders—because too many seventh-graders already were having sex.

• Jo Mecham, a nurse at a Bettendorf, Iowa, middle school, says she overhears "pretty explicit sexual talk" from boys and girls in her "conservative" community. And despite a dress code, girls come to classes looking like bare-bellied rock stars: "They'll leave the house totally OK, and when they get to school, they start disrobing."

• Joey Zbylut-Birky, a middle-school teacher in Omaha, recently asked students to think about "where

they feel most comfortable" as part of an assignment to write song titles about themselves. A group of giggling boys piped up with comments about receiving oral sex.

The list goes on. Middle schools that used to do without dress codes now must send home exhaustive inventories of forbidden garments, from tube tops to too-low hip-huggers. Schools that used to handle crude language on a case-by-case basis now must have "no-profanity" policies. And sexual-harassment training is a normal part of middle-school curriculum.

The world "is rougher, it is sexier and it has reached down to touch boys and girls at younger ages," says Margaret Sagarese, who, with Charlene C. Giannetti, has written several books on parenting, including the new *The Patience of a Saint: How Faith Can Sustain You During the Tough Times of Parenting.*

Baby-boomer parents who thought that nothing would ever shock them are shocked by the way their young

teens talk, dress and perhaps even behave, Sagarese says.

"Things have changed," says Jude Swift, 52, a mother of five whose youngest is an eighth-grade boy. "I think a great deal of it is due to the media and what kids see on TV, in magazine ads, in videos.... It's all about being sexy."

The world 'is rougher, it is sexier' and it's harder for teens to avoid it

Swift, of Camillus, N.Y., says she picked up a *Teen People* magazine the other day and "I was amazed. It was page after page of young teens dressed in very provocative ways and in very provocative poses."

Young girls "do not see anything wrong in looking that way," says Zbylut-Birky, the Omaha teacher. And, she says, "they don't see the difference between how they should

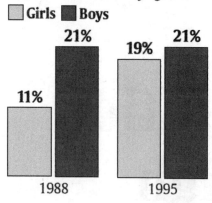

Sex by age 14

Kids (15 and older) who say they had had intercourse by age 14:

■ Girls ■ Boys

1988: Girls 11%, Boys 21%
1995: Girls 19%, Boys 21%

BY JULIE SNYDER, USA TODAY

look for a party and how they should look in an educational setting."

Boys want to look sexy, too

Even boys face increasing pressure to look sexy, says Sagarese: "There are 12-year-old boys going to GNC and taking all kinds of supplements because they want abs the same way girls want breasts."

Of course, many girls who dress like Britney Spears and many boys who talk like Eminem don't go beyond nervous note-passing in their actual romantic lives.

Zbylut-Birky, who overheard the oral-sex banter, says, "A lot of times they use that kind of language to impress their peers, but there's really nothing going on there."

But for some substantial minority of middle schoolers, something very risky—including intercourse and oral sex—is going on, some experts say. In 1995, government researchers asked teens over age 15 whether they'd had sexual intercourse by age 14; 19% of girls and 21% of boys said yes. In 1988, the numbers were 11% for girls and the same 21% for boys, says the Washington, D.C.-based research group Child Trends. Data for 2002 are just being collected.

Another study, using different methods, followed 12- to 14-year-olds between 1997 and 1999 and

found 16% of girls and 20% of boys reported sex at 14 or younger, says Child Trends researcher Jennifer Manlove.

As for oral sex, a 2000 study from the Alan Guttmacher Institute in New York caused a firestorm by suggesting that more young teens were engaging in that activity—possibly as a way of remaining technical virgins in the age of abstinence education. That study was based on scattered, anecdotal reports of increased oral herpes and gonorrhea of the throat.

No nationwide, scientific study has actually asked young teens, or older teens for that matter, whether they have oral sex.

"A lot of alarm parents feel on this issue is based on anecdotal information," says Bill Albert, spokesman for the Washington, D.C.-based National Campaign to Prevent Teen Pregnancy, a private, non-profit group working to reduce teen pregnancy.

But some of the anecdotes are hair-raising.

"The other day at school, a girl got caught in a bathroom with a boy performing oral sex on him," says Maurisha Stenson, a 14-year-old eighth-grader at a Syracuse, N.Y., middle school.

When the lights went on

Denyia Sullivan, 14, attends a different Syracuse middle school but says she's seen and heard about similar things. One time, a girl performed oral sex on a boy in the gym bleachers during a movie. "The teacher turned on the light and there they were," Sullivan says. "Everybody was looking and laughing."

The two girls also say there's more than oral sex going on. Sullivan can think of five pregnant girls at her school, which includes sixth-, seventh- and eighth-graders. Stenson guesses that "almost 50%" of kids at her school, for seventh- and eighth-graders, are engaging in some kind of sex.

"This is happening; they are telling the truth," says Courtney Ramirez, who directs the Syracuse Way to Go after-school program, designed to help kids succeed in school and avoid risks. Both girls are peer educators in the program.

"Youths are really getting involved in things a whole lot sooner than we thought," Ramirez says.

But other experts say that without good, current numbers on nationwide trends, they can't even say with any confidence that early sex is increasing. "It could be getting worse, it could be getting better, we just don't know," Albert says.

One problem is that the best government studies are done infrequently. Another is that researchers—and the public—are squeamish about asking detailed sex questions of young teens. And when they do ask, they aren't sure youngsters always understand the questions or answer truthfully. Albert's organization will try to fill in the gap later this year with a report based on data from around the country.

But many educators and parents have heard the alarms and are acting now. Krystal McKinney directs a program that offers sex education and life-skills training to middle-school girls in the Washington, D.C., area. Since the 2000 Guttmacher oral sex report, she and her staff have redoubled efforts to make sure that girls understand the risks.

"We have kids who think you can't get diseases from oral sex," she says. "Kids think they know everything, but we challenge that."

With the youngest teens, clear information is crucial, says Xenia Becher, a mental health educator at the Syracuse after-school program.

Recently, she says, she asked some 13- to 15-year-olds to define sex. "They had trouble coming up with an answer," she says. "Some said it had to be between a male and female and a penis and vagina had to be involved.

"So I asked, 'What about if two men were involved?' 'Well,' they said, 'I don't know what that is, but it's not sex.'"

Becher also trains parents to discuss sex with their kids. She tells them that their voices matter, even in a sex-soaked culture.

"When you get down to what's right or wrong, popular culture is going to have an influence, but the stronger internal voice comes from you," she says.

Becher admits that setting limits and encouraging independence can be a real balancing act. When her own 13-year-old daughter dressed for a dance in a pair of "those nasty hip-huggers" and a short top, Becher says, she asked her to think how she'd look when "she was waving her arms around on the dance floor." But she didn't make her daughter change.

"You've got to pick your battles," she says.

Parents shouldn't back off

"Kids really do care what their parents think," says Kristin Moore, president of Child Trends. "They don't really want their parents to back away. But a lot of parents do back away at this age."

Some parents, she says, are so intimidated by a child's hostile behavior and demands for privacy that they give far too much ground. "Sometimes parents are home during a party but have no idea what is going on at the party."

Mark Gibbons, an Augusta, Ga., father of two girls ages 8 and 12, says that he and his wife are doing everything they can to stay involved. They try to talk to their daughters about everything. "We've told them that it may sometimes be embarrassing, but that we'd rather they get their information from us," he says.

"I talk to them all the time," says Lauryn, a seventh-grader who takes classes for gifted and talented kids. She does say that she prefers to discuss boyfriends with her mom.

Nevertheless, when Lauryn has friends over, Gibbons says he keeps his ears open. When she's instant messaging on the computer, he says, "Every once in a while, I'll just wander over there and ask who she's talking to. And I do look at her little directory and make sure all those user names are people that I know. We try not to show that we're being nosy, but we are."

Gibbons also chaperones middle-school dances. It's a window into his daughter's larger world—one that, even in a community of "pretty well-behaved kids," can be shocking, he says. "Some of the dancing they do is kind of risque, to say the least."

Lauryn says she appreciates her parents' involvement: "I believe it does makes a difference.... I have never gotten into trouble." And she says she does know kids who are getting into sexual trouble. "At some of the parties I go to, people playing 'Truth or Dare' will say that they've already 'done it,'" she says.

Meanwhile, Gibbons says he recently got a reminder that it is never too early to discuss sexual values. Third-grader Tayler "came home and said one little girl took a boy behind a tree and they were French kissing.... I said, 'Well, do you think that is wrong?' She said, 'Yes.'"

But while parents are right to watch and worry, some may be worrying too much and enjoying too little about their children's pubescent years, says Sagarese, the parenting author. "I can't tell you how many parents have come up to me at speeches and they are apoplectic that their daughter is kissing. They feel like the first kiss is a runaway train that will lead to AIDS or pregnancy."

Her co-author, Giannetti, says, "Parents need to take a deep breath and a step back and remember what it was like to be a young adolescent."

Sometimes, Sagarese says, a first kiss is just a first kiss—and the same lovely rite of passage it was in a more innocent time.

From *USA Today* magazine, March 15-17, 2002, pp. 1-2. © 2002 by the Society for the Advancement of Education. Reprinted by permission.

Choosing Virginity

A New Attitude: Fewer teenagers are having sex. As parents and politicians debate the merits of abstinence programs, here's what the kids have to say.

BY LORRAINE ALI AND JULIE SCELFO

THERE'S A SEXUAL REVOLUTION GOING ON IN AMERICA, AND believe it or not, it has nothing to do with Christina Aguilera's bare-it-all video "Dirrty." The uprising is taking place in the real world, not on "The Real World." Visit any American high school and you'll likely find a growing number of students who watch scabrous TV shows like "Shipmates," listen to Eminem—and have decided to remain chaste until marriage. Rejecting the get-down-make-love ethos of their parents' generation, this wave of young adults represents a new counter-culture, one clearly at odds with the mainstream media and their routine use of sex to boost ratings and peddle product.

According to a recent study from the Centers for Disease Control, the number of high-school students who say they've never had sexual intercourse rose by almost 10 percent between 1991 and 2001. Parents, public-health officials and sexually beleaguered teens themselves may be relieved by this "let's not" trend. But the new abstinence movement, largely fostered by cultural conservatives and evangelical Christians, has also become hotly controversial.

As the Bush administration plans to increase federal funding for abstinence programs by nearly a third, to $135 million, the Advocates for Youth and other proponents of a more comprehensive approach to sex ed argue that teaching abstinence isn't enough. Teens also need to know how to protect themselves if they do have sex, these groups say, and they need to understand the emotional intensity inherent in sexual relationships.

The debate concerns public policy, but the real issue is personal choice. At the center of it all are the young people themselves, whose voices are often drowned out by the political cacophony. Some of them opened up and talked candidly to NEWSWEEK about their reasons for abstaining from sex until marriage. It's clear that religion plays a critical role in this ex-

traordinarily private decision. But there are other factors as well: caring parents, a sense of their own unreadiness, the desire to gain some semblance of control over their own destinies. Here are their stories.

The Wellesley Girl

ALICE KUNCE SAYS SHE'S A FEMINIST, BUT NOT THE "ARMY-boot-wearing, shaved-head, I-hate-all-men kind." The curly-haired 18-year-old Wellesley College sophomore—she skipped a grade in elementary school—looks and talks like what she is: one of the many bright, outspoken students at the liberal Massachusetts women's college. She's also a virgin. "One of the empowering things about the feminist movement," she says, "is that we're able to assert ourselves, to say no to sex and not feel pressured about it. And I think guys are kind of getting it. Like, 'Oh, *not* everyone's doing it'."

But judging by MTV's "Undressed," UPN's "Buffy the Vampire Slayer" and just about every other TV program or movie targeted at teens, everyone *is* doing it. Alice grew up with these images, but as a small-town girl in Jefferson City, Mo., most teen shows felt alien and alienating. "You're either a prudish person who can't handle talking about sex or you're out every Saturday night getting some," she says. "But if you're not sexually active and you're willing to discuss the subject, you can't be called a prude. How do they market to that?" The friend from back home she's been dating since August asked not to be identified in this story, but Alice doesn't mind talking candidly about what they do—or don't do. "Which is acceptable? Oral, vaginal or anal sex?" she asks. "For me, they're all sex. In high school, you could have oral sex and still call yourself a virgin.

Now I'm like, 'Well, what makes one less intimate than the other?'"

Alice, a regular churchgoer who also teaches Sunday school, says religion is not the reason she's chosen abstinence. She fears STDs and pregnancy, of course, but above all, she says, she's not mature enough emotionally to handle the deep intimacy sex can bring. Though most people in her college, or even back in her Bible-belt high school, haven't made the same choice, Alice says she has never felt ostracized. If anything, she feels a need to speak up for those being coerced by aggressive abstinence groups. "Religious pressure was and is a lot greater than peer pressure," says Alice, who has never taken part in an abstinence program. "I don't think there are as many teens saying 'Oh come on, everybody's having sex' as there are church leaders saying 'No, it's bad, don't do it. It'll ruin your life.' The choices many religious groups leave you with are either no sex at all or uneducated sex. What happened to educating young people about how they can protect themselves?"

The Dream Team

KARL NICOLETTI WASTED NO TIME WHEN IT CAME TO HAVING "the talk" with his son, Chris. It happened five years ago, when Chris was in sixth grade. Nicoletti was driving him home from school and the subject of girls came up. "I know many parents who are wishy-washy when talking to their kids about sex. I just said, 'No, you're not going to have sex. Keep your pecker in your pants until you graduate from high school'."

"If you're abstinent, it's like you're the one set aside from society because you're not 'doing it'."

AMANDA WING, 17,
who plans to stay a virgin until marriage

Today, the 16-year-old from Longmont, Colo., vows he'll remain abstinent until marriage. So does his girlfriend, 17-year-old Amanda Wing, whose parents set similarly strict rules for her and her two older brothers. "It's amazing, but they did listen," says her mother, Lynn Wing. Amanda has been dating Chris for only two months, but they've known each other for eight years. On a Tuesday-night dinner date at Portabello's (just across from the Twin Peaks Mall), Amanda asks, "You gonna get the chicken parmesan again?" Chris nods. "Yep. You know me well." They seem like a long-married couple—except that they listen to the Dave Matthews Band, have a 10:30 weeknight curfew and never go beyond kissing and hugging. (The guidelines set by Chris's dad: no touching anywhere that a soccer uniform covers.)

"Society is so run by sex," says Chris, who looks like Madison Avenue's conception of an All-American boy in his Abercrombie sweat shirt and faded baggy jeans. "Just look at everything—TV, movies. The culture today makes it seem OK to have sex whenever, however or with whoever you want. I just disagree with that." Amanda, who looks tomboy comfy in baggy brown cords, a white T shirt and chunky-soled shoes, feels the same way. "Sex should be a special thing that doesn't need to be public," she says. "But if you're abstinent, it's like *you're* the one set aside from society because you're not 'doing it'."

The peer pressure in this town of 71,000 people in the shadow of the Rocky Mountains is substantially less than in cosmopolitan Denver, 45 minutes away. ("It figures you had to come all the way out here to find a virgin," one local said.) Chris joined a Christian abstinence group called Teen Advisors this year. "We watched their slide show in eighth grade and it just has pictures of all these STDs," he says. "It's one of the grossest things you've ever seen. I didn't want to touch a girl, like, forever." He now goes out once a month and talks to middle schoolers about abstinence. Amanda saw the same presentation. "It's horrible," she says. "If that doesn't scare kids out of sex, nothing will." Could these gruesome images put them off sex for life? Chris and Amanda say no. They're sure that whoever they marry will be disease-free.

To most abstaining teens, marriage is the golden light at the end of the perilous tunnel of dating—despite what their parents' experience may have been. Though Amanda's mother and father have had a long and stable union, Karl Nicoletti separated from Chris's mother when Chris was in fifth grade. His fiancée moved in with Chris and Karl two years ago; Chris's mother now has a year-and-a-half-old son out of wedlock. Chris and Amanda talk about marriage in the abstract, but they want to go to college first, and they're looking at schools on opposite sides of the country. "I think we could stay together," Chris says. Amanda agrees. "Like we have complete trust in each other," she says. "It's just not hard for us." Whether the bond between them is strong enough to withstand a long-distance relationship is yet to be seen. For now, Chris and Amanda mostly look ahead to their next weekly ritual: the Tuesday pancake lunch.

The Survivor

REMAINING A VIRGIN UNTIL MARRIAGE IS NEITHER AN EASY nor a common choice in Latoya Huggins's part of Paterson, N.J. At least three of her friends became single mothers while they were still in high school, one by an older man who now wants nothing to do with the child. "It's hard for her to finish school," Latoya says, "because she has to take the baby to get shots and stuff."

Latoya lives in a chaotic world: so far this year, more than a dozen people have been murdered in her neighborhood. It's a life that makes her sexuality seem like one of the few things she can actually control. "I don't even want a boyfriend until after college," says Latoya, who's studying to be a beautician at a technical high school. "Basically I want a lot out of life. My career choices are going to need a lot of time and effort."

Latoya, 18, could pass for a street-smart 28. She started thinking seriously about abstinence five years ago, when a national outreach program called Free Teens began teaching classes at her church. The classes reinforced what she already knew from growing up in Paterson—that discipline is the key to getting through your teen years alive. Earlier this year she dated a 21-year-old appliance salesman from her neighborhood, until Latoya heard that he was hoping she'd have sex with him. "We decided that we should just be friends," she explains, "before he cheated on me or we split up in a worse way."

So most days Latoya comes home from school alone. While she waits for her parents to return from work, she watches the Disney Channel or chills in her basement bedroom, which she's decorated with construction-paper cutouts of the names of her favorite pop stars, such as Nelly and Aaliyah. She feels safe there, she says, because "too many bad things are happening" outside. But bad things happen inside, too: last year she opened the door to a neighbor who forced his way inside and attempted to rape her. "He started trying to take my clothes off. I was screaming and yelling to the top of my lungs and nobody heard." Luckily, the phone rang. Latoya told the intruder it was her father, and that if she didn't answer he would come home right away. The man fled. Latoya tries not to think about what happened, although she feels "like dying" when she sees her attacker on the street. (Her parents decided not to press charges so she wouldn't have to testify in court.) Her goal is to graduate and get a job; she wants to stay focused and independent. "Boys make you feel like you're special and you're the only one they care about," she says. "A lot of girls feel like they need that. But my mother loves me and my father loves me, so there's no gap to fill."

The Beauty Queen

EVEN THOUGH SHE LIVES 700 MILES FROM THE NEAREST ocean, Daniela Aranda was recently voted Miss Hawaiian Tropic El Paso, Texas, and her parents couldn't be prouder. They've displayed a picture of their bikini-clad daughter smack-dab in the middle of the living room. "People always say to me 'You don't look like a virgin'," says Daniela, 20, who wears supersparkly eye shadow, heavy lip liner and a low-cut black shirt. "But what does a virgin look like? Someone who wears white and likes to look at flowers?"

Daniela models at Harley-Davidson fashion shows, is a cheerleader for a local soccer team called the Patriots and hangs out with friends who work at Hooters. She's also an evangelical Christian who made a vow at 13 to remain a virgin, and she's kept that promise. "It can be done," she says. "I'm living proof." Daniela has never joined an abstinence program; her decision came from strong family values and deep spiritual convictions.

Daniela's arid East El Paso neighborhood, just a mile or so from the Mexican border, was built atop desert dunes, and the sand seems to be reclaiming its own by swallowing up back patios and sidewalks. The city, predominantly Hispanic, is home to the Fort Bliss Army base, breathtaking mesa views—and some of the highest teen-pregnancy rates in the nation. "There's a lot of girls that just want to get pregnant so they can get married and get out of here," Daniela says.

But she seems content to stay in El Paso. She studies business at El Paso Community College, dates a UTEP football player named Mike and works as a sales associate at the A'gaci Too clothing store in the Cielo Vista Mall. She also tones at the gym and reads—especially books by the Christian author Joshua Harris. In "Boy Meets Girl," she's marked such passages as "Lust is never satisfied" with a pink highlighter. She's also saved an article on A. C. Green, the former NBA player who's become a spokesman for abstinence. "My boyfriend's coach gave it to him because the other guys sometimes say, 'Are you gay? What's wrong with you?' It's proof that if a famous man like Green can do it, so can he."

"I feel that part of me hasn't been triggered yet," she says. "Sex is one of those things you can't miss until you have it."

LENÉE YOUNG, 19,
who has never had a boyfriend

Daniela has been dating Mike for more than a year. He's had sex before, but has agreed to remain abstinent with her. "He's what you call a born-again virgin," she says. "Or a secondary abstinent, or something like that. We just don't put ourselves in compromising situations. If we're together late at night, it's with my whole family."

Daniela knows about temptation: every time she walks out onstage in a bathing suit, men take notice. But she doesn't see a contradiction in her double life as virgin and beauty queen; rather, it's a personal challenge. "I did Hawaiian Tropic because I wanted to see if I could get into a bikini in front of all these people," she says. "I wasn't thinking, 'Oh, I'm going to win.' But I did, and I got a free trip to Houston's state finals. I met the owner of Hawaiian Tropic. It's like, wow, this is as good as it gets."

The Ring Bearer

LENEE YOUNG IS TRYING TO WRITE A PAPER FOR HER SPANISH class at Atlanta's Spelman College, but as usual she and her roommates can't help getting onto the subject of guys. "I love Ludacris," Lenée gushes. "I love everything about him. Morris Chestnut, too. He has a really pretty smile. Just gorgeous." But Lenée, 19, has never had a boyfriend, and has never even been kissed. "A lot of the guys in high school had already had sex," she says. "I knew that would come up, so I'd end all my relationships at the very beginning." Lenée decided back then to remain a virgin until marriage, and even now she feels little temptation to do what many of her peers are doing behind closed dormitory doors. "I feel that part of me hasn't been triggered yet," she says. "Sex is one of those things you can't miss until you have it."

Last summer she went with a friend from her hometown of Pittsburgh to a Silver Ring Thing. These popular free events meld music videos, pyrotechnics and live teen comedy sketches with dire warnings about STDs. Attendees can buy a silver ring—and a Bible—for $12. Then, at the conclusion of the program, as techno music blares, they recite a pledge of abstinence

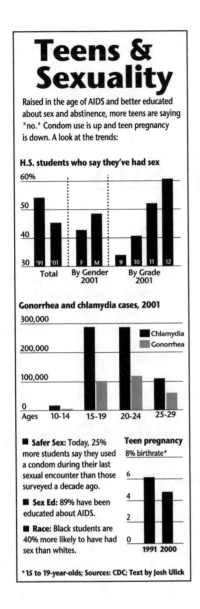

Teens & Sexuality

Raised in the age of AIDS and better educated about sex and abstinence, more teens are saying "no." Condom use is up and teen pregnancy is down. A look at the trends:

H.S. students who say they've had sex

Total '91 '01
By Gender 2001 F M
By Grade 2001 9 10 11 12

Gonorrhea and chlamydia cases, 2001

■ Chlamydia
■ Gonorrhea

Ages 10-14 15-19 20-24 25-29

■ **Safer Sex:** Today, 25% more students say they used a condom during their last sexual encounter than those surveyed a decade ago.

■ **Sex Ed:** 89% have been educated about AIDS.

■ **Race:** Black students are 40% more likely to have had sex than whites.

Teen pregnancy
8% birthrate*

1991 2000

*15 to 19-year-olds; Sources: CDC; Text by Josh Ulick

Young was the only woman who said no, and everybody in the room was stunned. "Are you serious? We gotta find you a boyfriend!" But Lenée wasn't embarrassed. "I don't feel like I've missed out," she says. "I just feel like my time will come." Until then, she sports that shiny silver ring.

The Renewed Virgin

Lucian Schulte had always planned to wait until he was married to have sex, but that was before a warm night a couple of years ago when the green-eyed, lanky six-footer found himself with an unexpected opportunity. "She was all for it," says Lucian, now 18. "It was like, 'Hey, let's give this a try'." The big event was over in a hurry and lacked any sense of intimacy. "In movies, if people have sex, it's always romantic," he says. "Physically, it did feel good, but emotionally, it felt really awkward. It was not what I expected it to be."

While the fictional teens of "American Pie" would have been clumsily overjoyed, Lucian, raised Roman Catholic, was plagued by guilt. "I was worried that I'd given myself to someone and our relationship was now a lot more serious than it was before," he says. "It was like, 'Now, what is she going to expect from me?'" Lucian worried, too, about disease and pregnancy. He promised himself never again.

Lucian, now an engineering major at the University of Alberta in Canada, is a "renewed virgin." His parents are strong proponents of chastity, and he attended school-sponsored abstinence classes. But the messages didn't hit home until he'd actually had sex. "It's a pretty special thing, and it's also pretty serious," he says. "Abstinence has to do with 'Hey, are you going to respect this person?'" He has dated since his high-school affair, and is now hoping a particular cute coed from Edmonton will go out with him. "But I'll try to restrict myself to kissing," he says. "Not because I think everything else is bad. But the more you participate with someone, the harder it's going to be to stop."

It's not easy to practice such restraint, especially when those around him do not. Lucian lives in a single room, decorated with ski-lift tickets and a "Scooby-Doo" poster, in an all-male dorm, but he says most students "get hitched up, sleep around and never see each other again." Meanwhile he does his best to push his own sexual urges from his mind. "I try to forget about it, but I have to say it sucks. Homework is a good thing to do, and going out for a run usually works." He also goes to Sunday mass. Lucian figures he can hold out until he's married, which he hopes will be by the time he's 30. "I'm looking forward to an intimate experience with my wife, who I'll truly love and want to spend the rest of my life with," says Lucian. "It's kind of corny, but it's for real."

With SARAH DOWNEY and VANESSA JUAREZ

and don their rings. "My friend, who's also a virgin, said I needed to go so I could get a ring," Lenée says. "It was fun, like the music and everything. And afterwards they had a dance and a bonfire."

The idea of abstinence was not new to Lenée. In high school she participated in a program sponsored by the University of Pittsburgh Medical Center called Postponing Sexual Involvement. Her mother had discussed it with her—once—the week before she left for college. Two of her closest friends are also virgins; the trio jokingly call themselves The Good Girls Club. But student life can sometimes be a shock to her sensibilities. "Another friend of mine and this guy were talking about how they didn't use a condom. He said, 'I like it raw.' I was like, 'Oh, my goodness'."

And then there was the recent party that began with truth-or-dare questions. The first one: have you ever kissed a boy?

Staying Up Late With Sue

By Anne Matthews

Sue Johanson, sex guru, has three grown kids, two grand-children, three books, a nursing degree and not one but two hit TV programs. Thirty weeks a year, live from Toronto's SkyDome, she broadcasts *The Sunday Night Sex Show,* a favorite in Canada since 1996.

In 2002 she added a second hour especially for the U.S. audience. *Talk Sex With Sue* airs late nights on the Oxygen cable network, and some 4.2 million Americans now stay up to catch her tips and quips, from the latest in lubricants to the odds of a male over 35 having a heart attack during intercourse.

Johanson, a leading sex educator in Canada for more than three decades, will discuss absolutely anything except the year she was born. "Sometime in the 20th century" is about as specific as she gets. Gray hair gives her credibility, and she knows it. "Nothing reduces inhibitions like a grandmother sitting on TV talking about whips, willies and warts," she says.

She's the Julia Child of sex, unflappable and candid. Fans know she likes to knit and sew, bake sourdough bis-cuits, putter at her Ontario lake cottage and go to yard sales—"I'm cheap!"

On camera, she is a born ham, especially when sharing condom advice: "If you wanna be mine, cover your vine!"; "Shroud the moose before you let loose!" Every week she delves into her Pleasure Chest—actually an old sewing bas-ket, thriftily relined with red velvet—and offers tabletop demos of sex toys. On a live broadcast, this can be risky. Audiences have seen her battle a smoldering vibrator and a badly out-of-control vacuum pump. Sex toys that are dish-washer-safe get a special nod of approval.

The heart of her shows is the call-in segment. Erectile dysfunction, pregnancy and yeast infections are the most common worries; always, Johanson's answers reassure and teach as well as amuse. This is an international public edu-cation project that only looks like standup comedy. Her ap-proach is slangy but never vulgar. She has never been bleeped. And you can't beat her command of statistics: What percentage of American teens have their first sexual experience in automobiles? "Twelve percent. You never see that in car commercials." What percentage of women over 80 continue to have sex? "Thirty percent. Finding a man that age with working parts is another story."

Johanson works in the tradition of the wisecracking ad-vice columnist who uses reader queries to explain human behavior. Like Dear Abby and Ann Landers, she tackles sensitive topics head-on, and like Dr. Ruth Westheimer, she displays a frankness that can be jaw-dropping. Sex aids for quadriplegics? Bondage play after a bypass? Sue covers it all. Canadians seem to love it, stopping her on the street or at the grocery store for detailed sex advice. Americans politely murmur that they really, really like the show.

CREDENTIALS AND CREDIBILITY

Born in Ontario to an English-Irish family, married young to a Swedish-Canadian electrician employed by a public util-ity, Johanson is a registered nurse with postgraduate train-ing in family planning, human sexuality and counseling and communications. These credentials underpin her cred-ibility. Her ability to talk easily with teenagers about sexual issues led her to create, in 1970, the first birth control clinic in any North American high school. She still does 60 shows live and 30 lectures a year; for her countless courses, talks and media presentations on smart sex, she received in 2001 the prestigious Order of Canada award, that nation's ver-sion of knighthood.

Good sex after midlife interests Johanson—and her audi-ence. "Who says you shouldn't have exciting sex at 70?" she asks. "If fitness and flexibility allow, do it, try it, don't limit yourself by age. 'Oh dear, I'm 50, I can't, I shouldn't.' " The key, she believes, is the quality of the relationship with one's partner. Enjoyable sex calls for drive, enthusi-asm, imagination.

And understanding. "As we get older the body changes—no more firm, young, bodacious tatas. Your waistline is gone, you've got turkey neck and wrinkled skin. … You're not sure what a partner will think? Well, your partner has the same worries. That manly chest has slipped south. … Talk about it ahead of time. Say, 'I'm going to find this a little difficult—my body works, but it isn't so beauti-ful.' And they'll likely reply, 'Thank goodness! Me too!' "

Getting more out of your love life

Tips from Sue Johanson:

1. Skip burgers and fries. Good nutrition makes you feel much better, and makes for better sex. "Eat junk food," she says, "and allyou want to do is fight over the remote control."

2. Games are good. Try phone sex—he on one extension, she on another. Try hide-and-seek, on the floor, in the dark, in the nude. "Find each other, then have fun under the coffee table."

3. Toys work, too. "Go to a sex store together, buy small, low-cost items to start, check them out, then invest more once ou know what you like."

4. Choose a time when both feel ready for lovemaking. Wake up your partner at midnight with caresses and a sultry "Hi, big guy!" Someone with arthritis may do best in the morning, after a good night's sleep. "When we were young," Johanson points out, "we could never have sex during the day—the kids would hear."

5. If you have a physical restriction, or just the aches and pains of aging:
- Take an anti-inflammatory 20 minutes ahead of time.
- Together, take a romantic hot bath, with lights low, and candles and incense by the tub.
- Keep extra pillows nearby in case of leg or foot cramps.
- Have cream or gel handy.

- Warm the bed with an electric blanket.

6. Pleasurable positions? Spoon-fashion. Side-by-side. The X position. Or female-on-top. Try chair sex: It's easy on the joints.

7. And try the following books:
- Her latest, *Sex, Sex and More Sex*, coming out this month.
- *The Ultimate Guide to Sex and Disability*, by Cory Silverburg, Miriam Kaufman and Fran Odette.
- *The New Love and Sex After 60*, by Robert Butler and Myrna Lewis. "Get the book and stand well back!"

NOT JUST FOR THE YOUNG

Arousal in both sexes takes longer with age, Johanson explains, and the need for orgasm diminishes dramatically. But the need for a sex life is evergreen, even if grown children try to interfere, or shame ("Mother! At your age!"). Sex in nursing homes and assisted-living communities is growing more common, she adds; in Canada, facilities often include a "love nest" on the premises, with double bed, flowers, candles and a good radio/CD player. Improvised intimacy works, too. "Privacy can be as simple as a Do Not Disturb sign on a room door, which means 'Meals and meds can wait. We are having fun in here.' "

Johanson's weekly call-ins still demonstrate the widespread belief that sex is the property of the young. That's changing. Aging boomers, she says, will permanently redefine post-50 sex. Women in their 70s and 80s have begun asserting their ongoing interest in a sex life. Sue calls such people "cougars"—older women who enjoy sex, always did and have no intention of giving it up. Recently she spoke to an 85-year-old woman whose male partner is 35. No complaints from either side; quite the contrary.

"So why accept arbitrary age parameters?" Johanson asks. The basic rules of sex apply at every life stage. "Use your head, plan ahead, know what you're doing, never let sex just happen." At 18 or 80, she advises, "Don't always expect multi-orgasmic bliss. Pleasure, sure. Affection, definitely. Sex should be energizing. Enjoyable. And a bit of a giggle."

Anne Matthews *is a nonfiction writer in Princeton, N.J.*

Sex in the '90's

Old people may not have much time to waste, but they've got plenty of time to screw around. And some have gotten really good at it. Jeff Johnson kneads sexy seniors for pointers. Grab a walker—you'll need it.

Jeff Johnson

Friday, 9 p.m., Florida's Gulf Coast

I'm wandering through an open-air apartment complex complete with AstroTurf and a pool. Somewhere behind these stucco walls lurks a cane-wielding, 75-year-old sexual tigress named Loretta. She'd rather enjoy the fruits of a sixsome than the brain-numbing death march of *Golden Girls* reruns. But it wasn't always that way.

"I married at 18," Loretta begins, mere inches from me on a couch in her cozy apartment. "My first husband put me on a pedestal and wouldn't do anything too dirty. So, I had no sexual outlet. When he died, I learned to quilt and was involved with church. Then someone got me a magazine subscription and there was an ad for Betty Dodson's *Self-Loving* video. I sent for it and she recommended some vibrators. And she said **get a mirror and look at yourself.**" She pauses to mention that **freshly ejaculated semen might make breasts bigger.**

"Eventually, I replied to some personal ads and met a nice man who said he was into indoor games. I thought he meant bridge or canasta," she continues. This man, who would become Loretta's second husband, had 30 acres in the country. "I learned that you could **go outside without clothes on**, and it was wonderful. I had never done any of this stuff in 69 years! I discovered that I enjoyed sex, and I could exude sex. I was a caterpillar that turned into a butterfly."

Sexual freedom like this is exactly why I'm in Florida, the perennial playground for sexy septuagenarians of all shapes and sizes, where, to many, the Cuban Missile Crisis is just a Latin lover who's having a tough time getting a hard-on.

Loretta's third hubby, Paul (number two eventually passed away also), is 20 years younger, but says he wouldn't trade Loretta for three 25-year-olds. As he whips up a batch of gin and tonics, he shows me poems he wrote about suicide before he met Loretta at a masturbation party.

"At my first sex party, I was so shy," Loretta remembers. "But everyone was so warm and outgoing. People came up and led me to the 'love chair.' My second husband was on one side, and this other guy was on the other side of me, there was one guy between my legs, then there was one guy playing with this breast, and one playing with that one. So, I had five men! It was like going off the high-dive, but it is what I wanted to experience." And if a 75-year-old is willing to take that plunge, there's no reason not to **try out taboos you've been denying yourself.**

While some of us may hump with the rote sterility of a junior high marching band, Loretta and Paul **improvise like seasoned jazzbos** when they **make love each morning.**

"The way that I do sex is I **do whatever comes into my head**," Loretta explains as she wanders into her bedroom in search of

their favorite toy, **the Crystal Wand**. "It's acrylic," Paul explains, while Loretta shows me that it has an end for both a man and a woman. "And it hits the G-spot perfect," he adds. "I've seen it bring women to heights they've never been to."

"When Paul and I get together, sometimes we have a plan, but we **never go by the plan**, because other things happen," Loretta continues, insisting I grope their wand. "Our lovemaking routine is very exciting, but we know that when that routine gets old, there are other things out there waiting for us." And I don't think she means hunting down a discount at the local buffet.

Saturday, noon, Tampa

Next stop on the senior sex tour is an upscale business hotel on the highway, where I meet Loretta's mentor, Lynda Gayle. Lynda Gayle, 60, has been a homemaker, a city clerk and the owner of a printing business. She now runs ClubRel8, a (pretty much) weekly masturbation party that encourages and praises sexual experimentation.

Lynda Gayle has a flowing white-blond mane and says she ejaculates puddles when she's aroused. The rest of the time she's a fountain of sex education, and I am currently getting soaked.

As Lynda Gayle and her hubby set up shop (miniature candy bars, baskets of lotions, hand towels), she explains that she's so good at Kegels, she could be doing hands-free, pants-on masturbating right now and I'd have no idea. "Every woman can do this—they should **masturbate while waiting at red lights**. It makes you tighter," she says.

Later, she disrobes for the lucky photographer and climbs into the hot tub/bathtub, firing off more tidbits. **"When choosing a vibrator, touch it to the end of your nose,"** she says, soaping up her ample bosom. "Whatever it does to your nose is what's gonna happen to you."

She adds, "I can **get off masturbating a man**. The feel, the smell, the energy flow. That's the beauty of it. I **have him sit in a chair.** It's easier on your elbow and hand than doing it in a bed. Occasionally, a man will say, 'I don't think I can come this way.' I just say, 'I don't fucking care, because I am doing this for me.' I **keep my hands very lubricated with almond oil.** It smells good and it tastes good, too. **Never use any kind of lubricant that you wouldn't want in your mouth."** And finally, Lynda Gayle lets a vibrator's charge run through her hand and onto the penis, as "sometimes the charge is too strong to touch the cock directly."

But women aren't chopped liver either. "My first experience with another woman was with two other ladies that my husband arranged," Lynda Gayle says. "I think touching another woman gave me an appreciation of what I felt like. **A lesbian experience allows women to appreciate their own bodies even more.**"

Just **don't forget to breathe.** "When you're having sex and it's great, you breathe little short breaths or you hold your breath. The kidneys, heart and lungs get together and say, enough of this shit, I'm not getting the air I need, and they cut the orgasm off," Lynda Gayle says. "This is frustrating because you're usually so high that you think you can never get that high again, or you get a tremendous headache right in the back of your skull. But if you learn to keep breathing, you can continue to have wonderful orgasms that last forever."

Hard to believe, but Lynda Gayle fled a chilly first marriage, which taught her another erotic lesson. **"Contract how much sex you want before you get married,"** she advises. "That way you know the sex is going to be there and what the person's sexual energy is. **Talk about what sexual things you both want to explore.** When you get married, it's like everything becomes sacred and you almost think you can't be dirty anymore. And yeah, you can."

"When you marry, you think you can't be dirty anymore, but you can," Lynda Gayle says. Then she greets a friend who's carrying a sex toy that gives an electrical charge.

Then Lynda Gayle excuses herself to greet a lady friend who arrives with a tackle box full of sexual devices, including one that plugs into the wall and runs a charge through her body so she can give "electric blow jobs."

Saturday, 2 p.m., St. Petersburg

Hours of frank, descriptive sex talk with old strangers has left me wanting a nap. It's like taking a deposition that keeps getting juicier and more surreal. But instead of a refractory snooze, I'm meeting with Forever Young, a mixed-gender troupe who dance (women) and strip down to thongs (men) at nursing homes for charity. While the group of seniors does nothing X-rated during performances, FY's members are comfy with their bods and share intimate details as easily as you would share a ballpoint pen at a bank.

While the ladies, Sandy, 68, and Dee, 57, pose, 73-year-old Fred slyly flashes his package to lighten the mood. The women, both single, laugh it off, and after a touch of prodding, offer their golden (years) rule: **Don't screw whiners.**

"Some men are still babies. Whaa, whaa, whaa. They just want somebody to listen to their aches and pains. Some of them still want a mother and a maid. But we're at a place where we just wanna be the girlfriend," Sandy says.

Saturday, 7 p.m., Fort Lauderdale

I park outside of the Goldcoast Ballroom, a hall that caters to seniors, thinking this elders-on-the-prowl story is a cinch. There's nothing that embarrasses them.

But my change of venue to a more "normal" locale brings me down to earth. An older friend of my all-powerful, stylish and youthful editor Bill escorts me inside the club, where there are 150 seniors dancing, eating (and hoarding) sandwiches and gossiping about the female snowbirds who hog the attention of the few remaining attractive men.

While Loretta and Lynda Gayle put porn stars to shame and the Forever Young gals are scantily clad and saucy, the Goldcoast crew appears a touch more chaste. Apparently, not every senior citizen in Florida is shooting a foot-fetish video or wearing a sparkly thong.

The women are polite or uninterested in me (a buxom Jersey retiree treats me like a bran thief when we dance). I don't have the guts to pump them for sex info, so I move on to Trapeze, a nearby swingers' club whose owner has assured me he has plenty of chatty older members.

The club is in a down-market strip mall and hasn't gotten going just yet. "Come back in an hour and I'll see what I can do," snaps Little Alan, the manager.

To make nice, I go get him a bottle of wine, and by the time I return, dozens of Corvettes and SUVs are being valet-parked, and middle-aged and youngish couples in pastel and leather are eyes-wide-shutting their way through the door. It's pulsating, and I'm hoping at least a few old-timers are in there somewhere.

Sure enough, Little Alan procures a couple eager to talk. They happily show off their portfolio of photos of the wife (she's a grandma) in sexy costumes, but they don't want their names used.

"We went to Vegas and bought **a $750 vibrator,**" the husband offers. "It has a motor that runs electronic shocks through a rod inside and then another rubberized piece goes into the anus, with electronic stimulators. Another piece is a vibrator. It does a lot."

Turns out there's a reason these two have a device that does the lion's share of the work.

"My husband was in an accident," the wife says. "I've accepted it, though some restrictions apply. He can't act accordingly having sexual intercourse. So, we **have different types of toys**. Things that make it more comfortable for him." In other words, **work with what you've got**.

Back in New York, I get an e-mail from another sex-club senior, explaining her sexual awakening: "When I was younger, I jumped into bed easily and willingly, wanting to please my lovers in whatever way they wanted me to," says Diana, 64, who runs an "adult encounters" group with her husband. "But I left feeling less fulfilled and sometimes empty. Men were not giving *me* the same amount of pleasure that I was giving them. So, I became **far more selective about taking on a lover. I look for a mutual giving and receiving of energy**. Then I feel fulfilled."

Part of being selective means ignoring Mr. Young, Dumb and Full of Cum, who leaves you sore, bored and unable to score. Instead, **seek out someone who knows what they're doing**.

"I didn't have any orgasms in my first marriage, even though I had two children," Diana continues. "Sex was performed out of duty. But I can have orgasms now, thanks to the expertise and knowledge of my second husband. He is 14 years older than me. Today, I am **genuine and honest with my sexuality**. I was a faker and a phony at sex in my 20s, but only because I was sexually ignorant."

Many people asked whether I needed therapy or a hot shower when I was done with this story, assuming exposure to these geezers would leave me repulsed and maybe sticky, too. Actually, I found their sexual nonchalance refreshing. They knew what they wanted and joked about their bodies—totally, finally secure in their odd folds and flaws. So, **go forth, drop your bloomers and, if you're feelin' it, fornicate**. And the next time you get a sweet Arbor Day card from Grandma, remember that she may have been sitting on someone's face when she wrote it.

what turns you on?
(*hint:* it's not work!)

By Carin Rubenstein

HERE IS THE GOOD NEWS: WE ARE NOT HAVING A MIDLIFE CRIsis (our gen-x kids may be). We are the people we set out to be, and we love to have sex and spend time with our families. In our exploration of how baby boomers see themselves and what really makes them feel alive, in the summer of 2001, *My Generation* and AARP conducted a major national telephone survey of 2,118 Americans age 18 and older. After September 11, we followed up with another survey of 1,071 Americans to gauge the shifts, if any, in sentiment.*

The results of our surveys should surprise and encourage boomers everywhere. Even before September 11, boomers weren't nearly as self-centered as some suspected; after the acts of terrorism, they aren't nearly as traumatized as many expected. The evidence: In the summer of 2001, the majority of boomers, men and women, said that they wished they could do more good deeds for others and that their lives were more meaningful. A year later, these wishes still hold.

In both 2001 and 2002, boomers were enthralled by love and focused on their sexuality—just what we would have hoped for ourselves when we were young.

what *midlife* crisis?

THE BEST NEWS OF ALL IS THAT THERE SEEMS TO BE NO MIDLIFE crisis. Despite the dread with which many of us approach our 50th birthday, the roughest emotional times of our lives are usually behind us. Midlife can be a time of relative personal tranquility, happiness and self-confidence, a time when boomers begin taking stock of their lives and feeling grateful for what they have.

"There is no 'midlife crisis,'" agrees Alice Rossi, Ph.D., an expert on midlife and editor of the book *Caring and Doing for Others: Social Responsibility in the Domains of Family, Work and Community*. "Much more critical and traumatic events occur in early adulthood than in midlife," she says. It's during their 20s and 30s that Americans are searching for the right

partner, a suitable career and a sense of identity. So, she says, "the peak in depression and anxiety occurs in early adulthood, not in midlife."

In our surveys, we, too, found that Americans under the age of 35 experience negative feelings more often than older Americans. A majority of boomers often feel happy, capable and competent, truly alive and peaceful. (See charts)

no more *pretending*

FOR MANY BOOMERS, MIDLIFE IS THE FIRST TIME WHEN THEY can rid themselves of what they don't like, embrace what they do like and learn to be comfortable with who they are. By the age of 40 or 50, Americans no longer have to pretend. "I don't do anything anymore that I don't want to do," explains a 54-year-old beautician in Ohio. "I spend all day talking with women, so on the weekends I don't socialize."

"The degree of freedom we have to do what we want increases with middle age, but just isn't there for a younger person," explains Rossi. Young adults may feel obliged to attend social events, but midlifers—who are much more secure about their social status—are more likely either to enjoy such shindigs or to skip them altogether, Rossi believes.

midlife *dreamin'*

MIDLIFERS ARE LESS LIKELY THAN YOUNGER AMERICANS TO harbor hidden fantasies and pipe dreams. For young Americans, crazy dreams "are motivators," says Margie Lachman, Ph.D., a psychologist at Brandeis University who researches adult development.

Those of us further on in life, however, "realize that there are limitations, and that we can't achieve everything or be everybody," Lachman adds. Boomers still dream, of course, but their fantasies become less whimsical and more civic-minded

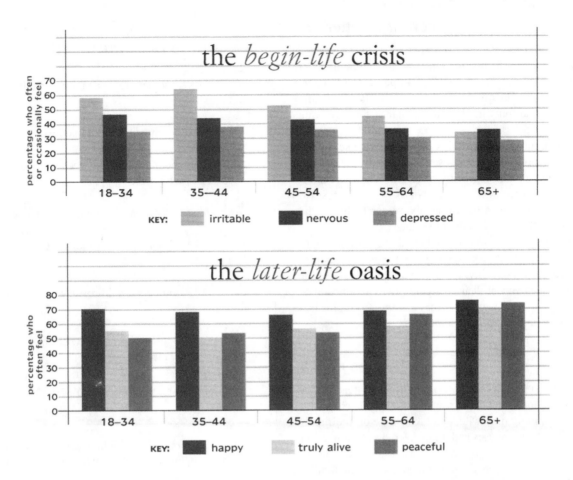

the *begin-life* crisis

KEY: irritable nervous depressed

the *later-life* oasis

KEY: happy truly alive peaceful

(trading in the goal of wanting to be a rock star for organizing a fund-raising concert to benefit a local charity).

giving back

MIDLIFE IS THE TIME WHEN WE BEGIN TO SEARCH FOR A WAY TO make a meaningful contribution to the world, regardless of national events. Both before and after September 11, six in 10 boomers wished they had a more socially meaningful life. Financially stable and having reached a comfortable level of well-being, "we realize we have a responsibility that goes beyond our own life and our own family, and we seek meaning by helping other people," says Lachman.

Last summer, eight in 10 Americans between 45 and 54 said they wished they could do good deeds for other people; slightly more say that this year. This is how we felt when we were younger, and we haven't lost our commitment to social responsibility. That's why one 49-year-old man we surveyed volunteers to help the local high school football team by videotaping every game and making a highlight tape for the players to watch. Another boomer admits that he's started to think "more about what we as Americans can do to help each other."

a little *romance*

BOOMERS ARE PASSIONATELY SEXUAL BEINGS. AMERICANS IN midlife were flourishing sexually before last September, and they still are now.

Our 2001 survey reveals that nearly six in 10 boomers really love to make love, and almost as many love to spend romantic evenings with their partners.

"Unless you've let yourself go to the dogs, why shouldn't you love sex?" says a 48-year-old real estate agent and devoted husband from Arizona. It's clear that boomers with partners are even more likely than single boomers to be enamored of love-making; 60 percent of married boomers love to make love, compared to 48 percent of those without a partner.

what *we* want

WHEN WE BREAK DOWN THESE FIGURES, WE FIND THAT IN MIDlife men have more sexual enthusiasm than women. Two-thirds of men (66 percent) between 45 and 54 love to make love, compared to 51 percent of women in that age group. This striking gender difference exists among younger Americans, as well, so it is not just a side effect of menopause.

Both boomer men and women love to spend romantic evenings with their mates, although they may be interpreting "romance" in very different ways. For a 54-year-old woman from Ohio, romance means eating at a restaurant with "white linen tablecloths and a bucket for the wine," a place where she can talk to her husband. But a 48-year-old man in Tucson confesses that he's only willing to get dressed up and go out for dinner as long as he knows he'll be able to "spice it up a bit" when he gets home.

more *sex,* better sex

BOOMERS HAVEN'T YET ACHIEVED A STATE OF PERFECT SEXUAL union. In fact, many of them often fantasize about having better sex. About half, 58 percent of men and 48 percent of women, say that they secretly dream of having a more satisfying sex life, because as one man puts it, "it's just human nature" to want better sex.

What do so many mid-lifers think they're missing sex-wise? When men talk about having better sex, they usually mean more frequent lovemaking and especially more oral sex, says sex researcher Dr. Robert Kolodny, a co-author of 14 books on sexuality. The more often men have oral sex, research shows, the happier they say they are with their marriage.

Being desired is what women need at this age, according to Susan M. Seidman, Ph.D., a psychologist who counsels couples and families in New York City. Women in midlife need to know that their husbands accept their changing physical appearance and think they're aging well, "and they get this from physical closeness and sexual intimacy," Seidman says.

all in the *family*

BOOMERS LOVE SPENDING TIME WITH THEIR FAMILIES. ABOUT four in 10, we found, think of themselves as nurturers above all, dedicated to spending time with, and taking care of, their children, as well as their spouses and a larger group of family and friends.

Since September 11, Americans are more focused on family. A 51-year-old woman tells us that her loved ones have become much more important, and "material things" less so.

t.g.i.*f.*

NINE OUT OF 10 BOOMERS, BOTH MEN AND WOMEN, DID NOT name work as a major passion; six in 10 don't love their jobs.

"People fall in and out of love with their careers," explains Seidman. And for boomers especially, "who had expectations of making big, big bucks and being big, big happy," the midlife reality of the work grind can be exhausting, she says. That's why many baby boomers look beyond work for personal fulfillment and a sense of self-worth.

A 53-year-old man who used to be consumed with his job as a quality assurance manager says he no longer finds it as challenging or inspiring. Now his passion is competitive swimming. "I'm in better shape than I ever was, and I'm happier about what I achieve in the pool than what I achieve at my desk," he explains.

does money buy *happiness?*

THE MORE MONEY AMERICANS EARN THE MORE LIKELY THEY ARE to be positive about their work, we found. On average, boomers earned the highest salaries of those in our survey. Among workers who earn more than $50,000 a year, many of whom are boomers, 45 percent really love their work; but only 34 percent of those who earn less than $30,000 a year are as en-

---

a *boomer* profile

7 in **10** boomers feel sexually attractive (often or occasionally)

6 in **10** boomers love to make love

55% of boomers love to spend romantic evenings with their partner

54% secretly dream of having a better sex life

6 in **10** boomers wish their lives were more meaningful

5 in **10** boomers are always trying to learn new things

83% of boomers say they wish they could do good deeds for other people

6 in **10** boomers don't really love their jobs

---

thusiastic. Plus, more of the highest earners often feel happy, capable and competent than those who earn the least.

how we have *fun*

BOOMERS LOVE BEING ACTIVE AND DOING THINGS OUTSIDE; GOLF, camping, gardening, waterskiing and hiking are just a few of our interests. Being active is a primary passion of 62 percent of boomer men, and it's second only to nurturing for boomer women, 46 percent of whom love being active.

Creative activities—crafts, writing, drawing and cooking—are also popular. A 50-year-old man is passionate about the computer programs he writes; a woman in her 50s pens historical romances for her own enjoyment.

the *learning* curve

CONSTANTLY CHALLENGING THEMSELVES WITH NEW EXPERIENCES and ideas, a majority of midlifers—about six in 10—say they're always trying to learn new things. A 49-year-old man tells us he's going back to school to learn how to make guitars, and a 52-year-old woman just joined a Bible-study organization.

spirituality

ONLY A FEW BOOMERS, ABOUT ONE IN 10, ARE PASSIONATE about worship. Spiritual pursuits divide along gender lines. While six in 10 boomer women often engage in spiritual and religious activities, only 39 percent of boomer men do. More boomer women than men really love this kind of religious involvement: 37 percent of women compared to 26 percent of men.

This gap is not surprising, says Diana Kirschner, Ph.D., a psychologist who regularly addresses spirituality. "Women tend to be more connected with other people and that lends itself to being more spiritual. Men are more instrumental, into doing rather than being," she says.

who has the most *fun?*

PASSION IS WHAT ENGAGES AND EXCITES US IN THE LONG TERM, but fun is what we do for quick pleasure. Men and women regard having fun very differently, we found. In fact, men are much more focused on fun than women are. Our evidence:

• 55 percent of men deliberately take time to have fun, either every day or every few days, compared to 43 percent of women.

• Men spend more time than women having fun: On average, men have 22 hours of fun each week, compared to 17 hours a week for women.

"Women are called on much more to be caregivers, and it's difficult to mix fun and changing diapers or disciplining children," explains John Robinson, Ph.D., a sociologist at the University of Maryland and director of the Americans' Use of Time Project. Fathers usually spend time with their kids doing things like playing baseball. Both mothers and fathers love being with their children, but fathers tend to have the most fun doing it.

An almost-50-year-old Iowa man sheepishly agrees that "in lots of families, like mine, the men are more free to have fun." He is certainly up for it: He rides horses and argues about anything from "politics to cosmology."

A woman in her mid-40s says that although she spends less time having fun as she has grown older, "I enjoy the fun more, because I'm doing things I like, not just doing anything. In my late 20s, I'd go clubbing and dancing," she says, "but I was trying to please other people. Now, I only do the things I want to do." These things, she says, include going to dinner and a movie with her boyfriend and shopping.

FOR BOOMERS, MIDLIFE IS STILL YOUTHFUL LIFE, OUR "FINALLY Doing What I Want" years. Instead of wallowing in a 50th-year crisis, we're living out our sexual and romantic dreams, as we de-emphasize the fantasies we once had about careers and money. And we cautiously but firmly pursue our ideals of community through service and family responsibility.

Midlife: A pretty great place to be, after all.

* Our special focus was on baby boomers, specifically women and men between the ages of 45 and 54. Both surveys were conducted for AARP/My Generation by RoperASW and included data weighted to census norms to correct for sampling errors. The word "boomer" here means "leading edge" boomers, those ages 45 to 54 years old.

George Sharrard provided assistance with computer analysis

Let us know what turns you on.
Take the poll at www.mygeneration.org.

UNIT 6
Old/New Sexual Concerns

Unit Selections

Key Points to Consider

- What does your college or university do about date or acquaintance rape? Are there education or prevention programs? How is a report of an assault handled? How do you think these issues should be handled on campuses?

- How do you feel about laws restricting sexual behaviors (for example, age limits, marital requirements for engaging in sex, or laws making specific sexual behaviors illegal)? Which laws would you add or change related to sexual issues or behaviors?

- What are your criteria for consent when two (or more) people engage in a sexual behavior? What do you recommend as safeguards against misunderstanding, confusion, and assault?

- Have you ever watched an "adult" video or logged onto an "adult" internet site? What purpose do you believe these products serve?

- Where do you believe "personal freedom" or "choice" about sexually related behaviors begins to collide with the "greater good" of society? How about sex online?

 **Links: www.dushkin.com/online/**
These sites are annotated in the World Wide Web pages.

The Child Rights Information Network (CRIN)
http://www.crin.org

Infertility Resources
http://www.ihr.com/infertility/index.html

Men's Health Resource Guide
http://www.menshealth.com/new/guide/index.html

Third Age: Love and Sex
http://www.thirdage.com/romance/

Women's Studies Resources
http://www.inform.umd.edu/EdRes/Topic/WomensStudies/

This final unit deals with several topics that are of interest or concern for different reasons. Also, as the title suggests, it combines "old" or ongoing topics and concerns with "new" or emerging ones. In one respect, however, these topics have a common denominator—they have all taken positions of prominence in the public's awareness as social issues.

Tragically, sexual abuse and violence are long-standing occurrences in society and in some relationships. For centuries, a strong code of silence surrounded these occurrences and, many now agree, increased not only the likelihood of sexual abuse and violence, but the harm to victims of these acts. Beginning in the middle of the twentieth century, two societal movements helped to begin eroding this code of silence. The child welfare/child rights movement exposed child abuse and mistreatment and sought to improve the lives of children and families. Soon after, and to a large extent fueled by the emerging women's movement, primarily "grass-roots" organizations that became known as "rape crisis" groups or centers became catalysts for altering the way we looked at (or avoided looking at) rape and sexual abuse.

Research today suggests that these movements have accomplished many of their initial goals and brought about significant social change. The existence and prevalence of rape and other sexual abuse is much more accurately known. Many of the myths previously believed (rapists are strangers that jump out of bushes, sexual abuse only occurs in poor families, all rapists are male and all victims are female, and so on) have been replaced with more accurate information. The code of silence has been recognized for the harm it can cause, and millions of friends, parents, teachers, counselors, and others have learned how to be approachable, supportive listeners to victims disclosing their abuse experiences. Finally, we have come to recognize the role that power, especially unequal power, plays in rape, sexual abuse, sexual violence, and, a term coined more recently, sexual harassment. However, as current events have shown us the battle is far from over and sexual abuse continues to have consequences for victims, those connected to them, as well as, society as a whole.

As we, as a society, have sought to expose and reduce abusive sex, it has become increasingly clear that all of society and each of us as individuals/potential partners must grapple with the broader issue of what constitutes consent: What is non-abusive sexual interaction? How can people communicate interest, arousal, desire, and/or propose sexual interaction, when remnants of unequal power, ignorance, misinformation, fear, adversarial sex roles, and inadequate communication skills still exist? Finally, another layer of perplexing questions that confront the proactive/reactive dilemma: What is, or should be, the role of employers, school personnel, or simply any of us who may be seen as contributing on some level due to awareness or complicity to an environment that allows uncomfortable, abusive, or inappropriate sexual interaction? Conversely, is it possible that we could become so "sensitive" to the potential for abuse that combined with our discomfort, anger, and fear we could become hysterical vigilantes pushing an eager legal system to indict "offenders" who have not committed abuse or harassment?

The articles in the first subsection, *Sexual Abuse and Harassment,* look at child sexual abuse from three perspectives. "Crimes Against Nature" tells the story of a young woman who was abducted and sexually assaulted as a child and includes a time line of the progress made in the area of child sexual abuse. The article "New Hope for Sex Offender Treatment" presents the encouraging findings about treated, incarcerated sex offenders and their recidivism.

The second subsection, *Legal and Ethical Issues Related to Sex,* focuses on one sexuality-related issue about which all of America (and the world) is struggling: explicit sex, especially on the internet. "A Cruel Edge" reports on the extensive research done by a University of Texas journalism professor on the ingredients of the most popular pornographic videos and web sites.

Each year *Annual Editions: Human Sexuality* closes with a final *Focus* section that is designed to give readers "food for thought" and/or fuel for discussion with classmates, friends, and/or family. Sometimes the focus identifies an emerging trend or timely issue in the "big picture" of sexuality. Other times the focus raises one or more very broad question(s) that defy simple answers. This year's *Focus* does both by exploring a wide range of religious and spiritual beliefs associated with sex from lust and erotic passion to the meaning of life, sex, and true intimacy. As with each previous focus section, readers are challenged to confront, consider, and discuss these complex personal and societal issues in order to conceptualize a better future for all of us. A future where humankind's quest for joyful, healthy, and fulfilling sexuality can be realized with the *reverence* referred to in the opening quote of this 05/06 edition.

SILENT
NO MORE

Survivors of sexual abuse can begin to heal the pain of the past by speaking out

BY ROBIN D. STONE

My journey from victim to survivor began when I was about 9 years old. My younger sister and I were sleeping over at an uncle's house in the country. I adored my uncle, and I curled up on his lap to watch the late-night movie. Everyone else was asleep when, sometime later, he led me by the hand to a dark corner of his house. There he fondled my growing breasts and rubbed my crotch. When he was finished, he sent me to bed, warning me never to tell anyone what he had done. "The incident," as I now refer to it, was five minutes of confusion, horror and profound embarrassment. Its impact has lasted a lifetime.

Like many children who've been violated and warned to keep quiet, I did as I was told. Through years of family gatherings and church functions, I kept my distance from my uncle as I built a wall of silence around myself. Inside it, my secret began to take root in my life, and as a tree's roots slowly conform to their surroundings, so was I shaped by my inability to give voice to what had happened to me. Deep down, I believed that I had done something to deserve what

happened, and even as I wrestled with that, there were periods when I managed to convince myself that it was really no big deal. Still, I decided that I shouldn't get too close to men, or anybody else for that matter. Even God was not exempt. I remember thinking that if God really existed, he wouldn't have let my uncle touch me.

Though some may find it difficult to understand how five minutes can forever affect the course of a life, those who have been sexually violated know all too well the residue of humiliation and helplessness that the experience leaves behind. Not telling about the abuse only compounds its effects. Indeed, some find that secrecy can become a way of life. Kristen (name has been changed), whose older cousin repeatedly forced her to have intercourse with him from ages 9 to 12, says, "There was a real connection between my not telling about the abuse and withholding other things about my life as well. You become good at hiding because you fear that if you don't, others will be able to see the shameful truth of what happened to you."

Sooner or later, though, the secret must be reckoned with, because the silence that helps us cope in the beginning can lead to anxiety, depression, addiction, memory loss, cancer, promiscuity and sexual and reproductive problems. "There's a mind-body-soul connection," explains Maelinda N. Turner, a Vancouver, British Columbia, social worker with a degree in divinity who has worked mostly with Black and Latino clients. "It may sound New-Agey, but if emotions aren't released, they hide in the body as disease."

A Quiet Epidemic

Because sexual violence—being forced or coerced to perform sexual acts—is fueled by the abuser's need for power and control, those who have less power, such as children, are often more vulnerable. Indeed, children under 12 make up about half of all victims of sexual assault. And not surprisingly, the rates of rape and other forms of sexual assault are higher in poor and urban areas, where so many feel powerless. As a result, experts say,

Healing the Hurt

By Iyanla Vanzant

1. Talk to someone. Find someone you trust and let them know what happened. Tell them exactly how you feel. Do not participate in the conspiracy by remaining silent.

2. Keep a journal of thoughts and prayers. Even after talking, the thoughts continue to circle in your mind. Write down what you think and feel, then write a prayer to have those thoughts and feelings healed.

3. Avoid asking yourself why. Asking why deepens the wound and feeds the feelings of shame and guilt. An unanswered why shifts the responsibility onto your shoulders.

4. Keep your body moving. The trauma of sexual abuse gets locked in the muscles and tissues of the body. You must exercise to free yourself of the effects of the emotional and mental trauma. Dancing, swimming or yoga can help you rebuild and regain a healthy relationship with your body.

5. Talk to yourself. Learn to love yourself by creating powerful, loving affirmations that support and encourage you. Affirmations let you know that you are still okay.

6. Rehearse the confrontation. Write out what you would say to your abuser, and write the response you believe the abuser would have. Keep writing both sides of the story until you experience peace. Repeat this exercise as many times as necessary.

7. Realize it was not your fault. Whether you were abused as a child or an adult, avoid blaming your appearance, behavior, inability to escape, lack of retaliation or fear for the violation.

8. Don't run from the memories. You only delay your healing when you avoid, deny or resist the memory of the experience. Instead, draw a picture that represents what you feel. When you are done, burn it!

9. Create a safe place. Choose a place in your home that you can decorate with comforting objects, or go to a park or some other easily accessible location. Claim it as a safe haven. When you go to your safe place, sit quietly, pray, meditate or just hold loving thoughts about yourself.

10. Get professional help or support. Do not deny yourself healing support and encouragement. Find a counselor, therapist or support group with whom you can continue to explore and share your thoughts and feelings.

Black women have a disproportionately higher risk of assault.

In recent years, even as overall crime rates have fallen, the incidence of rape and sexual abuse has risen. At least one in four women, and one in six men, will experience some form of sexual abuse in their lifetime. And according to some estimates, as many as one in four young women on college campuses will become a victim of rape or attempted rape, although half of those violated won't think of it as such. That's partly because almost 70 percent of rape and sexual-assault victims know their offender as an acquaintance, friend, relative or intimate partner, and we're loath to see people close to us as rapists. Think about it: If a mugger beats a woman as he steals her purse, she'd report that to the police. But if an associate rapes a woman after she has invited him up for a drink, she thinks about the line of questioning ("You did invite him up, didn't you?") and decides to keep it to herself. The bottom line: Fear often keeps us quiet and can even keep us from admitting to ourselves that we have been criminally violated. There's the fear of what people will think and what they'll say. There's the fear of retaliation. The fear that you won't be believed. Fear that you'll jeopardize existing relationships. Fear that somebody will go to jail. Fear that you'll be alone. And fear that you actually invited it. The fear can be so overwhelming that many victims of abuse actually repress the memory as a way of coping.

So why are we so reluctant to talk about sexual violence? Well, first we'd have to be willing to talk about sex, which many of us find uncomfortable. "We're certainly not the only group that's silent regarding abuse," says Gail E. Wyatt, Ph.D., author of *Stolen Women: Reclaiming Our Sexuality, Taking Back Our Lives* (John Wiley & Sons). "But we're the only group whose experience is compounded by our history of slavery and stereotypes about Black sexuality, and that makes discussion more difficult."

Because so few of us tell, nobody knows how big the problem of sexual violence really is. All statistics are based only on *reported* assaults, and, according to the 1999 National Crime Victimization Survey from the U.S. Department of Justice, sexual assault is reported only about 28 percent of the time, making it the least reported violent crime in the United States. Untold numbers continue to suffer in silence, sleepwalking through their days, alive but not truly living, compressing their feelings so they won't feel pain.

For survivors of sexual abuse, there is no one formula for recovery, but every path to healing ultimately requires that

Safeguarding Our Children

Few of us actually teach our children how to protect themselves from sexual abuse, despite the fact that 67 percent of all reported victims of sexual assault are under 18, according to a recent Department of Justice survey. How do we empower our kids to defend themselves, and to create an environment in which they'll feel free to tell us anything? Here are ways to start:

Give children the appropriate vocabulary so that words like *vagina, breast* and *penis* aren't foreign to them. Naming intimate body parts helps your child claim them in a healthy way.

Respect their boundaries. If Aunt Sally wants a kiss and your little one resists, don't force the issue. Children pushed to submit to affection may begin to feel that grown-ups' demands are more important than their own physical limits.

Teach them about inappropriate touching. "Say to your child, 'Nobody should touch you there,' or 'Nobody kisses you on the mouth,'" says New York clinical psychologist Dorothy Cuningham, Ph.D. Introduce concepts gradually, starting around age 3 and depending on your child's ability to understand. But don't put off talking about inappropriate touching, Cunningham warns. Toddlers can be the most vulnerable.

Encourage children to express their feelings. "You can't have closed communication and then expect it to be open if there's sexual misconduct," Cunningham points out. "Invite your children to talk to you. Don't just ask 'How's school?' Ask 'How's your teacher?' and 'What did you do today?' Get a sense of their relationships and friendships." Give feedback so your child knows you're listening and responsive. And don't be afraid to ask direct questions. For example, you might periodically ask your child "Has anyone ever tried to touch you in a way you did not like, or asked you to touch them in a way that made you uncomfortable?" One woman, abused by an older relative for years during her childhood, says that if her mother had asked her a direct question, her painful secret would have come out.

Teach children that it's okay to question authority—especially those in authority who make them feel uncomfortable. This can be a challenge for those of us raised to "do as you're told" by grown-ups. But children should never feel that they have no choice.

Know your child. "If you're tuned in, you know when she's upset," Cunningham says. If a once-carefree child becomes moody, withdrawn and unresponsive, don't dismiss it as phase. If your child suddenly doesn't want to go to Uncle Fred's house, pay attention. If your youngster becomes preoccupied with mature sexual concepts, don't assume it's just something picked up at school. Question your child gently, and above all, let her know you love her unconditionally.

—R.S.

---

we speak out about the ways in which we have been violated. On the following pages, three women (names and identifying details have been changed) give voice to their stories of abuse and silence—and they discover, in the telling, a way to finally move beyond the secrets that have haunted them for so long.

Dangerous Games

Stephanie, a 31-year-old artist, rarely makes her way from her East Coast home to the rural midwestern town where she grew up. Home reminds her of the "games" she and her two sisters used to play with their father. "When Mama was away, Daddy would put us on his lap and feel us up," says Stephanie, the middle sister. "He'd call us into his room one at a time. He'd start with a hug or a tickle, and then he'd touch my breast. We knew what was happening. My sis-

ters and I had a code. We'd say, 'Okay, in five minutes, you've got to come and get me.'" Throughout the girls' childhood, their father would call the eldest sister the most often. Today that sister escapes the pain of those memories through the use of illegal drugs and alcohol. Stephanie's youngest sister struggles with overeating. On the surface, Stephanie, who is single, seems highly functional compared with her sisters. She is full of energy and has a host of friends and a calendar packed with theater dates, parties and book-club meetings.

When I ask Stephanie how she feels about what her father did to her and her sisters, she seems surprised. She has never thought much about it, she says, adding, "What's done is done." But she quickly contradicts herself. "Things have built up over the last few years," she admits. "I'm at the point where I hate

when my father even answers the phone. Yet when I do go home, I don't want him to know that I feel uncomfortable. He's this old man and he does love me. It's all bizarre."

Stephanie believes her abuse is to blame for her struggle to become truly intimate with men. "For a long time, I didn't like to be touched," she says. "It made me feel kind of helpless." Her sisters, too, have had trouble sustaining relationships. Neither has ever married, but each has a child.

"The great wound of sexual abuse," explains social worker Maelinda Turner, "is that it leads you to believe you're not worthy to celebrate the gifts of the power of your sexuality without fear, question or judgment." I ask Stephanie if she and her sisters have ever considered talking with a professional. She shrugs: "I feel like you're supposed to just go on with your life."

Turner sees patterns typical of sexual-abuse victims in Stephanie and her sisters. "You can find ways to escape from the pain," she explains. "Work, drugs, food. You can be successful, smart and busy, but eventually it sneaks up on you. At some point you need to slow down and deal with what happened and how it has affected your life."

She stresses that unless their father gets counseling, the sisters have to contend with the fact that when their children are around him, they, too, will be in danger. That concern became quite real a few years ago, when one sister suspected their father had begun to abuse her 6-year-old son. Her fear for her son led her to finally confront her father about the abuse she and her sisters had suffered. As the secret tumbled out, her mother reacted with disbelief. "You all must have done something," she said lamely, apparently not knowing how else to respond. Stephanie's father insisted nothing had happened with his daughters or his grandson, and her mother let the issue drop. Stephanie's sister, dismayed by her parents' denial and needing to protect her son, now avoids her parents' home.

That episode was the first and last time the sisters ever openly discussed the abuse with their parents. Turner believes that the entire family will need to go into therapy if real healing is to occur, but she acknowledges that it is unlikely that Stephanie's parents will ever move past their denial. Mothers who can't acknowledge their daughters' abuse have often been abused themselves, she reflects. Until they can deal with their own demons, they can't help their daughters. "It's like a cancer," Turner says. "If your grandmother had it and your mother had it, you're susceptible."

As for her father, Stephanie is resigned. "People are who they are," she says. "Rather than have him live out his last days being miserable, I've made a conscious decision to make him feel comfortable." A soft sigh escapes her as she adds: "That just leaves me waiting until he dies."

Sex, Money, Drugs

Evelyn's eyes say she's 50. In fact, she is only 35. She grew up in a comfortable home in New York City with her parents, sister and two brothers. When she was 10, her brother's teenage friend began to creep up to her bedroom to fondle her. He'd give her candy to keep silent. Evelyn finally threatened to tell when he pressured her to "let him put his thing in me." Then he left her alone. In junior high, she fell into a clique of girls who regularly visited the principal's office. "We let him feel us up, and he gave us money and good grades," she says. The principal was fired when one of the girls became pregnant and told. No one else in the clique breathed a word.

At 16 Evelyn befriended a man who owned a neighborhood store. He invited her into the basement for drugs and sex. Not long after, she got pregnant and dropped out of school to have his child. She was in the ninth grade and could barely read. "I was always used to a man taking care of me," she says. At 18 she met Benny, who fed her crack habit and then beat her. Desperate to escape him, Evelyn left her baby with her mother and took off on her own. Soon she was prostituting to buy crack. "It didn't matter what they did to me," she says of the countless tricks she turned. "I just wanted my money."

Author Gail Wyatt, a professor of psychiatry at UCLA, observes that by the time Evelyn was a teenager, she had been conditioned to see herself as a sexual object and sex as a means to an end. Evelyn's case is extreme, Wyatt notes, but in all sexual relationships it's important to ask, "Is my body just being used to get me something?"

Evelyn quickly sank into a miserable routine of sex, violence and drugs that consumed two decades of her life and drained her self-worth. In crack houses she would often emerge from her haze naked and bruised, knowing she had been raped. "I was too afraid to go to the cops," she says. "Why would they believe me? I wanted to die. I asked God why I wasn't dying." She was too ashamed to tell her family she needed

help: "I didn't want them to see me; I didn't want to disgrace them."

Indeed, her unwillingness to reveal to her family her earliest incidents of abuse—first by her brother's friend, then by the principal and later the store owner—may have led to Evelyn's pattern of abusive sexual encounters. As Wyatt observes, family dynamics are frequently at the root of our silence around issues of sex and sexuality. "An abuse victim's decision not to tell says a lot about whom they trust, their loneliness and isolation," she explains. "Sometimes there's an emotional distance in the family. It's difficult to talk about sex if you're not talking in general. And abusers will tell you they can sense vulnerable, needy kids."

Evelyn, still vulnerable and needy as an adult, eventually entered an upstate treatment program, where her pattern of abusive sexual encounters continued: She had sex for money with men on staff. She got caught and kicked out and headed back to the streets. Eventually she landed in Project Greenhope, a Manhattan rehabilitation and drug-treatment residence for women who've had trouble with the law. More than a year later, she's clean and fortunately AIDS-free, and through counseling she's coming to understand the roles sexual abuse and silence have played in her life. Soon she will be on her own, and with only $117 a month in welfare, she will need to find a job and a home. "I'm learning to love myself, but I'm scared to death," she admits. "I've never paid a bill in my life."

While Wyatt applauds Evelyn's efforts so far in turning her life around, she cautions that Evelyn will need long-term psychotherapy to help her reclaim her own power over her body: "This young woman was conditioned to give her power away," Wyatt says, adding that Evelyn needs to develop positive relationships with women, perhaps other graduates of her treatment center, and steer clear of the temptations of old friends and habits. She encourages Evelyn to avoid sexual relationships altogether until she gets in touch with her own sexuality. "This is not just about sex," Wyatt says. "This is her whole life."

Longing for Nurturing

Behind Kim's fiery spirit and quick wit is a wounded, still grieving young woman. She's overweight, but she has "too many other things to work on" besides dropping pounds. She's single and often lonely, though she has a boyfriend of seven years. Before him, by her own account, she had a string of mostly empty sexual relationships, 40 in all. "I used to confuse sex with love," she says. Now 34, she still finds it hard to believe that a man could want more than sex from her, saying, "I'm afraid people will leave if they see the real me."

Kim can identify exactly when these feelings of worthlessness began. Her stepfather started fondling her during bath time when she was about 7, and by the time she was 11 he had graduated to intercourse. "I went from crying to just giving in to fighting to get him away from me," she says. She felt she had no choice but to remain silent: Her stepfather had warned that if she told her mother, a prominent southern political activist, he'd kill them both. To prove his point, he'd sharpen his knives and clean his gun in front of Kim.

And so she endured routine rapes by the man who was supposed to be taking care of her while Mommy was out saving the world, beatings when she threatened to tell, and a pregnancy and horrifying miscarriage that she suffered through alone at age 16. "I knew my stepfather was the father," she wrote in a journal, "and just like everything else he had done to me, I could not tell anyone about it."

When Kim was 19, her stepfather pressed one time too many for sex. She resisted and he slapped her, and in her anger she found the courage to tell her mother. Kim was stunned when her mother responded by accusing her of seducing her stepfather and ordered her out of the house. Forced to live with friends and family for a while, Kim eventually moved out on her own. Many years later, she would learn that her mother herself had been sexually abused by a relative. Through therapy she would come to understand that her mother had no inkling of how to protect or support her daughter. At the time, though, Kim was devastated.

"Sometimes I think I shouldn't have said anything," Kim says through tears. "I paid a price: I had to change my life. I had no degree, no job, no skills, nobody but me. What I've lived through is incomprehensible. I lost a good part of my life." She tries to describe the physical and psychological impact of her past: "I constantly have indigestion. When I'm afraid, I want to throw up. I'm always waiting for the other shoe to drop, for something to rock my semblance of being normal."

Dorothy Cunningham, Ph.D., a clinical psychologist with a private practice in New York, explains that Kim's situation was made worse by her mother's denial: "When a parent refuses to accept what's going on, they're often thinking about what it could do to their career and to their family," Cunningham says. "It took a lot of courage for Kim to say this happened, and the mother left her child to heal herself."

Kim has been trying to do just that. Now working toward her college degree, she has been in therapy for years, though she admits she doesn't go as often as she should. "Sometimes it's too hard," she says. Yet therapy is crucial to Kim's healing process, Cunningham says. "There's a loss of innocence, a loss of childhood and family," she explains, and Kim needs to mourn that loss. Therapy can be a safe place to grieve.

Cunningham also sees in Kim a woman who needs to get angry. "People who stay in victim mode blame themselves," she says. "They see themselves as bad and dirty. In some ways that's safer than unleashing the anger that's inside. You need to give yourself permission to be angry. Say 'I deserved to be listened to; I deserved protection.' When you're a victim, you don't feel like you deserve anything. When you're angry, you're moved to action; you're empowered."

One of the most difficult memories for an abuse victim to deal with is the sensation of physical pleasure that she may have experienced. Even now, Kim struggles to understand how she could have felt pleasure while being raped. "It was like looking forward to a lover," she says, her voice almost a whisper. "And

as much as I looked forward to it, it repulsed me too."

As disturbing as Kim finds this aspect of her abuse, her experience is not uncommon. "It's very difficult for many to accept," Cunningham confirms. "You can be terrified and confused but still have an orgasm. Kim should know that her body did what bodies are supposed to do—it responded to touch. That's how bodies are made. She needs to know she's not a perverted soul."

Seven years ago, after Kim's stepfather died, she began to reach out to her mother. But their conversations often spiral into accusations and tears. Though she still longs for the nurturing that she feels she missed while growing up, Kim recognizes that she is more likely to get it from supportive friends and family members than from her mother. "She is what she is," Kim sums up, "but I still love her. And I know I'm going to be okay."

Common Ground

While every experience of sexual abuse is different, some common therapeutic themes emerge: We need to understand the role of power in our relationships, and hold our abusers accountable for their actions. And we must learn to treat ourselves kindly as we work to come to terms with what happened. "You can't mark progress or breakthroughs," Maelinda Turner says of the healing process, "but you can look back six months or a year and know that you're in a different place."

My own healing took years. I was 21 when my mother and stepfather finally sensed my discomfort around my uncle and gently encouraged me to tell them about it. My parents were surprisingly calm, and I felt enormous relief that I could finally let go of my secret. But when my mother called my uncle to confront him, he denied everything, which left my parents to decide whom they should believe. Fortunately for me, they believed their daughter. Some heated family discussions followed, and it was eventually agreed that a few relatives should be informed so they'd know not to leave their kids vulnerable. My uncle steered clear of me, and life went on.

But even after I shared my experience with my parents, I didn't really deal with the *effects* of it for another 12 years. During that time, the 9-year-old girl in me was still feeling a 9-year-old's feelings. And so, about four years ago, with the help of a psychotherapist, I began the hard work of untangling the secret from my life, pulling up its deeply rooted feelings of shame and fear and self-doubt.

When I look back on my experience, I see that the most difficult aspect of my abuse was not the telling, of what happened to me—it was carrying the burden of silence for all those years. In my own journey toward healing, I'm learning to counter the 9-year-old's thoughts that even now sometimes play in my mind. I'm learning not to be afraid of inviting attention by speaking up or standing out or even by writing. I'm learning that I didn't deserve what happened to me, and that I have a right to be angry at my uncle. I'm also learning that I can have warm, close relationships.

I married a man whose love was strong enough to breach the wall I'd built around myself, and who understood why I needed to take this healing journey. We have a young son who is my heart and joy, and I'm doing work that fulfills me. I used to wonder where I might be if not for what happened in that dark corner so many years ago. But I now see that in spite of what happened, I'm embracing life, moving out of the long shadow of silence and doing what I can to help myself, and others, heal. And like so many survivors, I carry on.

GETTING HELP

If your child tells you she has been abused, assure her that she did the right thing in telling and that she's not to blame for what happened. Offer her protection, and promise that you will promptly take steps to see that the abuse stops. Report any suspicion of child abuse to your local child-protection agency or to the police or district attorney's office. Consult with your child's physician, who may refer you to a specialist with expertise in trauma. A caring response is the first step toward getting help for your young one.

If you know a sister who has been sexually assaulted, encourage her to seek out a group or individual therapist who is trained to counsel her. These resources can help:

BOOKS

Surviving the Silence: Black Women's Stories of Rape by Charlotte Pierce-Baker (W.W. Norton & Co., $23.95).

I Never Called It Rape: The Ms. Report on Recognizing, Fighting and Surviving Date and Acquaintance Rape by Robin Warshaw (HarperPerennial, $13).

I Never Told Anyone: Writings by Women Survivors of Child Sexual Abuse edited by Ellen Bass and Louise Thornton (Harper-Collins, $13).

I Can't Get Over It: A Handbook for Trauma Survivors by Aphrodite Matsakis, Ph.D. (New Harbinger, $16.95).

ORGANIZATIONS

Rape, Abuse and Incest National Network (RAINN), 635-B Pennsylvania Ave., S.E., Washington DC 20003; (202) 544–1034; (800) 656-HOPE (hot line directs you to a crisis counselor). Or contact the group on-line at rainn.org or rainnmail@aol.com.

Association of Black Psychologists, P.O. Box 55999, Washington DC 20040; (202) 722–0808.

National Association of Black Social Workers, 8436 W. McNichols St., Detroit MI 48221; (313) 862–6700.

National Black Women's Health Project, 600 Pennsylvania Ave., S.E., Suite 310, Washington DC 20003; (202) 543–9311.

Survivors of Incest Anonymous, P.O. Box 190, Benson MD 21018; (410) 893–3322.

Men Can Stop Rape, P.O. Box 57144, Washington DC 20037; (202) 265–6530 or mencanstoprape.org.

Robin D. Stone, editor-in-chief of essence. com, is writing a book about Black women survivors of sexual abuse. She is reachable by E-mail at womenwise@aol.com.

From *Essence*, August 2001, pp. 123-124, 126, 153-1. © 2001 by Robin D. Stone. Reprinted by permission of the author.

Crimes Against Nature

When Rose Martelli was just 7 years old, she was abducted and sexually assaulted by a stranger in her suburban neighborhood. Now, more than 20 years later, she tells her story for the first time, providing rare and important insight that can help protect children everywhere. In our special investigation, we hear from crime experts, psychologists and activists about the progress we've made, and what more still needs to be done

Rose Martelli

Warning to readers: The following true crime story contains graphic language and details. We opted not to delete these details or to use euphemistic or clinical language because these can't honestly convey the horror of sexual crimes against children. Only fully informed citizens can make thoughtful assessments of appropriate justice and needed legal change. If this story inspires outrage, we encourage readers to direct it toward work that will continue to protect children from predators (see "How to Keep Our Kids Safe"). — The Editors

"Come here," was all I heard someone say.

It was February 22, 1982, a mild, sunny morning; I was 7 years old, walking to school along one of the main, tree-lined thoroughfares of Maplewood, New Jersey, my hometown. My older brother had just transferred to a public school, and my two younger sisters hadn't started school yet, so every day I walked the first five blocks to Immaculate Heart of Mary by myself before meeting my friend Jennifer for the last four.

A white, two-door sedan with a black vinyl hardtop pulled into the driveway in front of me. The passenger-side door swung open. "Come here," a man's voice said. Maybe it was a dad driving a classmate to school? Maybe there was a ride in it for me. Curious, I leaned in toward the open door. At that moment, the driver's hand reached out, over my head, and grabbed the back of my neck. I felt my body hurl into a 360-degree flip and I landed on the floorboard of the front passenger seat. Then the door shut and the car sped off. At least this is how I remember it, even though, from the vantage of adult logic, it hardly seems possible.

I don't recall thinking anything those first few minutes I was pulled into that car. Random crime was not a feature of my suburban neighborhood. I was a tomboy; I loved the endless, untroubled afternoons of riding bikes through neighbors' backyards or playing hide-and-seek across a wide, five-block radius of my home. It never occurred to me that anything bad could happen to me there. While I'm sure I'd been privy to a safety orientation or two at school and had probably watched my share of McGruff the Crime Dog commercials on TV, nothing like that came to mind.

A hand was pressing down on my head to keep me on the floor, even though I didn't dare resist. After several minutes, the voice that had lured me into the car said, "What's your name?" I asked where he was taking me.

"What's your name?"

"Where are you taking me?"

"What's your name?"

"I'll tell you my name when you tell me where you're taking me."

He demanded my name a final time, his voice angrier: gruff, masculine and scary. I told him and when he asked me for my parents' names, my address, my phone number, and where I had been headed, I told him all those things, too.

We merged onto a highway, and he said I could sit up on the seat. That's when I got my first look at him. He was maybe in his 40s. He was scruffy; his dark hair and beard were scraggly. He was big in every direction—huge shoulders, a thick belly, very tall—but the biggest thing about him was his eyes. And they were pitch black.

As soon as I'd righted myself on the seat, he instructed me to lie down instead, with my head at his hip and my feet against the door—so, I assumed, nobody could see me. I became convinced that his plan was to drive me to the Delaware Memorial Bridge (about two hours south) and drop me off it. Bridges had always terrified me as a child.

CHILD ABDUCTION IN AMERICA: A TIMELINE

May 25, 1979 Six-year-old Etan Patz is abducted in New York City. His body is never found. His case receives intense national attention.

July 1979 to May 1981 Twenty-nine African-American youths are abducted and murdered in Atlanta, sending fear through the city and sparking the creation of armed "bat patrols" by neighborhood residents.

July 27, 1981 Six-year-old Adam Walsh is kidnapped in the toy department of a Hollywood, Florida, department store. Two weeks later, the little boy's remains are found in a drainage canal 120 miles from his home.

August 1982 Thanks partly to John Walsh, the Missing Children Act is passed, requiring the FBI to enter lost kids' descriptions into its national crime computer.

September 1984 The National Center for Missing & Exploited Children is founded. The center distributes photos of missing kids and trains government agencies in handling kidnapping cases.

February 1988 John Walsh's TV show, *America's Most Wanted: America Fights Back*, debuts. The show reenacts kidnapping cases (and other crimes) to locate missing children and catch their abductors.

November 1990 The National Child Search Assistance Act is passed, prohibiting police from insisting on waiting periods before taking reports on missing children.

October 1, 1993 12-year-old Polly Klaas is taken from her bedroom in Petaluma, California, during a slumber party. She's found dead two months later.

December 1993 The International Parental Kidnapping Crime Act cracks down on parents who abduct their own children and remove them from the United States.

January 13, 1996 Amber Hagerman, 9, is abducted while riding her bicycle in her Arlington, Texas, neighborhood. Four days later she is found murdered. Her killer is never caught.

July 1997 The National Conference of Commissioners on Uniform State Laws approves state legislation to further curtail parental kidnapping. Today 34 states have passed bills based on the model law.

June 5, 2002 14-year-old Elizabeth Smart is seized by two ex-communicated Mormons from her Salt Lake City bedroom.

January 13, 2003 The PROTECT Act, calling on states to coordinate the adoption of AMBER Alert, a national emergency broadcast system to help locate missing children, is introduced into Congress.

March 12, 2003 Elizabeth Smart is found and returned to her family. The next morning her father, Ed Smart, publicly calls on Congress to pass the PROTECT Act, "*today*, not tomorrow, not a year from now."

April 30, 2003 After clearing both houses, the PROTECT Act is signed into law by President George W. Bush.

September 2003 AMBER Alert recovers its 100th victim.

With me prostrate across the bench seat and him still driving, he unzipped his jeans and took out his penis. "Say, I want to suck your c—," he said. I had never seen a penis before, I didn't even know what one was, and I really did not like the way his words sounded—foreign and bad. But I knew I had no choice; this man was in charge. So I said it, and he instructed me to lick it "just like a lollipop." I did. Then he pulled down my underpants and started touching me.

As all this was happening, I slowly, slowly crept my feet up the side of the car door until they just barely showed in the window. Maybe another driver would see, get suspicious, look more closely. Maybe we'd get a witness that way. I remember later being told that we did.

We weren't in the car an hour when it ran out of gas (so we wouldn't make it to the bridge, I thought, thankfully). He pulled over, zipped up and I collected my bookbag and lunchbox. We crossed the highway and walked together

about a mile to his apartment, hand in hand at his insistence. I knew instinctually that what was happening was wrong and bad—my 7-year-old mind had no other vocabulary to classify it. And I knew I was supposed to be at school, not walking alongside a highway with a strange man. But I felt I had no other option but to do as I was told.

We entered his apartment through the back door, which opened into the kitchen. He pointed me toward a chair while he went to the phone on the wall and dialed someone. From his conversation I learned that his name was Vic, and that the car belonged to the person on the other end. He hung up and motioned me into the living room. I remember wallpaper that looked like a collage of old-fashioned, Wild West-style "Wanted" posters, and gambling equipment as furniture; he used a low-standing craps table as a coffee table. Downstairs, where he led me next, contained a bedroom with a kitchenette. The bedroom was domi-

nated by a waterbed and had a single lightbulb hanging from a cord casting dim light. I hated his place; if one of my friends from school lived here, I would not want to go there to play.

He told me to sit down on the bed and started undressing me. I didn't struggle or cry; it didn't occur to me to do either. I don't think I was in shock, because I felt very aware of everything: where his hands touched my clothes, how closely his frame approached mine on the bed. I was conscious, but passive. He started undoing my braids and seemed to enjoy this most of all, lingering over pieces of hair and stroking my head. When he was done with me, he undressed himself.

What he did to me sexually for the next six or seven hours I only recall in fleeting visual flashes that are strung together in my memory like a loop of a tape. What he did, he did over and over again. He'd tell me to perform the same act from the car, and I would. He'd lay me down on my back on his bed and put his fingers inside me; when I told him that it hurt he'd coat them with Vaseline, but that didn't make his fingers any smaller. He never attempted intercourse, and I never worried that he might because I didn't know what it was.

I never had thoughts about dying, no thoughts about how all this would end. After all, I had never been in danger before. I cried only once the whole day, toward the end of the afternoon, when I suddenly felt punched in the stomach by the thought that I would never see my mom again. He demanded to know, in an angry tone of voice, why I was crying. Trying to restrain my tears, I said that I wanted to see my mom. He yelled at me to shut up until he scared me enough that I did.

Then, sometime around 3 or 4 P.M., he started crying. We were sitting on the edge of the bed, and he leaned into me, letting out immense sobs on my shoulder. I consoled him. I didn't hate him. I didn't want to hurt him. I just patted his back and said, "It's okay, it's okay," over and over.

After a few minutes of crying, he stopped rather quickly and silently started to get dressed. I took that as my cue to do the same. He then began calling different numbers asking for information about a bus. Now that I was close to being let go (why else would he be asking about a bus? I reasoned), I felt remarkably relaxed. I ate the entire contents of my Holly Hobby lunchbox, cupcakes first. After each call I'd casually ask if he had found a bus yet until finally he responded to me by lurching across the table, digging his thumbs into my neck and hissing, "No, I didn't find a fucking bus yet, okay?" I squeaked out, "I can't breathe," and he dropped his hands.

When he finally found the right bus, we left his apartment as we arrived, hand in hand, and walked to a bus stop. As the bus pulled up, I frantically concocted a plan: I'd take an aisle seat, and once the bus started moving I'd jump up and scream, "This man just kidnapped me!" As he paid our fare, with one hand possessively spanning the back of my neck, I tried to bore my stare into the bus driver's skull, silently begging him to look at me. Surely he could see that something was wrong, that a 7-year-old girl in a parochial school uniform was not supposed to be traveling with a man like this. But the driver didn't look up, and when the two of us sat down, Vic surprised me by ushering me into a window seat. My plan was foiled, and I no longer had the guts to scream.

We took the bus to a supermarket plaza. We walked to a pay phone and he again asked me for my parents' names and phone number. He dialed, and after a moment he said, "Is this Marcie Martelli? Is your daughter Rose Martelli? She's at the A&P in Elizabeth." He hung up, turned to me, and said, "If you tell anyone anything about me, I'll come back and get your mom."

And then he was gone.

Oddly, I wasn't overjoyed or excited. I didn't think about finding a trusted adult, like a cashier or a police officer, as kids are told to do if they're in trouble. Instead I went inside the A&P and browsed the cosmetics aisle. After a few minutes, two policemen walked into the store. I knew they were looking for me, but for some reason I didn't want them to find me. I passed quickly through an aisle or two trying to avoid them, but they caught up with me. "Are you Rose Martelli?" one of them asked.

"Yes," I replied.

"Were you just kidnapped?"

"Yes."

"Come with us."

The policemen took me to a hospital where I was met by a slew of doctors, nurses and more police officers. They were all extremely friendly and upbeat. The head cop asked me how good my memory was. I boasted that I had an excellent memory, and took great pride in detailing for him everything I'd had for breakfast that day. For dinner, I got a huge roast beef sandwich—I had never had roast beef before, and I loved it—and

a hot-fudge sundae. The only thing that dampened my mood at the hospital was when I went to use the bathroom and realized, as I turned around to flush, that there was blood in the bowl. I was so embarrassed; I remember telling a nurse, "I think I broke your toilet." The nurse didn't explain to me that my hymen probably had been broken. I wound up figuring it out for myself about six years later in health class.

About an hour after I arrived at the hospital, and after the police questioned me about Vic and what happened to me, a policeman said, "We have two people here who can't wait to see you." I've never been so happy to see somebody as I was when my mom and dad walked into that room that day. They were wonderfully sunny and cheerful, which was just what I needed at that moment. To see them break down or cry, I think I would have felt as if I'd done something wrong or even felt guilty for upsetting them.

Then the police officers told me they needed to take pictures of my vagina. After a thorough medical examination, I was released at around 10 P.M. I remember being dressed and ready to go home when the police officers asked me and my parents to drive around with them as they looked for Vic. But it was dark, and I was falling asleep, so my mom called it off and my parents took me home. I slept well in my own bed that night.

I didn't go to school the rest of that week. Every morning the police came over and showed me mug shots and pictures of cars. My dad and I drove around on several occasions with the police as I pointed out landmarks I remembered. Later that week the police said that I had to tell them every single thing that happened on the day I was kidnapped, so they could type it all down. I rattled off the whole story with as many details as possible—down to the odd furniture in Vic's apartment, the number tacked on his front door, a red star on a slide in his apartment complex's playground and even the ID number on the bus.

The cops would later tell me that my detailed descriptions helped them catch Vic. But until I wrote this story, I didn't learn what he was charged with or if he was convicted, or if there was a trial. (See "How the Crime Was Solved.") All I knew was that he went to jail soon afterward and might not be eligible for parole until I turned 22. But the summer I was 17, the Maple-wood police told my mom that Vic had died in prison.

Being kidnapped made me famous. For days afterward, flowers and stuffed animals from neighbors, our church and my school poured into the house. I read about myself in the papers. When we went to Mass the next Sunday, the whole congregation gave me a standing ovation as I walked in with my family. For months, I was a town celebrity, particularly among other kids. They'd come up to me at the playground or the pool and ask if I was Rose Martelli, the Rose Martelli who was kidnapped. I remember one kid asking if it was true that I had been raped. I answered, "I don't know, what does 'rape' mean?"

Telling the story never bothered me. In fact, I loved the way it kept people riveted. The following summer I joined the swim team, and on the bus returning from away meets, I'd have dozens of teammates surrounding me, listening intently. I told it to get attention from boys I liked.

My parents, meanwhile—my dad taught history at a public high school a few miles away, and my mom, a former teacher—seemed to want to brush the whole experience under the rug, to get on with a normal life, of course, but also to forget that the whole thing ever happened. My mom, to this day, mostly refers to it as "what happened to you when you were 7." Later that winter, they took all four of us kids to a psychologist's office without saying exactly where we were going. When we got there, we were told to play in the waiting room while my parents went inside. Eventually I went in and the psy-

chologist asked me questions about my kidnapping. She seemed weird to me, and I didn't like talking to her. On the ride home, I asked my parents, "Do I have to go there again?" They seemed very relieved and quickly assured me that I didn't.

The only other time I ever went to therapy was a few sessions as a high-school senior at the insistence of my best friend. We did work through some of my issues of fear, but still, the events of that day would continue to influence me throughout my life in various ways. For one, I became intensely terrified of strangers—male strangers—for about five or six years afterward. The summer after I was kidnapped, I had to take an IQ test for a gifted-student program. My father drove me to the testing location where I was to sit alone for three hours in a room with an administrator, a large man with dark hair and a beard. I froze the minute I saw him. I don't remember how I got the words out—my fear of strangers was actually something I tried never to mention, especially not to my parents—but I refused to stay without my dad. The administrator had to call for special permission to allow my dad to come in and stay with me. (He did; I passed the test and got into the program.) When I got to middle school, at age 11, I started walking two miles each way to school, often alone. I would tense up each time a car passed by. I was convinced everybody had a gun.

Now 29, I no longer have such random fear. And with the exception of writing this story, I don't spend a lot of time thinking about the events of that day. The only time I do is when there is a highly publicized case in the news like Elizabeth Smart's. I know that getting back to your own bed safely is just the first part; then comes figuring out the rest of your life with this ordeal now part of it. I just hope that Elizabeth, and other kids who survive such experiences, can move past it as well as I feel I did. Not that I got through it perfectly, or

that it had no negative effect on me, but I do think my life stayed its course; I do think I wound up happy, ambitious about life, and the person I was mostly meant to be all along. Really, when I hear about cases like Elizabeth's, I feel the most empathy for the parents. As I've gotten older, I have thought more and more about how horrifying it must be for parents; while I was missing, mine probably, felt more helpless than I did.

I'm still grateful to my parents for acting so upbeat at the hospital that night; quite frankly, I will never know how they did it. But now that I'm an adult, I've thought that it would have been nice to see my dad punch a wall or something. Deep down, my greatest insecurity has been that I don't think myself somebody worth fighting for. Sometimes, during moments I am less than proud of, I will pick a fight with someone I love just to feed a psychological impulse to see if they run away or stick it out. That impulse can feel as strong as a physical addiction at times and is something I have to fight hard. Whether these urges stem from being an abuse and kidnap victim, that's all something I gave up trying to solve years ago. I was a late bloomer with boys; was that because my first sexual experience was a forced, cruel and illegal one? I don't think so, but who knows?

There is no clean equation that can determine what about my life or personality is due to what happened to me that sunny February morning. That knot of causes and effects, more than 20 years old, is tied far too tightly to pick apart and separate the strands. And I don't feel the need to pick. I like who I am. I'm happy with myself. Getting to that point has not appeared to be any more difficult for me than it is for anybody else. And if I am scarred by the experience, they are scars that I own, and that have given me a sense of pride and accomplishment for overcoming what could have been a torturous ordeal. And that's a good feeling.

HOW TO KEEP OUR KIDS SAFE

Here are the recommendations of Leigh Baker, Psy.D., author of *Protecting Your Children From Sexual Predators*.

• **Establish an ironclad rule that your child can never go off alone with *any* adult without your permission**. Three-quarters of abductions are committed by someone the child knows.

• **Act out possible scenarios using dolls, puppets and toy cars**. Have a puppet be an adult who says, "Come with me—I've got a surprise." Using a child puppet, have your child say, "I need to call Mommy first." When the adult puppet says, "I asked your mom, and she said it's okay," the child should say, "I need to hear her tell *me* it's okay."

• **Establish a phrase that means "Stop—this might be dangerous."** Have a child say "red light" during preventive play acting whenever she senses something isn't right. If she ever encounters a similar real-life situation, the phrase will pop into her head and override her natural tendency to obey adults.

GET INVOLVED IN MAKING LAWS STRONGER

To help minimize all children's chances of being abducted or abused, lobby your elected representatives at the local, state and national levels to support legislation that would:

1) create a national, easily accessed database of offenders

2) abolish statutes of limitation for child abuse

3) require police departments to provide training and follow established procedures in child-abduction cases.

4) To learn how to launch an AMBER Alert program, which helps locate missing children, in your community, log onto www.missingkids.com.

Innocence Interrupted: A Doctor's Analysis

We asked Joyanna Silberg, Ph.D., a clinical psychologist who specializes in children's trauma, to comment on Rose Martelli's experience. Dr. Silberg, the editor of the book *"The Dissociative Child: Diagnosis, Treatment and Management,* is also the executive vice president of the Leadership Council on Child Abuse and Interpersonal Violence (www.leadershipcouncil.org), in Philadelphia.

Q: *Rose tells the story of her abduction in such an unemotional and matter-of-fact way. Why is that?*
A: Her flat tone suggests that she was dissociating during her abduction and molestation. Dissociation is a term for a specific defense mechanism—a psychological reaction that allows people to endure terrifying and humiliating experiences by distancing themselves from events as if they were happening to someone else, even in retrospect. Although Rose does not recall experiencing this phenomenon herself, many young patients I treat tell me that as they were being raped or abused, they felt as if they were looking down from the ceiling and seeing

themselves. Dissociation also can quell the intense fear that victims feel, which helps explain why Rose doesn't recall being terrified, even though she says she expected to be dropped off a bridge. I also suspect that, during the hours she describes as "a loop of tape," Rose has blocked out many details of the assault, erasing them from her memory.

Q: *Why didn't Rose know better than to approach a stranger's car?*
A: Her behavior is utterly typical, even for children who have been told repeatedly not to talk to strangers. Children are accustomed to obeying adults, so when Rose heard a man say "Come here," she obeyed him. Also, to a 7-year-old, warnings about danger are abstract; Rose knew her neighborhood to be nothing but safe and friendly.

Q: *Why wouldn't a child dial 911 or approach a salesperson for help after she was left in the A&P? Rose even avoided the police who came looking for her.*
A: Again, her behavior is not unusual. Rose had gotten used to following the instructions of her abductor. He told her to wait for her mother. Also, she heard him speak to her mother on the phone

and saw him leave the store, so she expected her mother to arrive shortly.

Q: *Rose told the nurse that she had broken the toilet when she noticed blood in her urine. What do you make of that?*

A: That is such a poignant detail. I can't help but wonder if Rose was saying, "I'm afraid I am broken." Adults are squeamish about discussing sex with children, so the nurse's silence is not surprising. Yet in the case of a molested child, openness would have been better. Instead, Rose had to wait until health class to figure it out for herself.

Q: *Is Rose's enjoyment of her "celebrity status" after the abduction normal?*

A: Completely. Kids and grownups alike enjoy retelling "war stories" as a way of being the center of attention. Sometimes, however, this retelling can be a form of "traumatic reenactment," which means the person is stuck in the past and unable to extricate herself from the cycle of telling and retelling. When I work with young children, I use play therapy to get them to retell their stories in a way that gives them control over events. This therapy helps them gain a sense of control and resolution, which seems to have eluded Rose.

Q: *Why does Rose say she worries that she "wasn't worth fighting for"?*
A: This probably stems from her sense that her abduction was "brushed under the rug." But she does express gratitude that her parents were upbeat upon her return; this allowed her to feel calmer than she otherwise might have at the time. Her memory of her parents' reaction—downplaying the situation—contrasts dramatically with the case of Elizabeth Smart. The

Smarts made their daughter's plight as public as possible both before and after her safe return home. How that approach will affect Elizabeth down the road is an open question. What we do know is that both the Martellis and the Smarts did what they believed was best under horrific circumstances.

Q: *Rose calls herself a "late bloomer with boys." What effects do these kinds of trauma have on a woman's sex life and her ability to form intimate attachments?*
A: Childhood victims of sexual assault often have great difficulty in

this area. A victim might see herself as an object of sexual gratification and thus have trouble believing that someone could love her for herself. Also, she may confuse abusive relationships with love and therefore choose inappropriate partners. For other victims, intercourse triggers painful flashbacks, so they avoid sex altogether. With therapy, survivors of sexual assault can move beyond these issues and learn to trust others.
—*Sondra Forsyth*

New hope for sex offender treatment

Research suggests psychological treatment helps reduce recidivism among convicted sex offenders.

BY KAREN KERSTING

Controversial questions swirl around the correctional system's management of sex offenders: How long should they be incarcerated for their crimes of forcing sex acts on adults or children? How should they be monitored following release? Does psychological treatment in prison actually affect the risk of committing further offenses? And how can courts balance offenders' potential for rehabilitation with a community's need to protect its citizens?

Responses to these questions have varied over the years, and, accordingly, so has policy-making by the states and the federal government. Recent policies have been trending toward longer prison sentences and more restrictive after-release monitoring, stemming in part from a dismal view of treatment programs, treatment advocates say.

But many psychologists and policy advocates, including law professor John Q. LaFond, JD, of the University of Missouri–Kansas City, say that approach disregards key information on the nature of sex offenders—statistics show most are not likely to repeat their crimes—and on the increasing efficacy of offender treatment, largely due to a modern behavior modification model stressing relapse prevention through recognition and avoidance of criminal impulses.

"In the 1980s, American states made the decision that sex offenders were not sick; they were bad," LaFond says. "Some states decided to offer treatment, but there wasn't much hope that it would work. Now, however, there's an emerging optimism that psychologists can deal with these people and offer alternatives to continued incarceration."

Some of that optimism comes from a meta-analysis on the effectiveness of treatment for sex offenders published in *Sexual Abuse: A Journal of Research and Treatment* (Vol. 14, No. 2) in 2002. That analysis showed for the first time a significant difference between recidivism rates for sex offenders who were treated and those who were not, says psychologist R. Karl Hanson, PhD, lead author of the study and senior researcher for the Solicitor General Canada—the government agency that manages Canadian courts and corrections.

The study revealed, among the most recent research samples, sexual recidivism rates of 17.3 percent for untreated offenders, compared with 9.9 percent for treated offenders. Though that's not a large reduction, the large sample size and widely agreed-upon research methods make it statistically reliable and of practical significance, Hanson says.

One in every 10 state inmates receives *psychotropic medication*.

Misperceptions

Even so, psychologists face challenges in convincing law enforcement authorities to take treatment seriously given the obvious public concern about sex offenses. One major obstacle is public misconceptions about recidivism, Hanson says. "Even when we're talking with law enforcement officials, they'll guess demonstrated rates to be in the 70s or 80s, so real rates of 10 to 20 percent surprise everybody," he notes.

That's why the recent meta-analysis finding is a breakthrough of sorts—low recidivism rates among untreated sex offenders make finding a statistically significant treatment effect difficult, says psychologist Robert Prentky, PhD, who is the director of research for Justice Resource Institute in Bridgewater, Mass.

"Through anecdotal evidence, we know that modern treatment lowers recidivism, and the meta-analysis backs that up now," Prentky says. "We are unlikely to find a large treatment effect as long as the re-offense rates for untreated sex offenders are relatively low, for example, around 15 percent."

Assessing dangerousness

Psychologists have gleaned a number of important treatment insights in their research—the most basic of which is one size does not fit all.

"A large part of the challenge to managing this group is educating the courts that sex offenders are a highly heterogeneous population and not all of them are at high-risk for re-offending," says psychologist Moss Aubrey, PhD, who does private assessment of male sex offenders in New Mexico.

People commit sexual crimes for different reasons, Aubrey says. "Some are highly predatory, highly psychopathic and have repeated offenses, making them more likely to re-offend," he explains.

In the last 10 years, psychologists have made substantial advances in clearly identifying factors that increase an offender's risk of committing an offense after release, Hanson says. These factors include the number of offenses, intimacy deficits, sexual preoccupations and age.

Actuarial scales for determining an offender's risk of committing more sex crimes after treatment are available, but not always trusted by judges and many clinicians, Prentky says. More often, courts base release decisions on progress reports from prison psychologists—relying heavily on their expertise.

"Psychologists are essentially being asked to determine what level of risk an individual poses to a community even though there is no definitive way to know for certain," LaFond says. "They're being asked to balance that risk with the individual liberty concerns of an offender. Science has come up with tools to help them, but it's still a huge responsibility and a terrible burden."

Challenges of treatment

Adding to that burden are clients who may not disclose all of their crimes or sexually deviant thoughts. Offenders who report crimes they have committed, other than those they were convicted of, face either additional prosecution or being held beyond their sentence under a civil commitment law.

"If you reveal in the course of treatment that you've done all sorts of things that the criminal justice system is unaware of, you place yourself at substantially increased risk of not being released or facing stricter regulation after release," Prentky says. "That is a serious roadblock to treatment."

This disclosure problem for the most part cannot be alleviated; it must be worked around. Providers have to spell out con-

fidentiality rules both in writing and verbally during treatment, Prentky says. Therapists must tell their patients to do the best they can discussing their problems and tendencies without revealing information that would place them at greater risk, says Prentky, adding that, "It's unethical not to make clients aware of the limits to confidentiality."

"Psychologists are essentially being asked to determine what level of risk an individual poses to a community even though there is no definitive way to know for certain. They're being asked to balance that risk with the individual liberty concerns of an offender. Science has come up with tools to help them, but it's still a huge responsibility and a terrible burden."

John Q. LaFond
University of Missouri–Kansas City

Disclosure is most problematic in the early phases of treatment, in which offenders are expected to take full responsibility for all of their criminal behavior. But it is less of a problem in the subsequent phases, in which treatment focuses on developing and refining relapse prevention strategies, Prentky says.

Another key consideration for both psychologists and judges is timing. It's crucial to start therapy as soon after incarceration as possible, LaFond says. Offenders often fail to realize the severity of their crimes, and an antagonistic prison environment can exacerbate feelings of being wrongly accused and hamper treatment.

"Attitudes that led to offending can become stronger, more virulent in prison," says LaFond. "Offenders can develop explanations for themselves that become solidified over time. You want to confront those ideas right away and make it clear that sex offenses are very serious crimes."

If treatment methods are as effective as Hanson's meta-analysis indicates, they are likely to become more popular in U.S. prisons, LaFond says.

"Most sex offenders do eventually return to the community," LaFond says. "So we need to change them while they're in treatment."

APA published the book "Preventing Sexual Violence: How Society Should Cope with Sex Offenders" by John Q. LaFond in early 2004.

A CRUEL EDGE

The painful truth about today's pornography—
and what men can do about it.

BY ROBERT JENSEN, PH.D.

AFTER AN INTENSE THREE HOURS, THE workshop on pornography is winding down. The 40 women all work at a center that serves battered women and rape survivors. These are the women on the front lines, the ones who answer the 24-hour hotline and work one-on-one with victims. They counsel women who have just been raped, help women who have been beaten, and nurture children who have been abused. These women have heard and seen it all. No matter how brutal a story might be, they have experienced or heard one even more brutal; there is no way to one-up them on stories of male violence. But after three hours of information, analysis, and discussion of the commercial heterosexual pornography industry, many of these women are drained. Sadness hangs over the room.

One women who has held back throughout the workshop, her arms wrapped tightly around herself. Now, finally, she speaks. "This hurts. It just hurts so much."

Everyone is quiet as the words sink in. Slowly the conversation restarts but her words hang in the air:

It hurts.

It hurts to know that no matter who you are as a woman you can be reduced to a thing to be penetrated, and that men will buy movies about that, and that in many of those movies your humiliation will be the central theme. It hurts to know that so much of the pornography that men are buying fuses sexual desire with cruelty.

Even these women, who have found ways to cope with the injuries from male violence in other places, struggle with that. It is one thing to deal with acts, even extremely violent acts. It is another to know the thoughts, ideas, and fantasies lie behind those acts.

People routinely assume that pornography is such a difficult and divisive issue because it's about sex. I think that's wrong. This culture struggles unsuccessfully with pornography because it is about men's cruelty to women, and the pleasure men sometimes take in that cruelty. And that is much more difficult for everyone to face.

"At least our society still brands rape a crime;

THERE ARE DIFFERENT PORNOGRAPHIC genres, but my studies of pornographic videos over the past seven years have focused on the stories told in mainstream heterosexual pornography. By that I mean the videos and DVDs that are widely available in the United States, marketed as sexually explicit (what is commonly called "hard-core"), rented and purchased primarily by men, and depict sex primarily between men and women. The sexual activity is not simulated: What happens on the screen happened in the world. This mainstream pornography does not include overt bondage and sadomasochism, explicit violence, urination or defecation, although such material is widely available in shops, through the mail, or on the Internet. (There's also, of course, an underground market for child pornography—the only porn clearly illegal everywhere in the United States.)

To obtain mainstream pornographic videos for study, I visited stores that sold "adult product" (the industry's preferred term) and asked clerks and managers to help me select the most commonly rented and purchased tapes. I wanted to avoid the accusation that feminists analyzing pornography only pick out the worst examples, the most violent material, to critique.

While many may find what is described here to be disturbing, these are not aberrations. These rapes are broadly representative of the 11,303 new hardcore titles that were released in 2002, according to *Adult Video News*, the industry's trade magazine. They are standard fare from a pornography industry with an estimated $10 billion in annual sales. They are what brothers and fathers and uncles are watching, what boyfriends and husbands and, in many cases, male children are watching.

What kind of stories does this mainstream pornography tell the all-American boy—and what does that mean for the girl next door? Here are three examples:

- The 2003 film "Sopornos 4" was produced by VCA Pictures, one of the "high-end" companies that create films for the "couples market." These films, sometimes called "features," typically attempt some plot and character development. The industry claims these films appeal to women as well as men.

  The plot of "Sopornos" is a takeoff on the popular HBO series about New Jersey mobsters. In the last of six sex scenes, the mob boss's wife has sex with two of his men. Moving through the standard porn progression—oral sex and then vaginal sex—one of the men prepares to penetrate her anally. She tells him: "That fucking cock is so fucking huge. … Spread [my] fucking ass. … Spread it open." He penetrates her. Then, she says, in a slightly lower tone, "Don't go any deeper." She seems to be in pain. At the end of the scene, she requests the men's semen ("Two cocks jacking off in my face. I want it.") and opens her mouth. The men ejaculate onto her at the same time.

- "Two in the Seat #3," a 2003 "gonzo" release (meaning, there is no attempt to create characters or story lines) from Red Light District, contains six scenes in which two men have sex with one woman, culminating in a double-penetration (the woman is penetrated vaginally and anally at the same time). In one scene, 20-year-old Claire, her hair in pigtails, says she has been in the industry for three months. Asked by the off-camera interviewer what will happen in the scene, she replies, "I'm here to get pounded." The two men then enter the scene and begin a steady stream of insults, calling her "a dirty, nasty girl," "a little fucking cunt," "a little slut." After oral and vaginal sex, she asks one to "Please put your cock in my ass." During double-penetration on the floor, her vocalizations sound pained. She's braced against the couch, moving very little. The men spank her, and her buttock is visibly red. One man asks, ''Are you crying?"

  Claire: "No, I'm enjoying it."

  Man: "Damn, I thought you were crying. It was turning me on when I thought you were crying."

  Claire: "Would you like me to?"

  Man: "Yeah, give me a fucking tear. Oh, there's a fucking tear."

- Finally, there's "Gag Factor 10," a 2002 release from JM Productions also in the "gonzo" category. One of the 10 sex scenes involves a woman and man having a picnic in a park. While she sits on the blanket, he stands and thrusts his penis into her mouth. Two other men who walk by join in. One man grabs her hair and pulls her head into his penis in what his friend calls "the jackhammer."

  At this point the woman is grimacing and seems in pain. She then lies on the ground, and the men approach her from behind. "Eat that whole fucking dick. … You little whore, you like getting hurt," one says. After they all ejaculate into her mouth, the semen flows out onto her body. She reaches quickly for the wine glass, takes a large drink, looks up at her boyfriend, and says, "God, I love you, baby." Her smile fades to a pained look of shame and despair.

I CAN'T KNOW EXACTLY WHAT THE WOMEN in these films were feeling, physically or emotionally. But here is what BellaDonna, one of the women who appeared in "Two in the Seat #3," told a television interviewer about such sex scenes: "You have to really prepare physically and mentally for it. I mean, I go through a process from the night before. I stop eating at 5 p.m. I do, you know, like two enemas, and then the next morning I don't eat anything. It's so draining on your body."

Even if the pain shown in the above scenes is acted and not real, why don't directors edit *out* pained expressions? I see only two possible answers: either they view such pain as being of no consequence to the viewers' interest—and hence to the goal of maximizing film sales—or they believe viewers enjoy seeing the women's pain. So why, then, do some men find the infliction of pain on women during sex either not an obstacle to their ability to achieve sexual pleasure or a factor that can *enhance* their pleasure?

I believe it's all about the edge.

There are only so many ways that human beings can, in mechanical terms, have sex. There are a limited number of body parts and openings, a limited number of ways to create the friction that produces the stimulation and sensations. That's why stories about sexuality generally tap into something beyond the mechanical. When most nonpornographic films deal with sex, they draw, at least in part, on the emotions most commonly connected with sex: love and affection. But pornography doesn't have that option, since my research has shown that men typically consume it to *avoid* love and affection and go straight to sexual release.

And that means pornography, without emotional variation, will become repetitive and uninteresting, even to men watching primarily to facilitate masturbation. So pornography needs an edge.

When the legal restrictions on pornography gradually loosened in the 1970s and '80s, anal sex captured that edge, because it was seen as something most women don't want. Then, as anal sex became routine in pornography, the gonzo genre started routinely adding double-penetrations and gag inducing oral sex—again, acts that men believe women generally do not want. These days, pornography has become so normalized and so mainstream in our culture that the edge keeps receding. As Jerome Tanner put it during a pornography directors' roundtable discussion featured in *Adult Video News*, "People just want it harder, harder, and harder, because… what are you gonna do next?"

It's not surprising that the new edge more and more involves overt cruelty—an easy choice given that the dynamic of male domination and female submission is already in place in patriarchy. All people are capable of being cruel, of course. But contemporary mainstream heterosexual pornography forces the question: Why has cruelty become so sexualized for some men?

Feminist research long ago established that rape involves the sexualization of power, the equation in men's imaginations of sexual pleasure with domination and control. The common phrase "rape is about power, not sex" misleads, though; rape is about the fusion of sex and domination, about the eroticization of control. And in this culture, rape is normal. That is, in a culture where the dominant definition of sex is the taking of pleasure from women by men, rape is an expression of the sexual norms of the culture, not violations of those norms. Sex is a sphere in which men are trained to see themselves as naturally dominant and women as naturally passive. Rape is both nominally illegal and completely normal at the same time.

PORNOGRAPHY, however, is **sold** to us as liberation."

By extension, there should be nothing surprising about the fact that some pornography includes explicit images of women in pain. But my question is: Wouldn't a healthy society want to deal with that? Why aren't more people, men or women, concerned?

Right-wing opponents of pornography offer a moralistic critique that cannot help us find solutions, because typically those folks endorse male dominance (albeit not these particular manifestations of it). Conversely, some feminists want us to believe that the growing acceptance of pornography is a benign sign of expanding sexual equality and freedom. Meanwhile, feminist critics of pornography have been marginalized in political and intellectual arenas. And all the while, the pornographers are trudging off to the bank with bags of money.

"Why has **cruelty** become so sexualized for **SOME MEN**?"

I think this helps explain why even the toughest women at rape crisis centers find the reality of pornography so difficult to cope with. No matter how hard it may be to face rape, at least our society still brands it as a crime. Pornography, however, is not only widely accepted, but sold to us as liberation.

I don't pretend to speak for women; my focus is on men. And I believe that the task for men of conscience is to define ourselves and our sexuality outside of the domination/submission dynamic. It is not easy: Like everyone, we are products of our culture and have to struggle against it. But as a man, I at least have considerable control over the conditions in which I live and the situations in which I function. Women sometimes do not have that control. They're at far more risk of sexual violence, and they have to deal with men who disproportionately hold positions of power over them. Mainstream pornography tips that power balance even further.

For example, when a female student has a meeting about a research project with a male college professor who the night before was watching "Gag Factor 10," who will she be to him? Or when a woman walks into a bank to apply for a loan from a male loan officer who the night before was watching "Two in the Seat #3," what will he be thinking? And when a woman goes in front of a male judge who the night before was watching "Sopornos 4," will she be judged fairly?

But some will argue: How can you assume that just because men watch such things they will act in a callous and cruel manner, sexually or otherwise? It is true that the connection between mass-media exposure and human behavior is complex, and social scientists argue both sides. But taken together, the laboratory evidence, the research on men who abuse, and the voluminous testimony of women clearly indicate that in some cases pornography influences men's sexual behavior. Pornography may not *cause* abuse, but it can be implicated as an accessory to the crime.

If we could pretend that these images are consumed by some small subset of deviant men, then we could identify and isolate those aberrant men, maybe repair them. But men who consume these images are everywhere: men who can't get a date and men who have all the dates they want. Men who live alone and men who are married. Men who grew up in liberal homes where pornography was never a big deal and men who grew up in strict religious homes where no talk of sex was allowed. Rich men and poor men, men of all colors and creeds.

When I critique pornography, I am often told to lighten up. Sex is just sex, people say, and I should stop trying to politicize pornography. But pornography offers men a politics of sex and gender—and that politics is patriarchal and reactionary. In pornography, women are not really people; they are three holes and two hands. Women in pornography have no hopes, no dreams, and no value apart from the friction those holes and hands can produce on a man's penis.

AS WITH ANY POLITICAL ISSUE, SUCCESSFUL strategies of resistance, I would suggest, must be collective and public rather than solely personal and private. Pornographers know that to be true—which is why they try to cut off the discussion. When we critique pornography, we typically are accused of being people who hate freedom, sexually dysfunctional prudes who are scared of sex, or both.

Pornographers also want to derail any talk of sexual ethics. They, of course, have a sexual ethic: Anything—and they mean anything—goes, and consenting adults should be free to choose. I agree that choice is crucial. But in a society in which power is not equally distributed, "anything goes" translates into "anything goes for men, while some women and children will suffer for it."

There are many controversial issues in the pornography debate, but there should be nothing controversial about this: To critique pornography is not repressive. We should be free to talk about our desire for an egalitarian intimacy and for sexuality that rejects pain and humiliation. That is not prudishness or censorship. It is at attempt to claim the best parts of our common humanity: love, caring, empathy. To do that is not to limit anyone. It is to say, simply, that women count as much as men.

ROBERT JENSEN, PH.D., *journalism professor at the University of Texas at Austin, is the co-author of* Pornography: The Production and Consumption of Inequality *and author of* Citizens of the Empire: The Struggle to Claim Our Humanity.

PREGNANT?
YOU'RE FIRED!

DESPITE LAWS THAT ARE SUPPOSED TO PROTECT PREGNANT WOMEN, GROWING NUMBERS OF MOMS-TO-BE ARE FINDING THE WORKPLACE ANYTHING BUT FAMILY-FRIENDLY. HERE'S HOW TO MAKE SURE THIS DISCRIMINATION DOESN'T HAPPEN TO YOU

BY STEPHANIE B. GOLDBERG

In 1995, Janet Rau, now thirty-two, was a rising star at Applebee's restaurant in suburban Atlanta. She was promoted to general manager after just a year and a half on the job. "I was the first female to hold that position within the franchise," says Rau. "In many ways, I was an experiment for them."

That March, she informed her district manager that she and her husband planned to start a family. "I didn't want to spring it on him as a surprise," she says. At her performance review in September, Rau says the manager remarked: "That's when I knew you weren't one hundred percent committed to your job."

Later that month, Rau announced her pregnancy. Rather than congratulate her, the district manager said glumly: "We'll just have to deal with it." Rau was upset, but figured her boss simply needed some time to get used to the idea. A few weeks later, she experienced uterine bleeding

and took a week off. When she returned, things were never the same. In November, her boss demoted her to second assistant manager—two levels down from her previous post —and transferred her to another location. "It was devastating," she says.

Rau's boss gave her an odd explanation for the demotion—her restaurant had not performed successfully during the Atlanta Olympics. While that was true, Rau says the real reason the establishment lost business was its location in Cobb County, which had been ruled out as an Olympic site because it had an anti-gay resolution.

"You're doing this because I'm pregnant," she told him.

He denied it. But Rau, angry, started looking for legal help. A friend referred her to Atlanta attorney Nancy Rafuse (who, coincidentally, was pregnant herself). The lawyer agreed to represent Rau and filed a claim with the Equal Employ-

ment Opportunity Commission (EEOC) against the owner of the Applebee's franchise for discrimination. From that point on, "it was very clear that they were going to make her so miserable she would just leave the job," says Rafuse.

Rau was denied promotions and reprimanded for missing work to care for her sick husband. She says the last straw came when an employee she had fired for pushing and threatening her was rehired by the company a week later. "I was afraid for my safety—and for the safety of my unborn child," says Rau, who resigned in 1998.

In August 1999, a jury decided that Rau had been discriminated against and awarded her $1.8 million in damages. Because federal law limits the amount of damages to $300,000, the award was later reduced to that amount plus $34,000 in back pay.

Rau, who is now a marketing consultant, contends the suit was never about money. "I knew I had done a good job, but invariably, doubts start creeping in," she explains. "To have a jury listen to the facts and draw the same conclusion I did is wonderful."

WHEN THE LAW IS NOT ENOUGH

Surprisingly, what happened to Rau is not uncommon. According to the EEOC, from 1992 to 1999, pregnancy discrimination complaints increased by 23 percent. This is in spite of the Pregnancy Discrimination Act (PDA) of 1978, which makes it illegal for companies with fifteen or more employees to hire, fire or withhold promotions on the basis of pregnancy or related conditions such as miscarriage.

Once women have children, "employers mistakenly have a sense that they aren't going to be as productive," says one expert

---

In addition, under the Family Medical Leave Act (FMLA), which went into effect in 1993, workers who have been employed for at least a year at companies with fifty or more employees are allowed to take up to twelve weeks of unpaid leave annually for family-related medical situations, such as the birth of a child. They must be reinstated when they return to work—or placed in comparable positions in terms of pay, status and benefits.

So why is pregnancy discrimination still happening? According to experts, employers can find ways around the laws by claiming that hiring, firing and promotion decisions were made for valid business reasons. "Discrimination has become more subtle," explains Sandhya Subramanian, policy counsel for the National Partnership for Women & Families, an advocacy group in Washington, D.C. She says the sto-

ries she hears today are on the order of: "I got pregnant and I felt pressure to leave my job. Then I was terminated, and I'm convinced it had something to do with my pregnancy."

Some employers view pregnancy as a problem because they assume that once women have children they won't work as hard as they used to. "They mistakenly have a sense that workers aren't going to be as useful or productive," says Subramanian. Often, it comes down to corporate culture, adds Marcia Bram Kropf, vice president of Catalyst, a New York City research and advisory group that promotes the advancement of women in business. "Many industries grew up around the assumption that husbands work, wives stay home with the children and workers should be free to travel or stay late without any advance notice," says Kropf. "And if you're not doing that, you're not going to be seen as committed to your work—even if you're outproducing your co-workers."

Bonnie Kerzer, a thirty-six-year-old sportswear designer and mother of two in Brooklyn, New York, was a victim of that outdated thinking about motherhood. After she announced her pregnancy in 1992, the president of the manufacturing company where she had worked for two years became unfriendly to her, Kerzer recalls. Three days before she was due back at work from maternity leave, "he called to tell me my job had been eliminated," she says. "I couldn't believe it."

The company claimed her services were no longer needed, but Kerzer was suspicious—especially when they hired another person to perform duties similar to hers. A former colleague confided to her that the president of the company had once remarked that Kerzer's pregnancy "was a sign that she was lazy." Kerzer was outraged.

She began looking for an attorney. "I had to see about eight different lawyers before I could find one who would take my case on contin-

gency," she says. "It's not easy to file suit. You need to be very persistent."

In 1998, she received a settlement from her employer, the terms of which are confidential. "It would have been so easy to give up," she says. "But I knew I had been wronged and that I had to continue to fight."

PUSHING THE LIMITS?

When it comes to accommodating pregnant workers, some companies say that they're forced to bear too heavy a burden. Take the case of the Chicago-area auto leasing company that fired Regina Sheehan, a purchasing agent, in 1994, when she was five months pregnant. Sheehan, now forty-three, was fired several months before she was to take her third maternity leave in three years.

According to Sheehan, the company made no secret of its hostility toward her pregnancies. During her third pregnancy she had to take a three-week disability leave because she was at risk for a miscarriage. When she returned, she was told by her supervisor, "Gina, you're not coming back after this baby."

Although her performance reviews had been satisfactory, Sheehan was closely monitored by the company to see if she was meeting her performance goals. When she was terminated, a supervisor told her: "Hopefully, this will give you some time to spend at home with your children."

"I was hysterical," says Sheehan. "I was going through a difficult pregnancy, and we really needed my income." She contacted a lawyer and filed a claim with the EEOC.

Her case went to trial in 1997. A jury awarded her $30,000 in back pay and attorney's fees, but the matter wasn't concluded until more than a year later, when the verdict was upheld on appeal.

Anita Blair, a lawyer and president of the Independent Women's Forum, a conservative group headquartered in Arlington, Virginia, believes that women like Sheehan are

THE **SMART WAY** TO NEGOTIATE A MATERNITY LEAVE

- DO YOUR HOMEWORK. Before springing the news on your boss, find out how other women have been treated. "You're likely to have problems if performance is evaluated by the notion that you have to be physically present at work to be a productive employee," says Cynthia Thompson, Ph.D., associate professor of business at Baruch College, in New York City.
- GIVE AS MUCH NOTICE AS POSSIBLE. By law, you're required to give notice at least thirty days prior to your departure. However, the experts recommend going beyond that. "Our research shows that women who experienced the fewest problems with maternity leave were more likely to have given their employers sufficient notice," says Ellen Galinsky, president of the Families and Work Institute, in New York City.
- DEFINE YOUR GOALS. Before talking to your boss, decide how long you want to be away and how available you want to be to your co-workers.
- PUT YOURSELF IN YOUR EMPLOYER'S SHOES. At the same time you notify your employer of your pregnancy leave, outline a plan for handling your work while you're away, suggests Cindia Cameron of 9-to-5, The National Association of Working Women.
- GET ALL INFORMATION ABOUT YOUR LEAVE IN WRITING. This avoids misunderstandings and puts you on much sounder footing if you have to contemplate legal action in the future.
- STAY IN TOUCH WITH YOUR BOSS WHILE YOU'RE ON LEAVE. It will be better for your career, says Cameron, "and it reduces the shock of returning to the office."

For more information, call the 9-to-5 Hotline at 800-522-0925.

---

expecting too much from their employers. "That person is gone three months of the year and is getting full-time benefits for part-time work," says Blair. "It's not simply a problem for management, but it also demoralizes the other employees who have to cover for her."

As difficult as it may be for companies to handle one employee's three maternity leaves in three years, the law is the law, other experts contend. "It's disruptive in the sense that [companies] are used to an individual's habits and now they have to break in another person," acknowledges Houston employment lawyer Beatrice Mladenka Fowler. "But legally, their responsibilities are clear."

"Society is still catching up with the law," adds Subramanian. "Many employers are ignorant of their obligations, and a lot of people are unsure of their rights or hesitant about taking advantage of them."

FIGHTING BACK

If you suspect that you are a victim of pregnancy discrimination, keep notes of conversations with managers and document any reduction of responsibilities. If you plan to discuss your situation with your human resources department, you may want to consult an attorney, since your remarks can have legal consequences later.

Then, contact the EEOC promptly. From the day you experience a discriminatory act, such as denial of pregnancy leave or termination, you have 180 to 300 days to file a claim with the regional office of the EEOC, depending on your state. If your state or municipality has its own civil rights agency (you can find this out by calling the NOW Legal Defense and Education Fund, in New York City, at 212-925-6635), you may want to file a charge with them first and then file a complaint with the EEOC.

The agency will investigate your complaint. More than half of all claims filed are dismissed—nearly 55 percent in 1999—for lack of evidence.

Regardless of the EEOC ruling, you can still get your day in court by requesting a right-to-sue letter from the agency. From a practical standpoint, however, a lack of EEOC certification "can hurt a lot," according to staff attorney Yolanda Wu of the NOW Legal Defense and Education Fund. "It might make it harder for you to get an attorney, and the defendant would certainly use the fact in court to try to prove you have a weak case."

The good news is that after overcoming so many hurdles, you're likely to prevail in court. Jury Verdict Research, a Horsham, Pennsylvania, company that maintains a database of jury awards, analyzed pregnancy discrimination verdicts and settlements from 1993 to April 2000, and found that 61 percent of the plaintiffs won, receiving median awards of $56,360.

An alternative to litigation is private mediation, in which a neutral party hears both sides and makes a decision. Because it's a private proceeding, it's quicker, cheaper, more informal than litigation and more conducive to preserving relationships (this is especially useful if you plan to return to work at the company). If you don't like the mediator's decision, you can disregard it and file a lawsuit.

Preparing yourself emotionally for litigation is important, too. Many lawyers discourage women from bringing suit because these cases are so difficult to win.

Kathleen Williamsen, a thirty-one-year-old art teacher and the mother of a sixteen-month-old daughter, was turned down by two attorneys before she found one who would represent her. Williamsen filed a claim last year with the EEOC over her treatment by the Sewanhaka Central High School District, in Elmont, New York. She says she received good performance ratings during 1997, her first year of teaching. But then she got pregnant. "The thinking is that you're not as accessible once you have children," says Williamsen. "That you won't stay as late or work as hard."

Within a week of her announcement in October 1998, Williamsen received her first unsatisfactory performance review. Several more followed. Matt Jacobs, the president of her local teachers' union, claims never to have seen such a blatant turn-around in performance evaluations. "Her performance was not just good—it had been outstanding," he says.

Williamsen transferred to another school for the fall 1999 semester. She was denied tenure and lost her job this past January. She is now suing the school district.

"I try not to be bitter," Williamsen says. "I have my dignity and the knowledge that I did the right thing."

From *Ladies' Home Journal*, July 2000, 78–81, 145–146. © 2000 by Stephanie B. Goldberg. Reprinted by permission.

The Bible's Lost Stories

Fueling faith and igniting debate, a new generation of scholars is altering
our beliefs about the role of women in the scriptures

By Barbara Kantrowitz and Anne Underwood

THE YEAR'S SURPRISE "IT" GIRL IS the star of a mega best seller, a hot topic on campuses and rumored to be the "special friend" of a famous and powerful man. Yet she's still very much a woman of mystery. For close to 2,000 years, Christians have known her as Mary Magdalene, but she was probably named Miriam, and came from the fishing village of Magdala. Most people today grew up believing she was a harlot saved by Jesus. But the Bible never says that. Scholars working with ancient texts now believe she was one of Christ's most devoted followers, perhaps even his trusted confidante and financial backer. This revisionist view helped inspire the plot of "The Da Vinci Code," which has been on The New York Times best-seller list for 36 weeks, with 4.3 million copies in print. Author Dan Brown draws on some credible discoveries about the first followers of Jesus as well as some rather fantastical theories about Mary Magdalene to suggest that she was far more than the first to witness the risen Jesus (her most important role, according to the New Testament). The blockbuster novel has enraged many theologians who consider it anti-Catholic, but it has also added new force to an already dynamic debate among women who see Magdalene's story as a parable for their own struggles to find a place in the modern church. None of this would be possible without a new generation of women Biblical scholars who have brought a very modern passion to the ancient tradition of scriptural reinterpretation—to correct what these scholars regard as a male misreading of key texts. It has not been easy work. Despite the undeniably central role of Mary, the mother of Jesus, the Biblical focus has largely been on what God has accomplished through the agency of men—from Adam to the Apostles. Of some 3,000 characters named in the Bible, fewer than 10 percent are women. Female scholars are trying to redress the imbalance by unearthing narratives that have been overlooked

for centuries and reinterpreting more-familiar stories, including Mary Magdalene's and even the story of Eve (where, one could argue, the problems really began). And they are rigorously studying the Biblical period to glean what they can about the role of women in ancient times.

ACROSS THE COUNTRY, FRESH RESEARCH is inspiring women of all faiths. Evangelical Protestant women hold their own Bible-study groups where the distaff version of history is a major draw. Jewish worshipers now add to the litany of Abraham, Isaac and Jacob the names of their wives: Sarah, Rebekah and Rachel. In addition to Moses at Passover, some celebrate his sister, Miriam, who defied a powerful and tyrannical ruler to rescue her baby brother from a death decree and became a prophet and leader in her own right. For Roman Catholics in particular, Mary Magdalene has emerged as a role model for women who want a greater church presence after the wave of sexual-abuse scandals. "I want my daughter to feel that she is as equally valued as her brother in terms of her faith," says Dr. Jo Kelly, 38, of Sinking Spring, Pa. Not long ago, Kelly's daughter, Mary Shea, 7, told her mother she wanted to be a priest. Kelly, a pediatrician who belongs to a religious-discussion group, didn't discourage her. "Keep believing that," she replied, "and maybe we can change people's minds."

Mary Magdalene inspires, these women say, because she was not a weakling—the weeping Magdalene whose name begat the English word "maudlin" but a person of strength and character. In an era when women were commonly identified in relation to a husband, father or brother, she was identified instead by her town of origin. Scholars believe she was one of a number of women who provided monetary support for Jesus' ministry. And when the male disciples fled, she steadfastly witnessed Jesus' crucifixion, burial and resurrection, providing the thread of continuity in the central story of Christian history—an extraordinary role in an age when women generally provided legal testimony only in the absence of male witnesses. Tradition, however, has consigned Mary to a lesser role. "Instead, we've been given the image of Mary as a forgiven sinner," says Sister Christine Schenk, cofounder of FutureChurch, an organization calling for women's equality in the Roman Catholic Church. "Well, Peter was a forgiven sinner, too, but that's not what we remember him for." Schenk helped institute nationwide observances of Mary Magdalene's feast day, July 22.

To honor their heroine, Catholic women like Kathy Kidder and her friends in Gainesville, Fla., are forming reading groups to discuss the dozens of new scholarly and literary books about her and debating her role on religious Web sites like `Magdalene.org` and `Beliefnet.com`. The new insights they gain can shatter old beliefs, but often also help them deepen their faith. College student Frances Garcia, 26, of Orlando, Fla., was raised Catholic, but now attends a Baptist church. "The Da Vinci Code" raised troubling questions for her about how women's contributions to early Christianity were suppressed by church leaders. "My faith was really shaken," she says. "I started doing a lot of research on my own." Learning more made her feel "closer to God," she says.

What started out as scholarship with an openly feminist political agenda has evolved into serious and respected inquiry. To understand this change, consider what has happened to the field during the career of Bernadette Brooten. As a graduate theology student at Harvard in the late 1970s, Brooten was told that scholars already knew everything there was to know about women in the Bible. Yet Brooten, now a professor of Christian studies at Brandeis University, made the remarkable discovery by reading older versions of the Bible that Junius, one of the many Christian "Apostles" mentioned by Saint Paul, was in fact a woman, Junia, whose name was masculinized over the centuries by translators with their own agenda. Brooten's discovery became "official" when Junia's real name was incorporated into the New Standard Revised Version of the Bible, which came out in 1989.

Today, there are female Biblical scholars at dozens of institutions, and at least two universities—Harvard and the Claremont Graduate University in California—offer degree programs on women in religion. These scholars have produced a new dictionary called "Women in Scripture," a woman's study Bible, and feminist commentaries to various books of the New Testament and early Christian literature. "There are increasing numbers of resources concerning Biblical women that are making their way into libraries, classrooms and bookstores," says Amy-Jill Levine, professor of New Testament studies at Vanderbilt University Divinity School. "They're no longer just cleaned up or romanticized stories, but rigorously historical, imaginative, cross-cultural collections." These insights are also filtering out into popular culture with a slew of literary interpretations of women's Bible stories in the wake of Anita Diamant's 1997 best seller, "The Red Tent," including many about Mary Magdalene.

The fascination with Magdalene has a long and rich history of its own. Diane Apostolos-Cappadona, a cultural historian at Georgetown University, curated an exhibit last year of Magdalene portraits at the American Bible Society in New York. "She's gone through conflations and misinterpretations and reinterpretations and retrievals," she says. "I've seen her represented in every medium of art through every Christian period—as the witness to the Resurrection, the seductive temptress, the haggard desert mother signifying penitence, the beautiful woman reborn signifying new life." But for most people, the image that sticks is the rehabilitated prostitute. Scholars blame Pope Gregory the Great for her bad rep; in A.D. 591, he gave a sermon in which he apparently combined several Biblical women into one, including Magdalene and an unnamed sinner who anoints Jesus' feet. Although the Vatican officially overruled Gregory in 1969, the image stuck until quite recently. "It became a snowball that grew and grew until her name in legend and art history evoked the whore," says Jane Schaberg, professor of religious studies at the University of Detroit Mercy and author of "The Resurrection of Mary Magdalene."

The ferocious warrior-heroine Judith is 'like **Wonder Woman**, only Jewish,' says one scholar

Part of the problem may stem from what scholars have called "the muddle of the Marys." There are a lot of women named Mary in the New Testament, and it's not always clear which is which.

But some scholars also think Mary Magdalene was defamed because she was a threat to male control of the church. As the "Apostle to the Apostles"—the first to encounter the risen Christ and to take the news to Peter and the other male Apostles—she was clearly more than just an ordinary follower. In several Gnostic Gospels—written by Christians whose alternative views of Jesus were eventually suppressed as heresy—Mary Magdalene rivals Peter for the leadership of the early church because of her superior understanding of Jesus' teaching. The Gospel of Philip, for example, describes her as Jesus' close companion whom he often "used to kiss." Karen King of Harvard Divinity School, author of "The Gospel of Mary of Magdala" and a leading authority on women's roles in the early church, sees her as a target of jealousy because she threatened Peter's status. By transforming her into a reformed whore, King believes, the church fathers "killed the argument for women's leadership"—and for recognizing women as fit recipients of divine revelation. King says the transformation also created a powerful symbol of the prostitute as redeemed sinner, the female version of the Prodigal Son. If Jesus could accept her, he could accept anyone.

In "The Da Vinci Code," Brown suggests that she still had one more hold on Jesus—as his wife. That theory has been circulating for centuries. Some historians think it is possible because Jewish men of that era were almost always married, but many others dismiss that reasoning. Some argue that Jesus wasn't conventional in any other sense, so why would he feel the need to be married? Others say that relegating her to the role of wife is belittling. "Let's not continue the relentless denigration of Mary Magdalene by reducing her only importance to a sexual connection with Jesus," says John Dominic Crossan, professor emeritus of religious studies at DePaul University in Chicago. "She's not important because she was Mrs. Jesus. That's like saying Hillary Rodham Clinton is only important because she's married to Bill Clinton. Both women are important in their own right."

That's certainly true for the women who see in Mary Magdalene's rediscovered importance a pathway to their own new roles in the church. Mary Magdalene's story gave Maggie Albo, a 49-year-old volunteer hospice chaplain from Spokane Valley, Wash., the courage to lobby the Diocese of Spokane for space in local Catholic cemeteries to bury abandoned remains from the county medical examiner's office. "Mary has taught me to step out in faith to do the work of Jesus," she says. "I aspire to be a Mary of Magdala … a woman unafraid to speak up."

Mary Magdalene is not the only Biblical heroine to benefit from a modern makeover. A number of scholars have gone back to the original Hebrew texts for a clearer understanding of Eve, the original woman in the Bible. The popular conception of Eve is the product of centuries of myth and artistic interpretation. One widely held misconception is that the fruit Eve offered Adam in the Garden of Eden was an apple. In fact, scholars say, the Bible never states that. "Just because Milton mentions it in 'Paradise Lost' or some Renaissance painter puts it in a picture doesn't make it an apple," says Carol Meyers, professor of Biblical studies at Duke. Meyers says that not only is the apple missing from the story of Adam and Eve in Genesis, but there is also no mention of the words "the temptation of Adam," "seduction," "curse of Eve," "Fall of Man," "sin" or "original sin." And yet the Creation story has traditionally been the basis for the argument that women are responsible for sin and should therefore be subservient to men. This error "has oppressed both women and men," says Phyllis Trible, professor of Biblical studies at Wake Forest University, "because the master-slave relationship isn't a relationship of freedom for either party." Trible gives a more egalitarian rendering of a passage that has long troubled many women readers. When God tells Eve "Your desire shall be for your husband and he shall rule over you," Trible sees a patriarchy turning description into prescription. In the original Hebrew, Trible insists, "it doesn't say he shall rule over you. It just says he does rule over you—a description of the way things are."

In the ancient cultures where the Bible was formed, men did indeed rule over women. They owned and sold them, often as slaves. One slave in particular, Hagar, has captured the imagination of contemporary Hispanic and African-American women. Just as women's perspective is not necessarily the same as men's, minority women do not necessarily share the same perspective as white women. According to the Bible, God promises Abraham land and a multitude of offspring. But because he and his childless wife, Sarah, are old, Sarah suggests

that he father a child with Hagar, her Egyptian handmaiden. After a son is born, Hagar feels superior to the jealous Sarah, who in turn abuses her handmaiden—forcing Abraham to send Hagar away. Eventually God addresses Hagar directly (the first woman after Eve so honored), names her child Ishmael and encourages her to return. Later, Sarah also conceives and, at the age of 90, delivers Isaac, through whom Jews claim their spiritual lineage to Abraham. Hagar's has always been the lost voice in this narrative, but no longer. "Her character resonates by ethnicity and class—as an African and a slave," says Renita Weems, an associate professor of the Hebrew Bible at Vanderbilt Divinity School. "And we understand slaves." Similarly, Megan McKenna, author of several books on Biblical women, found that the figure of Hagar powerfully appealed to the Hispanic maids in her Bible-reading group at a California motel. She remembers one illegal immigrant from El Salvador saying in halting English: "Oh, now Sarah knows what it's like to be treated like dirt all the time."

Equally appealing to modern women looking for inspiration are overlooked stories that celebrate the bravery of women. In the Book of Joshua, it is Rahab, a prostitute, who helps Joshua conquer Jericho by hiding his spies in her house. For her courage, she and her children are the only ones spared in the Israelites' sacking of the city. One of the most prominent warriors in the Book of Judges is Deborah, a military commander and judge who leads an army into battle because her general will not go without her. Deborah predicts that only a woman will capture the enemy leader, Sisera. That woman, it turns out, is Jael, into whose tent Sisera flees for refuge. Jael feeds him, puts him to bed and then, as he sleeps, picks up a mallet and drives a tent peg through his head.

Perhaps the most striking protofeminist text in Scripture is the Book of Judith, wholly devoted to a heroine who saves Israel. "She's like Wonder Woman, only Jewish," says Vanderbilt's Levine. Judith's moment comes as Israel is being threatened by a neighboring power. The male Jewish leadership prepares to surrender, but Judith, a beautiful and pious widow, has another plan. Dressed in her alluring best, she enters the enemy's camp. The general, Holofernes, becomes infatuated and plans to seduce her. But when she is alone in his chambers, Judith decapitates Holofernes and takes his head home in her food bag. The enemy flees. All of Israel, including Jerusalem and its temple, are saved, and Judith, whom scholars see as a personification of Israel, returns to her previous life.

The spotlight of new scholarship has even revealed the human side of the most revered female in Christianity—Mary, the mother of Christ. Next to her son, Mary is probably the best-known character in the Bible, but for many, she is an alabaster figure. Some theologians have been looking for a more multidimensional Madonna. "Let's stop treating her as this virgin mother we have no relationship with, that we can't touch and understand because she's so different from us," says Weems, author of "Showing Mary: How Women Can Share Prayers, Wisdom and the Blessings of God." Weems starts her reinterpretation not with Mary the exalted and untouchable Queen of

Decoding 'The Da Vinci Code'

For millions, the phenomenal best seller is their introduction to the arcane and mysterious 'shadow history' of the early church. Herewith, an attempt to separate truth from fiction.

Did Leonardo include Mary Magdalene in his "Last Supper"? Most art scholars say no. The figure reputed to be Mary Magdalene is actually the beloved disciple John, who is usually depicted young and clean-shaven.

Were Jesus and Mary M. married? Although there is no way to prove or disprove this, most experts consider it highly unlikely. Their main argument: there is no mention of it in canonical writings.

Was Mary M. a prostitute? This misperception probably began with a sermon by Pope Gregory the Great in A.D. 591 in which he conflated several figures into one. In 1969 the Vatican officially overruled Gregory.

Are Opus Dei and the Priory of Sion real organizations? Yes, but there is no indication that either is involved in any plot to conceal or reveal secrets of the Holy Grail.

What is the Holy Grail? The most widely accepted idea is that it was the cup used by Christ at the Last Supper. Others have hypothesized that it was a secret book. In the 12th century a French abbot claimed to possess it; his silver chalice now resides in the National Gallery of Art in Washington, D.C.

Did male leaders cover up the true role of women in the early church? Yes, in the sense that history is written by the winners, and in a patriarchal society, men had a big edge.

What happened to Mary M. after the Resurrection? Nobody knows. In the Eastern Orthodox tradition, she went to Turkey. A Western legend says she went to Provence.

Is there a secret cache of documents that reveal the true history of Christianity? No one knows, but scholars are busy analyzing ancient documents found in Egypt in the last century. These texts, known as the Gnostic Gospels, were lost for centuries, and could shed new light on the origins of the church.

Did Leonardo hide clues about church secrets in his paintings? Art historians doubt it.

also suddenly and miraculously pregnant and ultimately gives birth to John, a prophet who would be called "the Baptist."

Embedded in the story of Mary and Elizabeth is a theme, finally being openly explored, that speaks directly to the experience of contemporary women. Unlike other Biblical figures, Mary is not bowing to the demands of a patriarchal society by providing her future husband with a male heir. On the contrary, she has scandalized her betrothed, Joseph, by freely accepting God's will that she bear a child by the power of the Holy Spirit. In the Mary and Elizabeth visitation scene in Luke's Gospel, Mary has come to visit her cousin for three months. As Luke paints it, this is more than just a domestic interlude. Through Elizabeth, the history of the Old Testament will end with the last of the Hebrew prophets, John. Through Mary, a new history of salvation will begin with the life, death and resurrection of Jesus. In a powerful closing hymn, Mary glories in a God who often uses the powerless—especially women—to accomplish His purposes. Acknowledging her "lowliness" as God's "servant," she goes on to predict—rightly—that henceforth "all generations will call me blessed."

The popular conception of Eve is the product of centuries of myth and artistic interpretation

Mary and Elizabeth's dependence on God and each other—a Biblical example of sisterhood in action—contrasts with the struggle of their spiritual ancestress, Tamar, who has to rely only on herself to outwit the patriarchal social structure. As her story is told in Genesis 38, her first husband dies, leaving her childless. According to the law of the time, she is then married to her husband's younger brother in order to produce a son who would continue her husband's lineage. It is not to be. God strikes her second husband dead for practicing *coitus interruptus* in order to avoid fathering a child who will take away his inheritance. By law, Tamar should then have been married to the third son, but her father-in-law, Judah, suspects that Tamar herself is behind his sons' deaths. He declines to give her to his third son, who is underage, and, at the same time, won't declare her a widow—which would leave her free to marry again. Instead, he sends her back to her father's house, where she must remain chaste while she waits for Judah to give her to the third son. Eventually, Tamar tricks Judah into impregnating herself. It ends well when he accepts her and Tamar gives birth to twins—two sons to replace the two he has lost.

Tamar has to deceive the most powerful man in her life in order to get what she deserves. Her Biblical sisters have had to wait thousands of years for their day in the sun, but their voices, too, are finally being heard. No one is trying to claim that the women of the Bible were anywhere near as powerful as the men in their world. But neither were they weak and passive. Perhaps they were just misunderstood. And ignored. Take the story every Sunday-school kid has heard about how Jesus fed a multitude of 5,000 with just five loaves of bread and two fish. What the Bible really says is that there were "five thousand, not

Heaven, but with Mary the simple teenage girl. On that fateful day when the Archangel Gabriel appeared to her and told her she would carry the Son of God, Mary was terrified—just as Moses, Isaiah and Jeremiah all protested that they were too young or not worthy of the task when presented with their own challenges from God. But Mary put her trust in God and was rewarded for it. God gives her the much-needed companionship of her older cousin Elizabeth, a long-barren woman who was counting women and children." In other words, assuming there was a wife and at least two children for every man, Jesus actually fed 20,000 people. Why didn't the man who recorded this tale capitalize on the opportunity to make Jesus' miracle seem even more impressive? It seems that women and children were simply too unimportant. "The amazing thing is that there are any women at all in the ancient texts," says Deirdre Good, professor of New Testament studies at General Theological Seminary. As the scholarly debate continues, one thing worshipers might keep in mind is how often these marginalized characters prevail and are entrusted to deliver the Word of God. From Eve to Miriam to Mary, they were all players—and are, in our unfolding spiritual drama.

Some say Magdalene was defamed because she was a threat to the male control of the church

NETWORKER NEWS

Breaking the Silence

Helping offending priests come to terms with their sexuality

By Mary Sykes Wylie

During the mid-1990s, in a big-city diocese already convulsed by proliferating sex-abuse charges, a man nearing 40 accused a priest we shall call Father McMahan of having sexually abused him when he was 17. McMahan acknowledged his guilt. Though no other complaints or suggestions of his sexual impropriety had come to light, his bishop immediately packed him off to St. Luke Institute in Maryland, one of several church-sponsored psychiatric centers that treat Roman Catholic clergy. McMahan remembers that one of his superiors warned him, "Father, if you find out you are gay or a pedophile, you will not be a happy man." A self-identified heterosexual, McMahan agreed, but insisted he'd still rather know who he really was than go through life not knowing.

In one sense, Father McMahan's case was not unusual. Professionals who treat clerical sex offenders maintain that most aren't hard-core pedophiles, who serially abuse scores, even hundreds of children, but adults who, like McMahan, have sexual encounters with postpubescent boys and older teenagers—perhaps only once or a few times in their careers. In another sense, however, McMahan's willingness to analyze his sexuality was unusual. If most sex offenders resist knowledge about their sexuality, how much harder must it be for a priest to admit his sexual offenses, particularly those committed against children? A priest's self-image is bound up with his calling as one of God's representatives, a living exemplar of chastity, faith, and selfless devotion.

"Being a priest is a pretty heavy thing," says psychologist Robert Goodkind, who treated priests during the 1980s and '90s at a now-closed Catholic psychiatric center in Jemez Springs, New Mexico. "People look up to you, put you on a pedestal, and, without ever really knowing you, assume you are one step closer to God than they are. This may encourage a certain narcissism sometimes, a sense of entitlement."

Being revered and admired doesn't turn anyone into a sex offender, but traditional religious attitudes can instill in priests a feeling that their ordination protects them from the foibles and failures of their humanity. McMahan remembers that other priests, early in their treatment, glossed over their offenses by taking what he calls "spiritual shortcuts"—saying they'd confessed their offenses, prayed to Jesus for help, and promised not to offend again, and thereby believing they'd solved their problem. "Faith can be a powerful resource for healing," says the Reverend Steven J. Rossetti, a psychologist and president of St. Luke, "but [priests] can also use spirituality as a defense and rationalization. We point out to them that confession removes the spiritual [sin], but doesn't affect the psychodynamic roots of their difficulty."

At St. Luke, priests take part in a five-to-seven-month inpatient treatment program, which includes multiple weekly sessions of individual and group therapy, educational seminars, 12-step programs, psychodramas, and art therapy. During group meetings, peers challenge a new patient's belief that wrapping himself in a cloak of faith and clerical airs will keep him from reoffending. "Other priests with similar problems are the best ones to make it clear to [new residents] that they can't use that priest stuff here, that they are no different from anybody else in the group," says Rossetti.

Experts on pedophilia and other sex offenses, as well as mental-health professionals who treat priests, widely agree that priests aren't any more likely than other adult males to abuse minors, and they accept that neither homosexuality nor celibacy *per se* make men more dangerous to children. "There is no more risk to a boy from a homosexual man than to a girl from a heterosexual man. Nor does celibacy create offenders—sexual offenses are committed as often by noncelibates as by celibates," says Fred Berlin, pioneering researcher and clinician in the treatment of pedophilia and consultant to the National Conference of Catholic Bishops' ad hoc committee on sexual abuse.

Nonetheless, critics of the church argue that training for the priesthood has too often encouraged and reinforced a perpetual adolescence and psychosexual immaturity that puts priests at risk for molesting later in life. Many older priests began contemplating their vocation in their early teens, and some even entered minor seminaries—all-male clerical high schools, which prepared promising young men to enter "major" seminaries when they turned 18. These institutions sequestered them from some of the social and sexual experiences that help boys grow up, while stressing prayer, sacrifice, and self-discipline as the sole recourse for the inevitable pains, desires, and conflicts of youth. "Clerical training typically rewarded adolescent values—enthusiasm, group identity, willingness to sacrifice for a common cause—and, I think, has educated people for a prolonged adolescence," argues Richard Sipe, a psychotherapist and former priest, whose 1990 book, *A Secret World: Sexuality and the Search for Celibacy* was based on a 25-year study of celibacy and sexuality among Roman Catholic clergy. Seminaries ignored, and actively discouraged, emotional and sexual self-discovery. "Many priests, when ordained, are emotional 13-year-olds," Sipe contends.

Within this educational system, priests rarely had an opportunity to explore their sexuality or come to terms with the emotional and physical costs of celibacy. Sex-education courses are becoming the norm in training programs for priests, but two decades ago sexuality was, literally, an unspeakable subject. In this cocoon, says Goodkind, many never had the chance to look squarely at their sexuality; many were never sure *which* sex attracted them. (Estimates of gay clergy range from 20 to 50 percent.) Young men confused about their sexuality, or suspecting they might be gay and wanting to consecrate their church-prescribed celibacy to a higher cause, frequently found a home in the priesthood.

A key component in treating offending priests is education. In middle age or later, offending priests often find themselves on a steep psychosexual learning curve, exhaustively exploring their sexuality for the first time. For those used to a culture of silence, talking about sex can

seem almost as bad as doing it. As McMahan remembers, during one group session, a dignified elderly priest cried out in dismay, "I have never talked about sex in my whole life, and now all I talk about is sex." McMahan, however, felt liberated by the knowledge he gained about himself: "I had been sexually abused when I was a young boy, and I got the chance to work through things about the abuse that had been locked away and hidden inside. Talking about it cleared things up for me, helped me understand myself better, and made me feel I could breathe fresh air again."

Priests who receive treatment for sex offenses are often able, for the first time in their lives, to know and accept themselves, and make mature, informed choices about how they want to live. "Many men come into treatment feeling horrible about whom they were attracted to, as well as by what they had done," says Goodkind. "But a key element of Catholicism is forgiveness and the sacrament of reconciliation. We work with them so that they can accept their sexuality for what it is, quit punishing themselves, and, at the same time, shun the behavior that got them into trouble."

Sometimes, however, gay priests attracted to consenting adult partners choose not to shun the behavior; instead, they leave the priesthood. "Part of the work they needed to do in treatment was muster the courage and prepare themselves to make the big leap to go live in the secular world," adds Goodkind. Some gay priests choose to remain in the priesthood and tacitly continue having sexual relationships with other adult clergy.

For those who have dedicated their lives to agape rather than eros, flouting vows of celibacy has high spiritual and psychological costs. A significant part of treatment is helping priests maintain celibacy by teaching them the importance of establishing strong, nonsexual bonds of friendship and love. Many parish priests, with a plummeting decline in their numbers over the last few decades, live alone in rectories, working 16-hour days, enjoying little if any personal life. According to McMahan, a quick gauge of whether a priest is at risk for abusing is the degree of his isolation and the poverty of his social and relational life. Learning how to make nonsexual connections is basic to St. Luke's treatment program, says Rossetti, who suggests that many priests who abuse minors have inadequate relationships with their peers. "If you take away [a priest's] relationship with a 15-year-old, what are you going to put in its place?" he asks. "You can't just white-knuckle it."

Celibacy, when freely undertaken in full knowledge of self, is not a negation of sexuality, "but a way of coming to terms with it," says Richard Sipe. Celibacy can be "truly a gift to God and to self, a way of freeing one to love in a more general and expansive, less individualistic, way," agrees McMahan. "But you have to know and accept your own sexuality before you can make the decision to direct it into that channel."

After several months at St. Luke, Father McMahan returned to work as a priest in his parish, with a sharpened appreciation of what the church can do to prevent further abuse. He believes that priests need training in setting appropriate boundaries between themselves and their parishioners, particularly children, and in recognizing boundary violations when they occur. "Young priests need to learn that there are ways that you can and ways that you cannot touch people, times when you can have conversations with parishioners behind closed doors and times when you leave the door open. There is also a time, a place, and a way to hug children—I think it really is not wise to be alone with kids a lot." Still, says McMahan, "tactility is very important to children—they need to be touched, and we have to touch them. The issue is how to do that effectively and appropriately."

The Mystery of Misogyny

Why do fundamentalists hate women?

BARBARA EHRENREICH
THE PROGRESSIVE

A feminist could take dim comfort from the fact that the Taliban's egregious misogyny only became newsworthy after the war against them began last fall. It certainly wasn't high on Washington's agenda a few months earlier, in May, when President Bush congratulated the ruling Taliban for banning opium production and handed them a check for $43 million—never mind that their regime accorded women a status somewhat below that of livestock.

In the weeks after September 11, however, you could find escaped Afghan women on *Oprah* and longtime anti-Taliban activist Mavis Leno doing the cable talk shows. CNN broadcast the documentary *Beneath the Veil*, and even Bush mentioned the Taliban's hostility to women—although their hospitality to Osama bin Laden was still seen as the far greater crime. Women's rights may play no part in U.S. foreign policy, but we should perhaps be grateful that they have at least been important enough to deploy in the media mobilization for war.

On the analytical front, though, the neglect of Taliban misogyny—and beyond that, Islamic fundamentalist misogyny in general—remains almost total. If the extreme segregation and oppression of women does not stem from the Koran, as nonfundamentalist Muslims insist, then why should it have emerged when it did, toward the end of the 20th century? Liberal and left-wing commentators have done a thorough job of explaining why the fundamentalists hate America, but no one has bothered to figure out why they hate women.

And *hate* is the operative verb here. Fundamentalists may claim that the sequestration and covering of women serves to "protect" the weaker, more rape-prone sex. But the protection argument hardly applies to the fundamentalist groups in Pakistan and Kashmir that specialize in throwing acid in the faces of unveiled women. There's a difference between "protection" and a protection racket.

The mystery of fundamentalist misogyny deepens when you consider that the anti-imperialist and anti-colonialist Third World movements of 40 or 50 years ago were, for the most part, at least officially committed to women's rights. Women participated in Mao's Long March; they fought in the Algerian revolution and in the guerrilla armies of Mozambique, Angola, and El Salvador. The ideologies of these movements were inclusive of women and open, theoretically anyway, to the idea of equality. Osama bin Laden hardly rates as a suitable heir to the Third World liberation movements of the mid-20th century, but he did purport to speak for the downtrodden and against Western capitalism and militarism. Except that his movement offered the most downtrodden sex nothing but the veil and a life lived largely indoors.

Of those commentators who do bother with the subject, most explain the misogyny as part of the fundamentalists' wholesale rejection of "modernity" or "the West." Hollywood culture is filled with images of strong or at least sexually assertive women, hence—the reasoning goes—the Islamic fundamentalist impulse is to respond by reducing women to chattel. The only trouble with this explanation is that the fundamentalists have been otherwise notably selective in their rejection of the "modern." The terrorists of September 11 studied aviation and communicated with each other by e-mail. The Taliban long favored Stingers and automatic weapons over scimitars. If you're going to accept Western technology, why throw out something else that has contributed to Western economic success—the participation of women in public life?

Liberal and left-wing commentators have done a thorough job of explaining why the Muslim fundamentalists hate America, but no one has bothered to figure out why they hate women.

Perhaps—to venture a speculation—the answer lies in the ways that globalization has posed a particular threat to men. Western industry has displaced traditional crafts—female as well as male—and large-scale, multinational-controlled agriculture has downgraded the independent farmer to the status of hired hand. From West Africa to Southeast Asia, these trends have resulted in massive male displacement and, frequently, unemployment. At the same time, globalization has offered new opportunities for Third World women—in export-oriented manufacturing, where women are favored for their presumed "nimble fingers," and, more recently, as migrant domestics working in wealthy countries.

These are not, of course, opportunities for brilliant careers, but for extremely low-paid work under frequently abusive conditions. Still, the demand for female labor on the "global assembly line" and in the homes of the affluent has been enough to generate a kind of global gender revolution. While males have lost their traditional status as farmers and breadwinners, women have been entering the market economy and gaining the marginal independence conferred even by a paltry wage.

Add to the economic dislocations engendered by globalization the onslaught of Western cultural imagery, and you have the makings of what sociologist Arlie Hochschild has called a "global masculinity crisis." The man who can no longer make a living, who has to depend on his wife's earnings, can watch Hollywood sexpots on pirated videos and begin to think the world has been turned upside down. This is *Stiffed*—Susan Faludi's 1999 book on the decline of traditional manhood in America—gone global.

Or maybe the global assembly line has played only a minor role in generating Islamic fundamentalist misogyny. After all, the Taliban's home country, Afghanistan, has not been a popular site for multinational manufacturing plants. There, we might look for an explanation involving the exigencies—and mythologies—of war. Afghans have fought

each other and the Soviets for much of the past 20 years, and, as Klaus Theweleit wrote in his brilliant 1987 book, *Male Fantasies*, long-term warriors have a tendency to see women as a corrupting and debilitating force. Hence, perhaps, the all-male *madrassas* in Pakistan, the schools where boys as young as 6 are trained for jihad, far from the potentially softening influence of mothers and sisters. Or recall terrorist Mohamed Atta's specification, in his will, that no woman approach his grave.

Then again, it could be a mistake to take Islamic fundamentalism out of the context of other fundamentalisms—Christian and Orthodox Jewish. All three aspire to restore women to the status they occupied—or are believed to have occupied—in certain ancient nomadic Middle Eastern tribes.

Religious fundamentalism in general has been explained as a backlash against the modern, capitalist world, and fundamentalism everywhere is no friend to the female sex. To comprehend the full nature of the threats we face since September 11, we need to figure out why.

Barbara Ehrenreich is a columnist for The Progressive *and the author of* Nickel and Dimed: On (Not) Getting By in America (*Metropolitan Books, 2001*). *From* The Progressive (*Dec. 2001*).

IN SEARCH OF
EROTIC INTELLIGENCE

BY ESTHER PEREL

Reconciling our desire for comfortable domesticity and hot sex

EVERYBODY'S NOT DOING IT. That's the word from Newsweek, The Atlantic, *and other trend watchers: Couples are having less sex these days than even in the famously uptight '50s. Why? Busy, exhausting lives is the easy answer. But how Americans view eroticism in the wake of recent sexual and social revolutions may be an even bigger factor, according to a growing number of researchers and social observers.*

—*The Editors*

A few years ago, at a psychology conference, I heard a speaker discuss a couple who had come to therapy in part because of a sharp decline in their sexual activity. Previously, the couple had engaged in light sadomasochism; now, following the birth of their second child, the wife wanted more conventional sex. But the husband was attached to their old style of lovemaking, so they were stuck.

The speaker believed that resolving the couple's sexual difficulty required working through the emotional dynamics of their marriage and new status as parents. But in the discussion afterward, the audience was far less interested in the couple's relationship than in the issue of sadomasochistic sex. Some people speculated that motherhood had restored the woman's sense of dignity, and now she refused to be demeaned by an implicitly abusive, power-driven relationship. Others suggested that the couple's impasse illustrated long-standing gender differences: Men tended to pursue separateness and control, while women yearned for loving connection.

When after two hours of talking about sex no one had mentioned the words *pleasure* or *eroticism*, I finally spoke up. Their form of sex had been entirely consensual, after all. Maybe the woman no longer wanted to be tied up because she now had a baby constantly attached to her

breasts—binding her better than ropes ever could. Why assume that there *had* to be something degrading about this couple's sex play?

Perhaps my colleagues were afraid that if women *did* reveal such desires, they'd somehow sanction male dominance everywhere—in business, politics, economics. Maybe the very ideas of sexual dominance and submission, aggression and surrender, couldn't be squared with the ideals of compromise and equality that undergird couples therapy today.

As an outsider to American society—I grew up in Belgium and have lived in many countries—I wondered if these attitudes reflected cultural differences. I later talked with Europeans, Brazilians, and Israelis who had been at the meeting. We all felt somewhat out of step with the sexual attitudes of our American colleagues. Did they believe such sexual preferences—even though they were consensual and completely nonviolent—were too wild and "kinky" for the serious business of maintaining a marriage and raising a family? It was as if sexual pleasure and eroticism that strayed onto slightly outré paths of fantasy and play—particularly games involving aggression and power—must be stricken from the repertoire of responsible adults in committed relationships.

SEXUAL DESIRE DOES NOT PLAY BY THE RULES OF GOOD CITIZENSHIP.

WHAT STRUCK US was that America, in matters of sex as in much else, was a goal-oriented society that prefers explicit meanings and "plain speech" to ambiguity and allusion. Many American therapists encourage clarity and directness, which they tend to associate with honesty and openness: "If you want to make love to your wife/

husband, why don't you tell her/him exactly what you want?" These professionals in large part "solve" the conflict between the drabness of the familiar and the excitement of the unknown by advising patients to renounce their fantasies in favor of more reasonable "adult" sexual agendas.

Whereas therapists typically encourage patients to "really get to know" their partners, I often say that "knowing isn't everything." Most couples exchange enough direct talk in the course of daily life. To create more passion, I suggest that they play a bit more with the ambiguity that's inherent to communication. Eroticism can draw its powerful pleasure from fascination with the hidden, the mysterious, and the suggestive.

Ironically, some of America's best features—the belief in equality, consensus-building, fairness, and tolerance—can, in the bedroom, result in very boring sex. Sexual desire and good citizenship don't play by the same rules. Sexual excitement is often politically incorrect; it often thrives on power plays, role reversals, imperious demands, and seductive manipulations. American therapists, shaped by egalitarian ideals, are often challenged by these contradictions.

In Europe, I see more of an emphasis on complementarity—the appeal of difference—rather than strict gender equality. This, it seems to me, makes European women feel less conflict about being both smart and sexy. They can enjoy their sexual power, even in the workplace, without feeling they're forfeiting their right to be taken seriously. Susanna, for example, is a Spanish woman with a high-level job at an international company in New York. She sees no contradiction between her work and her desire to express her sexual power—even among her colleagues. "If compliments are given graciously, they don't offend. We're still men and women who are attracted to one another, and not robots," she says.

Of course, American feminists accomplished major improvements in women's lives in many ways. Yet without denigrating their achievements, I believe that the emphasis on egalitarian and respectful sex—purged of any expressions of power, aggression, and transgression—is antithetical to erotic desire for men and women alike. (I'm well aware of the widespread sexual coercion and abuse of women and children. Everything I suggest here depends on getting clear consent and respecting the other's humanity.) The writer Daphne Merkin writes, "No bill of sexual rights can hold its own against the lawless, untamable landscape of the erotic imagination." Or as filmmaker Luis Buñel put it more bluntly, "Sex without sin is like an egg without salt."

MANY THERAPISTS assume that the fantasy life that shapes a new relationship is a form of temporary insanity, destined to fade over a long-term partnership. But can sexual fantasy actually enhance the intimate reality of relationships? Clinicians often interpret the desire for sexual adventure—ranging from simple flirting and contact with previous lovers to threesomes and fetishes—as fear of commitment and infantile fantasy. Sexual fantasies about one's partner, particularly those that involve role-playing, dominance, and submission, are often viewed as signs of neurosis and immaturity, erotically tinged idealizations that blind one to a partner's true identity. Here's an example from a client I worked with (the name changed, of course):

Terry had been in therapy for a year, struggling with the transition from being half of an erotically charged couple to being one-quarter of a family with two children and no eroticism at all. He began one session with what he deemed a "real midlife story" that began when he and his wife hired a young German au pair. "Every morning she and I take care of my daughters together," he said. "She's lovely—so natural, full of vitality and youth—and I've developed this amazing crush on her. You know how I've been talking about this feeling of deadness? Well, her energy has awakened me. I want to sleep with her and I wonder why I don't. I'm scared to do it and scared not to."

I didn't lecture him about his "immature" wishes, or explore the emotional dynamics beneath this presumably "adolescent" desire. Instead, I tried to help him relish the awakening of his dormant senses without letting the momentary exhilaration endanger his marriage. I marveled with him at the allure and beauty of the fantasy, while also calling it just that: a *fantasy*.

"It's great to know you still can come to life like that," I said. "And you know that you can never compare this state of inebriation with life at home, because home is about something else. Home is safe. Here, you're on shaky ground. You like it, but you're also afraid that it can take you too far away from home. And you probably don't let your wife evoke such tremors in you."

A few days later, he was having lunch in a restaurant with his wife and she was telling him of her previous boyfriend. "I'd been thinking hard about what we talked about," he told me, "and at the table I had this switch. Normally, I don't like hearing these stories of hers—they make me jealous and irritated. But this time I just listened and found myself getting very turned on. So did she. In fact, we were so excited we had to look for a bathroom where we could be alone."

I suggested that perhaps the experience of desiring a fresh young woman was what enabled him to listen to his wife differently—as a sexual and desirable woman herself. I invited Terry to permit himself the erotic intensity of the illicit with his wife: "This could be a beginning of bringing lust home," I said. "These small transgressions are acceptable; they offer you the latitude to experience new desire without having to throw everything away."

IT AMAZES ME how willing people are to experiment sexually *outside* their relationships, yet how tame and puritanical they are with their partners. Many of my patients describe their domestic sex lives as devoid of excitement and eroticism, yet they are consumed by a richly imaginative sex life beyond domesticity—affairs, pornography, prostitutes, cybersex, or feverish daydreams. Having denied themselves freedom of imagination at home, they go outside to reimagine themselves, often with random strangers. Yet the commodification of sex can actually hinder our capacity for fantasy, contaminating our sexual imagination. Furthermore, pornography and cybersex are ultimately isolating, disconnected from relations with a real, live other *person.*

A fundamental conundrum is that we seek a steady, reliable anchor in our partner, at the same time we seek a transcendent experience that allows us to soar beyond our ordinary lives. The challenge, then, for couples and therapists, is to reconcile the need for what's safe and predictable with the wish to pursue what's exciting, mysterious, and awe-inspiring.

It's often assumed that intimacy and trust must exist before sex can be enjoyed, but for many women and men, intimacy—more precisely, the familiarity inherent in intimacy—actually sabotages sexual desire. When the loved one becomes a source of security and stability, he/she can become desexualized. The dilemma is that erotic passion can leave many people feeling vulnerable and less secure. In this sense there is no "safe sex." Maybe the real paradox is that this fundamental insecurity is a precondition for maintaining interest and desire. As Stephen Mitchell, a New York psychoanalyst, used to say, "It is not that romance fades over time. It becomes riskier."

Susan and Jenny came to see me about their sexual relationship. Susan, a longtime lesbian, set out to seduce Jenny right after they met. Jenny responded, though it was her first lesbian relationship. They moved in together just as Susan was waiting for the arrival of her adopted baby. Once they were a threesome, Jenny thought they were a wonderful family, but completely lost any sexual interest in Susan. Jenny, already in some conflict about her lesbianism, couldn't be a second mom to the new baby, family builder, companion, and passionate lover all at once.

The transition to motherhood can have a desexualizing effect. I reminded them that the mother isn't an erotic image in our culture. Mom is supposed to be caring, nurturing, loving, but, frankly, rather asexual. "Being new parents can be pretty overwhelming," I said. "But can you try to add making love to the list of all the other things you enjoy doing together to unwind and relax? The idea is to make each other feel good, not to solve the fate of your relationship. That's an offer you can't refuse."

At the next session, Jenny reported: "That really loosened us up. We can talk about it, laugh and not be instantly scared."

So many couples imagine that they know everything there is to know about their mate. In large part, I see my job as trying to highlight how little they've seen, urging them to recover their curiosity and catch a glimpse behind the walls that encircle the other. As Mexican essayist Octavio Paz has written, eroticism is "the poetry of the body, the testimony of the senses. Like a poem, it is not linear, it meanders and twists back on itself, shows us what we do not see with our eyes, but in the eyes of our spirit. Eroticism reveals to us another world, inside this world. The senses become servants of the imagination, and let us see the invisible and hear the inaudible."

Esther Perel is on the faculties of the New York Medical Center, Department of Psychiatry, and the International Trauma Studies Program, New York University. She is in private practice in New York.

From *Utne Reader*, September/October 2003, pp. 67–70, originally appeared in *Psychotherapy Networker*, May/June 2003. Copyright © 2003 by Psychotherapy Networker. Reprinted by permission.

THE MERRY-GO-ROUND OF DESIRE

An interview with Mark Epstein

A contemporary psychiatrist uses ancient Buddhist wisdom to make sense of desire in our every day lives.

Mark Matousek

In the nine years since publishing his first book, *Thoughts Without a Thinker*, Mark Epstein, M.D. has done more to pioneer the meeting of Buddhist and Western psychologies than any doctor in this country. Now turning this cross-cultural gift to the polarizing topic of Eros, Epstein continues to break new ground in his forthcoming book, *Open to Desire*, envisioning a middle path where lust for life—questioned in some dharma circles—is no longer seen as the enemy.

Trained at Harvard, Epstein, whose other books include *Going to Pieces Without Falling Apart* and *Going On Being*, is a longtime meditator who lives in New York City with his wife of twenty years, Arlene Schechet, and their two teenage children. One chilly afternoon last fall, attired in a black T-shirt and khakis, he met with me in his basement office to talk about this thorny issue of desire.

—MARK MATOUSEK

You're working on a book about desire. Why desire?

After studying Buddhism for thirty years, I realized that people have this idea that Buddhism is about getting rid of desire. I don't think that's true, so the book is a defense of desire, really—an exploration of the Middle Way, trying to chart out an approach to desire that isn't about indulging, necessarily, or repressing.

Why does desire need defending? From the Western, Puritan point of view, it's always been seen as dangerous, devilish, the enemy. From the Eastern spiritual point of view—as adopted by many Western practitioners, at least—it has the connotation of something to be avoided, a poison. As a psychotherapist, I've been trained not to avoid the so-called "real stuff"— anger, fear, anxiety—and this certainly includes desire. Desire is the juice. It's how we discover who we are, what makes a person themselves. I wanted to try to explore how to work with it more creatively.

Many of the ancient stories of the Indian subcontinent, like the *Ramayana*, the epic tale of separation and reunification of the lovers Sita and Rama, explore desire in an expansive, imaginative way. In the *Ramayana*, Sita is kidnapped by the demon Ravana and separated from her lover, Rama. Ravana wants to possess Sita totally. He is enthralled by her but can only see her as an object. Sita resists this, and in her isolation and imprisonment she deepens her own desire for Rama. The separation that Ravana brings about helps her to get more in touch with the nature of her own desire. I was intrigued by the way desire and separation are intertwined in the tale, as if you can't have one without the other. There seems to be a teaching there about what constitutes a true union. I've been reading over these stories to try to bring back some of this ancient wisdom.

WHAT WE REALLY WANT IS FOR THE OBJECT TO BE MORE SATISFYING THAN IT EVER CAN BE.

We should probably define our terms. Are we talking about sexual desire? Carnal desire? I'm taking the psychodynamic view that all desire is really sexual at some level. Freud once said that he wanted to show that not only was everything spirit, but it was also instinct. One of the wonderful things about the Indian perspective is that it doesn't make the same distinctions between lower and higher that we are used to. Lower and higher are one. There is a much more unified view, so that there is no question but that the sensual contains within it the seeds of the divine. The view in the West, at best, is that things are organized in a hierarchical way, with sensual pleasure being a lower rung on a ladder that reaches toward the sublime. In the Indian view, it's not a rung, it's the entire ladder. So I'm trying to keep a focus on sexual desire throughout.

With the same general implications of clinging and attachment? The question is whether clinging and attachment are an intrinsic part of desire. Sometimes in Buddhist scripture they really seem to be talking about desire in a more celebratory way. When I make my defense, I like to make that distinction. The Buddha warned against the clinging and craving that arise when we try to make the object of desire more of an "object" than it really is. If we stay with our desire, however, instead of rejecting it, it takes us to the recognition that what we *really* want is for the object to be more satisfying than it ever can be.

The Buddha's teachings emphasize that because the object is always unsatisfying to some degree, it is our insistence on its being otherwise that causes suffering. Not that desiring is negative in itself. We can learn to linger in the space between desire and its satisfaction, explore that space a bit more. In my interpretation, this is the space that Sita was in during her separation from Rama. When we spend more time there, desire can emerge as something other than clinging.

Or addiction? Yes. Desire becomes addiction after you have that first little taste of something—alcohol, great sex, getting stoned—that comes so close to complete satisfaction … then you start chasing it. The same thing happens in meditation: having that first bit of bliss, then it's gone. You want the perfection back. But you're chasing something you've already lost. If you stay with that widening dissatisfaction and think, "Oh, yeah, of course," then insight can begin to happen. In that gap.

So our relationship to desire is the problem. That's the point I'm trying to make. Different teachers have different approaches to this: some recommend avoidance of temptation or renunciation, while others talk about meeting desire with compassion. Another strategy is to recognize the impermanence of the object of desire—for instance, by countering lust with images of how disgusting the body really is.

Other teachers say that desire is really just energy that we have to learn how to use without getting caught by it. This is traditionally found under the rubric of Tantra, but it appears throughout the Buddhist canon. There's the famous Zen story in which the Buddha holds up a flower, and only one disciple grasps his meaning and smiles. There are many interpretations of this story, and mine is perhaps unorthodox. But the flower, in Indian mythology, seems to be the symbol of desire. Mara, the tempter, shoots arrows of desire at the Buddha, and the Buddha turns them into a rain of flowers. Kama, the god of Eros, shoots five flowered arrows from his bow. When the Buddha holds up the flower, he might be saying, "No big deal." Desire is something that can be met with a smile.

As a therapist, do you believe that it's possible to reject desire in a healthy way? Of course. There's something very useful about the capacity for renunciation. I think that renunciation actually deepens desire. That's one of its main purposes. By renouncing clinging, or addiction, we deepen desire.

Think of Shiva. In the Indian myths, Shiva is the great meditator, the supreme renunciant. He was so absorbed in his meditation that the gods once tried to rouse him to come to their aid in a battle by sending Kama to wake him. But Shiva reduced Kama to ashes with one glance from his third eye. He was so powerful, he could incinerate desire with one look. But the world could not survive without Eros. The gods pleaded with Shiva, and he resurrected Kama as easily as he had destroyed him. He then left his meditative absorption and turned toward his lover, Parvati. They had sex for the next thousand years. The bliss of their lovemaking was the same as the bliss of his solitary meditation. This is the essential teaching of Shiva: that *tapas*, the heat of renunciation, is the same as *kama*, the heat of passion. One deepens the other. The Buddha's point, I think, was that by renouncing clinging we actually deepen desire. Clinging keeps desire in a frozen, or fixated, state. When we renounce efforts to control or possess that which we desire, we free desire itself.

So it's selective renunciation. I think so. Because you don't want to snuff out the love. They say that the Buddha taught each of his disciples differently. He could look at each of us and see where the clinging was.

It may not be so much that we *have* desire as that we *are* desire. Trying to renounce desire is like trying to renounce yourself. This isn't the way to see the emptiness inside. But clinging is different. We can renounce clinging without estranging ourselves from desire.

Selective renunciation deepens desire because you separate out what's addictive. You free up the erotic? The question would be, What is the truly erotic?

Enlighten us. I think it has something to do with playing with separateness: trying to erase it while at the same time knowing that we cannot. There is a tension between the control we wish we had and the freedom that is naturally present. There were great religious debates in seventeenth-century India about which would bring you closer to divine desire: being in a committed relationship or having an adulterous one. And the adulterous relationship won out because of the quality of separateness, of otherness, that the illicit relationship had. The relationship between husband and wife in those days was more about property. The woman was completely objectified; everything was scripted. There was no room in that relationship for the quality of hiddenness that makes something erotic—or of teasing.

In Japanese garden design there is a principle called "Hide and Reveal." They make a path near a waterfall so that you can never see the waterfall entirely from any one vantage point. You can only get glimpses of it—there's something in that that relates to the erotic. In psychodynamic language, this is the ability to have a relationship between two subjects, instead of a subject and an object. Can you give your lover the freedom of their subjectivity and otherness? Admit that they are outside of your control?

Which in turn could help us remain unattached …

Any attempt to attach too much will only lead to frustration and disappointment. But attachment is a tendency that is endemic to our minds. We can't just pretend it's not there, but if you can keep coming back to the truth—that what we desire is not *ours* in that sense—we can confront our own grasping nature, which, if seen clearly, self-liberates.

What are some of the practices, skills, that someone caught on the merry-go-round of desire can use to find the Middle Way? Meditation is the basic tool for that. In training the mind in bare attention, not holding on to pleasurable experiences and not pushing away unpleasant ones, we can learn to stay more in touch with ourselves. When we practice in this way, pretty quickly we can find out where we are stuck. The mind keeps coming around to the same basic themes. One of my first Buddhist teachers, Jack Kornfield, writes very movingly in his book *A Path with Heart* about his early experiences in long-term meditation at a monastery in Thailand. His mind was just filled with lust. He was freaking out about it, but his teacher just told him to note it. Despairing that it would never change, he tried his best to follow his teacher's instructions. And what he found was that, after a long period of time, his lust turned to loneliness. And it was a familiar loneliness, one that he recognized from childhood and that spoke of his feeling of not being good enough, not deserving enough of his parents' love. I think he said something like, "There's something wrong with me, and I will never be loved." Something like that. But his teacher told him to stay with those feelings, too; just to note them. The point wasn't to recover the childhood pain, it was to go through it. And eventually the loneliness turned into empty space. While it didn't go away permanently, Jack's insight into something beyond the unmet needs of childhood was crucial. This is one way to unhook ourselves from repetitive, destructive, addictive desire. It lets us go in a new direction—it frees desire up.

SEXUAL RELATION IS AS CLOSE AS ONE CAN COME TO EXPERIENCING THE MINGLING OF BLISS AND EMPTINESS.

The way we try to extort love or affection from people can be very subtle. Or we may use food or drugs or television or whatever else to try to get that extra something. When we don't get it, we wonder what's wrong with *us*. And the layers of addiction are never-ending. An alcoholic can stop drinking, but that doesn't mean he's not using sex to the same end, you understand. These layers extend all the way down to someone in a monastery, who can still be addicted to some pleasant feeling in meditation. In Buddhism they say that the most difficult addiction to break is the one to self.

The other tendency in meditation is to push away what we don't want, but aversion constitutes self as much as desire. This can lead to the anti-erotic, anti-celebratory, anti-emotional tendency among some Buddhists. This keeps them feeling more cut off than they want to be.

In a culture of addiction—with overavailability of nearly everything—isn't the learning curve especially steep when it comes to confronting desire? One thing that has helped me think about this is the psychoanalyst Jessica Benjamin's theory that there are two kinds of desire. A male desire (present in both sexes), which knows what it wants and is going after it, which is all about trying to obtain satisfaction. And a female desire, not just in women, which is more about interpersonal, and intrapersonal, space. The male desire is about doing and being done to, while the feminine desire is about being. Think of a baby at the breast. In one version, the breast is trying to feed the baby—it's forcing itself into the baby's consciousness, or the baby's mouth. In the other version, the breast just is. The baby has to find it, discover it, for herself. It's almost like our culture is hip to "male" desire, assaulting us constantly with "you want this, you want that." It's so much in the object mode that it doesn't yield the room for what she's calling a feminine desire, which is "Give me some space to know what I really want."

WE CAN LEARN TO LINGER IN THE SPACE BETWEEN DESIRE AND ITS SATISFACTION.

What do you think about transcendence of bodily desire as a healthy path? Transitionally, it might be valuable for people at certain times. So much of our conditioned experience is spent in the lower part of our body. And it's certainly helpful for the sick body. You want to know that your mind is more powerful than any of that, that you're not *only* that but exist psychically, emotionally—on many levels all at once. I remember when I would take classes with Ram Dass, and he would only teach from the heart up. He would lead guided meditations where the energy would only circulate from the fourth through the seventh chakras. It was always implicit, though, that we would bring the energy back down to the lower chakras eventually.

But transcendence as the ultimate thing, I haven't found that to be helpful. It seems like the only idea that really makes sense to me is this one: samsara and nirvana are one. Dissociating yourself from any aspect of who you really are is only a setup for future trouble. The ultimate thing has to be a complete integration of all aspects of the self.

In your own evolution as a lover and practitioner, has your relationship to desire changed, hit walls—have there been tangles? Not to get too intimate … It's always been a question for me. When I first started to practice, I was mostly aware of my anxiety. But as my mind started to calm down, I began to notice my own desire more. As if desire and anxiety are two sides of the same coin. I've always had a basic view, I suppose, that the Middle Path was the only way to go. Getting to know my first meditation teachers helped. I remember after one of my first Vipassana retreats with Joseph Goldstein and Jack Kornfield, I went into town with them to eat in a restaurant. I think they must have ordered meat or something—they had no pretension about them. It was such a relief. I didn't need to idealize them; their humanness was very obvious and very touching. For me it meant that I didn't have to try to be something other than what I was.

That's one of the main things that encouraged me to become a therapist—the relief I felt at not trying to be other than I was. Suzuki Roshi used to talk about using the manure of the mind as the fertilization for enlightenment. That's how I felt about accepting who I was. I understood that I had to make use of whatever I actually was—not pushing it away was as important as not holding on to it.

I'm interested in this question of transformation. Can laypeople actually transform desire? How much of this is imagination? Tantra is all about the capacity to imagine. Once you understand the emptiness of phenomena, you have the freedom to imagine another reality—superimpose another reality on this one. It's just as real as this one, which you've already understood is empty.

So the energy isn't actually changing? The energy isn't actually changing, no.

"Transformation" is a misnomer, then. Is imagination as important in connecting sex and love, do you think? I think sexual desire is the physical attempt to reach the other, coupled with the intuition that they are forever out of reach. A famous psychoanalyst named Otto Kernberg speaks of sexual union as the experience of a lover revealing himself or herself as a body that can be penetrated and a mind that is impenetrable. You feel these two things simultaneously. Sexual desire has both the male and the female element: the attempt to possess or take over the other, coupled with the impossibility of ever really grasping them. And it's out of that combination that love, empathy, compassion— all those other feelings—emerge. Through realizing the lover's otherness.

That's the basis of love? I don't think that's the basis of love, but that's what happens when you're in love. Being able to appreciate, feel compelled by, the infinite unknowability of the other. It's a mystery you want to get closer to, where there's a yielding but not an ultimate merger. Both of you remain free.

Sex is a real vehicle for experiencing this. Which is why, in Tibetan Tantra, they use sexual relation as a metaphor for what is realizable through advanced practices. Sexual relation is as close as one can come in worldly life to experiencing the mingling of bliss and emptiness that is also understandable through solitary meditation practice.

Yet sex and mindfulness are not necessarily great bedfellows. Lots of us use, or have used, sex as a great way to get unconscious. Yet even with the senses overwhelming us, there's still some awareness there. And it may be that very sort of awareness, of mind at the brink of going

under, that's most powerful. The moment of orgasm is classically seen as a doorway to higher consciousness, but most of us don't stay there for very long. In fact, we run away from it, a little bit afraid of how overwhelming it is. As I understand it, Tantra is about staying within that doorway longer, to rest in the bliss. That's what you train yourself to do. The nonconceptual bliss that you can only really taste through intimate sex, or spiritual practice.

Which is obviously very easy to become addicted to. Yes.

How does pleasure differ from joy, do you think? Buddhist psychology says that every moment of consciousness has pleasurable, unpleasurable, and neutral qualities. Even after enlightenment, these feelings persist. They don't go away. But joy—the Pali word is *sukkka*, the opposite of *dukkba*, or unsatisfactoriness—is a fruit of realization. The capacity for joy increases as the attachment to the self diminishes. In the end, everything becomes sukkha. You know, even dukkha becomes sukkha. So I think it all becomes pleasure.

Yet pleasure has such a bad rep in the Buddhist world. And that's unfortunate. Because the Buddha taught not only about suffering, but about the end of suffering. Desire is only a problem when we mistake what's ephemeral for an object, something we can permanently grasp. It's only suffering because *we don't understand.* You know, this knowledge is encoded in the great Buddhist monuments, or *stupas*, that were built at the height of Buddhism's flowering in India. Surrounding the central mound of the stupa—where the ashes or bones of the Buddha or another enlightened being were stored—was a processional area where visitors to the stupa could circumambulate in a kind of devotional walking meditation. But enclosing the processional area was a great circular railing carved with all kinds of sculptures. These sculptures were often of all of the pleasures of worldly life, and they often included erotic scenes, couples in all forms of embrace, goddesses with trees growing out of their vaginas, these kinds of things. And you had to pass through these scenes, or under them, to reach the processional area. The pleasures of worldly life were the gateways, or portals, to the Buddha's understanding, as symbolized by the central mound. They are blessings that lead us further toward the Buddha's joy.

Test Your Knowledge Form

We encourage you to photocopy and use this page as a tool to assess how the articles in *Annual Editions* expand on the information in your textbook. By reflecting on the articles you will gain enhanced text information. You can also access this useful form on a product's book support Web site at *http://www.dushkin.com/online/*.

NAME: DATE:

_____

TITLE AND NUMBER OF ARTICLE:

_____

BRIEFLY STATE THE MAIN IDEA OF THIS ARTICLE:

_____

LIST THREE IMPORTANT FACTS THAT THE AUTHOR USES TO SUPPORT THE MAIN IDEA:

_____

WHAT INFORMATION OR IDEAS DISCUSSED IN THIS ARTICLE ARE ALSO DISCUSSED IN YOUR TEXTBOOK OR OTHER READINGS THAT YOU HAVE DONE? LIST THE TEXTBOOK CHAPTERS AND PAGE NUMBERS:

_____

LIST ANY EXAMPLES OF BIAS OR FAULTY REASONING THAT YOU FOUND IN THE ARTICLE:

_____

LIST ANY NEW TERMS/CONCEPTS THAT WERE DISCUSSED IN THE ARTICLE, AND WRITE A SHORT DEFINITION:

We Want Your Advice

ANNUAL EDITIONS revisions depend on two major opinion sources: one is our Advisory Board, listed in the front of this volume, which works with us in scanning the thousands of articles published in the public press each year; the other is you—the person actually using the book. Please help us and the users of the next edition by completing the prepaid article rating form on this page and returning it to us. Thank you for your help!

ANNUAL EDITIONS: Human Sexuality 05/06

ARTICLE RATING FORM

Here is an opportunity for you to have direct input into the next revision of this volume.
We would like you to rate each of the articles listed below, using the following scale:

1. **Excellent: should definitely be retained**
2. **Above average: should probably be retained**
3. **Below average: should probably be deleted**
4. **Poor: should definitely be deleted**

Your ratings will play a vital part in the next revision.
Please mail this prepaid form to us as soon as possible.
Thanks for your help!

RATING	ARTICLE	RATING	ARTICLE
	1. Women's Ideal Bodies Then and Now		38. The Sexual Revolution Hits Junior High
	2. Sex Around the World		39. Choosing Virginity
	3. The Beauty Pageant Prevails		40. Staying Up Late with Sue
	4. A Deadly Passage to India		41. Sex in the '90s
	5. AIDS: 20 Years of Terror		42. What Turns You On? (Hint: It's Not Work!)
	6. A Man of Words: A Man of Action		43. Silent No More
	7. Slaves of the Brothel		44. Crimes Against Nature
	8. Rock the Casbah		45. New Hope for Sex Offender Treatment
	9. The Princess Paradox		46. A Cruel Edge
	10. The Manliness of Men		47. Pregnant? You're Fired!
	11. The New Gender Wars		48. The Bible's Lost Stories
	12. "The Uniform for Today is Belly Buttons"		49. Breaking the Silence
	13. Hear Sensuality, Think Sex?		50. The Mystery of Misogyny
	14. The New Sex Scorecard		51. In Search of Erotic Intelligence
	15. The Hormone Conundrum		52. The Merry-Go-Round of Desire
	16. Sex, Drugs & Rock 'n' Roll		
	17. What Problem?		
	18. When Sex Hurts		
	19. The Rise of the Gay Family		
	20. Why Are We Gay?		
	21. Dr. Sex		
	22. Great Expectations		
	23. Looking for Ms. Potato Head		
	24. How to Tell Your Potential Love About Your Chronic STD		
	25. The New Flirting Game		
	26. Passion Flowers		
	27. Save Your Relationship		
	28. How to Rediscover Desire		
	29. The Viagra Dialogues		
	30. The Secret Lives of Wives		
	31. Access Denied		
	32. What's New in Contraception? Understanding the Options		
	33. Barren		
	34. Under the Radar		
	35. Which Babies? Dilemmas of Genetic Testing		
	36. Sex Without Sex? Keeping Passion Alive		
	37. A Tale of Two Mothers		

(Continued on next page)

BUSINESS REPLY MAIL
FIRST CLASS MAIL PERMIT NO. 551 DUBUQUE IA

POSTAGE WILL BE PAID BY ADDRESEE

McGraw-Hill/Dushkin
2460 KERPER BLVD
DUBUQUE, IA 52001-9902

NO POSTAGE
NECESSARY
IF MAILED
IN THE
UNITED STATES

Ildluıdıllludluıllbldıbldllıudıdıll

ABOUT YOU

Name

Date

Are you a teacher? ❐   A student? ❐
Your school's name

Department

Address   City   State   Zip

School telephone #

YOUR COMMENTS ARE IMPORTANT TO US!

Please fill in the following information:
For which course did you use this book?

Did you use a text with this ANNUAL EDITION? ❐ yes ❐ no
What was the title of the text?

What are your general reactions to the *Annual Editions* concept?

Have you read any pertinent articles recently that you think should be included in the next edition? Explain.

Are there any articles that you feel should be replaced in the next edition? Why?

Are there any World Wide Web sites that you feel should be included in the next edition? Please annotate.

May we contact you for editorial input? ❐ yes ❐ no
May we quote your comments? ❐ yes ❐ no